Utilizing AI for Assessment, Grading, and Feedback in Higher Education

Nasser Hamed Al Harrasi
University of Technology and Applied Science, Oman

Mohamed Salah El Din
Majan University College, Oman

A volume in the Advances in Educational Technologies and Instructional Design (AETID) Book Series

IGI Global
PUBLISHER of TIMELY KNOWLEDGE

Published in the United States of America by
IGI Global
Information Science Reference (an imprint of IGI Global)
701 E. Chocolate Avenue
Hershey PA, USA 17033
Tel: 717-533-8845
Fax: 717-533-8661
E-mail: cust@igi-global.com
Web site: http://www.igi-global.com

Library of Congress Cataloging-in-Publication Data

CIP Pending
ISBN: 979-8-3693-2145-4
EISBN: 979-8-3693-2146-1

This book is published in the IGI Global book series Advances in Educational Technologies and Instructional Design (AETID) (ISSN: 2326-8905; eISSN: 2326-8913)

British Cataloguing in Publication Data
A Cataloguing in Publication record for this book is available from the British Library.

For electronic access to this publication, please contact: eresources@igi-global.com.

Advances in Educational Technologies and Instructional Design (AETID) Book Series

ISSN:2326-8905
EISSN:2326-8913

Editor-in-Chief: Lawrence A. Tomei, Robert Morris University, USA

MISSION

Education has undergone, and continues to undergo, immense changes in the way it is enacted and distributed to both child and adult learners. In modern education, the traditional classroom learning experience has evolved to include technological resources and to provide online classroom opportunities to students of all ages regardless of their geographical locations. From distance education, Massive-Open-Online-Courses (MOOCs), and electronic tablets in the classroom, technology is now an integral part of learning and is also affecting the way educators communicate information to students.

The **Advances in Educational Technologies & Instructional Design (AETID) Book Series** explores new research and theories for facilitating learning and improving educational performance utilizing technological processes and resources. The series examines technologies that can be integrated into K-12 classrooms to improve skills and learning abilities in all subjects including STEM education and language learning. Additionally, it studies the emergence of fully online classrooms for young and adult learners alike, and the communication and accountability challenges that can arise. Trending topics that are covered include adaptive learning, game-based learning, virtual school environments, and social media effects. School administrators, educators, academicians, researchers, and students will find this series to be an excellent resource for the effective design and implementation of learning technologies in their classes.

COVERAGE

- Instructional Design Models
- Bring-Your-Own-Device
- Virtual School Environments
- Hybrid Learning
- Higher Education Technologies
- Educational Telecommunications
- Game-Based Learning

IGI Global is currently accepting manuscripts for publication within this series. To submit a proposal for a volume in this series, please contact our Acquisition Editors at Acquisitions@igi-global.com or visit: http://www.igi-global.com/publish/.

The Advances in Educational Technologies and Instructional Design (AETID) Book Series (ISSN 2326-8905) is published by IGI Global, 701 E. Chocolate Avenue, Hershey, PA 17033-1240, USA, www.igi-global.com. This series is composed of titles available for purchase individually; each title is edited to be contextually exclusive from any other title within the series. For pricing and ordering information please visit http://www.igi-global.com/book-series/advances-educational-technologies-instructional-design/73678. Postmaster: Send all address changes to above address.

Titles in this Series

For a list of additional titles in this series, please visit:
http://www.igi-global.com/book-series/advances-educational-technologies-instructional-design/73678

Exploring Contemporary English Language Education Practices
Truong Cong Bang (University of Economics and Law, Ho Chi Minh City, Vietnam & Vietnam National University, Ho Chi Minh City, Vietnam) Cuong Huy Nguyen (International University, Vietnam National University, Ho Chi Minh City, Vietnam) and Hung Phu Bui (University of Economics Ho Chi Minh City, Vietnam)
Information Science Reference • copyright 2024 • 296pp • H/C (ISBN: 9798369332948) • US $245.00 (our price)

Addressing Issues of Learner Diversity in English Language Education
Thao Quoc Tran (HUTECH University, Vietnam) and Tham My Duong (Ho Chi Minh City University of Economics and Finance, Vietnam)
Information Science Reference • copyright 2024 • 357pp • H/C (ISBN: 9798369326237) • US $235.00 (our price)

AI-Enhanced Teaching Methods
Zeinab E. Ahmed (Department of Computer Engineering, University of Gezira, Sudan & Department of Electrical and Computer Engineering, International Islamic University Malaysia, Malaysia) Aisha A. Hassan (International Islamic University of Malaysia, Malaysia) and Rashid A. Saeed (Taif University, Saudi Arabia)
Information Science Reference • copyright 2024 • 405pp • H/C (ISBN: 9798369327289) • US $245.00 (our price)

Effective and Meaningful Student Engagement Through Service Learning
Sharon Valarmathi (Christ University, India) Jacqueline Kareem (Christ University, India) Veerta Tantia (Christ University, India) Kishore Selva Babu (Christ University, India) and Patrick Jude Lucas (Christ University, India)
Information Science Reference • copyright 2024 • 293pp • H/C (ISBN: 9798369322567) • US $275.00 (our price)

Integrating Cutting-Edge Technology Into the Classroom
Ken Nee Chee (Universiti Pendidikan Sultan Idris, Malaysia) and Mageswaran Sanmugam (Universiti Sains Malaysia, Malaysia)
Information Science Reference • copyright 2024 • 425pp • H/C (ISBN: 9798369331248) • US $300.00 (our price)

IGI Global
PUBLISHER of TIMELY KNOWLEDGE

701 East Chocolate Avenue, Hershey, PA 17033, USA
Tel: 717-533-8845 x100 • Fax: 717-533-8661
E-Mail: cust@igi-global.com • www.igi-global.com

Table of Contents

Detailed Table of Contents

This chapter explores the transformative impact of artificial intelligence (AI) on various research domains. The chapter highlights the leading role of AI research platforms in the development of AI in research practices. In addition, the chapter describes the fundamental concepts of AI powered tools such as generative artificial intelligence and large language models. The narrative extends to AI integration in modern research practices, spotlighting its use in hypothesis formulation, generation of research questions, and data analysis. AI's contributions to data analysis in many fields are explored, particularly in automating processes and generating insights. The discussion further explores several AI applications in various research domains such as RPA, Semantic Scholar, and DeepChem. However, potential bias and transparency are main challenges of AI-powered applications. Therefore, it is imperative to champion explainable AI and human-in-the-loop approaches to improve confidence. The chapter recommends further interdisciplinary collaboration between researchers and AI developers.

The evolution of the higher education sector, especially during the COVID-19 pandemic, pinpointed the necessity for agility and innovation in performing the increased load in administrative duties. Artificial intelligence (AI) showed up as a prominent solution for higher education institutions (HEI). This chapter explores AI's potential in administrative functions like scheduling, library services, enrollment, and others, acknowledging the benefits and highlighting challenges such as stakeholder participation, lack of knowledge, privacy concerns, and budgetary limitations. It promotes a holistic, phased approach to AI integration, underscoring strong leadership, clear vision, and collaboration for successful adoption and enhancing educational quality.

Preface

Welcome to *Utilizing AI for Assessment, Grading, and Feedback in Higher Education*. In recent years, artificial intelligence (AI) has emerged as a transformative force across various sectors, and higher education is no exception. As editors, Dr. Nasser Hamed Al Harrasi and Mohamed Salah El Din, we are pleased to present this edited reference book, which explores the myriad ways AI is reshaping teaching, learning, research and administrative processes in academia.

The impact of AI in higher education cannot be overstated. By automating tasks such as grading and scheduling, AI frees up valuable time for educators to focus on enhancing the student experience and improving the quality of teaching. However, alongside these benefits come significant challenges. The proliferation of generative AI models, such as ChatGPT and Google Bard, has raised concerns about academic integrity and the fundamental nature of learning itself.

Through meticulous analysis of existing literature, this book offers a comprehensive overview of the effective uses of AI in higher education, as well as insights into the potential drawbacks and ethical challenges. It serves as a vital resource for professors, lecturers, academic policymakers, and other stakeholders seeking to navigate the complexities of integrating AI into educational practices.

One of the distinguishing features of this book is its multidisciplinary approach. By bringing together experts from diverse fields such as computer science, education, psychology, and ethics, we aim to bridge the gap between AI specialists and higher education professionals. This collaboration fosters innovation and opens new avenues for research and exploration in the realm of AI-driven education.

The chapters in this book cover a wide range of topics related to integrating AI in higher education, including grading and evaluation, research, assessment tools, communication enhancements, academic administration, and ethical considerations. Each chapter provides valuable insights and practical recommendations for harnessing the potential of AI while mitigating its risks.

In conclusion, "Utilizing AI for Assessment, Grading, and Feedback in Higher Education" is more than just a collection of scholarly essays—it is a call to action. It is our hope that this book will inspire educators, researchers, policymakers, administrators, and practitioners to embrace the transformative power of AI in higher education and chart a course towards a more inclusive, innovative, and ethically responsible future.

ORGANIZATION OF THE BOOK

Chapter One: Automated Evaluation Techniques and AI Enhanced Methods

In this chapter, Ahmed, Zaki, and Bentley explore the transformative potential of Artificial Intelligence (AI) in reshaping assessment, grading, and feedback processes in higher education. They delve into real-time feedback mechanisms and AI-driven practices, highlighting the importance of personalized grading criteria and the analysis of student data to accommodate diverse learning styles. The chapter emphasizes the role of faculty training in adopting AI-driven enhanced methods, promoting a more equitable and student-centered learning environment.

Chapter Two: Enhancing Assessment Systems in Higher Education: A Review on Artificial Intelligence Usage

Al-Amin, Saqui, and Khan provide a comprehensive review of the usage of Artificial Intelligence (AI) in educational assessment, focusing on recent developments and challenges. They investigate AI-based learning assessments and assess the readiness of educators to incorporate AI tools into their assessment procedures. This chapter contributes to the ongoing discussion on how AI could impact the assessment landscape in higher education, offering insights into current practices and future directions.

Chapter 3: Evolution of Assessment and Feedback Methods in Higher Education

Suhail, Guangul, and Nazeer examine the evolution of assessment and feedback methods in higher education, driven by technological advancements and changing societal needs. They discuss the shift towards innovative, technology-based assessment methods and highlight the role of AI and digital tools in creating inclusive, personalized learning experiences. The chapter addresses the challenges posed by online and distance learning, advocating for flexible and integrity-focused approaches to assessment.

Chapter 4: AI and Personalized Grading Criteria

Ahmed, Zaki, and Bentley discuss the potential of AI in transforming assessment, grading, and feedback processes in higher education. They explore the significance of real-time learning and virtual teaching platforms, evaluating AI-based assessments and natural language processing techniques. This chapter provides valuable insights into how AI enables personalized interventions and deeper insights into student performance, promoting a more effective and efficient assessment process.

Chapter 5: Future Horizons: Exploring Artificial Intelligence's Role in Shaping Research Landscapes

Al Harrasi and Salah El Din delve into the transformative impact of Artificial Intelligence (AI) on various research domains, highlighting its role in hypothesis formulation, research question generation, and data analysis. They explore AI applications such as RPA and Semantic Scholar, while also addressing challenges such as bias and transparency. The chapter emphasizes the need for interdisciplinary collaboration to harness the full potential of AI in research.

Chapter 6: AI-Driven Transformation in Higher Education: New Frontiers in Administration and Management

Salah El Din and Al Harrasi explore the potential of Artificial Intelligence (AI) in transforming administrative functions in higher education, including scheduling, library services, and enrollment. They discuss the benefits and challenges of AI integration, emphasizing the importance of strong leadership and collaboration for successful adoption. This chapter advocates for a holistic approach to AI integration, aiming to enhance educational quality through innovative administrative practices.

Chapter 7: AI Powered Teaching-Plan, Present and Post Evaluation

Sivakumar and Al Harthy examine the process of AI-powered teaching and learning in higher education, focusing on plan, progress, and post-evaluation stages. They discuss major components involved in AI-powered teaching and learning, as well as cutting-edge technologies and case studies. The chapter also addresses implications and recommendations for policymakers to navigate challenges in incorporating AI into higher education.

Chapter 8: Integrating AI in Higher Education Applications, Strategies, and Ethical Considerations

Al Daraai, Al Maqrashi, Al Zakwani, and Al Shaikh provide a comprehensive overview of integrating artificial intelligence (AI) in higher education, covering applications, strategies, and ethical considerations. They explore how AI technologies can enhance teaching, learning, and grading, while also addressing ethical concerns such as data privacy and algorithmic bias. This chapter emphasizes the importance of aligning AI applications with educational objectives and providing teacher training for successful implementation.

Chapter 9: Navigating the Impact of AI Integration in Higher Education: Ethical Frontiers

Ghandour examines the ethical considerations of incorporating AI into higher education institutions, aiming to develop a conceptual framework for stakeholders. The chapter explores various ethical dimensions, providing guidelines for navigating the ethical challenges associated with AI integration.

Chapter 10: Artificial Intelligence in Higher Education and Its Socioscientific Evaluation

Çildir delves into the socioscientific dimensions of the widespread use of artificial intelligence (AI) in higher education, emphasizing the ethical and moral issues. The chapter recommends urgent measures to address potential negativities and highlights the importance of AI literacy among students and academics.

Chapter 11: Strategies Considerations of Implementing AI in Higher Education

Al Harthy and Al Hasani discuss ways to improve teaching, learning, and administrative elements of higher education through the integration of AI techniques. They provide insights into the advantages, challenges, and ethical issues of various AI tools and applications, offering a complete strategy for implementation.

Chapter 12: AI-Driven Innovation in Higher Education Marketing - An Exploration of Oman's Academic Landscape

AlBalushi and Al Bolushi systematically review AI's transformative impact on higher education marketing, addressing challenges and opportunities within the

Omani context. The chapter emphasizes strategic planning, campaign execution, and balancing technology with human aspects, offering insights for effective AI utilization in education marketing.

IN CONCLUSION

In concluding this edited reference book, it is evident that Artificial Intelligence (AI) is revolutionizing higher education in profound ways. From transforming assessment and grading processes to enhancing research practices and administrative functions, AI presents both opportunities and challenges for educators, researchers, policymakers, and administrators.

Through the chapters contributed by esteemed scholars and experts in the field, readers have gained valuable insights into the diverse applications of AI in higher education. From the exploration of AI-driven teaching and learning methodologies to the examination of ethical considerations and implementation strategies, each chapter has contributed to a deeper understanding of how AI is reshaping the educational landscape.

As editors, our aim was to provide a comprehensive overview of the effective uses of AI in higher education while addressing the potential drawbacks and ethical challenges. We believe that this book serves as a valuable resource for educators, researchers, policymakers, administrators, and practitioners seeking to navigate the complexities of integrating AI into educational practices.

Moving forward, it is imperative that stakeholders in higher education continue to engage in interdisciplinary collaboration and dialogue to harness the transformative power of AI while ensuring its responsible and ethical implementation. By doing so, we can leverage AI to create more inclusive, innovative, and student-centered learning environments, ultimately advancing the quality and accessibility of higher education for all.

Acknowledgment

The editors of this book appreciate the invaluable contributions from all respected scholars who participated in this book. Their dedication and valuable insights are truly valued. This work would not have been possible without their collaboration and commitment. We hope that this book will shed light on the inspiring uses of artificial intelligence in higher education, both in teaching and non-teaching activities. Special thanks to University of Technology and Applied Sciences, and Majan University College in Oman for their support to complete this project.

Chapter 1
Automated Evaluation Techniques and AI-Enhanced Methods

Sajeel Ahmed
University of Bedfordshire, UK

Abira Zaki
Iqra University, Pakistan

Yongmei Bentley
University of Bedfordshire, UK

ABSTRACT

The chapter explores the transformative potential of artificial intelligence (AI) in reshaping assessment, grading, and feedback processes in higher education. They cover real-time feedback mechanisms, AI-driven practices, and evaluation of AI-based assessments, promoting a more equitable, student-centered learning environment. AI is revolutionizing higher education by providing personalized grading criteria, analyzing student data, and adjusting assessment criteria to accommodate diverse learning styles. This approach promotes student engagement, fairness, and equity, enabling educators to tailor teaching strategies and address learning gaps. The chapter emphasizes faculty training and AI-driven enhanced methods.

DOI: 10.4018/979-8-3693-2145-4.ch001

BACKGROUND INFORMATION

Artificial Intelligence (AI) refers to computer systems that can perform complex tasks traditionally performed by humans, such as reasoning, decision-making, and problem-solving (Schuett, 2019). AI in Education (AIED) is revolutionizing education by streamlining assessment processes, enhancing learning outcomes, and creating personalized experiences. Originating in the 1970s, AIED aims to foster student success and drive innovation in teaching and learning (Humble & Mozelius, 2022; Rosen, 2023). AI is revolutionizing higher education by reshaping traditional assessment methods, empowering students, and enhancing efficiency. Technology-enhanced language learning (TELL) educators have been using various educational technologies for three decades (Zou et al., 2021). Artificial Intelligence (AI) is anticipated to emerge as a very useful technological advancement in the next years, alongside other transformative technologies such as robots, virtual reality, 3D printing, and networks (Hooda et al., 2022). AI can help educators manage resource requirements for assessments, grading, and feedback, transforming resource management with growing class sizes and diverse student groups.

AI integration can enhance critical thinking, promote ethical considerations, and equip students with necessary competencies for professional AI implementation (De Gagne, 2023). Next-generation educational technology, including artificial intelligence, has led to widespread use of computers and information and communication technologies in education (Ouyang et al., 2023a; Zawacki-Richter et al., 2019). AI assessment systems enhance educational experiences by identifying targeted interventions ensuring academic excellence. However, their implementation faces ethical constraints, despite rapid growth in education and research (Humble & Mozelius, 2022). Ali's (2020) study explores AI integration in language teaching, focusing on Automatic Speech Recognition (ASR) technology. Chatbots use keyword-matching to evaluate students' spoken language proficiency, enhancing communication between humans and machines (Ali, 2020). AI integration in flipped classrooms improves academic performance and student enthusiasm, fostering positive attitudes towards language acquisition among scholars (Ali, 2020).

In their study, Zawacki-Richter et al. (2019) conducted a comprehensive analysis of AI applications in the field of higher education. Their research spanned the years 2007 to 2019 and included a worldwide perspective (Zawacki-Richter et al., 2019). The findings revealed that the prominent areas of AI-enhanced education included profiling and prediction, assessment and evaluation, adaptive systems and customisation, as well as intelligent tutoring systems (ITS) (Zawacki-Richter et al., 2019). AI-powered systems can assess and grade the essays through analysing the structure, content, grammar and overall quality of the writing. However, these systems use NLP and machine learning in providing the detailed feedback to the students.

Automated essay scoring (AES), developed since 1966, assigns scores to student responses based on grammar, diction, structure, and other characteristics. Despite challenges, researchers continue to work on resilient AES systems (Ramesh & Sanampudi, 2022). The Transformer-based approach for Automatic Encoding System (AES) offers advantages over Bag-of-Words (BOW) in knowledge examinations and other tasks. Future research should explore the benefits of hierarchical coherence modeling and transformer-based language models, as well as the potential for transitioning between different models to enhance human evaluations and score "very easy" texts (Ludwig et al., 2021).

Automated essay scoring systems for educational assessment collect data on students' learning processes, evaluating cognitive abilities. Technology-enhanced assessment systems improve traditional methods, reduce costs, and offer personalized feedback. They adapt to various subject domains, manage large data volumes efficiently, and generate automated reports for educational decision-making (Ifenthaler, 2022).

Challenges in Implementing Automated Evaluation Techniques and AI-Enhanced Methods in Education

One potential area of over-emphasis that could be the focus on the technical capabilities and benefits of AI in assessment, grading and feedback while neglecting the potential limitations and challenges. Also AI systems can be flawed and overemphasizing their benefits without considering potential drawbacks that can lead to unrealistic expectations or unintentional adoption of AI systems. Ethical considerations such as fairness, transparency, and privacy are crucial for implementing AI in educational assessment. Failing to address these can lead towards potential biases, discrimination or privacy breaches. The importance of human involvement in assessment should not be underestimated, as AI systems can provide efficiency but should not replace human evaluators.

Accuracy and Reliability

Accuracy and reliability are paramount in AI grading assessments, as they must be sound. Precision in evaluation, no room for doubt, ensuring fairness, integrity, and trust abound.

The challenges of AI-enhanced learning analytics (LA) tools for career decision support are revealed, including five main benefits: career information, research, idea diversification, direction, decision support, and self-reflection (Gedrimiene et al., 2024). The review of 42 studies from 1990-2022 reveals that AI can be applied to 39 stages of medical education, but the challenges include performance improvement, effectiveness verification, and algorithms (Zhang et al., 2023). The opportunities, benefits, and challenges of AI in education are focused on developed countries and the Industry 4.0 era. It provides an in-depth understanding of AI technology in education, discussing challenges and ethical issues, and offers recommendations for future research directions (Tahiru, 2021). Autonomous learning in modern education, combining online and offline methods. It introduces a model for knowledge diffusion and proposes an effective algorithm for resource allocation (Wan et al., 2021).

Figure 1. Challenges in implementing automated evaluation techniques and AI-enhanced methods in education
(Author)

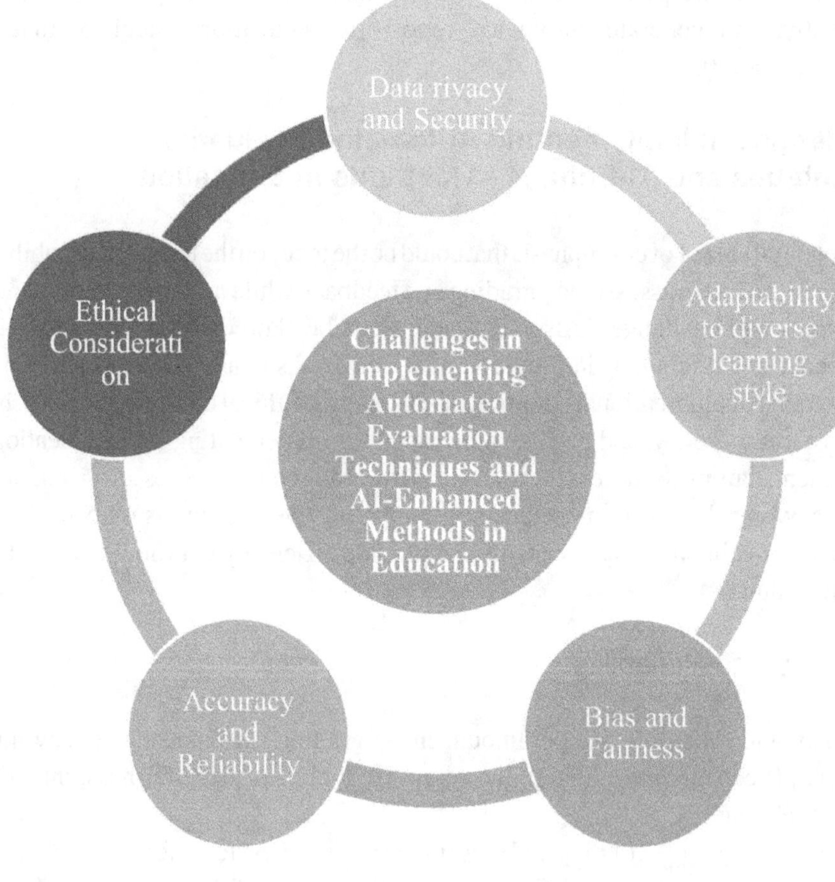

Let's consider a scenario where a university decides to implement an AI system to automatically evaluate and grade student essays in a particular course. The AI system is trained on a large dataset of essays that have been previously graded by human instructors, and it is expected to provide accurate and reliable assessments. However, the challenge arises when AI system encounters essays that are unique or unconventional in their structure, content, or writing style. These essays mat deviate significantly from the patterns and examples present in the training data, making it difficult for the AI system to accurately evaluate them. The AI system's ability to evaluate innovative essays or novel arguments is comprised through biases in training data or the system's design, potentially leading towards biased grading if the data is not diverse enough or reflects certain biases. Continuous monitoring and improvement of the AI system in education is crucial for enhancing accuracy and reliability. Also, regular updates towards training data and human oversight such as instructor reviews can mitigate potential errors and biases.

Bias and Fairness

AI algorithms face significant challenges in addressing bias and also ensuring fairness in automated evaluation systems, which can perpetuate biases and unfair outcomes, particularly for underrepresented students. The shift from academic ownership to a managerial ethos in academia has increased student evaluation of teaching (SET) power, raising questions about its validity, reliability, and fairness in reward and recognition (Cook et al., 2022). Higher education's diversified student body necessitates individualized assessments and rejects one-size-fits-all approaches, as current methods cause stress and divide students (Naseer et al., 2024). AI and learning analytics enhance peer assessment in teaching by proposing methods such as individual review guidelines, grade accuracy inference models, feedback strategies, and spot-checking mechanisms (Darvishi, Khosravi, Sadiq, et al., 2022). The impact of anonymous marking on students' feedback perceptions and future learning suggests it may reduce dialogue and undermine learning potential of feedback (Van der Kleij & Lipnevich, 2021). The survey explores the fairness of AI systems, their real-world applications, bias sources, and fairness definitions in machine learning, highlighting challenges and solutions to mitigate bias in AI systems, with future directions still being explored (Mehrabi et al., 2021). The blurred lines between assessment and feedback in higher education, highlighting six issues: students' focus on grades, late feedback, subordination, documentation, and anonymous marking requirements, and proposes strategies for preserving feedback's learning function (Winstone & Boud, 2022).

One of the scenarios included in which high school using an AI system to evaluate student math assignments facing challenge when it encounters problems containing references or unfamiliar scenarios. This could lead to potential biases, favoring or penalizing students from certain cultural backgrounds. To mitigate this the training data should be included for diverse cultural and also regular audits and evaluations should be conducted. Human oversight, that has included having a math teacher review AI-generated assessments that can also help ensuring fairness. Addressing bias and fairness concerns can create a more inclusive and equitable learning environment, enhancing the educational experience for all students.

Adaptability to Diverse Learning Styles

The use of AI in adaptive educational systems, highlighting the drawbacks of these systems, emphasising the importance of intelligent and adaptive e-learning environments for effective learning (Khosravi et al., 2022). Assessment approaches for Massive Open Online Courses (MOOCs) concludes that peer assessment is the most universally applicable method, discussing challenges, developments, and future research directions (Jansen et al., 2020). This is a comprehensive overview of automated feedback systems, focusing on their state-of-the-art applications. It reviews 109 systems, proposes a classification framework, and advocates for personalized, data-driven solutions for effective learning while highlighting the field's fragmentation (Deeva et al., 2021). Large language models in AI can enhance education by creating content, enhancing student engagement, and personalizing learning experiences. However, challenges include developing technology competencies, implementing strategies, and addressing biases (Kasneci et al., 2023). A literature review of 121 research papers from 2017-2021 examined automated grading and feedback tools for programming education. Most assessed correctness using dynamic techniques, but the feedback was limited to passing or failing tests and expected output (Messer et al., 2024).

Imagine a university could use an AI-powered tutoring system to help students learn programming languages. However, the system's current approach might not cater to the diverse leaning styles, such as visual or auditory. To address this the university could incorporate multimedia elements, such as visual diagrams and video demonstrations to cater visual learners and audio explanations and podcasts for auditory learners. Adaptive algorithms could also be implemented to analyse student's learning preferences and adjust content delivery. Feedback from students and instructors can inform ongoing improvements to enhance adaptability. However, this approach would make automated evaluation techniques and AI-enhanced methods more inclusive and effective in supporting students with different learning styles.

Data Privacy and Security

A machine learning-driven decision-making model for higher education institutions enhances outcomes, performance, prediction, accuracy, efficiency, and data security through high-quality input training data (Teng et al., 2023). AI's impact on higher secondary education, highlights its benefits, challenges, and ethical implications, emphasizing the need for effective integration and student preparation (Sarwar et al., 2024). AI's potential to tackle challenges but warn of advanced hacking techniques, discuss adversarial AI, cyber defense models, countermeasures, and key research areas in AI privacy and security (Al-Khassawneh, 2023). Learning analytics in higher education uses big data to understand student behavior, but raises privacy concerns, intrusive practices, justification, student autonomy, and whether it advances or counters educational goals (Ifenthaler & Yau, 2020). AI's applications in medical education, focusing on learning support, assessment, and curriculum review. However, challenges include lack of digitalization, sensitive examinations, and data integrity issues. Methodological improvements are needed to increase AI adoption (Chan & Zary, 2019). A text summarization and deep learning approach to identify GDPR violations based on recent privacy incidents and article terminology, showing promising accuracy compared to conventional text modeling techniques (AlEroud et al., 2021).

Imagine a school district that implements an AI-powered system to automate the grading of student exams. The system collects and analyses student responses to various test questions, providing instant feedback and grades. However, the challenges arise when it comes to ensuring the privacy and security of student data. In the scenario, the AI system collects a vast amount of personal information about each student, including their answers, performance metrics, and potentially sensitive demographic data. It is crucial to protect this data from unauthorized access, breaches, or misuse because it contains personally identifiable information and academic records.

Implementing the robust data privacy and security measures, complying with privacy regulations, and addressing algorithmic biases and data leakage are crucial for protecting student data. Further, encryption, access control, regular security audits, transparency, accountability, and informed consent enhanced the trust.

Ethical Considerations

AI advancements have raised authenticity and origin questions, prompting a rethinking of digital scholarship and publication processes. The MetaScribe system architecture allows for the reconsideration identity and anonymity, broadening ethical discussions (Israel & Amer, 2023). The validity of educational tests in dynamic systems, focusing on systemically valid tests that foster cognitive traits and proposes design principles for student assessment systems (Walker et al., 2023). A 2017 scoping review of 118 peer-reviewed papers found 53 use cases for large language models in automating educational tasks. However, practicality and ethics concerns may hinder adoption. Recommendations include updating innovations, open-sourcing, and human-centered approaches (Yan et al., 2024). The ethical and societal implications of AI integration in K-12 education, highlighting its applications, challenges, and instructional resources from MIT Media Lab and Code.org. It aims to guide practitioners (Akgun & Greenhow, 2022). The ethical implications of chatbot use in tertiary education, revealing significant impacts on privacy, transparency, trust, and the digital gap, necessitating further evaluation (Okonkwo & Ade-Ibijola, 2021).

Imagine a university that implements an AI-powered system to automate the admission process. Though the Ai system analyse applicant's academic records, personal statements, and other related information to make admissions decisions. However, a challenge arises when it comes to ensuring ethical considerations throughout the process. The Ai system in the admission process introduces biases and discrimination, potentially causing inequitable outcomes and perpetuating existing inequalities. To address this, universities should ensure diverse training data, conduct regular audits, maintain transparency, and ensure responsible use of student data. Human oversight and contextual factors are also crucial for a fair and transparent admissions process.

Leveraging AI for Assessment, Grading, and Feedback in Higher Education

In today's rapidly evolving educational landscape, harnessing the power of AI for assessment, grading and feedback presents the opportunities for maximizing benefits in higher education. By deploying automated evaluation techniques and AI-enhanced methods, educational institutions can significantly enhance efficiency and save valuable time for both educators and students. AI technologies provide accurate evaluations, personalised learning experiences and immediate feedback, enabling learners to identify strengths and weaknesses, promoting continuous improvement.

Enhanced Efficiency and Time Savings

Technology can improve science and engineering education by promoting critical thinking and utilizing new tools. It involves a collaborative learning project that includes peer review, enhancing learning outcomes and collective intelligence (Mora et al., 2020). UNCode notebook auto-grader, providing instant summative and formative feedback for Jupyter notebooks, a user-friendly tool used in AI courses, highlighting its effectiveness in error identification (González-Carrillo et al., 2021). A model to enhance students' cognitive capability in higher education, aiming to promote critical thinking and creativity, comparing it to existing algorithms, and addressing challenges (Al Ka'bi, 2023). AI's applications in classroom assessment, including large language models and test blueprint generation. It highlights challenges faced by teachers and suggests collaboration between educators, policymakers, and stakeholders to maximize AI's benefits and mitigate risks (Owan et al., 2023). The growing use AI in educational settings, including adaptive learning, smart campuses, teacher evaluation, and virtual classrooms (Alam, 2023).

Figure 2. Benefit
(Author)

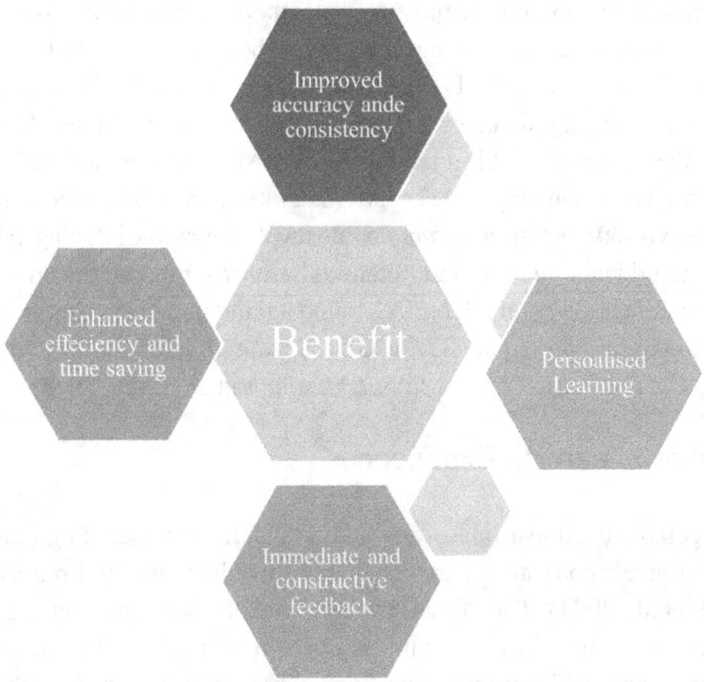

Improved Accuracy and Consistency

Artificial Intelligence is revolutionizing education by making learning accessible anytime, anywhere. This paper evaluates the role of AI in formative and summative assessment, with a focus on automated essay scoring systems and computerized adaptive tests. It also discusses the Big Data analysis approaches to machine learning that underpin these applications (Gardner et al., 2021). ChatGPT, an AI language model, to automate essay scoring (AES) for 12,100 essays in the ETS Corpus of Non-Native Written English (TOEFL11). The results show GPT has a certain level of accuracy and reliability, and linguistic features can enhance AES accuracy. This suggests that AI language models can revolutionize writing evaluation and feedback in research and practice (Mizumoto & Eguchi, 2023). Machine Learning to automatically grade middle school students' models and descriptions, incorporating disciplinary concepts and crosscutting ideas. However, accuracy is affected by five characteristics: alternative expression, confusing labels, inconsistent size, position, and redundant information (Zhai et al., 2022).

Immediate and Constructive Feedback

AI-powered writing tool significantly improves the academic writing skills of English second postgraduate students, promoting learning behavior and attitudinal technology acceptance (Nazari et al., 2021). This study reviews 63 AI-STEM research from 2011-2021, identifying six categories of AI applications and their distribution. It highlights the potential of AI in enhancing STEM education and calls for further exploration (Xu & Ouyang, 2022). AI integration in medical education, using ChatGPT for virtual teaching assistants, could revolutionize the learning of biomedical sciences, but ethical concerns and potential harm must be addressed (Lee, 2023). AI in higher education from 2016-2022 found a rapid increase in publications, with China leading. The study found 72% undergraduate students studied, with language learning being the most common subject (Crompton & Burke, 2023).

Personalized Learning Experiences

AI-based personalized learning offers potential solutions including compensating for peer absence, motivating learners, increasing diversity, and removing biases (Maghsudi et al., 2021). The effectiveness of personalized learning (PL) activities in online courses can address students' psychological need satisfaction and intrinsic motivation. Using self-determination theory, the study found that PL principles can support students' psychological needs and intrinsic motivation, and students found these interventions engaging and effective (Alamri et al., 2020). AI-powered video recommendations to boost students' motivation and engagement in a systems programming course, demonstrating significant improvement in learning performance and engagement for moderate motivation levels (Huang et al., 2023). Two studies show chatbots can enhance business education by providing interactive, confidential learning experiences. This research highlights the potential of chatbots in supporting inclusive learning and addressing student needs (Chen et al., 2023). The rapid development of AI has significantly impacted teaching and learning methods. It has been applied in adaptive learning, teaching evaluation, and virtual classrooms, improving teachers' and students' learning quality. However, AI applications may face challenges and require reform (Huang et al., 2021).

Advancements in AI-Automated Evaluation Techniques

The term Artificial Intelligence (AI) was first used at the Dartmouth Artificial Intelligence Conference in 1956 (Bhutani & Sanaria, 2023). Prominent scholars from several fields gathered to explore subjects related to extracting meaning from sensory information, the connection between randomness and innovative thought, and other themes that contributed to the development of the notion of "thinking machines" (Natale & Ballatore, 2020). The majority of participants envisioned the potential for computers to emulate human intellect, but their primary inquiry was the methods and timeline of this occurrence. Presently, AI is rapidly advancing and proliferating over all regions of the globe at a concerning pace (Tahiru, 2021) as it assumes a more significant part in our everyday existence. The increasing popularity of AI and machine learning has led to its broad implementation in many devices, apps, and services (Mishra & Tyagi, 2022). AI apps like Google Duplex and FaceApp perform speech activities, while autonomous hoover cleaners and humanoid robots like Yuki and Sophia demonstrate their significance in education, enhancing the efficiency and effectiveness of various tasks (Fujimoto, 2022). The AI-driven assessment tools has ushered in a new age of automated evaluation procedures. For example, within multiple-choice questions, AI algorithms have the capability to swiftly analyse and assess student replies, in terms of providing immediate feedback (Schneider et al., 2019). Moreover, the use of Natural Language Processing (NLP) techniques, which fall under the umbrella of AI, has greatly improved the evaluation of concise written responses. Assessment started a circle of improvement and proves learning since it affects students, teachers, administrators, and others, assessment and feedback are vital in higher education (Gour, 2020). Teachers spend a lot of time on assessment and feedback, but there is little progress in strategizing testing, providing trustworthy feedback, and analysing the effect of both in higher education (Hooda et al., 2022).

The incorporation of technologies that possess the capacity to assess grammar, coherence, and relevance has significantly transformed the assessment of students' written expressions (Luthfiyyah et al., 2021). Artificial intelligence models significantly transform the evaluation process for longer written assignments, ensuring uniformity and providing valuable feedback for students' intellectual development (Hourani et al., 2019). These developments combined signify a significant step towards the development of more efficient and precise evaluation procedures within the field of education.

Figure 3. Advancement in AI-automated evaluation technique
(Author)

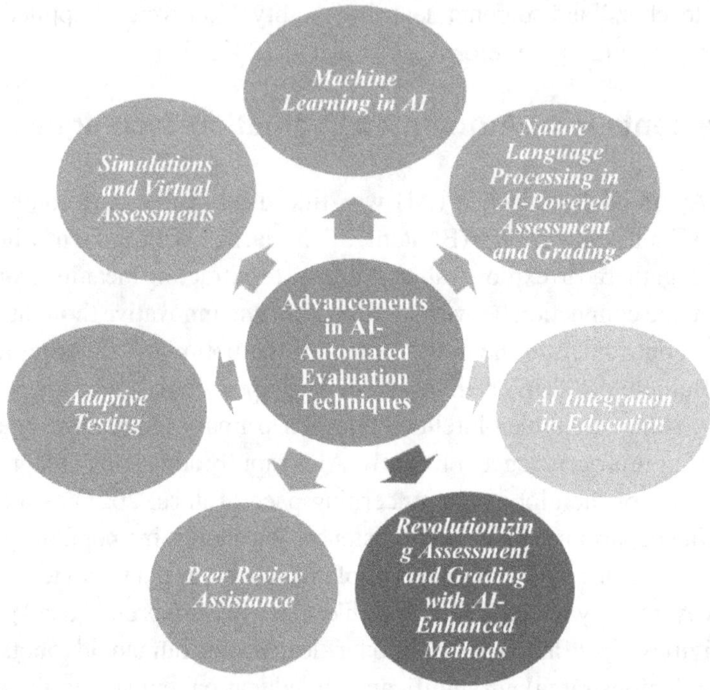

Revolutionizing Assessment and Grading with AI-Enhanced Methods

AI is revolutionizing educational evaluation by efficiently assessing assignments, providing constructive feedback, and fostering a dynamic learning environment, enabling personalized interventions and IoT-supported simulations (Kamruzzaman et al., 2023). Artificial intelligence (AI), machine learning (ML), and Internet of Things (IoT) technologies can automate labor-intensive tasks, including the processes of grading and attendance management. Educational software uses e-learning technology to facilitate students' intelligent learning, even in epidemic settings. One of the primary concerns that emerges within the educational system offered to pupils in a smart city is wireless learning settings (Kamruzzaman et al., 2023). GAI offers prospective lesson preparation, personalised learning assistance, fast assessment and evaluation, and student questions answered (Rahman & Watanobe, 2023). Artificial intelligence enhances educational evaluation with adaptive testing, adjusting question complexity to suit individual student learning, accurately estimating aptitude and providing a comprehensive learning experience (Alam, 2022).

Personalised assessment software framework generates individualized problem sets and automatically evaluates answers, potentially mitigating plagiarism in mathematics, engineering, science, and computer courses compared to conventional assignments (Manoharan, 2016). Automated grading, which is cheaper than and as effective as hand grading, shows how technology and education are integrated. This improvement simplifies evaluation and improves teaching for students and teachers (Messer et al., 2024). AI systems can grade examinations quickly and correctly, giving students immediate feedback this saves instructors time and assures fairness and consistency in assessment (Katz et al., 2022).

AI Integration in Education

AI integration in education improves efficiency, fairness, and personalized learning, but requires careful consideration of technology, ethics, and pedagogy. Anthology uses AI for equitable grading, reducing administrative workloads, and communication advancements, but requires teacher training and further research (González-Calatayud et al., 2021). AI's impact on education, focusing on its application in administration, instruction, and learning. It uses a qualitative approach and literature review, highlighting improvements in administrative functions, grading, and personalized curriculum (González-Calatayud et al., 2021). AI education policy in Hong Kong universities, focusing on text generative AI technologies, using data from 457 students and 180 teachers (Chan, 2023). AI performance prediction with learning analytics to enhance student learning in an online engineering course, enhancing engagement, performance, and satisfaction (Ouyang et al., 2023b). The Intelligent-TPACK framework suggests that teachers need both TK and PK to effectively integrate AI in education, highlighting the need for teachers to possess both technological and pedagogical knowledge (Celik, 2023).

Machine Learning in AI

Machine learning has significantly impacted Augmentative and Alternative Communication (AAC), but ethical concerns remain due to potential bullying, misinformation, and high hiring costs (Sennott et al., 2019). AI and machine learning are revolutionizing orthopedics, improving patient care through payment models, imaging analysis, and remote monitoring, urging surgeons to utilize AI applications (Helm et al., 2020). Machine learning models for low-performance hardware in the Internet of Things pave the way for the Internet of Conscious Things, and provides an example of edge machine learning implementation on a microcontroller (Merenda et al., 2020). The University of Illinois collaborated with educators and computer scientists to explore AI's potential in education, arguing that while AI cannot replace teachers, it can enhance human-like learning experiences (Cope et al., 2021). Moreover, around 49 articles on machine learning-based science assessment, focusing on technical, validity, and pedagogical features. It identifies research gaps and suggests future studies address these aspects (Zhai et al., 2020). Machine learning algorithms for teacher teaching evaluation, focusing on weighted naive Bayes (WNB) for improved classification accuracy, addressing existing evaluation issues and introducing relevant theories (Hu, 2021).

Nature Language Processing in AI-Powered Assessment and Grading

The AI-powered rubric method, while incorporating human aspects, is appealing due to its ability to be personalized based on learning goals and assessment standards, ensuring a tailored and compassionate grading process that balances technology and human competence. Recent studies transitioned from NLP-based methods to deep learning models for sentiment analysis in text-based corpora, leading to a rise (Ghelani, 2022). Pre-training and transfer learning techniques like ELMo, GPT, BERT, XLM, and XLNet have significantly improved natural language processing tasks, outperforming unsupervised models in Stanford Natural Language Inference datasets, but they lack reasoning skills and uniformity (Abdul Salam et al., 2022; Ndukwe et al., 2020). Sentence-Bidirectional Encoder Representations (SBERT) addresses computational costs in sentence-pair regression, offering automatic grading and personalized feedback to avoid guessing and inadequate feedback.

Open-ended inquiries require free text replies, but instructors face challenges due to natural language adaptability, variability, and specialized systems prone to false-positive and false-negative grading (Sychev et al., 2020). Template systems improve response accuracy but require expertise and resources. Open-ended text responses struggle with feedback, and quiz systems often fail to address specific errors. Natural-language processing algorithms can provide comprehensive feedback, comparing right answers with learners. Differentiating between tiers of textual analysis is beneficial (Zheng et al., 2019).

Simulations and Virtual Assessments

AI can be used in virtual simulations and assessments to evaluate performance and provide real-time feedback. VR, a computer-generated world, is widely used in education for scientific exploration, campus development, instruction, and training (Tabatabai, 2020). The study aims to develop a new teaching method using digital virtual technology in higher vocational education, integrating virtual simulation practice, practical training, skills training, emotional education, and information technology (Hao, 2019).

Adaptive Testing

AI-driven adaptive testing uses Item Response Theory to customize assessments, adjusting question difficulty based on student responses, resulting in more personalized and accurate evaluations of knowledge (Papanastasiou & Solomonidou, 2023). Adaptive learning systems, widely used in the US and China, cater to individual learning needs and capabilities. With over 2 million users in China in the last three years, this research aims to evaluate the effectiveness of personalized adaptive learning compared to traditional classroom methods (Wang et al., 2023). Education 4.0 emphasizes academic performance for university selection, addressing challenges in competitive markets. Research uses mathematical techniques to predict achievement and improve curriculum quality (Chen et al., 2020).

Peer Review Assistance

A peer review method that integrates instruction, self-assessment, and AI quality-control to enhance peer comments, resulting in longer feedback from 374 participants (Darvishi, Khosravi, Abdi, et al., 2022). Artificial Intelligence in Education (AIEd) is used in higher education, focusing on Computer Science and STEM fields. The research reveals four domains: profiling and prediction, assessment and evaluation, adaptive systems and personalization, and intelligent tutoring systems. However, the study highlights limitations in critical analysis, insufficient integration with theoretical pedagogical frameworks, and the need for more ethical and educational strategies for AIEd in higher education (Zawacki-Richter et al., 2019). High-quality written subject summaries enhance engagement in peer review tasks, leading to higher-quality reviews. Instructional design methods can improve student engagement in MOOCs (Indriasari et al., 2020).

DISCUSSION

The integration of AI and automated evaluation techniques in higher education presents both benefits and challenges, including efficiency, standardization, and ethical issues (Kamalov et al., 2023). Technical complexity, concerns about data privacy and bias, as well as resistance from educators and stakeholders, pose significant challenges to widespread adoption. Educational institutions should address challenges proactively and leverage AI-enhanced methods to harness the transformative potential of automated evaluation techniques based on improved teaching and learning experiences. The Educational Renaissance explores the transformative impact of AI integration in education, aiming to enhance learning outcomes, foster innovation, and redefine educators' roles as facilitators in technology-enhanced learning environments (Husain, 2023). AI and learning analytics are revolutionizing personalized education in higher education, enhancing student engagement and optimizing outcomes, but ethical considerations, implementation challenges, and faculty training are crucial (Vashishth et al., 2024). AI's role in student performance assessment and its future in education, highlighting its adaptability and ability to automate assessment, aid in fast decision-making, and provide continuous feedback on student progress (Halagatti et al., 2023). Big data and AI are gaining momentum in education research, policy-making, and industry. Key trends include assessment, individualized learning, and precision education. Governments should support lifelong learning, protect personal data, and foster reciprocal relationships (Luan et al., 2020). The education system relies on human assessment, but manual evaluations are time-consuming and unreliable. Online examination systems exist, but grading essays and short answers remains challenging (Ramesh & Sanampudi, 2022). The state of automated assessment of computer science assignments, focusing on exercises, security measures, testing techniques, feedback, and teacher information. It also identifies a new era using static analysis techniques and containerization (Paiva et al., 2022). Students' expectations and perceived effectiveness of computer-assisted review tools for improving English writing ability, finding computer scoring feedback more effective than teacher feedback (Wang, 2022). The AI-supported RTP-AIEW approach to enhance English writing skills, with results showing improved performance, self-efficacy, self-regulated learning, and reduced cognitive load in university EFL writing classes (Liu et al., 2023). The benefit in AI includes ChatGPT, a generative AI tool that gained over one million subscribers in a week, promoting personalized learning and formative assessment prompts. However, limitations include incorrect information generation and privacy issues (Baidoo-Anu & Ansah, 2023). AI studies in education from 1970-2020 identify clusters, themes, and ethical considerations, focusing on adaptive learning, deep learning algorithms, human-AI interaction, and AI-generated data use (Bozkurt et al., 2021). The potential of AI technologies in education includes chatbots and algorithms that simulate human interactions. It discusses the ethical and practical challenges of incorporating AI into education, aiming to provide insights for effective use while promoting responsible and ethical use (Adıgüzel et al., 2023). Engineering education is utilizing generative AI technology such as ChatGPT for personalized learning experiences. However, it's crucial to consider its limitations, such as potential biases and misinformation. Additionally, ethical concerns arise, such as unethical use and potential unemployment. The current state of ChatGPT is a preview of future advancements, and it's crucial for educators to understand these implications and adapt the education ecosystem to ensure the next generation benefits from generative AI (Qadir, 2023).

CONCLUSION

The use of AI in higher education signifies a significant progression in the pursuit of enhanced and tailored learning encounters. Artificial intelligence (AI) has the potential to mitigate the resource-intensive challenges encountered by educators by automating exams, grading, and feedback. This enables educators to focus their efforts on more complex aspects of education. Furthermore, the ability of AI to provide customised learning experiences guarantees that students are provided with the personalised assistance necessary for achieving academic excellence. The integration of AI in higher education institutions can foster a more inclusive, dynamic, and empowering learning environment, paving the way for a novel age of learning and enhanced educational experiences.

Based on the discussion and analysis above on automated evaluation techniques and AI-enhanced methods, the following recommendations are made:

- Educational institutions should invest in professional development programs for educators to improve their understanding and skills in using AI for assessment, grading and feedback, covering topics such as algorithms, data privacy, and ethical considerations.
- It is essential to foster collaboration between educators and AI developers for successful implementation of AI in higher education to establish partnerships to co-design and develop AI systems tailored to specific needs and goals.
- Institutions should continuously monitor and address biases in AI-based methods for assessment, grading, and feedback through regular evaluations and audits, and involve diverse stakeholders in decision-making to ensure fair and inclusive use of AI technologies.

REFERENCES

Abdul Salam, M., El-Fatah, M. A., & Hassan, N. F. (2022). Automatic grading for Arabic short answer questions using optimized deep learning model. *PLoS One*, *17*(8), e0272269. doi:10.1371/journal.pone.0272269 PMID:35917309

Adıgüzel, T., Kaya, M. H., & Cansu, F. K. (2023). Revolutionizing education with AI: Exploring the transformative potential of ChatGPT. *Contemporary Educational Technology*, *15*(3), ep429. doi:10.30935/cedtech/13152

Akgun, S., & Greenhow, C. (2022). Artificial intelligence in education: Addressing ethical challenges in K-12 settings. *AI and Ethics*, *2*(3), 431–440. doi:10.1007/s43681-021-00096-7 PMID:34790956

Al Ka'bi, A. (2023). Proposed artificial intelligence algorithm and deep learning techniques for development of higher education. *International Journal of Intelligent Networks*, *4*, 68–73. doi:10.1016/j.ijin.2023.03.002

Al-Khassawneh, Y. A. (2023). A review of artificial intelligence in security and privacy: Research advances, applications, opportunities, and challenges. *Indonesian Journal of Science and Technology*, *8*(1), 79–96. doi:10.17509/ijost.v8i1.52709

Alam, A. (2022). Employing adaptive learning and intelligent tutoring robots for virtual classrooms and smart campuses: Reforming education in the age of artificial intelligence. In *Advanced computing and intelligent technologies* [Springer.]. *Proceedings of ICACIT, 2022*, 395–406.

Alamri, H., Lowell, V., Watson, W., & Watson, S. L. (2020). Using personalized learning as an instructional approach to motivate learners in online higher education: Learner self-determination and intrinsic motivation. *Journal of Research on Technology in Education*, *52*(3), 322–352.

Baidoo-Anu, D., & Ansah, L. O. (2023). Education in the era of generative artificial intelligence (AI): Understanding the potential benefits of ChatGPT in promoting teaching and learning. *Journal of AI*, *7*(1), 52–62.

Bhutani, A., & Sanaria, A. (2023). *The Past*. Present and Future of Artificial Intelligence.

Bozkurt, A., Karadeniz, A., Baneres, D., Guerrero-Roldán, A. E., & Rodríguez, M. E. (2021). Artificial intelligence and reflections from educational landscape: A review of AI Studies in half a century. *Sustainability (Basel)*, *13*(2), 800. doi:10.3390/su13020800

Celik, I. (2023). Towards Intelligent-TPACK: An empirical study on teachers' professional knowledge to ethically integrate artificial intelligence (AI)-based tools into education. *Computers in Human Behavior*, *138*, 107468. doi:10.1016/j.chb.2022.107468

Chan, C. K. Y. (2023). A comprehensive AI policy education framework for university teaching and learning. *International Journal of Educational Technology in Higher Education, 20*(1), 38. doi:10.1186/s41239-023-00408-3

Chan, K. S., & Zary, N. (2019). Applications and challenges of implementing artificial intelligence in medical education: Integrative review. *JMIR Medical Education, 5*(1), e13930. doi:10.2196/13930 PMID:31199295

Chen, Y., Jensen, S., Albert, L. J., Gupta, S., & Lee, T. (2023). Artificial intelligence (AI) student assistants in the classroom: Designing chatbots to support student success. *Information Systems Frontiers, 25*(1), 161–182. doi:10.1007/s10796-022-10291-4

Chen, Z., Zhang, J., Jiang, X., Hu, Z., Han, X., Xu, M., Savitha, V., & Vivekananda, G. (2020). Education 4.0 using artificial intelligence for students performance analysis. *Inteligencia Artificial, 23*(66), 124–137.

Cook, C., Jones, J., & Al-Twal, A. (2022). Validity and fairness of utilising student evaluation of teaching (SET) as a primary performance measure. *Journal of Further and Higher Education, 46*(2), 172–184. doi:10.1080/0309877X.2021.1895093

Cope, B., Kalantzis, M., & Searsmith, D. (2021). Artificial intelligence for education: Knowledge and its assessment in AI-enabled learning ecologies. *Educational Philosophy and Theory, 53*(12), 1229–1245. doi:10.1080/00131857.2020.1728732

Crompton, H., & Burke, D. (2023). Artificial intelligence in higher education: The state of the field. *International Journal of Educational Technology in Higher Education, 20*(1), 22. doi:10.1186/s41239-023-00392-8

Darvishi, A., Khosravi, H., Abdi, S., Sadiq, S., & Gašević, D. (2022). Incorporating training, self-monitoring and AI-assistance to improve peer feedback quality. Proceedings of the Ninth ACM Conference on Learning@ Scale, Darvishi, A., Khosravi, H., Sadiq, S., & Gašević, D. (2022). Incorporating AI and learning analytics to build trustworthy peer assessment systems. *British Journal of Educational Technology, 53*(4), 844–875. doi:10.1111/bjet.13233

De Gagne, J. C. (2023). Values clarification exercises to prepare nursing students for artificial intelligence integration. *International Journal of Environmental Research and Public Health, 20*(14), 6409. doi:10.3390/ijerph20146409 PMID:37510641

Deeva, G., Bogdanova, D., Serral, E., Snoeck, M., & De Weerdt, J. (2021). A review of automated feedback systems for learners: Classification framework, challenges and opportunities. *Computers & Education, 162*, 104094. doi:10.1016/j.compedu.2020.104094

Fujimoto, T. (2022). Reproduction of humanness based on eXtended intelligence: Concept of artificial personality and its mechanism. *International Journal of Computational Systems Engineering*, *7*(1), 30–40. doi:10.1504/IJCSYSE.2022.131034

Gardner, J., O'Leary, M., & Yuan, L. (2021). Artificial intelligence in educational assessment: 'Breakthrough? Or buncombe and ballyhoo?'. *Journal of Computer Assisted Learning*, *37*(5), 1207–1216. doi:10.1111/jcal.12577

Gedrimiene, E., Celik, I., Kaasila, A., Mäkitalo, K., & Muukkonen, H. (2024). Artificial intelligence (AI)-enhanced learning analytics (LA) for supporting career decisions: Advantages and challenges from user perspective. *Education and Information Technologies*, *29*(1), 297–322. doi:10.1007/s10639-023-12277-4

Ghelani, D. (2022). *A review on student automatic grading system D.*

González-Calatayud, V., Prendes-Espinosa, P., & Roig-Vila, R. (2021). Artificial intelligence for student assessment: A systematic review. *Applied Sciences (Basel, Switzerland)*, *11*(12), 5467. doi:10.3390/app11125467

González-Carrillo, C. D., Restrepo-Calle, F., Ramírez-Echeverry, J. J., & González, F. A. (2021). Automatic grading tool for jupyter notebooks in artificial intelligence courses. *Sustainability (Basel)*, *13*(21), 12050. doi:10.3390/su132112050

Gour, A. (2020). AI-based Natural Language Processing (NLP) Systems. *Journal of Algebraic Statistics*, *11*(1), 48–58.

Halagatti, M., Gadag, S., Mahantshetti, S., Hiremath, C. V., Tharkude, D., & Banakar, V. (2023). Artificial Intelligence: The New Tool of Disruption in Educational Performance Assessment. In Smart Analytics, Artificial Intelligence and Sustainable Performance Management in a Global Digitalised Economy (pp. 261-287). Emerald Publishing Limited.

Helm, J. M., Swiergosz, A. M., Haeberle, H. S., Karnuta, J. M., Schaffer, J. L., Krebs, V. E., Spitzer, A. I., & Ramkumar, P. N. (2020). Machine learning and artificial intelligence: Definitions, applications, and future directions. *Current Reviews in Musculoskeletal Medicine*, *13*, 69–76.

Hooda, M., Rana, C., Dahiya, O., Rizwan, A., & Hossain, M. S. (2022). Artificial intelligence for assessment and feedback to enhance student success in higher education. *Mathematical Problems in Engineering*, *2022*, 2022. doi:10.1155/2022/5215722

Hourani, H., Hammad, A., & Lafi, M. (2019). The impact of artificial intelligence on software testing. *2019 IEEE Jordan International Joint Conference on Electrical Engineering and Information Technology (JEEIT)*. IEEE.

Huang, A. Y., Lu, O. H., & Yang, S. J. (2023). Effects of artificial Intelligence–Enabled personalized recommendations on learners' learning engagement, motivation, and outcomes in a flipped classroom. *Computers & Education, 194*, 104684. doi:10.1016/j.compedu.2022.104684

Huang, J., Saleh, S., & Liu, Y. (2021). A review on artificial intelligence in education. *Academic Journal of Interdisciplinary Studies, 10*(3).

Humble, N., & Mozelius, P. (2022). Discover. *Artificial Intelligence*.

Husain, N. (2023). Educational Renaissance: Unleashing the Potential of Interdisciplinary AI Integration. *Journal of Environmental Science and Technology, 2*(1), 159–166.

Ifenthaler, D. (2022). Automated essay scoring systems. In *Handbook of open, distance and digital education* (pp. 1–15). Springer. doi:10.1007/978-981-19-0351-9_59-1

Ifenthaler, D., & Yau, J. Y.-K. (2020). Utilising learning analytics to support study success in higher education: A systematic review. *Educational Technology Research and Development, 68*(4), 1961–1990. doi:10.1007/s11423-020-09788-z

Indriasari, T. D., Luxton-Reilly, A., & Denny, P. (2020). Gamification of student peer review in education: A systematic literature review. *Education and Information Technologies, 25*(6), 5205–5234. doi:10.1007/s10639-020-10228-x

Israel, M. J., & Amer, A. (2023). Rethinking data infrastructure and its ethical implications in the face of automated digital content generation. *AI and Ethics, 3*(2), 427–439. doi:10.1007/s43681-022-00169-1

Jansen, R. S., van Leeuwen, A., Janssen, J., Conijn, R., & Kester, L. (2020). Supporting learners' self-regulated learning in Massive Open Online Courses. *Computers & Education, 146*, 103771. doi:10.1016/j.compedu.2019.103771

Kamalov, F., Santandreu Calonge, D., & Gurrib, I. (2023). New era of artificial intelligence in education: Towards a sustainable multifaceted revolution. *Sustainability (Basel), 15*(16), 12451. doi:10.3390/su151612451

Kamruzzaman, M., Alanazi, S., Alruwaili, M., Alshammari, N., Elaiwat, S., Abu-Zanona, M., Innab, N., Mohammad Elzaghmouri, B., & Ahmed Alanazi, B. (2023). AI-and IoT-Assisted Sustainable Education Systems during Pandemics, such as COVID-19, for Smart Cities. *Sustainability (Basel), 15*(10), 8354. doi:10.3390/su15108354

Kasneci, E., Seßler, K., Küchemann, S., Bannert, M., Dementieva, D., Fischer, F., Gasser, U., Groh, G., Günnemann, S., Hüllermeier, E., Krusche, S., Kutyniok, G., Michaeli, T., Nerdel, C., Pfeffer, J., Poquet, O., Sailer, M., Schmidt, A., Seidel, T., & Kasneci, G. (2023). ChatGPT for good? On opportunities and challenges of large language models for education. *Learning and Individual Differences*, *103*, 102274. doi:10.1016/j.lindif.2023.102274

Katz, O., Presil, D., Cohen, L., Nachmani, R., Kirshner, N., Hoch, Y., Lev, T., Hadad, A., Hewitt, R. J., & Owens, D. R. (2022). Evaluation of a new neural network classifier for diabetic retinopathy. *Journal of Diabetes Science and Technology*, *16*(6), 1401–1409. doi:10.1177/19322968211042665 PMID:34549633

Khosravi, H., Shum, S. B., Chen, G., Conati, C., Tsai, Y.-S., Kay, J., Knight, S., Martinez-Maldonado, R., Sadiq, S., & Gašević, D. (2022). Explainable artificial intelligence in education. *Computers and Education: Artificial Intelligence*, *3*, 100074.

Lee, H. (2023). The rise of ChatGPT: Exploring its potential in medical education. *Anatomical Sciences Education*, ase.2270. doi:10.1002/ase.2270 PMID:36916887

Liu, C., Hou, J., Tu, Y.-F., Wang, Y., & Hwang, G.-J. (2023). Incorporating a reflective thinking promoting mechanism into artificial intelligence-supported English writing environments. *Interactive Learning Environments*, *31*(9), 5614–5632. doi:10.1080/10494820.2021.2012812

Luan, H., Geczy, P., Lai, H., & Li, P. (2020). Challenges and future directions of big data and artificial intelligence in education. *Frontiers in Psychology*, *11*, 580820. doi:10.3389/fpsyg.2020.580820 PMID:33192896

Ludwig, S., Mayer, C., Hansen, C., Eilers, K., & Brandt, S. (2021). Automated essay scoring using transformer models. *Psych*, *3*(4), 897–915. doi:10.3390/psych3040056

Luthfiyyah, R., Aisyah, A., & Sulistyo, G. H. (2021). Technology-enhanced formative assessment in higher education: A voice from Indonesian EFL teachers. *EduLite: Journal of English Education. Literature and Culture*, *6*(1), 42–54.

Maghsudi, S., Lan, A., Xu, J., & van Der Schaar, M. (2021). Personalized education in the artificial intelligence era: What to expect next. *IEEE Signal Processing Magazine*, *38*(3), 37–50. doi:10.1109/MSP.2021.3055032

Manoharan, S. (2016). Personalized assessment as a means to mitigate plagiarism. *IEEE Transactions on Education*, *60*(2), 112–119. doi:10.1109/TE.2016.2604210

Mehrabi, N., Morstatter, F., Saxena, N., Lerman, K., & Galstyan, A. (2021). A survey on bias and fairness in machine learning. *ACM Computing Surveys*, *54*(6), 1–35. doi:10.1145/3457607

Merenda, M., Porcaro, C., & Iero, D. (2020). Edge machine learning for ai-enabled iot devices: A review. *Sensors (Basel)*, *20*(9), 2533. doi:10.3390/s20092533 PMID:32365645

Messer, M., Brown, N. C., Kölling, M., & Shi, M. (2024). Automated grading and feedback tools for programming education: A systematic review. *ACM Transactions on Computing Education*, *24*(1), 1–43. doi:10.1145/3636515

Mishra, S., & Tyagi, A. K. (2022). The role of machine learning techniques in internet of things-based cloud applications. *Artificial intelligence-based internet of things systems*, 105-135.

Mizumoto, A., & Eguchi, M. (2023). Exploring the potential of using an AI language model for automated essay scoring. *Research Methods in Applied Linguistics*, *2*(2), 100050. doi:10.1016/j.rmal.2023.100050

Mora, H., Signes-Pont, M. T., Fuster-Guilló, A., & Pertegal-Felices, M. L. (2020). A collaborative working model for enhancing the learning process of science & engineering students. *Computers in Human Behavior*, *103*, 140–150. doi:10.1016/j.chb.2019.09.008

Naseer, F., Khalid, M. U., Ayub, N., Rasool, A., Abbas, T., & Afzal, M. W. (2024). Automated Assessment and Feedback in Higher Education Using Generative AI. In Transforming Education With Generative AI: Prompt Engineering and Synthetic Content Creation (pp. 433-461). IGI Global. doi:10.4018/979-8-3693-1351-0.ch021

Natale, S., & Ballatore, A. (2020). Imagining the thinking machine: Technological myths and the rise of artificial intelligence. *Convergence (London)*, *26*(1), 3–18. doi:10.1177/1354856517715164

Nazari, N., Shabbir, M. S., & Setiawan, R. (2021). Application of Artificial Intelligence powered digital writing assistant in higher education: Randomized controlled trial. *Heliyon*, *7*(5), e07014. doi:10.1016/j.heliyon.2021.e07014 PMID:34027198

Ndukwe, I. G., Amadi, C. E., Nkomo, L. M., & Daniel, B. K. (2020). *Automatic grading system using sentence-BERT network*. Artificial Intelligence in Education: 21st International Conference, AIED 2020, Ifrane, Morocco.

Ouyang, F., Wu, M., Zheng, L., Zhang, L., & Jiao, P. (2023a). Integration of artificial intelligence performance prediction and learning analytics to improve student learning in online engineering course. *International Journal of Educational Technology in Higher Education*, *20*(1), 1–23. doi:10.1186/s41239-022-00372-4 PMID:36683653

Ouyang, F., Wu, M., Zheng, L., Zhang, L., & Jiao, P. (2023b). Integration of artificial intelligence performance prediction and learning analytics to improve student learning in online engineering course. *International Journal of Educational Technology in Higher Education*, *20*(1), 4. doi:10.1186/s41239-022-00372-4 PMID:36683653

Owan, V. J., Abang, K. B., Idika, D. O., Etta, E. O., & Bassey, B. A. (2023). Exploring the potential of artificial intelligence tools in educational measurement and assessment. *Eurasia Journal of Mathematics, Science and Technology Education*, *19*(8), em2307. doi:10.29333/ejmste/13428

Paiva, J. C., Leal, J. P., & Figueira, Á. (2022). Automated assessment in computer science education: A state-of-the-art review. [TOCE]. *ACM Transactions on Computing Education*, *22*(3), 1–40. doi:10.1145/3513140

Papanastasiou, E. C., & Solomonidou, G. (2023). Evaluating Emergency Remote Assessment Adaptations in Higher Education due to COVID-19: Faculty Insights and Challenges. *Education Sciences*, *13*(2), 184. doi:10.3390/educsci13020184

Qadir, J. (2023). Engineering education in the era of ChatGPT: Promise and pitfalls of generative AI for education. *2023 IEEE Global Engineering Education Conference (EDUCON)*. IEEE.

Rahman, M. M., & Watanobe, Y. (2023). ChatGPT for education and research: Opportunities, threats, and strategies. Applied Sciences (Basel, Switzerland), 13(9), 5783

Ramesh, D., & Sanampudi, S. K. (2022). An automated essay scoring systems: A systematic literature review. *Artificial Intelligence Review*, *55*(3), 2495–2527. doi:10.1007/s10462-021-10068-2 PMID:34584325

Rosen, C. (2023). Applying Cognitive Theory to the Teaching of Programming: Metaphors, Robots and Problem-Based Learning. In Higher Education Computer Science: A Manual of Practical Approaches (pp. 51-61). Springer.

Sarwar, M. A., Saima, M., & Gul, A. (2024). The Role of Artificial Intelligence in Shaping the Future of Education at Higher Secondary Level. *Journal of Education and Social Studies*, *5*(1), 34–45. doi:10.52223/jess.2024.5104

Schneider, A., Kühl, M., & Kühl, S. J. (2019). Utilizing research findings in medical education: The testing effect within a flipped/inverted biochemistry classroom. *Medical Teacher*, *41*(11), 1245–1251. doi:10.1080/0142159X.2019.1628195 PMID:31282246

Schuett, J. (2019). A legal definition of AI. arXiv preprint arXiv:1909.01095.

Sennott, S. C., Akagi, L., Lee, M., & Rhodes, A. (2019). AAC and artificial intelligence (AI). *Topics in Language Disorders*, *39*(4), 389–403. doi:10.1097/TLD.0000000000000197 PMID:34012187

Sychev, O., Anikin, A., & Prokudin, A. (2020). Automatic grading and hinting in open-ended text questions. *Cognitive Systems Research*, *59*, 264–272. doi:10.1016/j.cogsys.2019.09.025

Tabatabai, S. (2020). Simulations and virtual learning supporting clinical education during the COVID 19 pandemic. *Advances in Medical Education and Practice*, *11*, 513–516. doi:10.2147/AMEP.S257750 PMID:32821192

Tahiru, F. (2021). AI in education: A systematic literature review. [JCIT]. *Journal of Cases on Information Technology*, *23*(1), 1–20. doi:10.4018/JCIT.2021010101

Teng, Y., Zhang, J., & Sun, T. (2023). Data-driven decision-making model based on artificial intelligence in higher education system of colleges and universities. *Expert Systems: International Journal of Knowledge Engineering and Neural Networks*, *40*(4), e12820. doi:10.1111/exsy.12820

Van der Kleij, F. M., & Lipnevich, A. A. (2021). Student perceptions of assessment feedback: A critical scoping review and call for research. *Educational Assessment, Evaluation and Accountability*, *33*(2), 345–373. doi:10.1007/s11092-020-09331-x

Vashishth, T. K., Sharma, V., Sharma, K. K., Kumar, B., Panwar, R., & Chaudhary, S. (2024). AI-Driven Learning Analytics for Personalized Feedback and Assessment in Higher Education. In *Using Traditional Design Methods to Enhance AI-Driven Decision Making* (pp. 206–230). IGI Global. doi:10.4018/979-8-3693-0639-0.ch009

Walker, M. E., Olivera-Aguilar, M., Lehman, B., Laitusis, C., Guzman-Orth, D., & Gholson, M. (2023). Culturally Responsive Assessment: Provisional Principles. *ETS Research Report Series*, *2023*(1), 1–24. doi:10.1002/ets2.12374

Wan, P., Wang, X., Lin, Y., & Pang, G. (2021). A knowledge diffusion model in autonomous learning under multiple networks for personalized educational resource allocation. *IEEE Transactions on Learning Technologies*, *14*(4), 430–444. doi:10.1109/TLT.2021.3103006

Wang, S., Christensen, C., Cui, W., Tong, R., Yarnall, L., Shear, L., & Feng, M. (2023). When adaptive learning is effective learning: Comparison of an adaptive learning system to teacher-led instruction. *Interactive Learning Environments*, *31*(2), 793–803. doi:10.1080/10494820.2020.1808794

Wang, Z. (2022). Computer-assisted EFL writing and evaluations based on artificial intelligence: A case from a college reading and writing course. *Library Hi Tech*, *40*(1), 80–97. doi:10.1108/LHT-05-2020-0113

Winstone, N. E., & Boud, D. (2022). The need to disentangle assessment and feedback in higher education. *Studies in Higher Education*, *47*(3), 656–667. doi:10.1080/03075079.2020.1779687

Xu, W., & Ouyang, F. (2022). The application of AI technologies in STEM education: A systematic review from 2011 to 2021. *International Journal of STEM Education*, *9*(1), 59. doi:10.1186/s40594-022-00377-5

Yan, L., Sha, L., Zhao, L., Li, Y., Martinez-Maldonado, R., Chen, G., Li, X., Jin, Y., & Gašević, D. (2024). Practical and ethical challenges of large language models in education: A systematic scoping review. *British Journal of Educational Technology*, *55*(1), 90–112. doi:10.1111/bjet.13370

Zawacki-Richter, O., Marín, V. I., Bond, M., & Gouverneur, F. (2019). Systematic review of research on artificial intelligence applications in higher education–where are the educators? *International Journal of Educational Technology in Higher Education*, *16*(1), 1–27. doi:10.1186/s41239-019-0171-0

Zhai, X., He, P., & Krajcik, J. (2022). Applying machine learning to automatically assess scientific models. *Journal of Research in Science Teaching*, *59*(10), 1765–1794. doi:10.1002/tea.21773

Zhai, X., Yin, Y., Pellegrino, J. W., Haudek, K. C., & Shi, L. (2020). Applying machine learning in science assessment: A systematic review. *Studies in Science Education*, *56*(1), 111–151. doi:10.1080/03057267.2020.1735757

Zhang, W., Cai, M., Lee, H. J., Evans, R., Zhu, C., & Ming, C. (2023). AI in Medical Education: Global situation, effects and challenges. *Education and Information Technologies*, •••, 1–23.

Zheng, Y., Niu, S., Shang, Y., Shao, Z., & Jian, L. (2019). Integrating plug-in electric vehicles into power grids: A comprehensive review on power interaction mode, scheduling methodology and mathematical foundation. *Renewable & Sustainable Energy Reviews*, *112*, 424–439. doi:10.1016/j.rser.2019.05.059

Zou, D., Huang, Y., & Xie, H. (2021). Digital game-based vocabulary learning: Where are we and where are we going? *Computer Assisted Language Learning*, *34*(5-6), 751–777. doi:10.1080/09588221.2019.1640745

Chapter 2
Enhancing Assessment Systems in Higher Education:
A Review on Artificial Intelligence Usage

Md. Al-Amin
University of Dhaka, Bangladesh

Fatematuz Zahra Saqui
University of Dhaka, Bangladesh

Md. Rabbi Khan
Bangabandhu Sheikh Mujibur Rahman Digital University, Bangladesh

ABSTRACT

Artificial intelligence (AI) has become an influential force in the rapidly changing 21st century, drastically changing the educational environment and providing novel approaches to transform teaching, learning, and the future of knowledge. Given the rising popularity of AI technology among educators and students, it is essential to investigate the current environment to comprehend how AI is being used in educational assessment – which is the aim of this book chapter. The study focuses on a few of the latest developments in artificial intelligence (AI)-based learning assessments through a narrative review of past research. Another aim of this chapter is to investigate the challenges related to the seamless incorporation of AI into assessment systems. These challenges allow educators to assess their readiness to incorporate AI tools into their assessment procedure. With its two-fold objective, this book chapter adds to the emerging discussion over how artificial intelligence (AI) could affect the assessment scenario in higher education.

DOI: 10.4018/979-8-3693-2145-4.ch002

INTRODUCTION

Artificial intelligence (AI) has emerged as an influential force in the 21st century in a wide range of sectors, including healthcare, security services, administration, and education (Bahroun et al., 2023; George & Wooden, 2023). Consequently, researchers in the educational sector have seen considerable changes in the advancement of language models, machine learning, natural language processing, and robotics due to the usage of artificial intelligence (Sharma et al., 2023; Soori et al., 2023). According to Xu et al. (2021), the development and use of intelligent systems that can carry out activities that have historically needed human intellect have increased due to technological advancements. AI can potentially improve learning outcomes, accelerate administrative procedures, and improve teaching and learning experiences in education (Ahmad et al., 2022; George & Wooden, 2023). Artificial intelligence (AI) is changing how things are taught and learned across educational institutes.

John McCarthy organized an "*artificial intelligence*" workshop at Dartmouth in 1956 and used this term for the first time (Moor, 2006). Since then, the word has become widespread. The history of AI started there in the mid-20th century, and educators then tried to explore the potential of computers to enhance learning experiences (Teachflow, 2023). The emergence of computer-based instruction (CBI) systems led to the early development of AI in educational settings in the 1960s (Moor, 2006). In the next two decades, intelligent tutoring systems and language learning tools were developed, and the transformative potentials of artificial intelligence became noteworthy (Teachfllow, 2023). Artificial intelligence has become more prevalent in educational development in recent years, especially after the evolution of large language models (Sheehan, 2023). Further, Automated tutoring and intelligent textbooks and resources opened a wide gateway to the next generation of personalized learning. However, ethical issues and equitable access remain criticisms of these innovations (Lynch, 2024).

Personalized learning experiences are one of the main advantages of AI in higher education (Pratama et al., 2023). Intelligent tutoring systems offer customized learning and feedback, recognizing students' misunderstandings and monitoring their development over time (Alkhatlan & Kalita, 2018; Graesser et al., 2018). Tailored feedback systems offer focused interventions according to student conduct (Celik et al., 2022; Chen et al., 2020; Hooda et al., 2022). Learners' engagement is increased by personalized resources adapted to their interests and skill levels (Aggarwal, 2023; Chen et al., 2020). Adaptive learning systems use AI algorithms to assess students' learning styles and provide information specifically suited to them (Aggarwal, 2023; Gligorea et al., 2023). AI-powered systems streamline administrative tasks, including student enrollment, by automating repetitive tasks and resolving student queries (Hannan & Liu, 2023; Srinivasa et al., 2022). Automated content production algorithms generate efficient instructional materials (Ng et al., 2023; Pedro et al., 2019). AI tools for grading and evaluation save teachers time by analyzing student replies, producing performance metrics, and offering immediate feedback (Chen et al., 2020; Vashishth et al., 2024). AI-driven virtual reality (VR) and gamification systems provide immersive and dynamic learning experiences concerning student engagement and outcomes (Almusaed et al., 2023). According to Shadbad et al. (2023), virtual reality settings imitate real-world events to facilitate experiential learning, while gamification components encourage student involvement. Examining how students engage with the material, intelligent feedback, and recommendation systems can pinpoint areas for development and make recommendations for pertinent resources (Kochmar et al., 2020). Artificial intelligence-based chatbots, virtual assistants, and collaborative platforms that link students with shared interests enable social and collaborative learning (Labadze et al., 2023). These resources facilitate peer communication, knowledge exchange, and cooperative problem-solving (Magnisalis et al., 2011; McLaren et al., 2010).

Advantages of AI in higher education comes along with their drawbacks and moral dilemmas (Pedro et al., 2019; Zawacki-Richter et al., 2019). Using AI to collect and store sensitive student data raises privacy and data security issues (Luan et al., 2020). Since AI-enabled devices need connectivity and access to technological resources, equity and access challenges could limit their potential (Roshanaei et al., 2023). This has the potential of increasing the existing digital divide among Global North and South. The requirement for faculty professional development in AI literacy, instructional design, and data analytics is another issue posed by AI's implications for higher education institutions (Drugova et al., 2023). As AI enhances the capacities of human instructors, it reshapes the interaction between students and teachers by encouraging cooperation and mutual assistance. Overhauling the curriculum to make it AI-friendly through adaptive learning and data-driven insights adds to the woes of champions of AI in higher education.

Higher education institutes are increasingly bombarded with AI tools, raising concerns about access, privacy, and ethics. Despite the promises of a more productive, learner-centered educational experience, institutions must carefully consider the broader implications of implementing these technologies and build necessary safeguards for potential hazards. The framework in Figure 1, adopted from Cheng et al. (2023), compiles the students' perspectives on the positives and negatives of artificial intelligence in the education system.

To understand the application and implications of artificial intelligence technology, educational researchers are emphasizing this topic with great scholarly interest. For instance, Zawacki-Richter et al. (2019) conducted a systematic literature review including 146 research articles that revealed common applications of AI in academic and administrative services, i.e., profiling and predicting students' performance, assessing learning outcomes, performing adaptive systems, and intelligent tutoring. Crompton and Burke (2023) highlighted five key applications of artificial intelligence in higher education: (1) assessment/evaluation, (2) prediction, (3) AI support, (4) intelligent tutoring systems (ITS), and (5) student learning management. Similarly, the comprehensive review of Ouyang et al. (2022) explored the role, impact, and consequences of AI use in online higher education. The study attempts to identify popular AI algorithms and their impact on online higher education. In other research, AlDhaen (2022) concentrated on policy implications and proposed policy recommendations for educational institutions and policymakers. Ismail et al. (2023) aimed at conducting a systematic review of the literature on artificial intelligence (AI), where the researchers proposed a chatbot model in higher education. These papers tried to demonstrate various aspects of AI usage in higher education by emphasizing its diverse uses, emerging trends, and potential policy implications. However, the application of artificial intelligence for assessment, grading, and feedback in higher educational institutions remains a prominent area of research, as the number of investigative studies in this area is insignificant. As a result, current research attempts to close the research gap by demonstrating the application of AI to enhance the assessment system in higher education.

TRADITIONAL ASSESSMENT METHODS IN HIGHER EDUCATION

Assessment is essential to education since it entails methodically obtaining data and using predetermined standards to create a judgment. Since they continuously affect effective learning outcomes and student satisfaction, evaluation and feedback are essential to learning, teaching, and curriculum improvement (Nedelsky, 1954). Some of the notable assessment types are briefly discussed below.

Summative assessment: Summative assessments thoroughly analyze students' learning outcomes and are carried out at the end of a course module. Combining insights from the teaching and learning processes gives educators the necessary knowledge about their students' academic accomplishments (Marriott, 2009). Grades, projects, term papers, and standardized exams are often used for summative evaluation (Kibble, 2017). Summative assessment has been shown to have the following benefits: (1) assisting teachers in avoiding mistakes; (2) improving performance in error correction; (3) providing accurate information for learners, teachers, and administrators in higher education environments; and (4) assisting with educational planning, such as curriculum development or funding allocation (Hancock, 2010; Knight, 2002; Marriott, 2008). Historically, summative assessment has been the focus of academics and higher education institutions to gauge students' learning outcomes over a predetermined period. Nevertheless, this method frequently ignores other aspects of the learning process, and the assessments given to students might not always improve their educational experiences (Mekonen & Fitiavana, 2021).

Formative Assessment: This assessment is a dynamic, continuing process integrated into the learning experience to guide instructional decisions and offer continual feedback. Instructors use various methods, including discussions, quizzes, and observations during the learning process, to execute formative assessments efficiently. Such assessment allows teachers to evaluate students' comprehension in real-time (Wood, 2018). A prominent benefit of formative assessment is its capacity to improve student learning outcomes. Formative assessments provide prompt feedback, foster self-efficacy, and reduce dropout rates through their motivating components (Evans et al., 2014; Lim & Rodger, 2010). classroom environment benefits from Formative assessment strategies benefit the classroom environment and promote student participation, as they include quizzes, debates, and peer evaluations (Marks, 2014). Moreover, formative assessment plays a crucial role in meeting the varied demands of a student by enabling teachers to modify their pedagogical approaches to improve understanding in general (Vonderwell & Boboc, 2013). However, formative assessment does present specific challenges such as the time and effort required for continuous evaluation, interpreting student's performance, and a lack of skilled teachers for balancing assessments with the curriculum as a whole (Do Quyen & Khairani, 2017; Schildkamp et al., 2020).

Self-assessment: Students usually evaluate their work against preset criteria, make personal objectives, and consider their learning experiences when they engage in self-assessment. Students can actively participate in their educational process using this reflective technique (Lew et al., 2010). The benefits of self-assessment are the development of metacognitive abilities, enhanced self-awareness, and a sense of accountability for one's learning. With the tenets of student-centered education, it advances the general objective of developing motivated, self-directed students who can successfully negotiate challenging academic and professional environments (Hanrahan & Isaacs, 2001). However, students could find it challenging to evaluate their work fairly, and self-evaluation is prone to biases or a lack of impartiality.

Peer assessment: Students rate each other's work according to specified standards in peer assessment strategy. This cooperative method encourages a sense of shared responsibility for learning and offers insightful information on individual performance. Students usually get explicit instructions and rubrics to facilitate peer evaluation, which allows them to provide helpful criticism on their peers' assignments, projects, or presentations (Iglesias Pérez et al., 2022). Peer assessment has several benefits; one is that it fosters a more inclusive and varied evaluation process by bringing in other viewpoints and stimulating active participation in the learning community. Additionally, since they must examine and defend their evaluations, it improves students' analytical and critical thinking abilities (Brindley & Scoffield, 1998). Nevertheless, limitations include possible prejudice, discrepancies in evaluation criteria, and the requirement for precise instructions to guarantee impartial and helpful criticism.

Figure 1. Students' understanding of AI in education
(Cheng et al., 2023)

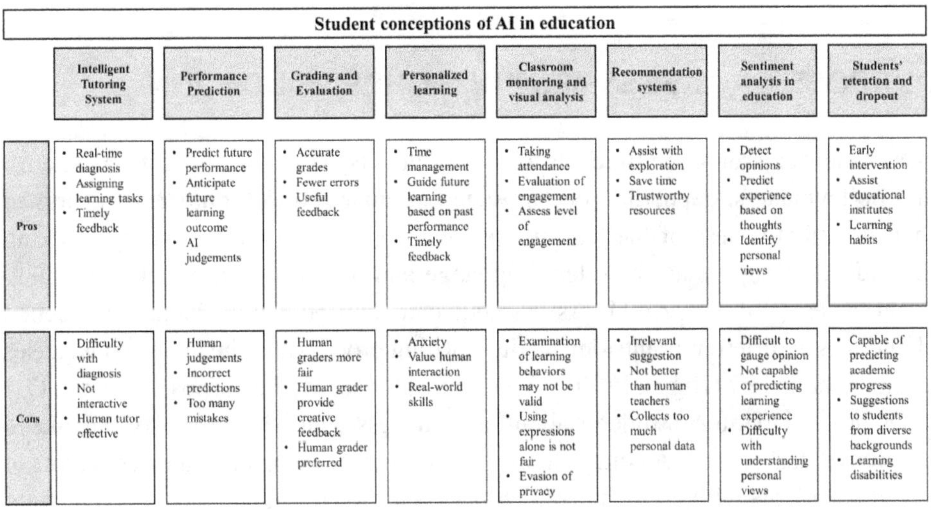

Criterion-referenced assessment: Criterion-based assessment is an evaluation technique that centers on specific learning objectives and contrasts a student's performance with predefined standards or criteria. Teachers provide explicit criteria defining the desired degree of performance in each skill or knowledge area to apply this evaluation. Instead of being rated against their peers' performance, students are assessed based on their capacity to meet these predetermined criteria. Criterion-referenced assessment has the benefits of openness, clarity, and connection with particular learning objectives (Lok et al., 2016). It helps ensure that students fulfill expectations and have the information and skills they need for their academic and professional goals (O'Donovan et al., 2001). Nevertheless, difficulties might occur in establishing standards appropriate to all situations, with the possibility of restricted comparability across different circumstances.

Norm-referenced Assessment: An approach to evaluation called "*norm-referenced assessment*" contrasts a person's performance with that of a larger group, or "*norm.*" Under this method, students are rated and given percentile ratings according to how well they do relative to the reference group's average performance (Lok et al., 2016).

Standardized tests are frequently used in norm-referenced assessment, where results are evaluated in light of the distribution of results in the reference population (Bond, 2019). Norm-referenced assessments are widely utilized in higher education for admissions, program evaluations, and standardized testing situations. One benefit of norm-referenced assessment is that it makes it easier to identify high and low performers by comparing an individual's performance on a national or international level. Its disadvantages include promoting unhealthy competitiveness and lacking in-depth insights into specific knowledge or skill areas (Turnbull, 1989).

PURPOSE OF ASSESSMENT IN HIGHER EDUCATION

Assessment can serve multiple purposes for students, educators, education systems, and policymakers, depending on its usage (summarized in Figure 2). It is argued that the effectiveness of the learning process depends on the systematic tracking of students' progress at every learning stage and the provision of active learning experiences (Wiliam, 2011). Assessment can help educators identify students' challenges at different points during the learning process and the underlying causes of those challenges (Biggs, 1999). Assessment also serves the purpose of motivation when utilized to inform students about their successes and the steps they can take to progress (Clark, 2012). A comprehensive assessment system can guide educators to provide students with constructive feedback and the assistance most conducive to their learning (Biggs, 1999). Moreover, the assessment clarifies constraints inherent in the pedagogical methodologies employed for student instruction. Grounded in the outcomes of assessments, educators can employ a reference framework to effectuate modifications in their instructional approaches, thereby augmenting the overall learning experience for students (Biggs, 1999; Black et al., 2003).

The education system's most widely used purpose of assessment is to grade students and give them certificates of achievement (Biggs, 1998). After completing an educational level, students obtain certificates to recognize their acquired knowledge and skills formally. Furthermore, assessment methodologies are instrumental in the quality management of the education system. The empirical data obtained through assessments can indicate whether the educational system is advancing on a favorable trajectory and simultaneously establish accountability measures within the education framework (Brown, 2004). Additionally, it assists in comparing the national education outcomes with their international counterparts. Policymakers rely on the information derived from assessments to establish and improve educational initiatives and policies (Schildkamp, 2019). Policymakers can make well-informed decisions about designing, modifying, and improving existing academic programs due to the valuable data and insights assessments provide.

Figure 2. Purpose of assessment
(Hooda et al., 2022)

	Purpose of assessment		
Learners and Instructors	Feedback and Diagnosis	Motive students	Monitoring and support
Education system	Certification	Selection	Quality Control
Policy makers and administrators	Curriculum and course design	Accountability	Monitor effectiveness

USE OF ARTIFICIAL INTELLIGENCE (AI) FOR ACADEMIC ASSESSMENT

Artificial intelligence (AI) is used in multiple avenues of higher education, particularly in the assessment, feedback, and grading of students. Various AI tools are developed to automate some aspects of the traditional evaluation processes, and their applications extend from training to education (a short comparison of a few AI assessment tools are provided in Table 1). AI-based systems provide tailored feedback and continuous monitoring, improving student learning and performance (Grenander et al., 2021; Kochmar et al., 2020). Artificial intelligence simplifies test-question selection, optimizing assessment creation and delivery in e-learning (Poth et al., 2019). AI can create assessment tools and assignments for suitable peers and automatically assign grades to student submissions. These methods transfer human labor to artificial intelligence and facilitate the maintenance of evaluation procedures (Swiecki et al., 2022). Nevertheless, issues with assessment, grading, and feedback in education continue to arise (Harry, 2023). The aforementioned highlights the possibility and necessity of utilizing AI-powered evaluation instruments to tackle accessibility issues and enhance learning outcomes. This section discusses an extensive summary of different assessment methods involving the use of Artificial Intelligence (AI).

Table 1. A comparison of major AI assessment tools (Blackboard Learn, n.d.; Capterra: Reviews of Blackboard Learn, n,d.; Capterra: Reviews of Digiexam, n.d.; Capterra: Reviews of Kahoot, n.d.; Digiexam, n.d.; Gradescope, n.d.; Haleem et.al., 2022; Kahoot: Kahoot! for schools Assessment, n.d.; Lo, 2023; Rahman & Watanobe, 2023; Tsai, 2024)

AI Tool	Basic features	Pros	Cons
Gradescope	• Grade written exams • Grade homework • Auto grading	• Customizable rubrics and instant feedback • Plagiarism detection • Quick student submissions • Integration with various Learning Management Systems (LMS)	• Has a learning curve • Technical glitches • Few features are expensive
Blackboard	• Support multiple type of tests (quiz, essay etc.) • Grading analysis (grading history, question analysis) • Grading setup (rubrics, test setting, prohibit late submission etc.)	• Flexibility to make changes in course work • Gradebook functions simplifies progress tracking • Notify if a student fall behind	• Quality issues of UI system • Limited user friendly in mobile device
Kahoot	• Get actionable insights from reports • Assess class progress in real time • Assign student-paced kahoots (exams) • Share insights with other educators • Combine several reports	• Gamification of the assessment • Make assessment fun and interactive • Easily accessible from mobile device	• Minor issues with the integration to other products • Individual progress tracking is time-consuming • The software is limited to only multiple choice or true and false.
Digiexam	• Exam management (high+ low stake) • AI monitoring technology during online exam • Auto grading and feedback mechanism	• Anonymous grading facility • Lockdown features during exam (locks computer for other activities)	• Issues with move from one question to another • Need improvement in feedback mechanism • Limited question types can be added
ChatGPT	• Conversational Interface • Quiz and test creation • Question answering and MCQ, written response evaluation • Feedback and Guidance	• Provide instant feedback • Can assess a wide variety of subjects and topics • Adapt responses according to input	• Inconsistency in response • Bias and stereotyping • Inability to evaluate complex tasks

QUIZZES OR AUTOMATED QUESTIONS GENERATION AND GRADING

Artificial Intelligence (AI) tools can be useful in improving quizzes, automated grading, and automated question formulation in education (Chaudhry et al., 2023; Crompton & Burke, 2023). According to González-Carrillo et al. (2021), AI has been successfully implemented for grading automation. These tools can create questions, conduct tests, and give students quick performance feedback (Chaudhry et al., 2023). The Kejarcita platform's quiz production and automated correction functionalities are some instances of AI-based automation (Fitria, 2021). Compared to traditional methods, AI-based systems can offer several advantages, such as the ability to process large amounts of assessment data quickly, assess the effectiveness of educational initiatives, and execute individualized and flexible learning experiences for students (Harry, 2023). Algorithms for automated questions can score students' answers quickly and accurately (Gao et al., 2024; Hahn et al., 2021). AI-based automated test administration may also consider each student's unique learning demands by modifying questions and maintaining the order of difficulty. Students may benefit from a more exciting and efficient learning experience through AI implementations (Crompton & Burke., 2023). AI-based automated grading systems can assess student answer sheets instantly, offer constructive criticism where development is required. Additionally, AI tries to analyze trends and patterns of students' performance (Deeva et al., 2021). This can assist teachers in adapting their methods of instruction, changing the course material, and developing beneficial evaluations (Chen & Chen, 2020).

Though AI has great potential for automated grading and quiz administration, drawbacks exist as it was developed based on a particular group of students' data. Therefore, rigorous design, validation, and cross-checking are necessary to guarantee the validity and reliability of AI-based evaluations (Lin et al., 2023). Furthermore, it is essential to regularly monitor AI evaluations to ensure that they do not yield biased or erroneous conclusions. These difficulties show that careful supervision and continual research are necessary to guarantee the effective incorporation of AI into educational evaluation procedures.

EVALUATION OF ASSIGNMENTS, REFLECTIVE WRITING, OPEN-ENDED ANSWERS, AND ESSAYS

Artificial intelligence (AI) systems can thoroughly examine various aspects of student writing by using complex natural language processing (NLP) algorithms. It covers a wide range of functions such as syntax and grammar corrections, coherence of writing, word usage, and components of argumentation and critical thinking

(Raheem et al., 2023; Son et al., 2023). A study by O'Dea & O'Dea (2023) asserts that automated essay scoring (AES) systems use machine learning and natural language processing methods to evaluate text-based essays automatically. Grading is often based on many criteria, including substance (consistency and usefulness of information), style (sentence structure and vocabulary), and statistics (average word and sentence length). Assessment tools powered by AI have a multitude of options that offer unique efficiency and scalability for assessing students. AI tools also allow teachers to handle many assignments efficiently and provide students with timely and helpful feedback (Kamalov et al., 2023). Artificial intelligence (AI) ensures academic integrity by automating plagiarism detection compared to large databases. It also encourages students to be creative (Van Hayden et al., 2021).

Educators can offer precise assignment instructions and rubrics that may maximize the efficiency of AI throughout the assessment process and enable alignment with particular learning goals (Kamalov et al., 2023). However, a few challenges of AI-based writing assessments must be addressed to make the process free of current controversies. Algorithmic bias is a significant issue since AI systems can be discriminatory or inaccurate. It can create discrimination while assessing work from people with different languages or cultural backgrounds. Additionally, Shofiah et al. (2023) suggest that AI tools could find it difficult to catch subtle meanings of writing, such as originality and creativity, which are crucial in fields like creative writing and literature. AI algorithms must continuously improve and validate to guarantee reliability and accuracy while evaluating challenging writing assignments. As a result, educators also need to look for opportunities to critically analyze the outputs of AI systems. Moreover, they can add human judgment to automated evaluations when required.

CONCEPT MAPPING

Concept maps (CM) are visual aids to teach knowledge in various situations. They are pictures that illustrate a specific topic and all of its subcomponents. According to Lukasenko et al. (2010), a concept map is a mental model built on a diagram with labeled nodes referring to ideas in a problem domain and arcs showing links between concept pairs. Many studies conducted in naturalistic settings have shown that concept maps are more effective for knowledge retention than other information-summarizing techniques (Jain et al., 2014). Concept maps can also assess students' learning (Akinsanya & Williams, 2004). Concept maps, as opposed to more conventional types of assessment like multiple-choice tests, can be used to ascertain a student's understanding of a specific topic after it has been taught (Jain et al., 2014).

The concept-mapping-based student assessment approach was employed in the research of Jain et al. (2014). The researchers created the artificial intelligence-based student learning evaluation tool (AISLE) to assess students' concept map comprehension of a given subject. It was reported that AISLE used Java and XML parsers to evaluate the amount of understanding a student has of a given topic. Consequently, AISLE, an AI-powered tool, may assist instructors in assessing a student's comprehension of a topic. The teacher used the idea map to obtain the statistics based on the probability density function and ran it through AISLE. In the first step, the teacher developed an ideal concept map, which was subsequently used by the AI tool as a reference for assessing the concept maps the students created (Lukasenko et al., 2010).

FORMATIVE FEEDBACK STRATEGY FOR FEEDBACK LOCALIZATION

Using formative feedback techniques to improve reviewers' comments is another method of utilizing AI in evaluation. Nguyen et al. (2017) explained the automated formative feedback technique and how it may be used to refine or clarify student or peer group comments. According to this study, student reviewers should have various learning opportunities from AI-generated interactive comments. As a result, the automated peer feedback strategy entails reviewing every remark from peers, emphasizing those that require editing, and permitting reviewers to edit and submit their work again—a process known as feedback localization (Nelson & Schunn 2009). Nguyen et al. (2017) state two kinds of feedback localization in an automated formative feedback strategy. Explicit localization by location can be accomplished with AI by incorporating absolute page, paragraph, and/or sentence numbers, a relative positional expression, or a section title. This procedure indicates where the feedback should be placed within the reviewed work. AI would refer to the subject matter of the paper's reviewed component through implicit localization. Quoting texts may also be used in an automated feedback strategy to improve the review (Nguyen et al., 2017). AI-driven automated feedback strategies that leverage both explicit and implicit localization for feedback might be employed to enhance peer assessment.

AI IN TRANSLATION AND INTERPRETATION (T&I) ASSESSMENT IN LANGUAGE LEARNING

Scholars of language education always place importance on translation and interpreting (T&I) in the second language learning process (Pym & Ayvazyan, 2017; Samardali

& Ismael, 2017; Widdowson, 2014). T&I is related to the cognitive development of the learners as well as having an important pedagogical value in language instruction (Cook, 2007). Takimoto and Hashimoto (2010) argued that T&I can improve students' problem solving, analytical, and critical thinking skills. Despite its well proven importance in language learning, the evaluation procedure for T&I may affect the actual benefit of this activity. Researchers share their concerns about the difficulties in the evaluation process of T&I (Gile, 1999; Han, 2015; Wu, 2010; cited in Han and Lu, 2023). The assessment of T&I demands careful analysis of the consistency of the source language and the target language (Han et al., 2021). As this task is more difficult and time consuming for human raters, the educators of language education may lose interest in taking advantage of the benefits of T&I in language learning. However, the advancement of AI technology provides the opportunity to rapidly evaluate human written works through automated writing evaluation tools. These tools are not especially designed to assess T&I works, as there is a need to find the fidelity or correspondence between the source and target language in T&I works (Han and Lu, 2023). Therefore, Han and Lu (2023) investigated to what extent automated machine translation (MT) metrics can be utilized to automate fidelity assessments in T&I classrooms. Examples of these metrics include the BLEU (Bilingual Evaluation Understudy), NIST (National Institute of Standards and Technology), METEOR (Metric for Evaluation of Translation with Explicit Ordering), and TER (Translation Edit Rate) metrics (Han and Lu, 2023). They found the feasibility of using these machine learning metrics in automated assessments of T&I works (Han & Lu, 2023). However, they also recommended using these metrics in small scale classrooms in addition to the teachers' manual evaluation process (Han & Lu, 2023).

SCIENTIFIC PRACTICE ASSESSMENT IN EDUCATION

With the advancement of AI in education, now it is possible to evaluate a student's science related written explanation. It is argued that written explanations and arguments on scientific topics are essential to assessing scientific practices in the science teaching-learning process (Pellegrino, 2013). However, there is a lack of effective tools to accurately measure these scientific practices. Research has shown the possibility of using machine learning translation to automatically assess the scientific written tasks of students (Ariely et al., 2023; Wiley et al., 2017). Beggrow et al. (2014) investigated the effectiveness of a free, open-source machine-learning tool in assessing the quality of a written task on the topic related to the causes of evolutionary change. They compared the results from the automated score to the human rated score, a multiple-choice score, and a clinical oral interview score (Beggrow et al., 2014). They concluded their study by mentioning three advantages of using an automated scoring system in assessing scientific written explanations: First, the automated scoring system can effectively assess written tasks as it is aligned with the human rated score; second, the automated score is also best aligned with the interview score, which is the systematic way to effectively measure student's ideas about a science related topic; third, automated scoring for scientific explanation is more efficient than the MCQ test as it can focus on assessing the student's understanding of concepts and the less understood concepts (Beggrow et al., 2014). Overall, the automated scoring system can provide detailed evaluation information related to a student's understanding of a concept, and it has the potential to replace the traditional assessment tools.

CHALLENGES OF IMPLEMENTING ARTIFICIAL INTELLIGENCE IN ASSESSMENT IN HIGHER EDUCATION

The concern about AI-enabled assessment lies in entrusting the evaluation responsibility to a dispassionate, objective machine. Nevertheless, the practical scenario unfolds where the primary responsibility for assessment is delegated to 'programmers, learning engineers, instructional designers, software vendors, and other human' entities who possess limited knowledge about the assessed students, their backgrounds, and the educational systems in which the students are nurtured (Swiecki et al., 2022, p.6). Furthermore, AI-enabled assessment limits the application of assessment as a pedagogical tool. Assessment is inherently a learning process, and numerous researchers advocate leveraging assessment as a means of learning rather than employing it solely as an objective measure of learning outcomes (Boud, 2000; Hargreaves, 2005; Wiliam, 2011). However, Swiecki et al. (2022) argued that AI-enabled assessment may cause concern as it restricts teachers' being lenient or punitive to the assessment process depending on students' progress and limits practices such as self-assessment and 'assessment for social justice.'

Furthermore, the systematic review by Celik et al. (2022) pinpointed the restricted technical capability of AI systems in evaluating graphics or figures as a considerable challenge. Their investigation also indicated concerns regarding the reliability and validity of AI-based assessment systems. AI algorithms designed for a particular context may lack reliability and validity when applied to different educational settings (Celik et al., 2022).

Hopfenbeck et al. (2023) mentioned the opportunities of AI in formative assessment while identifying some challenges. Among these challenges is the inadequacy of teachers' knowledge and skills in utilizing AI techniques. Moreover, educators may encounter difficulties when dealing with big data in the context of AI-based assessments. Despite the promising prospects of leveraging big data to enhance formative assessment by monitoring students' learning processes, there is a notable problem in figuring out which data is the most useful for helping students improve. Also, how big data works now differs significantly from traditional assessment data, making it tricky to use the usual data analysis methods (Cope & Kalantzis, 2016).

PRIVACY AND SURVEILLANCE

Another primary concern pervading AI usage in higher education and assessment includes the ethical question of privacy (Federspiel et al., 2023; Wu et al., 2023; Akgun & Greenhow, 2022; May & George, 2011). Nguyen et al. (2023) defined the principle of privacy as "*AIED must ensure well-informed consent from the user and maintain the confidentiality of the user's information, both when they provide information and when the system collects information about them.*" AI in higher education uses data from both instructors and students to develop their models. Hence, their data privacy and data breach form the foremost questions on AI usage. It is often assumed that users (teachers and students) are providing their data with consent (Akgun & Greenhow, 2022) when they agree to use AI facilities in their teaching and learning process. The assumption of consent is further challenged when these users are forced to adopt AI technologies as required by their institutes (Bulger, 2016). Understanding the broad impact of data breaches and privacy violations, the United Nations Educational, Scientific, and Cultural Organization (UNESCO) proposed global AI ethics standards, signed by its 193 member states on November 25, 2021. The proposed guidelines acknowledge privacy as a human right that "*must be respected, protected, and promoted throughout the life cycle of AI systems*." The AI system life cycle includes the entire operation, from research to development and maintenance, operation, evaluation, and termination (UNESCO, 2021). This indicates that privacy concerns remain intertwined with AI throughout its lifetime. Hence, educational institutes must heed that even if they are only at the user end of AI tools, their faculties and students' data must be protected along the entire chain. Therefore, the onus of responsibility should be shouldered by these institutes, which are increasingly adopting AI tools in their curricula. The institutes must question if they are building the necessary capacity. Incorporating AI in the ethics curriculum and developing an institution-specific AI ethic framework could be the steppingstones in future-proofing educational institutes from potential ethical dilemmas arising from the usage of AI.

The working system of AI technology manifested the risk of surveillance in various way. For instance, AI predictive system can track students' activity and performances therefore the feeling of insecurity among students can emerge that they are being watched (Hoti et al.,2023). The consequences of being felt insecure among students can also lead to little engagement in learning activity (Akgün & Greenhow, 2021). However, the issues of surveillance are the result of the lack of clear consent and transparency in using data (Huang, 2023). Scholars suggested that it is an ethical imperative to let the students and educators inform about to what extent their data is being tracked, used, and shared with the third parties (Luan et al., 2020; Nguyen et al., 2022).

BIAS AND DISCRIMINATION

Researchers have identified that the collection and analysis procedure of AI data can create biases and discrimination (Baker and Hawn, 2022; Kundi et al., 2023). For instance, Srinivasan and Chander (2021) identified that data creation, problem formulation, data analysis, data validation, and testing techniques can give rise to the risk of bias if careful consideration is not given to the whole process. Moreover, Kundi et al. (2023) argued that there are three biases that can arise in AI systems: from the input data, algorithms, and cognitive procedures. The input data bias is related to the sampling procedures, and it occurs when the data lacks the representative criteria of a population (Kundi et al., 2023). The algorithm designed for an AI system can also be susceptible to biases because of its inherent design and assumptions (Kundi et al., 2023). Though the AI system works based on data and mathematics model, it can present inaccurate and bias information due to the way they process and interpret information, similar to how human cognition can be influenced by various biases (Kundi et al., 2023). However, these biases can create discrimination and impact the result of AI in education (Akgun & Greenhow, 2022; Kamalov & Gurrib, 2023). In addition to these biases, there is a risk of trust and confirmation biases. AIED is designed to support educators and students with data for the improvement of the teaching learning process. However, teachers' skepticism on the implementation of AI-driven data leads to confirmation bias (Nazaretsky et al., 2021). Whether these biases are created intentionally or unintentionally, they need careful examination and monitoring while preparing, analyzing, and implementing data in an AI system.

THE FUTURE DIRECTION OF ARTIFICIAL INTELLIGENCE USAGE IN ASSESSMENT AND BEYOND

In the context of the increasing landscape of artificial intelligence (AI) products, educators are responsible for discerning the optimal utilization of these resources to enhance their pedagogical practices (Hopfenbeck et al., 2023). Teachers are obligated to critically examine the requisite skills necessary for adeptly navigating the dynamic role of AI in the educational domain. Specifically, educators must acquire proficiency in data skills through collaboration with data scientists to ensure the meaningful and purposeful incorporation of big data in AI-driven assessment methodologies (Gardner, 2021). Moreover, it is also suggested that guidelines be established for identifying and utilizing the most relevant and valuable data for improving student learning outcomes in AI assessment. However, it is necessary to develop self-regulated skills among learners to understand when and how to use AI feedback to progress their learning (Hopfenbeck et al., 2023).

Another recommendation is that teachers should be involved in designing AI systems for their teaching-learning practices (Celik et al., 2022; Swiecki et al., 2022). In the realm of Al development, a programmer's exclusive role can limit the consideration of benefits and drawbacks for students. It is imperative for software companies and Al developers to actively involve educators in this process (Swiecki et al., 2022). Furthermore, as questions arise about the accuracy and reliability of Al usage for assessments in different learning environments (Celik et al., 2022), it is advised to collaborate and develop mutual understanding among diverse stakeholders in the education sector for effective Al development.

The successful adoption of AI assessment in higher education hinges on building robust guardrails and monitoring systems *before*, *during*, and *after* its implementation. These safeguards are crucial to mitigate the ethical challenges inherent in this technology. The strength and comprehensiveness of these guardrails will not only shape the ethical use of AI assessment but also influence the broader landscape of AI in higher education. While educators and institutions play a critical role, the challenge of ensuring ethical AI goes beyond academia. It is a shared responsibility that extends to the developers and implementers of this technology.

REFERENCES

Aggarwal, D. (2023). Integration of innovative technological developments and AI with education for an adaptive learning pedagogy. *China Petroleum Processing and Petrochemical Technology*, *23*(2).

Ahmad, S. F., Alam, M. M., Rahmat, M. K., Mubarik, M. S., & Hyder, S. I. (2022). Academic and administrative role of artificial Intelligence in education. *Sustainability (Basel)*, *14*(3), 1101. doi:10.3390/su14031101

Akgun, S., & Greenhow, C. (2022). Artificial intelligence in education: Addressing ethical challenges in K-12 settings. *AI and Ethics*, *2*(3), 431–440. doi:10.1007/s43681-021-00096-7 PMID:34790956

Akinsanya, C., & Williams, M. (2004). Concept mapping for meaningful learning. *Nurse Education Today*, *24*(1), 41–46. doi:10.1016/S0260-6917(03)00120-5 PMID:14690643

AlDhaen, F. (2022). The use of artificial intelligence in higher education–Systematic review. *COVID-19 Challenges to University Information Technology Governance*, 269-285.

Alkhatlan, A., & Kalita, J. (2018). Intelligent Tutoring Systems: A Comprehensive Historical Survey with Recent Developments. *ArXiv*. /abs/1812.09628

Almusaed, A., Almssad, A., Yitmen, I., & Homod, R. Z. (2023). Enhancing Student Engagement: Harnessing "AIED"'s Power in Hybrid Education—A Review Analysis. *Education Sciences*, *13*(7), 632. doi:10.3390/educsci13070632

Ariely, M., Nazaretsky, T., & Alexandron, G. (2023). Machine learning and Hebrew NLP for automated assessment of open-ended questions in biology. *International Journal of Artificial Intelligence in Education*, *33*(1), 1–34. doi:10.1007/s40593-021-00283-x

Bahroun, Z., Anane, C., Ahmed, V., & Zacca, A. (2023). Transforming education: A comprehensive review of generative artificial Intelligence in educational settings through bibliometric and content analysis. *Sustainability (Basel)*, *15*(17), 12983. doi:10.3390/su151712983

Baker, R. S., & Hawn, A. (2022). Algorithmic bias in education. *International Journal of Artificial Intelligence in Education*, 1–41.

Beggrow, E. P., Ha, M., Nehm, R. H., Pearl, D., & Boone, W. J. (2014). Assessing scientific practices using machine-learning methods: How closely do they match clinical interview performance? *Journal of Science Education and Technology*, *23*(1), 160–182. doi:10.1007/s10956-013-9461-9

Biggs, J. (1998). Assessment and classroom learning: A role for summative assessment? *Assessment in Education: Principles, Policy & Practice*, *5*(1), 103–110. doi:10.1080/0969595980050106

Biggs, J. (1999). What the student does: Teaching for enhanced learning. *Higher Education Research & Development*, *18*(1), 57–75. doi:10.1080/0729436990180105

Black, P., Harrison, C., Lee, C., Marshall, B., & William, D. (2003). *Assessment for Learning – Putting It into Practice*. Open University Press.

Blackboard Learn. (n.d.). Anthology. https://www.anthology.com/products/teaching-and-learning/learning-effectiveness/blackboard-learn

Bond, L. A. (2019). Norm-and criterion-referenced testing. *Practical Assessment, Research & Evaluation*, *5*(1), 2.

Boud, D. (2000). Sustainable assessment: Rethinking assessment for the learning society. *Studies in Continuing Education*, *22*(2), 151–167. doi:10.1080/713695728

Brindley, C., & Scoffield, S. (1998). Peer assessment in undergraduate programmes. *Teaching in Higher Education*, *3*(1), 79–90. doi:10.1080/1356215980030106

Brown, G. T. (2004). Teachers' conceptions of assessment: Implications for policy and professional development. *Assessment in Education: Principles, Policy & Practice*, *11*(3), 301–318. doi:10.1080/0969594042000304609

Bulger, M. (2016). *Personalized learning: the conversations we're not having*. Data and Society Research Institute. https://datasociety.net/pubs/ecl/PersonalizedLearning_primer_2016.pdf

Capterra: Reviews of Blackboard Learn. (n.d.). Capterra. https://www.capterra.com/p/14500/Blackboard-LMS-for-Business/reviews/

Capterra: Reviews of Digiexam. (n.d.). Capterra. https://www.capterra.com/p/161396/DigiExam/reviews/

Capterra: Reviews of Kahoot. (n.d.). Capterra. https://www.capterra.com/p/156399/Kahoot/reviews/

Celik, I., Dindar, M., Muukkonen, H., & Järvelä, S. (2022). The promises and challenges of artificial Intelligence for teachers: A systematic review of research. *TechTrends*, *66*(4), 616–630. doi:10.1007/s11528-022-00715-y

Chaudhry, I. S., Sarwary, S. A. M., El Refae, G. A., & Chabchoub, H. (2023). Time to revisit existing student's performance evaluation approach in higher education sector in a new era of ChatGPT—A case study. *Cogent Education*, *10*(1), 2210461. doi:10.1080/2331186X.2023.2210461

Chen, L., Chen, P., & Lin, Z. (2020). Artificial Intelligence in education: A review. *IEEE Access : Practical Innovations, Open Solutions*, *8*, 75264–75278. doi:10.1109/ACCESS.2020.2988510

Cheng, L., Umapathy, K., Rehman, M., Ritzhaupt, A., Antonyan, K., Shidfar, P., ... Abramowitz, B. (2023). Designing, developing, and validating a measure of undergraduate students' conceptions of artificial Intelligence in education. *Journal of Interactive Learning Research*, *34*(2), 275–311.

Clark, I. (2012). Formative Assessment: Assessment Is for Self-Regulated Learning. *Educational Psychology Review, 24*(2), 205–249. doi:10.1007/s10648-011-9191-6

Cook, G. (2010). *Translation in language teaching: An argument for reassessment*. Oxford University Press.

Cope, B., & Kalantzis, M. (2016). Big data comes to school: Implications for learning, assessment, and research. *AERA Open*, *2*(2). doi:10.1177/2332858416641907

Crompton, H., & Burke, D. (2023). Artificial Intelligence in higher education: The state of the field. *International Journal of Educational Technology in Higher Education*, *20*(1), 22. doi:10.1186/s41239-023-00392-8

Deeva, G., Bogdanova, D., Serral, E., Snoeck, M., & De Weerdt, J. (2021). A review of automated feedback systems for learners: Classification framework, challenges and opportunities. *Computers & Education*, *162*, 104094. doi:10.1016/j.compedu.2020.104094

Digiexam. (n.d.). DigiExam. https://www.digiexam.com/

Do Quyen, N. T., & Khairani, A. Z. (2017). Reviewing the challenges of implementing formative assessment in Asia: The need for a professional development program. *Journal of Social Science Studies*, *4*(1), 160–177. doi:10.5296/jsss.v4i1.9728

Drachsler, H., & Greller, W. (2016, April). Privacy and analytics: it's a DELICATE issue a checklist for trusted learning analytics. In *Proceedings of the sixth international conference on learning analytics & knowledge* (pp. 89-98). 10.1145/2883851.2883893

Drugova, E. (2023). Learning analytics driven improvements in learning design in Higher Education: A systematic literature review [Preprint]. *Journal of Computer Assisted Learning*. Advance online publication. doi:10.1111/jcal.12894

Ellis, E. (2022). The potential of artificial intelligence in assessment feedback. *Times Higher Education*. https://www.timeshighereducation.com/campus/potential-artificial-intelligence-assessment-feedback

Evans, D. J., Zeun, P., & Stanier, R. A. (2014). Motivating student learning using a formative assessment journey. *Journal of Anatomy*, *224*(3), 296–303. doi:10.1111/joa.12117 PMID:24111930

Federspiel, F., Mitchell, R., Asokan, A., Umana, C., & McCoy, D. (2023). Threats by artificial Intelligence to human health and human existence. *BMJ Global Health*, *8*(5), e010435. doi:10.1136/bmjgh-2022-010435 PMID:37160371

Fitria, T. N. (2021). Artificial Intelligence (AI) In Education: Using AI Tools for Teaching and Learning Process. In Prosiding Seminar Nasional & Call for Paper STIE AAS, 4(1), 134-147.

Gao, R., Merzdorf, H. E., Anwar, S., Hipwell, M. C., & Srinivasa, A. (2024). Automatic assessment of text-based responses in post-secondary education: A systematic review. *Computers and Education: Artificial Intelligence*, 100206.

Gardner, J., O'Leary, M., & Yuan, L. (2021). Artificial Intelligence in educational assessment: 'Breakthrough? Or buncombe and ballyhoo?'. *Journal of Computer Assisted Learning*, *37*(5), 1207–1216. doi:10.1111/jcal.12577

George, B., & Wooden, O. (2023). Managing the strategic transformation of higher education through artificial Intelligence. *Administrative Sciences*, *13*(9), 196. doi:10.3390/admsci13090196

Gligorea, I., Cioca, M., Oancea, R., Gorski, A. T., Gorski, H., & Tudorache, P. (2023). Adaptive Learning Using Artificial Intelligence in e-Learning: A Literature Review. *Education Sciences*, *13*(12), 1216. doi:10.3390/educsci13121216

González-Carrillo, C. D., Restrepo-Calle, F., Ramírez-Echeverry, J. J., & González, F. A. (2021). Automatic grading tool for jupyter notebooks in artificial intelligence courses. *Sustainability (Basel)*, *13*(21), 12050. doi:10.3390/su132112050

Gradescope. (n.d.). Gradescope. https://www.gradescope.com/

Graesser, A. C., Hu, X., & Sottilare, R. (2018). Intelligent tutoring systems. In *International Handbook of the Learning Sciences* (pp. 246–255). Routledge. doi:10.4324/9781315617572-24

Grenander, M., Belfer, R., Kochmar, E., Serban, I. V., St-Hilaire, F., & Cheung, J. C. (2021, May). Deep discourse analysis for generating personalized feedback in intelligent tutor systems. *Proceedings of the AAAI Conference on Artificial Intelligence*, *35*(17), 15534–15544. doi:10.1609/aaai.v35i17.17829

Hahn, M. G., Navarro, S. M. B., Valentín, L. D. L. F., & Burgos, D. (2021). A systematic review of the effects of automatic scoring and automatic feedback in educational settings. *IEEE Access : Practical Innovations, Open Solutions*, *9*, 108190–108198. doi:10.1109/ACCESS.2021.3100890

Haleem, A., Javaid, M., & Singh, R. P. (2022). An era of ChatGPT as a significant futuristic support tool: A study on features, abilities, and challenges. *BenchCouncil transactions on benchmarks, standards and evaluations,* *2*(4), 100089.

Han, C., & Lu, X. (2023). Can automated machine translation evaluation metrics be used to assess students' interpretation in the language learning classroom? *Computer Assisted Language Learning*, *36*(5-6), 1064–1087. doi:10.1080/09588221.2021.1968915

Han, C., Xiao, R., & Su, W. (2021). Assessing the fidelity of consecutive interpreting. Interpreting. *Interpreting*, *23*(2), 245–268. doi:10.1075/intp.00058.han

Hannan, E., & Liu, S. (2023). AI: New source of competitiveness in higher education. *Competitiveness Review*, *33*(2), 265–279. doi:10.1108/CR-03-2021-0045

Hanrahan, S. J., & Isaacs, G. (2001). Assessing self-and peer-assessment: The students' views. *Higher Education Research & Development*, *20*(1), 53–70. doi:10.1080/07294360123776

Hargreaves, E. (2005). Assessment for learning? Thinking outside the (black) box. *Cambridge Journal of Education*, *35*(2), 213–224. doi:10.1080/03057640500146880

Harry, A. (2023). Revolutionizing Healthcare: The transformative role of artificial intelligence in the health sector. *BULLET: Jurnal Multidisiplin Ilmu*, *2*(2), 326–335.

Holmes, W., Porayska-Pomsta, K., Holstein, K., Sutherland, E., Baker, T., Shum, S. B., Santos, O. C., Rodrigo, M. T., Cukurova, M., Bittencourt, I. I., & Koedinger, K. R. (2022). Ethics of AI in education: Towards a community-wide framework. *International Journal of Artificial Intelligence in Education*, *32*(3), 1–23. doi:10.1007/s40593-021-00239-1

Hooda, M., Rana, C., Dahiya, O., Rizwan, A., & Hossain, M. S. (2022). Artificial Intelligence for Assessment and Feedback to Enhance Student Success in Higher Education. *Mathematical Problems in Engineering*, *2022*, e5215722. doi:10.1155/2022/5215722

Hopfenbeck, T. N., Zhang, Z., Sun, S., Robertson, P., & McGrane, J. A. (2023). Challenges and opportunities for classroom-based formative assessment and AI: A perspective article. [). Frontiers.]. *Frontiers in Education*, *8*, 1270700. doi:10.3389/feduc.2023.1270700

Hoti, A. H., Zenuni, X., Hamiti, M., & Ajdari, J. (2023, June). Student performance prediction using AI and ML: state of the art. In *2023 12th Mediterranean Conference on Embedded Computing (MECO)* (pp. 1-6). IEEE. 10.1109/MECO58584.2023.10154933

Huang, L. (2023). Ethics of artificial intelligence in education: Student privacy and data protection. *Science Insights Education Frontiers*, *16*(2), 2577–2587. doi:10.15354/sief.23.re202

Iglesias Pérez, M. C., Vidal-Puga, J., & Pino Juste, M. R. (2022). The role of self and peer assessment in Higher Education. *Studies in Higher Education*, *47*(3), 683–692. doi:10.1080/03075079.2020.1783526

Ismail, F. (2023). Artificial Intelligence in higher education. A protocol paper for a Systematic Literature Review. *Journal of Applied Learning and Teaching*, *6*(2), 56–63. doi:10.37074/jalt.2023.6.2.34

Jain, G. P., Gurupur, V. P., Schroeder, J. L., & Faulkenberry, E. D. (2014). Artificial intelligence-based student learning evaluation: A concept map-based approach for analyzing a student's understanding of a topic. *IEEE Transactions on Learning Technologies*, *7*(3), 267–279. doi:10.1109/TLT.2014.2330297

Kahoot: Kahoot! for schools Assessment. (n.d.). Kahoot. https://kahoot.com/schools/assessment/

Kamalov, F., & Gurrib, I. (2023). A new era of artificial intelligence in education: A multifaceted revolution. *arXiv preprint arXiv:2305.18303*.

Kamalov, F., Santandreu Calonge, D., & Gurrib, I. (2023). New era of artificial Intelligence in education: Towards a sustainable multifaceted revolution. *Sustainability (Basel)*, *15*(16), 12451. doi:10.3390/su151612451

Kelly, S. M. (2023). *Teachers are adapting to concerns about a powerful new AI tool*. CNN. https://edition.cnn.com/2023/01/19/tech/chatgpt-teachers-adjusting/index.html

Kibble, J. D. (2017). Best practices in summative assessment. *Advances in Physiology Education*, *41*(1), 110–119. doi:10.1152/advan.00116.2016 PMID:28188198

Knight, P. T. (2002). Summative assessment in higher education: Practices in disarray. *Studies in Higher Education*, *27*(3), 275–286. doi:10.1080/03075070220000662

Kochmar, E., Vu, D. D., Belfer, R., Gupta, V., Serban, I. V., & Pineau, J. (2020). Automated personalized feedback improves learning gains in an intelligent tutoring system. In *Artificial Intelligence in Education: 21st International Conference, AIED 2020, Ifrane, Morocco, July 6–10, 2020* [Springer International Publishing.]. *Proceedings*, *21*(Part II), 140–146.

Kundi, B., El Morr, C., Gorman, R., & Dua, E. (2023). Artificial Intelligence and Bias: A scoping review. *AI & Society*, 199–215.

Labadze, L., Grigolia, M., & Machaidze, L. (2023). Role of AI chatbots in education: Systematic literature review. *International Journal of Educational Technology in Higher Education, 20*(1), 56. doi:10.1186/s41239-023-00426-1

Lai, T., Xie, C., Ruan, M., Wang, Z., Lu, H., & Fu, S. (2023). Influence of artificial intelligence in education on adolescents' social adaptability: The mediatory role of social support. *PLoS One, 18*(3), e0283170. doi:10.1371/journal.pone.0283170 PMID:36930593

Lew, M. D., Alwis, W. A. M., & Schmidt, H. G. (2010). Accuracy of students' self-assessment and their beliefs about its utility. *Assessment & Evaluation in Higher Education, 35*(2), 135–156. doi:10.1080/02602930802687737

Lim, S. M., & Rodger, S. (2010). Use of formative assessment to enhance learning. *Focus on Health Professional Education: A Multi-disciplinary Journal, 12*(2), 30-33.

Lin, C. C., Huang, A. Y., & Lu, O. H. (2023). Artificial intelligence in intelligent tutoring systems toward sustainable education: A systematic review. *Smart Learning Environments, 10*(1), 41. doi:10.1186/s40561-023-00260-y

Lo, C. K. (2023). What is the impact of ChatGPT on education? A rapid review of the literature. *Education Sciences, 13*(4), 410. doi:10.3390/educsci13040410

Lok, B., McNaught, C., & Young, K. (2016). Criterion-referenced and norm-referenced assessments: Compatibility and complementarity. *Assessment & Evaluation in Higher Education, 41*(3), 450–465. doi:10.1080/02602938.2015.1022136

Luan, H., Geczy, P., Lai, H., Gobert, J., Yang, S. J., Ogata, H., Baltes, J., Guerra, R., Li, P., & Tsai, C. C. (2020). Challenges and future directions of big data and artificial Intelligence in education. *Frontiers in Psychology, 11*, 580820. doi:10.3389/fpsyg.2020.580820 PMID:33192896

Lukasenko, R., Anohina-Naumeca, A., Vilkelis, M., & Grundspenkis, J. (2010). Feedback in the concept map based intelligent knowledge assessment system. *Rigas Tehniskas Universitates Zinatniskie Raksti, 43*(1), 17. doi:10.2478/v10143-010-0020-z

Lynch, L. (2024) *Ai in education: Introduction.* Britannica. https://britannicaeducation.com/blog/ai-in-education/

Ma, X., & Jiang, C. (2023). On the Ethical Risks of Artificial Intelligence Applications in Education and Its Avoidance Strategies. *Journal of Education. Humanities and Social Sciences, 14*, 354–359.

Magnisalis, I., Demetriadis, S., & Karakostas, A. (2011). Adaptive and Intelligent Systems for Collaborative Learning Support: A Review of the Field. *IEEE Transactions on Learning Technologies*, *4*(1), 5–20. doi:10.1109/TLT.2011.2

Marks, I. (2014). Formative (classroom) assessment techniques. *Acta Educationis Generalis*, *4*(1), 46–50.

Marriott, P. (2009). Students' evaluation of the use of online summative assessment on an undergraduate financial accounting module. *British Journal of Educational Technology*, *40*(2), 237–254. doi:10.1111/j.1467-8535.2008.00924.x

May, M., & George, S. (2011). Privacy Concerns in E-learning: Is UsingTracking System a Threat? *International Journal of Information and Education Technology (IJIET)*, *1*(1), 1–8. doi:10.7763/IJIET.2011.V1.1

McLaren, B. M., Scheuer, O., & Mikšátko, J. (2010). Supporting collaborative learning and e-discussions using artificial intelligence techniques. *International Journal of Artificial Intelligence in Education*, *20*(1), 1–46.

Mekonen, Y. K., & Fitiavana, R. A. (2021). Assessment of Learning Outcomes in Higher Education: Review of literature. *Assessment of Learning Outcomes in Higher Education: Review of Literature*, *71*(1), 8–8. doi:10.47119/IJRP100711220211766

Moor, J. (2006). The Dartmouth College artificial intelligence conference: The next fifty years. *AI Magazine*, *27*(4), 87–87.

Nazaretsky, T., Cukurova, M., Ariely, M., & Alexandron, G. (2021, September). Confirmation bias and trust: human factors that influence teachers' attitudes towards AI-based educational technology. In CEUR Workshop Proceedings (Vol. 3042).

Nedelsky, L. (1954). Absolute grading standards for objective tests. *Educational and Psychological Measurement*, *14*(1), 3–19. doi:10.1177/001316445401400101

Nelson, M. M., & Schunn, C. D. (2009). The nature of feedback: How different types of peer feedback affect writing performance. *Instructional Science*, *37*(4), 375–401. doi:10.1007/s11251-008-9053-x

Ng, D. T. K., Lee, M., Tan, R. J. Y., Hu, X., Downie, J. S., & Chu, S. K. W. (2023). A review of AI teaching and learning from 2000 to 2020. *Education and Information Technologies*, *28*(7), 8445–8501. doi:10.1007/s10639-022-11491-w

Nguyen, A., Ngo, H. N., Hong, Y., Dang, B., & Nguyen, B. P. T. (2023). Ethical principles for artificial Intelligence in education. *Education and Information Technologies*, *28*(4), 4221–4241. doi:10.1007/s10639-022-11316-w PMID:36254344

O'Dea, X. C., & O'Dea, M. (2023). Is Artificial Intelligence Really the Next Big Thing in Learning and Teaching in Higher Education? A Conceptual Paper. *Journal of University Teaching & Learning Practice*, *20*(5). doi:10.53761/1.20.5.05

O'Donovan, B., Price, M., & Rust, C. (2001). The student experience of criterion-referenced assessment (through the introduction of a common criteria assessment grid). *Innovations in Education and Teaching International*, *38*(1), 74–85. doi:10.1080/14703290130000287З

Ouyang, F., Zheng, L., & Jiao, P. (2022). Artificial intelligence in online higher education: A systematic review of empirical research from 2011 to 2020. *Education and Information Technologies*, *27*(6), 7893–7925. doi:10.1007/s10639-022-10925-9

Pedro, F., Subosa, M., Rivas, A., & Valverde, P. (2019). *Artificial Intelligence in education: Challenges and opportunities for sustainable development.* United Nations Educational, Scientific and Cultural Organization (UNESCO). https://unesdoc.unesco.org/ark:/48223/pf0000366994?posInSet=22&queryId=9d8ca6cf-6a26-4f09-9b10-5e339c0e75da

Pellegrino, J. W. (2013). Proficiency in science: Assessment challenges and opportunities. *Science*, *340*(6130), 320–323. doi:10.1126/science.1232065 PMID:23599485

Poth, A., Beck, Q., & Riel, A. (2019). Artificial Intelligence helps making Quality Assurance processes leaner. In *Systems, Software and Services Process Improvement: 26th European Conference, EuroSPI 2019, Edinburgh, UK, September 18–20, 2019* [Springer International Publishing.]. *Proceedings*, *26*, 722–730.

Pratama, M. P., Sampelolo, R., & Lura, H. (2023). Revolutionizing education: harnessing the power of artificial Intelligence for personalized learning. *Klasikal: Journal of Education. Language Teaching and Science*, *5*(2), 350–357.

Pym, A., & Ayvazyan, N. (2017). Linguistics, translation and interpreting in foreign-language teaching contexts. In *The Routledge Handbook of Translation Studies and Linguistics* (pp. 393–407). Routledge. doi:10.4324/9781315692845-26

Raheem, B. R., Anjum, F., & Ghafar, Z. N. (2023). Exploring the Profound Impact of Artificial Intelligence Applications (Quillbot, Grammarly and ChatGPT) on English Academic Writing: A Systematic Review. [IJIR]. *International Journal of Integrative Research*, *1*(10), 599–622.

Rahman, M. M., & Watanobe, Y. (2023). ChatGPT for education and research: Opportunities, threats, and strategies. *Applied Sciences (Basel, Switzerland)*, *13*(9), 5783. doi:10.3390/app13095783

Roshanaei, M., Olivares, H., & Lopez, R. R. (2023). Harnessing AI to Foster Equity in Education: Opportunities, Challenges, and Emerging Strategies. *Journal of Intelligent Learning Systems and Applications, 15*(04), 123–143. doi:10.4236/jilsa.2023.154009

Ross, J. (2019). The Reliability, Validity, and Utility of Self-Assessment. *Practical Assessment, Research & Evaluation, 11*(1). Advance online publication. doi:10.7275/9wph-vv65

Samardali, M. F. S., & Ismael, A. M. H. (2017). Translation as a tool for teaching English as a second language. *Journal of Literature. Language and Linguistics (Taipei), 40*, 64–69.

Schildkamp, K. (2019). Data-based decision-making for school improvement: Research insights and gaps. *Educational Research, 61*(3), 257–273. doi:10.1080/00131881.2019.1625716

Shadbad, F., Bahr, G., Luse, A., & Hammer, B. (2023). Inclusion of gamification elements in the context of virtual lab environments to increase educational value. *AIS Transactions on Human-Computer Interaction, 15*(2), 224–246. doi:10.17705/1thci.00089

Sharma, S., Malik, A., Sharma, C., Batra, I., Kaswan, M. S., & Garza-Reyes, J. A. (2023). Adoption of industry 4.0 in different sectors: a structural review using natural language processing. *International Journal on Interactive Design and Manufacturing (IJIDeM)*, 1-23.

Sheehan, T. (2023). Generative AI in education: Past, present, and future. *EDUCAUSE Review*. https://er.educause.edu/articles/sponsored/2023/9/generative-ai-in-education-past-present-and-future

Shofiah, N., Putera, Z. F., & Solichah, N. (2023). Challenges and opportunities in the use of artificial Intelligence in education for academic writing: A scoping review. In Conference Psychology and Flourishing Humanity (PFH 2023) (pp. 174-193). Atlantis Press. doi:10.2991/978-2-38476-188-3_20

Son, J.-B., Ruzic, N. K., & Philpott, A. (2023). Artificial intelligence technologies and applications for language learning and teaching. *Journal of China Computer-Assisted Language Learning, 0*(0). doi:10.1515/jccall-2023-0015

Soori, M., Arezoo, B., & Dastres, R. (2023). Artificial Intelligence, Machine Learning and deep learning in advanced robotics, a review. *Cognitive Robotics, 3*, 54–70. doi:10.1016/j.cogr.2023.04.001

Srinivasan, R., & Chander, A. (2021). Biases in AI systems. *Communications of the ACM*, *64*(8), 44–49. doi:10.1145/3464903

Swiecki, Z., Khosravi, H., Chen, G., Martinez-Maldonado, R., Lodge, J. M., Milligan, S., Selwyn, N., & Gašević, D. (2022). Assessment in the age of artificial Intelligence. *Computers and Education: Artificial Intelligence*, *3*, 100075. doi:10.1016/j.caeai.2022.100075

Takimoto, M., & Hashimoto, H. (2010). An" eye-opening" learning experience: Language learning through interpreting and translation. *Electronic Journal of Foreign Language Teaching*, *7*(1), 86–95.

Teachflow. (2023, September 18). *The evolution of AI in education: Past, present, and future*. Teachflow.AI. https://teachflow.ai/the-evolution-of-ai-in-education-past-present-and-future/

Topping, K. (1998). Peer assessment between students in colleges and universities. *Review of Educational Research*, *68*(3), 249–276. doi:10.3102/00346543068003249

Tsai, S. (2024, February 1). Gradescope Review: Is It Worth It? *SCI Journal*. https://www.scijournal.org/articles/gradescope-review

Turnbull, J. M. (1989). What is… normative versus criterion-referenced assessment. *Medical Teacher*, *11*(2), 145–150. doi:10.3109/01421598909146317 PMID:2586296

United Nations Educational, Scientific and Cultural Organization, & Organization, C. (2021). *Recommendation on the Ethics of Artificial Intelligence*. United Nations Educational. https://unesdoc.unesco. org/ark:/48223/pf0000379920.page=14

Van der Heyden, B., Cohilis, M., Souris, K., de Freitas Nascimento, L., & Sterpin, E. (2021). Artificial intelligence supported single detector multi-energy proton radiography system. *Physics in Medicine and Biology*, *66*(10), 105001. doi:10.1088/1361-6560/abe918 PMID:33621962

Vashishth, T. K., Sharma, V., Sharma, K. K., Kumar, B., Panwar, R., & Chaudhary, S. (2024). AI-Driven Learning Analytics for Personalized Feedback and Assessment in Higher Education. In *Using Traditional Design Methods to Enhance AI-Driven Decision Making* (pp. 206–230). IGI Global. doi:10.4018/979-8-3693-0639-0.ch009

Vonderwell, S. K., & Boboc, M. (2013). Promoting formative assessment in online teaching and learning. *TechTrends*, *57*(4), 22–27. doi:10.1007/s11528-013-0673-x

Widdowson, H. G. (2014). The role of translation in language learning and teaching. In *Translation: A multidisciplinary approach* (pp. 222–240). Palgrave Macmillan UK. doi:10.1057/9781137025487_12

Wiley, J., Hastings, P., Blaum, D., Jaeger, A. J., Hughes, S., Wallace, P., Griffin, T. D., & Britt, M. A. (2017). Different approaches to assessing the quality of explanations following a multiple-document inquiry activity in science. *International Journal of Artificial Intelligence in Education, 27*(4), 758–790. doi:10.1007/s40593-017-0138-z

Wiliam, D. (2011). What is assessment for learning? *Studies in Educational Evaluation, 37*(1), 3–14. doi:10.1016/j.stueduc.2011.03.001

Wood, D. F. (2013). Formative assessment. In T. Swanwick (Ed.), *Understanding Medical Education: Evidence, Theory and Practice* (pp. 317–328). The Association for the Study of Medical Education. doi:10.1002/9781118472361.ch23

Wu, X., Duan, R., & Ni, J. (2023). Unveiling security, privacy, and ethical concerns of ChatGPT. *Journal of Information and Intelligence.*

Xu, Y., Liu, X., Cao, X., Huang, C., Liu, E., Qian, S., Liu, X., Wu, Y., Dong, F., Qiu, C.-W., Qiu, J., Hua, K., Su, W., Wu, J., Xu, H., Han, Y., Fu, C., Yin, Z., Liu, M., & Zhang, J. (2021). Artificial intelligence: A powerful paradigm for scientific research. *Innovation (Cambridge (Mass.)), 2*(4), 100179. doi:10.1016/j.xinn.2021.100179 PMID:34877560

Zawacki-Richter, O., Marín, V. I., Bond, M., & Gouverneur, F. (2019). Systematic review of research on artificial intelligence applications in higher education–where are the educators? *International Journal of Educational Technology in Higher Education, 16*(1), 1–27. doi:10.1186/s41239-019-0171-0

Chapter 3
Evolution of Assessment and Feedback Methods in Higher Education

Adeel H. Suhail
Middle East College, Oman

Fiseha Mekonnen Guangul
https://orcid.org/0000-0001-8497-4117
Middle East College, Oman

Abdul Nazeer
Middle East College, Oman

ABSTRACT

This chapter examines the evolution of assessment and feedback in higher education, driven by technological advancements and changing societal needs. It highlights the shift from traditional to innovative, technology-based assessment methods, emphasizing the role of artificial intelligence (AI) and digital tools in creating more inclusive, personalized learning experiences. The discussion covers the historical context of assessment methods and the move towards more adaptable, skills-oriented evaluation strategies. It also addresses the rise of online and distance learning, accelerated by challenges like the COVID-19 pandemic, which require flexible and integrity-focused approaches to assessment. The aim is to shed light on the dynamic evolution of educational assessment, emphasizing the imperative to integrate AI and digital technologies in a way that aligns with diverse learning methodologies, thereby enhancing the efficacy and applicability of assessments and feedback mechanisms.

DOI: 10.4018/979-8-3693-2145-4.ch003

INTRODUCTION

The landscape of higher education has been subject to continuous evolution, shaped largely by the relentless progression of technology and changing societal needs. This transformative journey has been particularly evident in the domain of assessment and feedback methodologies. Traditional modes of assessment, once the cornerstone of educational evaluation, are being rapidly supplemented, and in some cases supplanted, by innovative, technology-driven approaches. The purpose of this chapter is to explore this evolution, investigating how emerging technologies, especially Artificial Intelligence (AI) and digital tools, are reshaping the assessment landscape in higher education.

Context Setting

Historically, higher education has been a bastion of knowledge dissemination and a crucible for intellectual development. The methods employed to assess and provide feedback to students have been a critical aspect of this educational process. For centuries, these methods remained largely unchanged, revolving around written examinations, oral presentations, and standardized tests (Guangul, Suhail, Khalit, & Khidhir, 2020). However, the advent of the digital age has ushered in a paradigm shift. The last few decades have seen an unprecedented integration of technology in education, fundamentally altering how educators evaluate student performance and provide feedback (Earle, 2002; Thurzo, Strunga, Urban, Surovková, & Afrashtehfar, 2023).

This transition is not merely a matter of replacing paper with pixels; it represents a deeper change in the educational ethos. Traditional assessments often emphasized rote memorization and standardized testing, potentially overlooking critical thinking, creativity, and practical problem-solving skills. In contrast, modern technology-enhanced assessment methods aim to provide a more holistic evaluation of a student's capabilities, encompassing not only their knowledge but also their ability to apply that knowledge in diverse contexts (Al Mamari, 2020; Collis, 1989).

Moreover, the rise of online and distance learning, accelerated by global challenges such as the COVID-19 pandemic, has further necessitated the adoption of innovative assessment methods. These methods need to be adaptable to remote learning environments while maintaining academic integrity and ensuring fair evaluation (Guangul et al., 2020; Mohmmed, Khidhir, Nazeer, & Vijayan, 2020).

Significance of the Topic

Understanding the transformation of assessment and feedback methods is vital for several reasons. First, it allows educators and policymakers to align assessment strategies with the current educational goals and learning outcomes. The shift towards skills such as critical thinking, problem-solving, and digital literacy requires corresponding changes in how we assess these competencies.

Second, as the student demographic becomes increasingly diverse and globalized, it is imperative to employ assessment methods that are inclusive and accessible to all. Technology has the potential to democratize education, offering personalized learning experiences and catering to different learning styles and needs.

Third, the rapid advancement in AI and other digital tools offers both opportunities and challenges. While these technologies can streamline assessment processes and provide instant, tailored feedback, they also raise questions about ethics, privacy, and the human element in education. Navigating these issues is crucial for the successful integration of technology in assessment methods.

Overview of Chapter

This chapter aims to provide a comprehensive exploration of how assessment and feedback methods in higher education have evolved and what future trends might emerge. The following sections will be covered:

1. **Historical Overview of Assessment Methods:** This section will trace the origins and development of traditional assessment methods, setting the stage for understanding the significance of recent changes.
2. **Transition to Technology-Enhanced Assessment:** Here, we will explore how technology first began to influence assessment methods, focusing on the early stages of digital integration.
3. **The Emergence of E-Learning and Online Assessments:** This part will delve into the growth of e-learning and how it has transformed assessment methodologies, emphasizing the shift from paper-based to digital assessments.
4. **Artificial Intelligence in Assessment and Feedback:** This section will focus on the role of AI in modern assessment methods, discussing how it is used for automating grading and providing personalized feedback.
5. **Data Analytics and Student Performance:** This part will explore how data analytics is employed to monitor and enhance student performance through personalized feedback and predictive analytics.
6. **Ethical, Privacy, and Security Considerations:** This critical section will address the ethical and privacy concerns arising from digital assessments and

data collection, discussing strategies to ensure data security and academic integrity.

7. **AI Applications and Practical Examples:** This section will present real-world examples and applications demonstrating the implementation and impact of modern assessment methods.
8. **Future Trends and Predictions:** Finally, we will speculate on future developments in assessment techniques, focusing on potential technological advancements and the need for continuous adaptation in assessment methodologies.

In essence, this chapter seeks to provide a thorough understanding of the evolution of assessment and feedback methods in higher education, highlighting both the benefits and challenges of integrating technology into these processes. It aims to serve as a resource for educators, policymakers, and academic institutions navigating this rapidly changing landscape.

OVERVIEW OF ASSESSMENT METHODS IN HIGHER EDUCATION

Retrospective Look at Traditional Assessment Methods

The history of assessment methods in higher education is deeply rooted in traditional approaches, which predominantly revolve around memory-based evaluations. These methods, emerging from the late 19th century and influenced significantly by the works of Alfred Binet in intelligence testing, focused on standardized testing formats (Elsayed & Cakir, 2023). They included methods like multiple-choice questions, true/false queries, and short answer tests, which primarily evaluated the student's ability to recall and reproduce information. While traditional assessments have been widely accepted, they are criticized for focusing on passing or failing rather than on effective teaching, and for their potential lack of effectiveness in a more communicative teaching approach (Brown & Knight, 2012). Despite their criticisms, traditional assessments encompass a variety of methods, including observations, dialogues, quizzes, tests, performance tasks, and projects, as well as students' reflections on their own learning (Norova, 2020).

Alternative Assessment

The landscape of educational assessment has undergone profound transformations, moving from traditional memory-based assessments towards more dynamic and innovative practices that prioritize analytical and critical thinking skills. This evolution reflects a broader shift in educational philosophies, acknowledging the need for assessments that not only measure factual knowledge but also the application, synthesis, and creation of new ideas.

Memory-Based Assessments

Initially, these memory-based assessments were seen as a reliable way to gauge a student's grasp of the factual content. Educators leaned heavily on rote learning techniques, where the primary goal was for students to memorize and regurgitate facts and figures during examinations. This approach was favored for its simplicity and the ease with which educators could measure and compare student performances across a standardized format (Juma, 2015).

The simplicity and uniformity of these assessments allowed for straightforward administration and comparative analysis across varied educational settings. Despite its widespread adoption, this paradigm has increasingly come under scrutiny. Critics argue that it falls short in fostering a deeper, more comprehensive understanding of subject matter, neglecting the development of critical thinking, problem-solving skills, and the ability to apply knowledge in practical contexts. This critique points to a growing consensus on the need for a shift towards more dynamic, analytical assessment methods that not only gauge factual knowledge but also evaluate students' proficiency in synthesizing, analyzing, and applying information in novel situations. Such a shift challenges educators to reimagine assessment as a tool not just for measuring learning in its most basic form, but as a means to cultivate and evaluate a broader spectrum of intellectual capabilities, thereby preparing students for the complexities of the modern world (García-Pérez, Fraile, & Panadero, 2021).

Transition to Analytical and Critical Thinking-Focused Approaches

Over time, there was a growing recognition of the limitations inherent in purely memory-based assessments. Critics argued that these methods did little to encourage critical thinking, problem-solving, or the application of knowledge in real-world scenarios. This criticism led to a gradual shift towards more analytical and critical thinking-focused approaches in assessments.

The transition saw a move away from strictly standardized tests to include essays, long-form written responses, and project-based evaluations. These newer methods aimed to assess not just what students knew, but how they could apply their knowledge analytically and creatively. The evolution of these assessment methods was influenced by educational reforms and the growing emphasis on developing higher-order thinking skills among students (Cohen, Salas, & Riedel, 2002).

Modern Assessment Practices

In recent years, the trend in higher education has moved towards even more diverse and innovative assessment methods. This includes the use of technology in assessments, such as digital portfolios and online examinations, which offer a broader range of evaluating student learning and capabilities (Sillat, Tammets, & Laanpere, 2021; Suhail, Guangul, & Kuckian, 2023). Additionally, there has been an increased focus on formative assessments, which are designed to provide ongoing feedback to students and help them in their learning process, rather than just summative assessments, which evaluate what a student has learned at the end of an instructional unit (Ismail, Rahul, Patra, & Rezvani, 2022).

The historical progression of assessment methods in higher education reflects a shift from memorization towards a more holistic evaluation of a student's analytical and critical thinking abilities. This evolution signifies a deeper understanding of the complexities of learning and the diverse capabilities of students.

Table 1. Advantages

Traditional Assessment	Alternative Assessment
Measures Learning Retention: Assessments gauge how much material students have grasped, facilitating easy performance comparison	**Holistic Skill Measurement:** Alternative assessments evaluate students based on analytical, reasoning, and logical thinking skills, applying theoretical knowledge practically.
Convenient for Educators: Provides a quick snapshot of student knowledge, easy to administer.	**Recognition of Individual Talents:** They help in identifying a student's unique abilities and interests.
Objective Evaluation: Pen-and-paper tests offer specific syllabus-related questions, ensuring fair grading	**Real-Life Application:** These methods assess problem-solving skills and the application of knowledge in real-world scenarios
Develops Cognitive Skills: Enhances memory retention and understanding, aiding intellectual growth.	**Enhanced Student Engagement:** They promote active student engagement and encourage constructing new meanings of taught materials.
Efficient and Cost-Effective: Simple, time-saving, and economical, requiring minimal resources.	**Improved Relationships:** They facilitate a better rapport among students, teachers, and classmates, enhancing communicative and interactive skills.
	In-Depth Capability Analysis: Educators gain a comprehensive view of students' strengths and weaknesses.

Summary of Advantages and Disadvantages of Traditional and Alternative Assessment

In comparison, with traditional assessments that offer a structured and economical approach for evaluating student performance, which may lack depth and creativity, while alternative assessments, on the other hand, provide a more comprehensive evaluation of student abilities but require more resources and time for effective implementation.

Table 2. Disadvantages

Traditional Assessment	Alternative Assessment
Limits Creative Thinking: Restricts innovative thought, lacks encouragement for creativity.	**Increased Teacher Effort:** Evaluating alternative assessments can be more demanding for teachers, requiring a deeper understanding of each student's work.
Surface-Level Analysis: Offers a narrow view of student capabilities, often constrained by curriculum, may not suit diverse learning styles	**Time-Consuming:** This method is more time-intensive due to its detailed and individualized nature.
Limited Options for Students: Emphasizes rote learning over comprehensive skills, restricts choices.	**Potential for Misunderstanding and Unfairness:** The subjective nature of some alternative assessments might lead to inconsistencies in evaluation.
Theory-Based Approach: May induce student anxiety due to pressure and competition, lacks a nurturing learning environment.	**Higher Costs:** They often require more resources and financial investment for practical applications and project work
Lack of Diversity: Fails to address unique student needs, uniform in nature.	

TRANSITION TO TECHNOLOGY-ENHANCED ASSESSMENT

The evolution of assessment and feedback methods in higher education has seen significant transformations, especially with the advent of technology. The integration of technology into educational assessment practices marks a pivotal shift from traditional paper-based evaluations to dynamic, digital formats. This transition has not only changed the landscape of how assessments are created, administered, and evaluated but also how feedback is provided to enhance the learning experience (Bukie, 2014; Buzzetto-More & Alade, 2006).

Early Stages of Technology Integration in Education

The initial phase of technology integration into education began with computer-aided assessments. These early implementations sought to leverage the computational power of computers to automate the scoring of standardized tests, thus offering a glimpse into the potential of technology to streamline assessment processes. Computer-based testing environments were among the first to be adopted, providing a controlled setting where students could take tests that were then automatically graded by software. This era laid the groundwork for more sophisticated applications of technology in assessment, catalyzing innovations that would later encompass a broader spectrum of educational activities (Zhai & Wiebe, 2023).

Technological Integration: Blended Learning and Agile Platforms

The rise of blended learning, which combines traditional classroom experiences with online elements, has necessitated the development of assessments that function effectively across varied learning environments. Agile learning platforms have emerged in response, offering flexible, customizable learning experiences that adapt to individual student needs. These platforms support a range of assessment types, from timed quizzes to peer reviews, integrating seamlessly with digital learning environments to provide a cohesive educational experience (Kumar et al., 2021).

Online Testing and Digital Portfolios: Online testing has evolved to offer sophisticated, secure environments for examinations, with features designed to ensure the integrity and fairness of the assessment process. Digital portfolios, meanwhile, offer students the opportunity to compile and present a comprehensive record of their learning achievements, supporting both formative and summative assessment strategies (Luthfiyyah, Aisyah, & Sulistyo, 2021).

Advantages of Technology-Enhanced Assessment

Enhanced Accessibility and Convenience: One of the foremost advantages brought about by technology-enhanced assessment is the increased accessibility it offers. Students can undertake assessments at their convenience, transcending geographical and temporal limitations. This flexibility is particularly beneficial for distance learning and for accommodating diverse student schedules (Jurāne-Brēmane, 2023).

Immediate and Rich Feedback: Digital platforms facilitate immediate feedback, allowing students to quickly identify areas of improvement. This instantaneity supports a more responsive learning process, where feedback can be immediately incorporated into study practices.

Diversity in Assessment Types: Technology enables a variety of assessment formats beyond traditional quizzes and exams. Interactive simulations, multimedia projects, and collaborative assignments can now be seamlessly integrated into the curriculum, providing a richer, more engaging assessment experience that aligns with diverse learning styles.

Challenges of Technology-Enhanced Assessment

Addressing the Digital Divide: Despite its advantages, the shift to digital assessment has highlighted the digital divide, with disparities in access to technology affecting equitable participation in digital learning environments (Jopp, 2020).

Maintaining Academic Integrity: The transition to online assessments has necessitated new strategies to uphold academic integrity, with concerns around cheating and plagiarism prompting the development of sophisticated proctoring software and honor codes (Guangul et al., 2020).

In inference, the transition to technology-enhanced assessment represents a significant milestone in the evolution of educational practices. While this shift offers numerous benefits in terms of flexibility, diversity, and immediacy of assessment and feedback, it also presents challenges that require ongoing attention and innovation. As technology continues to advance, the potential for further transforming assessment and feedback methods remains vast, promising a future where educational evaluations are more inclusive, engaging, and reflective of students' diverse learning journeys.

THE EMERGENCE OF E-LEARNING AND ONLINE ASSESSMENTS

The emergence of e-learning and online assessments marks a significant shift in the educational landscape, reshaping how knowledge is delivered, absorbed, and evaluated, offering opportunities for innovation in teaching and evaluation methods. As this field continues to evolve, it will be crucial to address challenges related to integrity and accessibility to fully realize the potential of digital learning and assessment. This transformation is not just a technological leap but also a pedagogical one, reflecting a deeper change in the way we approach learning and assessment (Heil & Ifenthaler, 2023).

Growth of E-Learning Platforms

E-learning, or electronic learning, has grown exponentially, particularly fueled by advancements in internet technology and the increasing accessibility of digital devices (ÖNAL & Nezih, 2023). This growth can be attributed to several factors:

- **Accessibility and Flexibility:** E-learning platforms offer the flexibility to learn anytime and anywhere, breaking geographical and time barriers.
- **Customized Learning Experiences:** These platforms often provide personalized learning experiences, adapting to individual learning styles and paces.
- **Resource Availability:** There is an abundance of resources available online, ranging from interactive modules to video lectures and digital libraries, catering to diverse learning needs.

Transformative Impact on Assessment Methods

The rise of e-learning has brought about a parallel transformation in assessment methods:

- **From Paper-Based to Digital Assessments:** Traditional paper-based assessments are increasingly being replaced by digital formats. This shift is not merely about changing the medium but also involves rethinking the assessment design to leverage technology effectively.
- **Enhanced Engagement and Interactivity:** Digital assessments often incorporate interactive elements, making the evaluation process more engaging. This can include multimedia content, real-time feedback, and adaptive testing.
- **Data-Driven Insights:** Online assessments provide educators with valuable data on student performance and learning patterns, enabling more informed teaching strategies.

Academic Integrity and Accessibility

With the transition to online assessments, two critical aspects emerge:

- **Academic Integrity:** The digital format raises concerns about maintaining academic integrity. Institutions are exploring various methods, including proctoring software, plagiarism checkers, and honor codes, to uphold standards (Guangul et al., 2020).
- **Accessibility:** Digital assessments have the potential to be more inclusive, accommodating diverse learning needs through assistive technologies. However, this also raises concerns about digital divide issues, where access to technology and internet connectivity can impact equity in assessment (AlSadrani, Alzyoudi, Alsheikh, & Elshazly, 2020).

Effective Digital Assessment Tools in Improving Student Learning Outcomes:

Improving the integration of digital assessment systems with other technological processes and workflows in educational organizations can significantly enhance the efficiency and effectiveness of data management and educational delivery. Examples of these systems include student information systems, administrative structures, and learning management systems. These integrations help centralize and easily access data across departments.

E-learning and its associated technologies have greatly evolved assessments into e-assessments, providing a wide range of formative and summative assessment activities such as online quizzes, presentations, e-portfolios, essays, and computer-marked examinations. Learning management systems (LMS) like Moodle, Blackboard, Canvas, and MOOC platforms such as Coursera and EdX are increasingly incorporating third-party software to facilitate summative assessments. This integration has proven effective for diagnostic, formative, and summative assessments, offering students diverse performance demonstration opportunities (Serutla, Mwanza, & Celik, 2024).

Key features of effective digital assessment tools include:

- **Time Efficiency:** Automation of routine tasks, use of intelligent exam software for digitizing evaluations, and proctoring services that save time.
- **Data Analysis:** Providing a wealth of performance information for both students and teachers. These tools enable data analysis to derive actionable insights, which can lead to improvements in teaching and learning processes.

Acceleration of Digital Transformation in Education due to the Pandemic:

The pandemic has significantly accelerated the digitization process, profoundly impacting the educational landscape (Mohmmed et al., 2020). This shift has led to changes such as:

- Emphasis on critical thinking over rote learning.
- Introduction of accurate, engaging, secure, and flexible digital assessments.
- Increased use of digital devices and the internet for delivering assessments and evaluations.
- Adaptation of educational institutions to rapidly changing technology and business landscapes, necessitating a robust digital mindset and innovation.

Advantages and Disadvantages of Digital Assessment in Terms of Security and Flexibility

Digital assessments offer several advantages over traditional paper-based assessments, particularly in terms of security and flexibility (Kiennert et al., 2017):

- **Security:** Digital assessments are more secure, with institutions securing files before and after exams. Tools like e-marking and fully traceable assessments with remote proctoring and time-bound tests enhance security and prevent breaches.
- **Flexibility:** Digital assessment allows the creation and design of new modules and the marking of papers at any time and place. It offers various methods for both summative and formative evaluations, thereby providing better assessment experiences and integrating seamlessly with other technologies.

While digital assessments provide significant advantages in terms of security and flexibility, they also present certain disadvantages that are important to consider:

- **Accessibility and Equity Issues**: Despite the flexibility offered by digital assessments, there can be a significant digital divide between students. Not all students may have reliable access to the necessary technology or stable internet connections, leading to disparities in assessment conditions. This can exacerbate existing inequalities and potentially disadvantage students from lower socioeconomic backgrounds (AlSadrani et al., 2020).
- **Technical Issues and Reliability**: Digital platforms and tools, while versatile, can encounter technical glitches, software crashes, and connectivity issues that can disrupt the assessment process. The dependency on technology means that the reliability of digital assessments is contingent upon the functioning of digital infrastructure, which may not always be foolproof (Stüber, 2018).
- **Potential for Academic Dishonesty**: While digital assessments can incorporate features like remote proctoring to enhance security, they also open new avenues for academic dishonesty. Students might find sophisticated ways to circumvent security measures, such as using unauthorized assistance or exploiting software vulnerabilities, thereby challenging the integrity of the assessment process (Guangul et al., 2020).
- **Cost and Resource Requirements**: Implementing and maintaining digital assessment systems requires significant investment in technology, software, and training for both educators and students. The costs associated with these systems can be prohibitive for some institutions, limiting their ability to adopt digital assessment methods.

ARTIFICIAL INTELLIGENCE IN ASSESSMENT AND FEEDBACK

The integration of Artificial Intelligence (AI) in educational assessment and feedback mechanisms heralds a new era in the evolution of teaching and learning processes. AI's role in automating grading and providing tailored feedback represents a significant leap forward in the pursuit of personalized education, efficiency in assessment, and the attainment of fairness and objectivity in grading (Yanli & Danni, 2021).

Automating Grading and Tailored Feedback:

AI technologies, through advanced algorithms and machine learning models, are now capable of automating the grading process for a wide range of assignments, from multiple-choice tests to more subjective forms of assessment like essays and open-ended responses. Beyond mere grading, AI systems are designed to provide personalized feedback to students, identifying not only areas of weakness but also offering suggestions for improvement. This capability not only streamlines the assessment process but also enhances the learning experience by providing immediate, actionable feedback that is tailored to the individual learner's needs (Rutner & Scott, 2022).

Precision, Efficiency, and Fairness in AI-Driven Assessment Tools

Precision: AI-driven assessment tools are developed with a focus on precision. Through continuous learning and adaptation, these tools are designed to accurately evaluate student responses, reducing human errors and biases that might affect grading. The precision of AI in understanding and assessing complex student responses continues to improve, offering a level of consistency difficult to achieve manually (Karadağ, 2023).

Efficiency: The efficiency of AI in the assessment process is unmatched. By automating the grading of assignments and tests, educators are freed from the time-consuming task of manual grading, allowing them to dedicate more time to teaching and personalized student engagement. The immediate provision of grades and feedback further enhances the learning process by ensuring timely intervention and support.

Fairness: One of the critical concerns addressed by AI-driven assessment tools is the issue of fairness in grading. By applying uniform criteria to the evaluation process, AI minimizes subjective biases that might influence grades. However, the fairness of AI tools is contingent upon the elimination of biases in the algorithms themselves, necessitating ongoing scrutiny and adjustment to ensure that these tools do not perpetuate existing inequities (Owan, Abang, Idika, Etta, & Bassey, 2023).

Latest Advancements in AI and Their Role in Streamlining Assessment and Feedback

Recent advancements in AI technology have focused on enhancing the sophistication of assessment tools, improving their ability to evaluate complex and creative student work. Developments in natural language processing (NLP) allow for more nuanced understanding and assessment of written responses, while advancements in machine learning algorithms enable the adaptation and personalization of feedback based on individual student performance patterns (Karadağ, 2023).

AI is also playing a crucial role in developing adaptive learning platforms that adjust the difficulty level of assessments in real-time, providing a more customized learning experience that aligns with each student's unique learning trajectory. Furthermore, AI-driven analytics tools are offering educators deeper insights into student learning outcomes, enabling more informed decision-making around curriculum design and instructional strategies (Cardona, Rodríguez, & Ishmael, 2023).

In summary, the role of Artificial Intelligence in transforming the landscape of assessment and feedback in higher education is profound. By automating grading, providing tailored feedback, and enhancing the precision, efficiency, and fairness of assessments, AI technologies are streamlining educational processes and paving the way for more personalized and effective learning experiences. However, the deployment of AI in education also requires careful consideration of ethical implications, particularly concerning data privacy and algorithmic bias, to ensure that the benefits of these technologies are realized equitably across diverse student populations. One significant challenge that persists is the current limitations of tools like Turnitin in identifying submissions generated by AI, which raises concerns about academic integrity and the need for more sophisticated detection methodologies. As AI continues to evolve, its potential to further revolutionize educational assessment and feedback remains vast, promising a future where technology and education converge to foster enhanced learning outcomes.

DATA ANALYTICS AND STUDENT PERFORMANCE

The advent of data analytics in the educational sector has revolutionized the way student performance is monitored, analyzed, and enhanced. By harnessing the power of data analytics, educators and institutions can now offer personalized feedback and interventions that are tailored to the unique needs and learning patterns of each student (Hasan et al., 2020). This section explores the multifaceted role of data analytics in elevating student performance and the mechanisms through which it predicts and addresses individual learning challenges.

Personalized Feedback Through Data Analytics

Data analytics employs sophisticated algorithms and machine learning techniques to process vast amounts of data generated by students' interactions with digital learning platforms. This data, encompassing aspects such as engagement metrics, submission times, quiz scores, and forum participation, provides a comprehensive picture of a student's learning journey. By analyzing these data points, educational technologies can generate personalized feedback that highlights strengths, identifies areas for improvement, and suggests targeted resources or activities to address specific learning gaps.

This personalized feedback mechanism is instrumental in fostering a responsive learning environment where students receive real-time insights into their performance. Such an approach not only motivates students by acknowledging their progress but also empowers them to take charge of their learning through informed decision-making (Namoun & Alshanqiti, 2020).

Analytical Prediction for Early Intervention

One of the most impactful applications of data analytics in education is its ability to predict which students may require additional support to meet their learning objectives. Predictive analytics models leverage historical and real-time data to identify patterns and indicators of potential academic risks, such as low engagement levels, declining grades, or patterns of late submissions (Punlumjeak, Rachburee, & Arunrerk, 2017).

By recognizing these early warning signs, educators can proactively intervene with personalized support and resources tailored to the student's specific needs. This may involve one-on-one tutoring sessions, adjustments to course materials, or the provision of supplementary learning aids. The goal of such interventions is not only to address immediate academic challenges but also to build resilience and learning capacities that will benefit students in the long term (Uskov et al., 2020).

The Role of Data Analytics in Continuous Improvement

Data analytics also plays a crucial role in the continuous improvement of teaching strategies and curriculum design. By analyzing aggregated data on student performance and feedback, educators can identify trends and correlations that inform curriculum adjustments, teaching method enhancements, and the development of more effective assessment strategies (Tao et al., 2022).

Furthermore, data analytics facilitates a deeper understanding of the diverse learning preferences and needs within a student population. This insight enables educators to design inclusive and flexible learning experiences that cater to a wide range of learning styles, ultimately contributing to a more equitable educational environment (Sharma, Thakur, Kapoor, & Singh, 2023).

To sum up this section, the application of data analytics in monitoring and enhancing student performance represents a paradigm shift in education, moving towards a more data-driven, personalized, and responsive learning model. Through personalized feedback and predictive intervention, data analytics empowers educators to support each student's unique learning journey effectively. As educational technologies continue to evolve, the potential of data analytics to transform teaching and learning practices further promises to unlock new possibilities for student achievement and educational excellence.

ETHICAL, PRIVACY, AND SECURITY CONSIDERATIONS

The integration of technology in education, particularly in assessment and data analytics, brings a host of ethical, privacy, and security considerations that must be navigated with care (Dhirani, Mukhtiar, Chowdhry, & Newe, 2023). The shift towards digital assessments and the extensive gathering of student data poses potential risks and challenges that necessitate a thoughtful approach to uphold ethical standards, protect privacy, and ensure data security.

Ethical Dilemmas and Privacy Issues

The collection and analysis of student data, while invaluable for personalized learning and performance monitoring, raises significant privacy concerns. Ethical dilemmas emerge regarding the extent of data collection, the consent process, and the potential for misuse of sensitive information. There is a fine line between leveraging data to enhance education and infringing on students' privacy rights. Ensuring that students and guardians are fully informed about what data is collected, how it is used, and who has access to it is paramount to maintaining trust and upholding ethical standards in educational practices (Caroline Hillier, 2022).

Privacy issues are particularly pertinent in the context of minors, who may not fully grasp the implications of their data being collected. Educators and institutions must navigate these concerns with utmost diligence, ensuring compliance with legal frameworks such as the General Data Protection Regulation (GDPR) in Europe and the Family Educational Rights and Privacy Act (FERPA) in the United States.

Ensuring Data Security and Academic Integrity

Data security is another critical consideration, as the digitalization of assessments and student information systems introduces vulnerabilities to cyberattacks and data breaches. Educational institutions must employ robust cybersecurity measures, including encryption, secure authentication protocols, and regular security audits, to protect sensitive student data from unauthorized access.

Maintaining academic integrity in digital assessments is equally crucial. The potential for cheating and plagiarism in online settings necessitates innovative solutions to verify student identities and monitor exam environments. Proctoring software, AI-based plagiarism detection tools, and secure exam platforms are among the methods being used to uphold integrity. However, these measures must be balanced with respect for student privacy, avoiding overly intrusive surveillance practices (Sabic & Azemovic, 2010).

Addressing Ethical and Practical Concerns

The trend towards tech-centric assessment methods introduces several ethical, logistical, and educational challenges. Ensuring equitable access to technology is a fundamental ethical concern, as students without reliable internet access or adequate devices are at a disadvantage. Institutions must strive to mitigate these disparities, possibly through loaner programs for devices or offering alternative assessment options (Nusi & Zaim, 2023).

From a practical standpoint, the implementation of technology-driven assessments requires significant investment in infrastructure, training, and support services to be effective. Educators must be equipped with the skills to utilize these tools effectively, and students need adequate orientation to navigate digital assessment platforms confidently.

Educationally, there is the challenge of ensuring that technology-enhanced assessments accurately measure learning outcomes and foster the development of critical thinking and problem-solving skills, rather than merely technical proficiency. Balancing the use of technology with traditional assessment methods can help maintain a holistic approach to evaluating student performance.

To summarize, Navigating the ethical, privacy, and security considerations of technology integration in education is a complex but essential task. By addressing these concerns proactively, institutions can harness the benefits of digital assessments and data analytics to enhance learning while safeguarding student privacy, ensuring data security, and upholding academic integrity. The future of education technology depends not only on innovation but also on the responsible and ethical use of data to support student success.

AI APPLICATIONS AND PRACTICAL EXAMPLES IN HIGHER EDUCATION

The implementation of modern assessment methods in higher education has seen a variety of innovative approaches aimed at enhancing learning outcomes and student engagement. This section explores case studies that highlight the successful integration of these methods, analyzing their effectiveness and student perceptions. This segment underscores the transformative influence and potential of Artificial Intelligence (AI) within the realm of education. It highlights AI's pivotal role in promoting inclusivity, universal accessibility, and personalized learning experiences. Furthermore, it delves into an array of aspects and applications of AI across the educational landscape, encompassing:

- Inclusion and Universal Access: AI tools are making education globally accessible, including to those who speak different languages or have visual or hearing impairments, and even to students unable to attend school due to illness. This inclusivity extends to providing tailored education to students needing different levels or subjects not offered in their schools, aiming for equal educational opportunities for all, irrespective of social class, race, gender, ethnicity, or physical and mental abilities (Luo, 2023).
- Individualized Learning: Personalized Learning: AI's role in fostering individualized learning experiences is increasingly significant. As AI technology becomes more prevalent in educational environments, it allows for a more tailored approach to education. This capability ensures that instruction is adapted to meet the unique needs and learning styles of individual students, thereby enhancing their engagement and comprehension (Gima Lee, 2023).
- Applications and Benefits: Highlighting the expansive scope of AI in education, including the adaptive learning systems, assistive technologies for students with special needs, and AI's utility in streamlining administrative and operational tasks within educational institutions. This includes enhanced scheduling, efficient facilities management, sophisticated writing aids, and the deployment of advanced school management systems, among others. AI's integration in these areas not only optimizes educational processes but also significantly contributes to a more inclusive and effective learning environment (Dabingaya, 2022).

- Ethical Considerations: This aspect delves into the ethical terrain that accompanies AI's integration into education, highlighting the paramount importance of embedding ethical principles at the core of AI technology development and implementation. It calls for continuous oversight to guarantee these technologies are in strict conformity with human ethical norms, ensuring AI acts as a positive force that upholds and amplifies human dignity, rights, and values within educational settings (Tretow-Fish & Khalid, 2023).
- The Future of AI in Education: This segment explores the extensive discourse surrounding the advantages and drawbacks of incorporating AI within educational frameworks yet adopts an optimistic stance regarding its prospective contributions. It proposes a gradually emerging agreement on the profound impact of AI's advantages, poised to reshape education in a markedly positive manner (Cukurova, Miao, & Brooker, 2023).

In higher education, Artificial Intelligence (AI) is being leveraged to revolutionize the learning experience, streamline administrative operations, and deliver customized educational pathways. Key examples of AI's application in this domain encompass:

Adaptive Learning Platforms: Utilizing AI to analyze students' learning styles, performance, and engagement to tailor content and assessments, thereby providing a personalized learning journey for each student.

Automated Administrative Tasks: AI-driven systems are deployed to automate routine tasks such as enrollment, scheduling, and student inquiries, freeing up valuable time for staff to focus on more critical tasks.

Intelligent Tutoring Systems: These AI systems offer one-on-one tutoring for students in subjects ranging from mathematics to language learning, adapting to each student's individual pace and learning needs.

Predictive Analytics for Student Success: Leveraging AI to predict student performance and identify those at risk of falling behind, enabling early intervention strategies to support student success.

AI-powered Research Assistants: Enhancing research capabilities by sifting through vast amounts of data to identify trends, provide insights, and even suggest areas of study, thereby augmenting the research process for faculty and students alike.

Virtual and Augmented Reality Learning Environments: Integrating AI with VR and AR to create immersive learning experiences that simulate real-world scenarios, facilitating complex learning in a controlled, interactive environment.

Voice-assisted Technology: Implementing AI-driven voice assistants in classrooms and on campuses to provide instant access to information, assist with learning materials, and support campus navigation.

Chatbots for Student Support Services: Deploying AI chatbots to offer 24/7 support to students, answering queries related to courses, campus life, and administrative processes, enhancing the student experience and engagement.

Assistive Technology: AI aids in offering equitable education to special needs students, for example, by reading text to visually impaired students, thus facilitating their access to the same educational content as their peers.

Data and Learning Analytics: Teachers and administrators utilize AI to analyze educational data, helping them make informed decisions to improve teaching strategies and student learning outcomes.

Behavior Management and Lesson Planning: AI technologies are being explored for classroom management and to aid teachers in lesson planning, offering innovative ways to engage students.

Language Learning and Test Prep: AI-powered platforms provide language learning assistance and test preparation tools, adapting to the learner's proficiency level for more effective study practices.

Assessment and Feedback: AI is used for grading assignments, including essays, by compiling data on student performance and providing immediate, meaningful feedback to students, which is crucial for their learning and improvement.

In the rapidly evolving landscape of education, the infusion of Artificial Intelligence (AI) technologies is expanding, introducing innovative tools and solutions that enhance teaching and learning. Here are several notable examples:

Adaptive Learning Platforms: Tools like **Thinkster Math**, which use AI to assess students' current knowledge and tailor the learning content, accordingly, providing a personalized learning journey.

Assistive Technologies: AI-powered solutions like **text-to-speech** tools for visually impaired students, enhancing accessibility and inclusivity in education.

Learning Management Systems (LMS): Platforms such as **Moodle**, **Blackboard**, **Canvas**, and MOOC platforms like **Coursera** and **EdX**, which incorporate AI to offer personalized learning experiences, analytics, and assessment capabilities.

Plagiarism Detection: AI tools that help maintain academic integrity by checking student submissions for originality like **Turnitin**.

Virtual Teaching Assistants: Like **Jill Watson** introduced by the Georgia Institute of Technology, which uses AI to answer student queries, providing support outside traditional classroom hours.

Speech Recognition Software: Tools like **Nuance**, which facilitate transcription of lectures, making content more accessible to students with different learning needs.

AI in Writing: Technologies that assist students in improving their writing skills, such as **grammar** and **style checkers**.

Content Technologies Inc.: Develops AI learning systems focused on converting vast data into actionable knowledge, aiding both teachers and students in the educational process.

FUTURE TRENDS AND PREDICTIONS IN EVALUATION TECHNIQUES

The landscape of evaluation in higher education is poised for transformative changes, driven by technological advancements and the evolving needs of a diverse student population. As we look towards the future, several trends and predictions emerge, highlighting the trajectory of evaluation techniques in the realm of education. These trends underscore the importance of flexibility and the need for continuous enhancement in assessment methodologies to meet the demands of the 21st-century learner.

Technological Progress in Evaluation Techniques

Artificial Intelligence and Machine Learning: AI and machine learning are expected to play a pivotal role in the development of more sophisticated and adaptive assessment tools. These technologies will enable the creation of personalized evaluation pathways that adjust in real-time to the student's performance, providing a truly customized learning experience. Furthermore, AI could automate the grading of complex assignments, including essays and projects, with a level of nuance and understanding that approaches human evaluation (Asanbe, Osofisan, & William, 2016).

Blockchain for Academic Integrity: The use of blockchain technology is anticipated to revolutionize the way academic credentials and achievements are recorded and shared. This could have significant implications for assessment, offering a secure and immutable ledger of student performance that is accessible across institutions. Blockchain could also enhance the security and integrity of online assessments, mitigating concerns around cheating and fraud.

Virtual and Augmented Reality: VR and AR technologies hold the promise of immersive assessment experiences, allowing students to demonstrate competencies in simulated environments that closely mimic real-world scenarios. These technologies could be particularly transformative in disciplines where practical skills are paramount, offering a platform for students to showcase their abilities in a dynamic and interactive manner.

Flexibility and Ongoing Enhancement in Assessment Methodologies

Adaptive Assessments: The future of evaluation in higher education will increasingly lean towards adaptive assessments that tailor difficulty levels and question types to the individual learner's abilities. This approach not only challenges students appropriately based on their skill levels but also provides instructors with detailed insights into each student's understanding and mastery of the subject matter (Veeramuthu & Periasamy, 2014).

Continuous Feedback Loops: As assessment methodologies evolve, there will be a greater emphasis on providing continuous, formative feedback to students. This shift from summative to formative assessment practices encourages a growth mindset, where feedback is integral to the learning process, guiding students towards improvement and deeper understanding.

Interdisciplinary Evaluations: Future trends also suggest a move towards interdisciplinary evaluations that reflect the interconnected nature of knowledge and skills in the real world. Assessments will increasingly require students to apply learning from multiple disciplines to solve complex problems, encouraging critical thinking, creativity, and the integration of diverse perspectives.

Ethical Considerations and Data Privacy: As technological advancements continue to shape assessment practices, ethical considerations and data privacy will remain at the forefront. Ensuring the ethical use of student data, protecting privacy, and maintaining equity in access to technology-enhanced assessments will be ongoing challenges that institutions must address.

In brief, the future of evaluation in higher education is marked by rapid technological progress and an unwavering need for flexibility and continuous improvement. As institutions navigate these trends, the ultimate goal will be to create assessment methodologies that are not only technologically advanced but also equitable, inclusive, and supportive of every student's learning journey. By embracing innovation and adapting to change, the future of education can meet the diverse needs of learners in an increasingly complex and interconnected world.

CONCLUSION

This chapter thoroughly explores the transformative journey of educational assessments, from traditional memory-based evaluations to the innovative frontier of digital assessments. It illuminates the vast potential of integrating technology in assessment practices, highlighting not only the enhanced security and flexibility offered by digital means but also addressing the inherent challenges and opportunities this integration presents. As the educational landscape continues to evolve, driven by technological advancements and changing societal needs, the chapter underscores the necessity of a balanced approach to assessment. This approach should not only leverage the benefits of digital technologies but also remain cognizant of the potential disparities and obstacles that may arise. Ultimately, the chapter advocates for a future where assessments are dynamically aligned with educational goals, inclusively accessible, and comprehensively designed to evaluate a wide spectrum of student capabilities. Through this lens, the document positions itself as a critical analysis and forward-looking guide for educators, policymakers, and technologists aiming to navigate and shape the future of educational assessment.

REFERENCES

Al Mamari, B. K. S. (2020). *Bringing innovation to EFL writing through a focus on formative e-assessment:'Omani post-basic education students' experiences of and perspectives on automated writing evaluation (AWE).* University of Exeter.

AlSadrani, B., Alzyoudi, M., Alsheikh, N., & Elshazly, E. E. (2020). The digital divide in inclusive classrooms. *International Journal of Learning. Teaching and Educational Research, 19*(3), 69–85.

Asanbe, M., Osofisan, A., & William, W. (2016). Teachers' performance evaluation in higher educational institution using data mining technique. *International Journal of Applied Information Systems, 10*(7), 10–15. doi:10.5120/ijais2016451524

Brown, S., & Knight, P. (2012). *Assessing learners in higher education.* Routledge. doi:10.4324/9780203062036

Bukie, O. F. (2014). Understanding technologies for e-assessment: A systematic review approach. *Journal of Emerging Trends in Computing and Information Sciences, 5*(12), 936–947.

Buzzetto-More, N. A., & Alade, A. J. (2006). Best practices in e-assessment. *Journal of Information Technology Education, 5*(1), 251–269. doi:10.28945/246

Cardona, M. A., Rodríguez, R. J., & Ishmael, K. (2023). *Artificial intelligence and the future of teaching and learning: Insights and recommendations.*

Caroline Hillier, U. o. G., Canada. (2022). Creating Computer Confidence: An Investigation into Current Privacy and Security Concerns of the Senior Demographic. [IJITE]. *International Journal of Innovative Trends in Engineering, 11*(3), 19–23.

Cohen, M. S., Salas, E., & Riedel, S. L. (2002). Critical thinking: Challenges, possibilities, and purpose. *Contract No. DASW01-00-C-3010, March.*

Collis, B. (1989). Using information technology to create new educational situations. *Higher Education Policy*, *2*(4), 63–70. doi:10.1057/hep.1989.75

Cukurova, M., Miao, X., & Brooker, R. (2023). Adoption of Adaptive Learning Platforms in Schools: Unveiling Factors Influencing Teachers Engagement. *arXiv preprint arXiv:2304.00903.*

Dabingaya, M. (2022). Analyzing the Effectiveness of AI-Powered Adaptive Learning Platforms in Mathematics Education. *Interdisciplinary Journal Papier Human Review*, *3*(1), 1–7. doi:10.47667/ijphr.v3i1.226

Dhirani, L. L., Mukhtiar, N., Chowdhry, B. S., & Newe, T. (2023). Ethical dilemmas and privacy issues in emerging technologies: A review. *Sensors (Basel)*, *23*(3), 1151. doi:10.3390/s23031151 PMID:36772190

Earle, R. S. (2002). The integration of instructional technology into public education: Promises and challenges. *Educational Technology*, *42*(1), 5–13.

Elsayed, S., & Cakir, D. (2023). Implementation of Assessment and Feedback in Higher Education. *Acta Pedagogia Asiana*, *2*(1), 34–42. doi:10.53623/apga.v2i1.170

García-Pérez, D., Fraile, J., & Panadero, E. (2021). Learning strategies and self-regulation in context: How higher education students approach different courses, assessments, and challenges. *European Journal of Psychology of Education, 36*(2), 533–550. doi:10.1007/s10212-020-00488-z

Gima Lee, Y. J. L., Hee-jeong Kim. (2023). *Analysis of adaptive learning in Korea's AI mathematics learning platforms.* Korean School Mathematics Society. doi:10.30807/ksms.2023.26.3.004

Guangul, F. M., Suhail, A. H., Khalit, M. I., & Khidhir, B. A. (2020). Challenges of remote assessment in higher education in the context of COVID-19: A case study of Middle East College. *Educational Assessment, Evaluation and Accountability, 32*(4), 519–535. doi:10.1007/s11092-020-09340-w PMID:33101539

Hasan, R., Palaniappan, S., Mahmood, S., Abbas, A., Sarker, K. U., & Sattar, M. U. (2020). Predicting student performance in higher educational institutions using video learning analytics and data mining techniques. *Applied Sciences (Basel, Switzerland)*, *10*(11), 3894. doi:10.3390/app10113894

Heil, J., & Ifenthaler, D. (2023). Online Assessment in Higher Education: A Systematic Review. *Online Learning : the Official Journal of the Online Learning Consortium*, *27*(1), 187–218. doi:10.24059/olj.v27i1.3398

Ismail, S. M., Rahul, D., Patra, I., & Rezvani, E. (2022). Formative vs. summative assessment: Impacts on academic motivation, attitude toward learning, test anxiety, and self-regulation skill. *Language Testing in Asia*, *12*(1), 40. doi:10.1186/s40468-022-00191-4

Jopp, R. (2020). A case study of a technology enhanced learning initiative that supports authentic assessment. *Teaching in Higher Education*, *25*(8), 942–958. doi:10.1080/13562517.2019.1613637

Juma, Z. R. (2015). *Exploring the development of biological literacy in Tanzanian junior secondary school students*. Open Access Te Herenga Waka-Victoria University of Wellington.

Jurāne-Brēmane, A. (2023). Digital assessment in technology-enriched education: Thematic review. *Education Sciences*, *13*(5), 522. doi:10.3390/educsci13050522

Karadağ, N. (2023). The impact of artificial intelligence on online assessment: A preliminary review. *Journal of Educational Technology and Online Learning*, *6*(4), 822–837. doi:10.31681/jetol.1351548

Kiennert, C., Rocher, P.-O., Ivanova, M., Rozeva, A., Durcheva, M., & Garcia-Alfaro, J. (2017). Security challenges in e-assessment and technical solutions. *Paper presented at the 2017 21st International Conference Information Visualisation (IV)*. IEEE. 10.1109/iV.2017.70

Kumar, A., Krishnamurthi, R., Bhatia, S., Kaushik, K., Ahuja, N. J., Nayyar, A., & Masud, M. (2021). Blended learning tools and practices: A comprehensive analysis. *IEEE Access : Practical Innovations, Open Solutions*, *9*, 85151–85197. doi:10.1109/ACCESS.2021.3085844

Luo, Q. Z. (2023). The Influence of AI-Powered Adaptive Learning Platforms on Student Performance in Chinese Classrooms. *Journal of Education*, *6*(3), 1–12. doi:10.53819/81018102t4181

Luthfiyyah, R., Aisyah, A., & Sulistyo, G. H. (2021). Technology-enhanced formative assessment in higher education: A voice from Indonesian EFL teachers. *EduLite: Journal of English Education. Literature and Culture*, *6*(1), 42–54.

Mohmmed, A. O., Khidhir, B. A., Nazeer, A., & Vijayan, V. J. (2020). Emergency remote teaching during Coronavirus pandemic: The current trend and future directive at Middle East College Oman. *Innovative Infrastructure Solutions*, *5*(3), 1–11. doi:10.1007/s41062-020-00326-7

Namoun, A., & Alshanqiti, A. (2020). Predicting student performance using data mining and learning analytics techniques: A systematic literature review. *Applied Sciences (Basel, Switzerland)*, *11*(1), 237. doi:10.3390/app11010237

Norova, M. (2020). Advantages And Disadvantages of Traditional and Alternative Ways of Assessment. *ЦЕНТР НАУЧНЫХ ПУБЛИКАЦИЙ (buxdu. uz)*, *2*(2).

Nusi, A., & Zaim, M. (2023). Philosophy of Education In Digital Transformation: Ethical Considerations For Students' Data Security In Online Learning Platforms. *Jurnal Ilmiah Pendidikan Scholastic*, *7*(3), 42–50. doi:10.36057/jips.v7i3.629

Owan, V. J., Abang, K. B., Idika, D. O., Etta, E. O., & Bassey, B. A. (2023). Exploring the potential of artificial intelligence tools in educational measurement and assessment. *Eurasia Journal of Mathematics, Science and Technology Education*, *19*(8), em2307. doi:10.29333/ejmste/13428

Punlumjeak, W., Rachburee, N., & Arunrerk, J. (2017). Big data analytics: Student performance prediction using feature selection and machine learning on microsoft azure platform. [JTEC]. *Journal of Telecommunication, Electronic and Computer Engineering*, *9*(1-4), 113–117.

Rutner, S. M., & Scott, R. A. (2022). Use of Artificial Intelligence to Grade Student Discussion Boards: An Exploratory Study. *Information Systems Education Journal*, *20*(4), 4–18.

Sabic, A., & Azemovic, J. (2010). Model of efficient Assessment System with accent on privacy, security and integration with E-University components. *Paper presented at the 2010 2nd International Conference on Education Technology and Computer*. IEEE. 10.1109/ICETC.2010.5529579

Serutla, L., Mwanza, A., & Celik, T. (2024). *Online Assessments in a Changing Education Landscape Reimagining Education-The Role of E-Learning, Creativity, and Technology in the Post-Pandemic Era*. IntechOpen.

Sharma, A., Thakur, K., Kapoor, D. S., & Singh, K. J. (2023). *Designing Inclusive Learning Environments: Universal Design for Learning in Practice The Impact and Importance of Instructional Design in the Educational Landscape*. IGI Global. doi:10.4018/978-1-6684-8208-7.ch002

Sillat, L. H., Tammets, K., & Laanpere, M. (2021). Digital competence assessment methods in higher education: A systematic literature review. *Education Sciences*, *11*(8), 402. doi:10.3390/educsci11080402

Stüber, J. (2018). *Barriers of digital technologies in higher education: a teachers' perspective from a Swedish university*.

Suhail, A. H., Guangul, F. M., & Kuckian, S. (2023). Contemporary and Technology Based Assessment and Feedback for Student Enhanced Learning: A Case Study of Mechanical Engineering Department at Middle East College. *Paper presented at the SHS Web of Conferences*. IEEE. 10.1051/shsconf/202315607005

Tanik Önal, N., & Önal, N.ÖNAL. (2023). Online learning and teaching experiences of preservice science teachers during Covid-19 pandemic. *Journal of Educational Technology and Online Learning*, *6*(2), 295–314. doi:10.31681/jetol.1078486

Tao, X., Shannon-Honson, A., Delaney, P., Li, L., Dann, C., Li, Y., & Xie, H. (2022). Data analytics on online student engagement data for academic performance modeling. *IEEE Access : Practical Innovations, Open Solutions*, *10*, 103176–103186. doi:10.1109/ACCESS.2022.3208953

Thurzo, A., Strunga, M., Urban, R., Surovková, J., & Afrashtehfar, K. I. (2023). Impact of artificial intelligence on dental education: A review and guide for curriculum update. *Education Sciences*, *13*(2), 150. doi:10.3390/educsci13020150

Tretow-Fish, T. A. B., & Khalid, M. S. (2023). Methods for Evaluating Learning Analytics and Learning Analytics Dashboards in Adaptive Learning Platforms: A Systematic Review. *Electronic Journal of e-Learning*, *21*(5), 430–449. doi:10.34190/ejel.21.5.3088

Uskov, V. L., Bakken, J. P., Gayke, K., Fatima, J., Galloway, B., Ganapathi, K. S., & Jose, D. (2020). Smart learning analytics: student academic performance data representation, processing and prediction. *Paper presented at the Smart Education and e-Learning 2020*. Springer. 10.1007/978-981-15-5584-8_1

Veeramuthu, P., & Periasamy, R. (2014). Application of higher education system for predicting student using data mining techniques. *International Journal of Innovative Research in Advanced Engineering*, *1*(5), 31–36.

Yanli, X., & Danni, L. (2021). Prospect of Vocational Education under the Background of Digital Age: Analysis of European Union's "Digital Education Action Plan (2021-2027)". *Paper presented at the 2021 International Conference on Internet, Education and Information Technology (IEIT)*. IEEE. 10.1109/IEIT53597.2021.00042

Zhai, X., & Wiebe, E. (2023). Technology-based innovative assessment. *Classroom-based STEM assessment*, 99-125.

Chapter 4
AI and Personalised Grading Criteria

Sajeel Ahmed
University of Bedfordshire, UK

Abira Zaki
Iqra University, Pakistan

Yongmei Bentley
University of Bedfordshire, UK

ABSTRACT

The chapters discuss the potential of artificial intelligence (AI) in transforming higher education assessment, grading, and feedback processes, enabling personalized interventions, data analysis, and deeper insights into student performance. The chapter discusses the significance of real-time learning in higher education, focusing on virtual teaching platforms and AI-powered assessment methodologies. It evaluates AI-based assessments, machine learning algorithms, and natural language processing techniques.

BACKGROUND INFORMATION

Artificial Intelligence (AI) can significantly improve education by enhancing learning outcomes, increasing efficiency, and providing access to high-quality education worldwide. It uses knowledge tracing and collaborative filtering to create personalized learning experiences, aligning with individual student needs and future performance. AI can also help instructors identify and address learning gaps in real-time, providing actionable insights. A proposed adaptive exercise suggestion system

DOI: 10.4018/979-8-3693-2145-4.ch004

improved recommendation efficacy by 8%. Intelligent tutoring systems have been recognized since 1990 for their potential in improving learning outcomes.

AI can improve student engagement, motivation, and retention by tailoring learning to individual preferences. This can be achieved through personalized feedback systems or AI-powered Tutoring platforms. Canadian AI-powered platform Korbit achieved better learning outcomes than platforms without personalized feedback. AI tools and resources like virtual tutors, voice assistants, text-to-image generation models, and adaptive assessment systems can enhance traditional learning methods. The available guides from Joint Information Systems Committee (JISC) and ChatGPT illustrate how AI can enhance operational procedures, productivity, and student collaboration, promoting teamwork, effectiveness, and problem-solving abilities (Kuo et al., 2023).

UTILISING AI FOR ASSESSMENT, GRADING, AND FEEDBACK IN HIGHER EDUCATION: ISSUES, PROBLEMS, AND TRENDS

AI in assessment and grading may perpetuate biases, leading to unfair outcomes for marginalized groups. Ethical considerations, implementation challenges, and faculty training are crucial for successful AI adoption in higher education (Chatterjee & Bhattacharjee, 2020). Data privacy concerns and transparency are essential. AI-driven systems should be designed for accessibility and inclusivity, requiring significant financial investment and resources.

Algorithmic Bias and Fairness

AI algorithms used for assessment and grading might inadvertently perpetuate the biases present in the data as they are trained on, leading towards unfair outcomes, particularly for marginalized groups. Addressing the biased algorithms and ensuring fairness in AI-grading systems is a crucial challenge. Ethical concerns surrounding AI use in higher education, highlight the need for responsible deployment, avoiding bias, and promoting transparency and accountability among stakeholders from various organizations (Slimi & Carballido, 2023). AI and learning analytics are revolutionizing personalized education in higher education. They enable personalized feedback and assessment, focusing on students' strengths and areas for improvement. However, ethical considerations, implementation challenges, and faculty training are crucial for successful adoption. This technology can enhance student engagement and optimize educational outcomes (Vashishth et al., 2024). The negative impacts of AI in higher education include biases, plagiarism, micromanagement, behavior manipulation, overreliance, and privacy concerns. It examines AI's impact on various processes, including student enrollment, employee hiring, teaching, research, and employee well-being. The paper also explores potential solutions and policy implications (Ivanov, 2023). AI advancements in mental health research challenge historical biases, highlighting the need for fair-aware AI development in psychological science to address health-equity implications (Timmons et al., 2023). The blurred lines between assessment and feedback in higher education, highlighting six issues: students' focus on grades, late feedback, subordination, documentation, and anonymous marking requirements, and proposes strategies for preserving feedback's learning function (Winstone & Boud, 2022).

Figure 1. Utilising AI for Assessment, Grading, and Feedback in Higher Education: Issues, Problems, and Trends
Source: Author Made

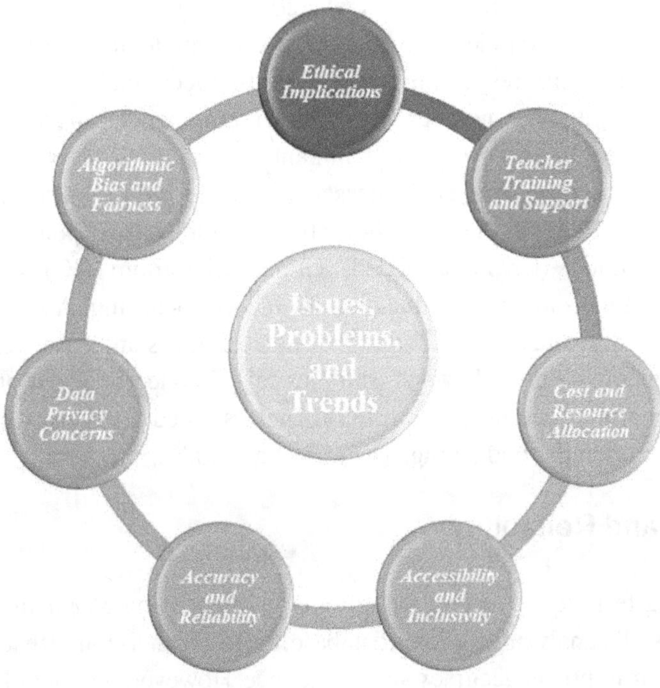

Data Privacy Concerns

AI can enhance education by providing personalized learning experiences, but ethical concerns like privacy and bias need to be addressed. Solutions include creating ethical guidelines, collaborating with educators, and involving stakeholders

(Rawat, n.d.). The use of AI in educational settings raises the concerns related to data privacy, as student the data is collected and analysed in order to provide the personalised feedback and grading. Also ensuring about the protection of the student privacy and compliance with the related regulations that has included GDPR and FEPRA is essential. The ethical concerns surrounding personalized learning, a popular application of Ed-tech, particularly at the K-12 level. It identifies six distinct ethical concerns: information privacy, anonymity, surveillance, autonomy, non-discrimination, and information ownership. The study also highlights whether these concerns are similar to those raised about educational tracking in the 1950s (Regan & Jesse, 2019). Contemporary culture is heavily influenced by data, indicators, and metrics, with big data, data science, and advanced technologies revolutionizing quantitative knowledge production and decision-making. Data fiction, primarily in commercial domains, has expanded to education, where understanding and analyzing its consequences is crucial, especially during mass university closures and COVID-19 crises (Williamson et al., 2020). The ethical tensions between education, Big Data, and student privacy. It advocates for demonstrating the efficacy of learning systems while respecting privacy, building accountability, and overseeing learning technologies. It concludes with policy recommendations to achieve these goals (Reidenberg & Schaub, 2018). Students perceive AI algorithms as fairer than teachers, indicating higher fairness with AI algorithms. Transparency and explanations are crucial in the evaluation process, emphasizing potential risks and ethical considerations (Chai et al., 2024). Google Classroom (GC) is increasingly being used in Malaysian higher education for blended learning. A study involving 17 students and three instructors found that its usefulness and ease were the main factors influencing its use. However, students raised concerns about privacy, peer interaction, and interface design, while instructors faced challenges in accessing learning analytics and cloud storage (Kumar et al., 2020).

Accuracy and Reliability

Deep learning techniques to improve glioma grading using Magnetic Resonance Images (MRIs). By analyzing a glioma database, the researchers found that focusing on the tumor region improves accuracy and confidence. However, accurate classification of grades 2, 3, and 4 remains challenging. The findings could advance a reliable data-driven system for glioma diagnosis and therapy planning. The accuracy and reliability of AI-based assessment and grading systems are one of the critical factors also ensuring that these systems should have been consistent and accurate with their results that is essential for maintaining the trust in their use (Pitarch et al., 2023). The Quality Assessment of Diagnostic Accuracy Studies 2 (QUADAS-2) tool in AI diagnostic accuracy systematic reviews discovered bias across all four domains, with 57.5% of 423 studies reporting a high or unclear bias risk, potentially hindering clinical implementation (Jayakumar et al., 2022). The study evaluated the suturing skills of 16 second-year veterinary students using three performance assessments (PAs) and electromyography armband data. The students performed suturing tasks on synthetic tissue models and were scored by expert surgeons using the OSCE and OSATS checklists. Surface electromyography data was used to analyze performance assessment scores. The results showed moderate reliability for the OSCE and OSATS checklists and poor reliability for the GRS (Kuzminsky et al., 2023).

Ethical Implications

Ethical implications that has included the use of student data for commercial purposes or the potential for AI in order to replace the human educators as there is a need to be carefully addressed. The ethical implications of AI integration in K-12 education, highlighting its potential benefits and challenges. It provides resources from MIT Media Lab and Code.org to help practitioners navigate these issues and ensure responsible implementation (Akgun & Greenhow, 2022). The use of AI in grading student papers, highlighting its benefits like discretion, convenience, and consistent feedback. However, it also addresses arguments against AI, including cost, privacy, legality, and ethics, and its implications for faculty career (Kumar, 2023). The paper examines the impact of explainable AI in education on students' trust and motivation. It uses a needs-elicitation study and explainable AI frameworks. The results show that full-text global explanations and accuracy statements do not affect trust or motivation. However, the grade provided by the system, particularly the difference between the student's self-estimated and system grade, significantly influences the effect of AI explanations (Conijn et al., 2023). AI has been used in various industries and consumer products for decades, but its applications in education are becoming more prevalent. Conversations about AI's disruption and ethical concerns are occurring, but the technology's development threatens to outpace academic discussion. This paper surveys academic and trade literature and uses a questionnaire to define existing and emerging ethical concerns of AI in education (Remian, 2019). The social and ethical implications of digitally mediated assessments, focusing on the challenges faced by students, educators, and institutions. It explores the control of assessment work, potential exclusion, and the benefits of assessment labor, offering practical solutions to navigate these ethical dilemmas (Bearman et al., 2020). Ethical AIED, analyzing current policies and guidelines, and proposes principles for stakeholders to guide the development and deployment of AI, addressing personal data and learner autonomy concerns (Nguyen et al., 2023).

Accessibility and Inclusivity

AI-driven assessment and grading systems should be designed with the accessibility and inclusivity in mind to get ensured that they accommodate the diverse learning needs and preferences. Also ensuring that these systems do not disadvantage the students with disabilities or those from the underrepresented backgrounds that is crucial. AI-based methodologies for scoring in educational assessments and proposes an evidence-centered design framework. It provides recommendations for defining construct, task, and evidence models to optimize AI-based automated scoring and support the validity of inferences from and uses of scores (Ercikan & McCaffrey, 2022). Over the past 50 years, higher education has grown and diversified, serving a diverse student body. This has led to the need for more individualized assessments and fewer one-size-fits-all approaches. Current methods, such as multiple-choice question assessments, high-stakes exams, and manual paper grading, are insufficient for measuring and supporting learning across this diverse group, causing stress and pitting students against each other (Naseer et al., 2024). The use of Chat-GPT, a GPT-4-based model, in the Fundamentals of Engineering Environmental Exam demonstrates significant improvements in accuracy and mathematical capabilities and highlights the model's potential for solving complex engineering problems. The study also highlights the need for future research to address AI challenges in education, enhance accessibility, and develop AI-resistant exam questions. The findings provide insights into the potential applications and limitations of AI models in education (Pursnani et al., 2023). AI systems for student assessment and grade assignment should prioritise the accessibility and inclusivity to avoid any discrimination. Although these systems should be accessible to all students, regardless of disabilities, and should be intuitively comprehensible. Inclusivity goes belong the accessibility, ensuring systems are unbiased and do not exacerbate social inequities. Regular oversight and feedback from diverse groups is crucial to catch the unintended issues early. With care, testing and transparency, AI can be developed to assess students in a standardised yet flexible manner with the potential to expand educational access worldwide.

Teacher Training and Support

Integrating AI into the assessment and grading practices requires adequate training and support for educators. Also providing teachers with the necessary skills and resources to effectively use AI tools that can enhance their efficacy and acceptance. The impact of AI on education, focusing on its application in administration, instruction, and learning. The research used a qualitative approach, utilizing literature review as the research design. AI has been widely adopted in education, transforming from computer technologies into web-based systems, humanoid robots, and chatbots. These technologies have improved administrative functions, grading, and teaching quality. Additionally, AI has enabled personalized curriculum and content, enhancing learners' experience and overall learning quality (Chen et al., 2020). The study explores K-12 science teachers' trust and attitudes towards AI-EdTech, emphasizing the need for increased knowledge, professional development programs, and discourse analysis of completed programs to enhance trust in AI-EdTech (Nazaretsky, Ariely, et al., 2022). The potential and challenges of implementing advanced AI models in education, focusing on concerns about their widespread use and opacity in the "new AI gold rush" era (Grassini, 2023). Also the effectiveness of machine learning algorithms in monitoring students' academic progress and identifying those at risk of unsatisfactory results. The study developed prediction models using different machine learning algorithms, with decision trees being the most effective. The final output consists of supportive measures to monitor students' performance and preventive measures to support struggling students. This helps improve education quality and prestige in modern educational institutes (Khan et al., 2021).

Cost and Resource Allocation

Implementing the AI-driven assessment and grading system required significant financial investment and resources while also balancing the costs associated with the AI adoption with the potential benefits that is a consideration for educational institutions. The meta-verse, the next-generation Internet, is a virtual world where users interact in real-time using avatars. It supports service provision and personalized experiences. This paper proposes a stochastic optimal resource allocation scheme (SORAS) for virtual education in the Metaverse. It aims to minimize service provider costs while accounting for user demand uncertainty. Simulation results show SORAS can effectively manage resource allocation (Ng et al., 2022). A stochastic optimal resource allocation scheme (SORAS) for virtual education in the Metaverse, aiming to minimize service provider costs and account for user demand uncertainty (Alias Rohini & Mohanavel, 2022). Artificial intelligence (AI) is revolutionizing education by improving accuracy, efficiency, and personalized feedback. This paper explores the applications of AI tools in classroom assessment, including large language models, test purpose determination, and test blueprint generation. It also discusses the role of teachers in AI-based assessment and the challenges faced by teachers. Strategies to address these challenges are presented, emphasizing the need for collaboration between educators, policymakers, and stakeholders to maximize AI's benefits while mitigating risks. The goal is to equip students with the skills needed for the 21st century (Owan et al., 2023). The online model is revolutionizing traditional learning pedagogies with the use of AI and Machine Learning (ML) tools. AI-enabled applications can assess learners' aptitudes using various testing frameworks. As AI instructional frameworks are still developing, they can enhance teaching skills. Organizations are adopting smart guidance plans, using AI and IoT to design course curriculums with different difficulty levels (Ahuja & Bala, 2021). The potential applications of AI in higher education, focusing on developing countries. It discusses the benefits, challenges, and ethical issues associated with AI use in teaching, learning, and research. The benefits include improved educational experiences, individualized learning, and administrative improvements. However, it also addresses potential issues like biases, human contact hazards, and creative thinking. The study suggests strategies for integrating AI into higher education, including upskilling educators, promoting collaboration, and ensuring fair access (Alordiah, 2023).

BENEFITS OF AI IN TEACHING

AI can revolutionise teaching through personalising learning paths for students, optimising outcomes, and providing real-time feedback. It can also enhance the student engagement through virtual teaching platforms like VR. AI automates the manual tasks, freeing up educators to focus more in impactful activities like individualised instruction and critical thinking skills.

Figure 2. Benefits of AI in Teaching
Source: Author Made

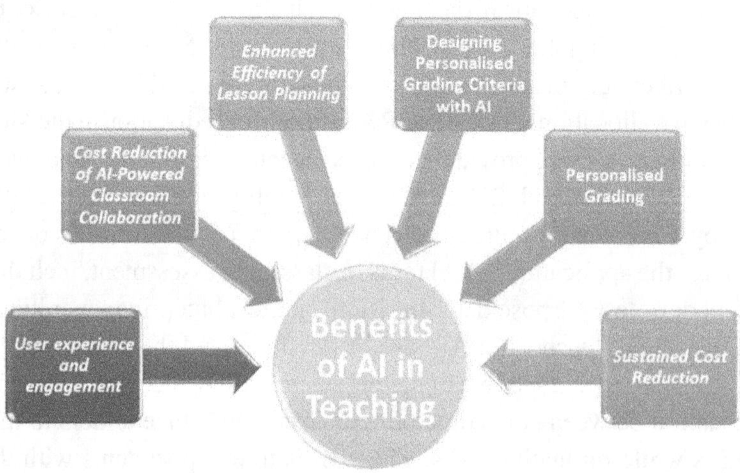

User Experience and Engagement

Advancements in computer science have led to the widespread adoption of AI technology, particularly in Automated Essay Scoring (AES) platforms. However, limited research has focused on AI explain ability and algorithm transparency's impact on AES usability. A qualitative study on an AI-based essay writing and grading platform explored these aspects, revealing key considerations for evaluating AES systems. These findings can guide the development of effective essay feedback and grading tools that prioritize explain ability and transparency, improving usability in computer science education (Hall, 2023). The potential of AI in enhancing student success, considering the student life-cycle and its benefits. This study examines current and future AI usage in education, considering technological, social, political, economic, cultural, and ethical factors. AI is being used in chat bots, paper grading, academic advising, and assessment trials (Liu et al., 2023). The study aims to develop and validate an instrument to measure undergraduate students' conceptions of AI in education. A conceptual framework was created using a literature review and expert review. The study involved 445 undergraduate participants from two public universities and one state college in the southeastern United States. The final model retained 37 items across eight factors of conceptions of AI in education. The results provide interpretations, limitations, and recommendations for future research and practice (Cheng et al., 2023).

Cost Reduction of AI-Powered Classroom Collaboration

Collaboration in the classroom is a frequently used pedagogical approach that facilitates students' cooperation and mutual learning. Given that instructors may only focus on one team at a time, AI can be used to support and guide the conversation in each group, forming a "hybrid team" based on the intended purpose and themes (intelligent triage). Artificial intelligence (AI) may facilitate effective coordination and guidance within a team. In their study, the researchers in investigated the potential of GPT-3 to serve as an innovator inside a hybrid (augmented) team throughout the process of developing new products. Integrating AI into education has the capacity to establish a more captivating, streamlined, and productive learning atmosphere that advantages both students and instructors.

Efficiency in terms of time and cost AI offers a significant benefit by automating manual processes. The integration of AI in education has brought about a significant change in the way things are done, with the potential to greatly enhance the efficiency of time and cost for both students and instructors. The use of automated tasks for instructors will result in time efficiency, enabling a heightened emphasis on individualized instruction. Artificial intelligence (AI) has the capability to optimize several educational procedures, such as producing questions based on prompts, evaluating assignments, and creating instructional material. This helps to alleviate the burden of educators, allowing them to concentrate on more advanced duties such as critical thinking and problem-solving. AI may be specifically taught to evaluate various topics and examinations, such as essays, problem-solving questions, and graphing exams. Given that grading takes up to 50% of instructors' work, the potential for time savings is substantial. Furthermore, the immediate evaluation offered on examinations guarantees that students have prompt and beneficial feedback on their performance.

Enhanced Efficiency of Lesson Planning

Let us read Asia website to teach 17 eighth-grade students at SMK Al Fattah, who struggled with reading English text due to laziness. The three-stage approach resulted in an average achievement increase of 13.24 points (Cantika et al., n.d.). AI-generated lesson plan development is an additional method for enhancing efficiency. AI may be used to generate lecture slides, tailor-made photos and videos, homework and test inquiries, and other educational materials, enabling academics to concentrate on duties that need human intervention. AI technologies offer cost-effective solutions for educational institutions, especially with limited resources. They provide scalable and accessible learning opportunities, reducing the need for extensive recruitment of teacher and staff. AI-powered educational materials, like MOOCs and digital textbooks, can be provided at lower costs, enhancing education availability, particularly in low-resource or rural areas (Bulathwela et al., 2024). The educator's role will be to supervise AI operations. Teachers must ensure quality control and optimize AI for global accessibility to high-quality education. AI-based education transcends geographical, social, and language barriers, promoting equitable knowledge dissemination (Miao et al., 2021). However, technical obstacles must be addressed to provide AI-driven education to rural areas. Future communication networks like 6G can help overcome these challenges.

Sustained Cost Reduction

Sustainability refers to the ability to maintain or support something over the long term, particularly in relation to environmental, social, and economic factors. Simply put, AI systems have the ability to expand efficiently at a reduced cost. Artificial intelligence (AI) has the capacity to equalize access to education by offering high-caliber learning materials and tailored guidance, regardless of geographical or socioeconomic constraints. Web-based AI platforms and chatbots have the potential to connect students with high-quality education, therefore mitigating disparities and fostering a more inclusive educational setting (Chen et al., 2020). Also, several participants still have significant challenges with their English presentation abilities, ChatGPT may assist in delivering a more compelling narrative when presenting their ideas to the jury, as well as in written reports (Kamalov et al., 2023). It signifies a level and fair opportunity for individuals from diverse backgrounds to compete. AI-powered adaptive learning systems may enhance students' engagement, motivation, and academic accomplishment by customizing educational material and pedagogical techniques to suit diverse cultures. This makes education more effective and accessible globally.

PERSONALISED GRADING

Personalised grading criteria represent a fundamental shift in the assessment landscape of higher education. By tailoring evaluation standards to individual students' strengths, weaknesses, and learning styles, educators can provide more targeted and constructive feedback. The significance of AI is well known, and it is important to incorporate AI into educational practices and the advancement of teaching methodologies. These efforts encompass several aspects, such as curricular development (Southworth et al., 2023) and even the utilisation of AI to facilitate examination processes (Greiner et al., 2023). Nevertheless, AI has the potential to contribute to decision-making processes and the evaluation of academic performance (Greiner et al., 2023). Guerrero Roldan et al. (2021) suggested that AI has the potential to enhance communication between teachers and students. This enables individuals to get prompt feedback on their workouts and assignments (Guerrero-Roldán et al., 2021). The advancement of AI systems has posed a significant challenge for academics in their ongoing efforts to systematically detect and address instances of academic dishonesty. Educators may have challenges in discerning between genuine effort and deceit due to the ability of students to manipulate AI-generated material to seem like their own work (Farrokhnia et al., 2023; Sullivan et al., 2023). Although AI systems empower students to take a more active role in their education. This fosters a sense of agency and motivation, leading to a more enriching and fulfilling learning experience overall. Motivationally intelligent systems have the potential to enhance students' motivation and learning abilities, so serving as a valuable addition to conventional educational objectives (Gašević et al., 2023).

AIED and Learning Analytics have developed machine learning frameworks for early warning systems, predicting students at risk based on academic achievements and graduate students' use of learning management systems. These systems, trained on factors like online study time and internet access, have achieved accuracy rates of up to 90%. The EDM and LA research streams share similar objectives but differ in methodology, ontological foundations, and study inquiries. Data usage varies, with online courses using machine learning methods and blended learning using regression, clustering, and classification approaches. Nevertheless, current methods lack the provision of feedback for both students and instructors, and often fail to consider the prediction of student academic achievement at the assignment or quiz level in present-day courses. Moreover, the majority of models used to determine student achievement or lack thereof are trained on data pertaining to past courses, which may result in unreliable forecasts (Afzaal et al., 2021).

DESIGNING PERSONALISED GRADING CRITERIA WITH AI

The incorporation of grading modifications into normal systems through which the implementation of the Personalised Grading Plan (PGP) Model has been shown to successfully provide accurate and equitable marks for students with impairments (Silva et al., 2005; Srivastava et al., 2020). Personalised grading criteria in higher education cater to individual student needs and cognitive preferences, ensuring a tailored assessment procedure that caters to their unique backgrounds, learning speeds, and abilities. AI plays a crucial role in personalising education by analyzing various aspects such as learning goals, student preferences, and performance records using advanced algorithms the academic performance of students is highly influenced by their personality characteristics and intelligence scores. Intelligence is shown to explain around 20% of the variation in total grades, while personality traits exhibit an additional 8% of validity in predicting academic achievement (Alamri et al., 2020).

The use of AI in many domains such as health, ecosystems, human-robot interaction, and natural catastrophes provides valuable perspectives on the implementation of data-driven decision-making and machine learning techniques (Ballesteros, 2019). As an instance, AI has the capability to analyse data pertaining to a student's performance across several assessment modalities, such as written assignments or practical demonstrations, in order to discern patterns and preferences. The system uses AI to analyze individual performance patterns, identifying areas for improvement . It creates customized grading rubrics, ensuring relevant and demanding assessments. Deep learning optimizes test scheduling, enhancing the effectiveness of computerized formative assessments. This strategy not only improves the educational experience for students but also provides instructors with crucial information to effectively promote personalised growth and development.

THE TRANSFORMATIVE FORCE OF AI

Artificial intelligence (AI), including machine learning (ML) and deep learning (DL), is widely recognised as a transformative force in several industries and sectors, including communications, construction, transportation, healthcare, manufacturing, advertising, and education. The role of AI in higher education will become more significant since it enables students to get a tailored approach to addressing learning challenges, taking into account their individual experiences and preferences. AI-powered digital learning systems have the ability to adjust to the specific knowledge level, learning pace, and intended objectives of each student, in order to optimise their educational experience. Artificial intelligence (AI) can enhance teaching and enable advanced digital education, including machine learning and deep learning. The COVID-19 pandemic has expedited the use of digital platforms in tertiary education, allowing institutions to focus on instruction and research. This research investigates advancements in AI use in higher education, including machine learning and deep learning, and identifies recurring motifs in literature related to AI-based algorithms in digital education.

Figure 3. The Transformative Force of AI
Source: Author Made

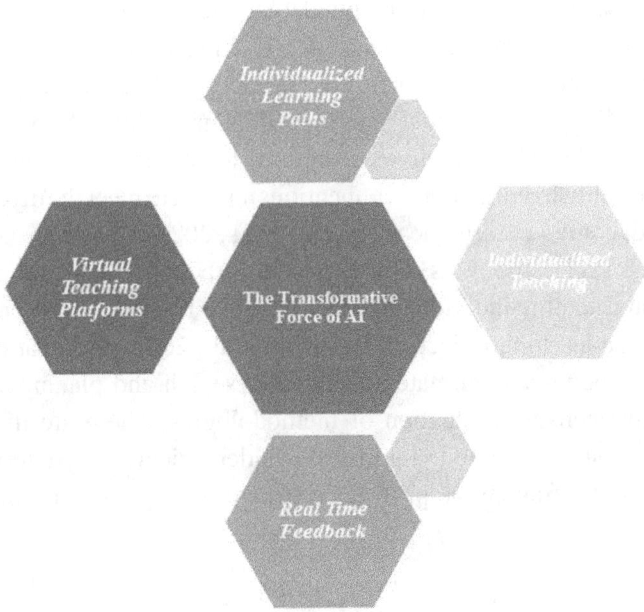

Individualised Teaching

AI-powered personalized education offers advantages of individualized teaching at a cost comparable to large university lectures. This approach is applicable to both online and classroom courses. Advances in science, technology, and healthcare have transformed professional lives, allowing for more flexible work options and longer career durations. Continuing education and lifelong learning are crucial for societal welfare. However, challenges such as insufficient data availability, time lag for feedback, and environmental fluctuations may pose challenges in providing individualized education.

Individualized Learning Paths

AI-driven systems have the capability to create personalized learning trajectories for students, taking into account their objectives, preferences, and existing knowledge. AI optimizes learning results by customizing the curriculum and speed to suit the individual requirements of each learner, providing them with suitable challenges and support (Kaswan et al., n.d.). The increasing popularity of e-learning has led to a rise in self-learning via the internet, offering advantages over traditional teacher-centered learning (Srivastava, 2020). However, the fragmented nature of learning information poses challenges to effectively acquiring knowledge across various domains. Researchers have found that the sequence of learning items significantly affects the quality of learning. To improve efficiency and enhance learners' comprehension, researchers are focusing on creating superior quality learning routes. Clustering-based approaches often gather superfluous or unrelated items, while knowledge graphs have been used to link learning items, but these methods only establish rudimentary connections and fail to meet the diverse learning requirements of contemporary e-learning (Shi et al., 2020). Personalized learning, a challenging task in classrooms, is being expanded by adaptive learning technologies, which focus on detecting individual students' unique learning needs and providing tailored real-time learning trajectories (Taylor et al., 2021). Adaptation pathways are increasingly popular in climate adaptation research and planning, but there's a lack of comprehensive evaluation of methodologies. There are three clusters: performance-threshold focused, multi-stakeholder oriented, and transformation oriented. A learning framework provides a structured approach for understanding these pathways.

Real Time Feedback

Feedback is crucial for enhancing knowledge and learning abilities, but students often express inadequacies in the quantity and quality of feedback they receive. The adoption of Intelligent Tutoring Systems (ITS) in education has led to the development of automated feedback systems that facilitate learning anytime, anywhere. Despite concerns about the effectiveness of ITS compared to human tutoring, recent research has shown that the impact of ITS is equivalent to that of human tutoring. Technology-enhanced learning has resulted in the development and implementation of numerous digital learning environments.

Automated feedback technologies in programming education offer a comprehensive global perspective, but their focus on individual subjects may overlook insights from systems created in other areas and applications, potentially duplicating existing efforts. An artificial neural network system that offers real-time feedback to students, allowing them to comprehend abstract ideas and engage in practical activities. This system, which is founded on Ohlsson's idea, enables pupils to acquire knowledge from mistakes produced by the system. Nevertheless, in online settings, the act of immediate engagement poses difficulties. Automated feedback has been facilitated by the use of sophisticated algorithms, such as educational agent-based cognitive architecture. The method also supports active training in interactive learning settings, boosting understanding diagnostics. Nevertheless, there is currently no study that has shown a correlation with educational ideas, and the majority of writers come from the field of computer science (Zhai et al., 2021).

Virtual Teaching Platforms

Virtual reality (VR) enhances human-computer interaction, fostering curiosity and creativity. It revolutionizes traditional teaching methods, improving talent development. VR has been used in fields like chemistry, medicine, and mathematics, improving students' motivation, engagement, and adaptability. Construction courses are particularly useful for enhancing practical knowledge in the building sector VR has shown significant potential in civil engineering for teaching construction personnel. Students involved in design review activities have demonstrated superior performance in VR settings. VR allows students to immerse themselves in a virtual environment that closely resembles an actual building site, enhancing their comprehension of concepts, confidence in interacting with models, and easier understanding of teacher guidance (An et al., 2023).

Immersive virtual reality (VR) techniques have been shown to positively impact students' teamwork skills, motivation, and overall quality of learning. Virtual teaching platforms, such as Problem-Based Learning (PBL) and gamification have been proven effective in enhancing engagement, retention, and motivation in various fields. Virtual labs for electrical circuits have improved retention rates and creativity. VR-based learning has shown higher retention rates in computer science. Desktop VR technologies improve learning effectiveness, while cybersecurity principles show that VR can improve memory (Halabi, 2020).

The pandemic has increased the demand for virtual learning in universities, requiring more technical infrastructure. Teachers play a crucial role in teaching students new learning environments, using virtual platforms to enhance collaborative engagement. However, the perception of virtual education remains impersonal. To improve inclusivity, comprehensiveness, student engagement, and motivation, educational institutions and governments should prioritize digital approaches and adequate pedagogical training (Chamorro-Atalaya et al., 2023). Virtual learning platforms can enhance collaboration between instructors and students, but also require careful course development and construction. A study by Phillips and O'Flaherty (2019) found that while the virtual flipped classroom approach did not significantly improve academic performance, course tutors played a significant role in the study. However, students often had negative experiences with these tutors, and they advocated for more professional development for those using virtual classrooms (Islam et al., 2023).

IMPLEMENTATION AND BEST PRACTICES FOR AI-DRIVEN ASSESSMENT

Artificial intelligence (AI) is revolutionizing education by providing teachers with insights into student engagement, enhancing business competencies, and improving school administration. AI-driven education offers customized learning experiences, adaptive assessments, predictive analytics, and chatbots, prioritizing individual learning abilities for improved results (Wang et al., 2023). The incorporation of AI-based evaluation tools into higher education settings requires careful attention to practical factors in order to ensure a successful deployment. One of the primary stages is the selection of suitable AI platforms or software (Johnson et al., 2022). The selection of AI assessment platforms depends on alignment with current educational technology, institution requirements, and platform capabilities. Educational institutions can choose from AI-based assessment platforms or integrate AI into existing systems (Haenlein & Kaplan, 2019). Educators and learners need comprehensive training in AI technologies, data interpretation, and pedagogical approaches. Integrating AI-based ideas in scientific teacher training programs fosters creative science learning, allowing instructors to adapt or disregard suggestions based on professional judgement and context (Gunawan et al., 2021). Educational institutions must have robust policies and processes to safeguard student data, ensuring compliance with privacy legislation and encryption mechanisms, and fostering trust through transparent communication channels.

Peer evaluation is a method where learners assess their peers' performance on learning tasks. This can be done online, in-person, or collaboratively (Iglesias Pérez et al., 2022). It enhances understanding, responsibility, writing proficiency, and constructive criticism. Assessors gain tailored feedback, while instructors can focus on improving education. Student engagement data can be used in learning analytics (Darvishi et al., 2022). Educational technology employs AI engineering techniques like machine learning, natural language processing, software agents, and planning to create structured information representations, intelligent tutoring, collaborative learning environments, and games (Chen et al., 2022). The role and implications of ChatGPT and AI tools in higher education, highlighting their potential to empower students and improve educational experiences. However, it also highlights the need for collaboration to address challenges in student training, curricula, assessment, technology development, and governance (Dai et al., 2023). Artificial intelligence (AI) has been utilized in various fields, including medicine, e-learning, engineering, and data management (Sapci & Sapci, 2020).

THE EVALUATION OF AI-BASED ASSESSMENTS

AI-driven evaluation methodologies undergo continuous assessment, involving preliminary research, feedback from instructors and students, and performance measures. This evaluation determines the effectiveness of these assessments in achieving desired objectives, facilitating modifications and enhancing personalized learning through AI-generated insights (Ruiz-Rojas et al., 2023). AI systems can provide educators with constructive feedback, identifying strengths and areas for improvement. This individualized approach ensures comprehensive and effective learning. AI-driven tutoring systems in higher education enhance learning outcomes by curating resources and generating exercises autonomously, allowing for continuous reassessment and personalized experiences (Schmohl et al., 2022). In order to effectively incorporate AI-based evaluation systems into higher education, it is essential to evaluate and address the practical elements involved thoroughly. AI systems can improve the Gleason score for prostate cancer patients, but may degrade in artifacts. A study suggests that the synergy between pathologist and AI enhances agreement with expert standards and pathology (Bulten et al., 2021).

AI integration in education improves learning experiences, requiring strategic selection, comprehensive training, and data protection. It offers personalized interventions and feedback mechanisms (Huang, 2022). This ensures that instructors and students are provided with the essential assistance and direction required to succeed in their respective positions. By diligently considering these elements, institutions may effectively use AI technology to enhance the learning experience for all parties involved. Institutions enhance educational experiences by fostering innovation and adapting to technological advancements, providing teachers with necessary tools for effective pedagogical approaches (García-Valcárcel et al., 2013). Modern instructional technology, professional development opportunities, and knowledge exchange platforms can enhance student-centered approaches in educational institutions. Personalized learning plans, interactive digital resources, and transparent communication can create a conducive educational environment (Dolezal et al., 2020). Institutions can use AI to improve learning experiences by providing personalized instruction, assessing performance, and offering suggestions. However, balancing AI with human interaction is crucial for boosting retention and academic achievement (Alqahtani et al., 2023).

Artificial intelligence (AI) is a computer science field that aims to improve cognitive abilities such as learning, problem-solving, and pattern recognition by creating human-like computer systems. It is developed by professionals including system designers, data scientists, and psychologists, with the goal of creating intelligent education systems for a constantly evolving world (Chen et al., 2020). AI enhances software and programs, improving mobile education and personalized experiences. It integrates virtual reality, AR, and XR technology to create a global educational environment. AI-driven algorithms analyze user data, while the Metaverse enhances higher education by creating virtual classrooms (Benavides et al., 2020).

DISCUSSION

The chapter has offered a thorough examination of the multifaceted challenges and emerging trends surrounding the integration of AI in to the assessment, grading and feedback practices within the higher education. It adeptly navigates through critical areas that has included algorithmic bias fairness, data privacy concerns, accuracy and reliability of AI systems, ethical implications, accessibility and inclusivity, teacher training and support, cost and resource allocation. Through exploring in to each area with insightful analysis, the chapter has effectively highlights the complexities inherent in deploying AI technologies in educational contexts. However, to enhance the depth chapter could benefit from more concrete examples, real-world case studies, and practical recommendations that is tailored towards educators and policymakers. The study analyzed 100 papers from 2010 to 2020 to explore AI's application in education, identifying four trends and challenges, such as inappropriate techniques, changing roles, and ethical issues (Zhai et al., 2021). A secure AIoT for implicit group recommendations, combining hardware and software security, to capture group-level preference features and ignore implicit feedback (Yu et al., 2021). AI implementation in English as a Second Language classrooms, revealing its potential to improve instruction, but also highlighting challenges and limitations, urging further research for long-term effects (Sharifuddin & Hashim, 2019-2022). ChatGPT's potential in science education, highlighting its applications in designing units, rubrics, and quizzes. However, it raises ethical concerns about environmental impact, content moderation, and copyright infringement (Cooper, 2023).

AI has significantly transformed the education through enhancing the personalised learning, efficiency, automation, scalability, enhanced learning analytics, and accessibility (Bates et al., 2020). It tailors the educational experiences towards individual student's needs, preferences and learning styles, maximizing academic success. AI automates tasks, allowing educators to focus on personalised instruction (Kaswan et al., n.d)). It also enables efficient scalability, handling large data volumes and also maintaining consistent quality. AI-driven learning analytics provide the insights into students' performance, enhancing the teaching and learning processes (Darvishi et al., 2022). AI has revolutionized education, but it also has drawbacks as this can perpetuate the biases, leading to unfair treatment for underrepresented students (Ferrara, 2023). Also, over-reliance on AI can cause depersonalization, hindering social interaction. Also, privacy and data security concerns arise from the collection of large data. AI cannot replicate human touch, potentially causing the loss of emotional support (Chan & Tsi, 2023). The high investment required for infrastructure, training and maintenance that might widen the digital divide and exacerbate the inequalities in access towards quality education. K-12 teachers prioritize capacity building, interdisciplinary learning, authentic problem-solving, creative tasks, AI principles, data literacy, ethics, and daily AI experiences, emphasizing a systematic AIED policy and flexible school systems (Kim et al., 2022). A participatory research on co-designing a learning analytics tool for science teachers, demonstrating how it can be developed through interviews and an AI algorithm, and how it was integrated into a free online learning platform (Nazaretsky, Bar, et al., 2022). Machine learning techniques for predicting student grades in first semester courses, comparing accuracy performance of six techniques and proposing a multiclass prediction model with a 99.5% f-measure for imbalanced multi-classification (Bujang et al., 2021). Learning Management Systems (LMS) to predict student grades, focusing on George Mason University networking students. The Support Vector Machine algorithm accurately predicts 70% of grades, marking the first study using online LMS data (Damuluri et al., 2020).

The chapter discusses the potential benefits of AI in education, including personalized grading, real-time feedback systems, virtual teaching platforms, and AI-based assessments. It highlights the importance of AI in enhancing learning experiences and student outcomes. However, improvements in organization, clarity, and concrete examples could enhance the chapter's accessibility and engagement. The chapter admits AI's significance in education but needs refinement for a more structured and informative approach.

CONCLUSION

Artificial Intelligence is being used to create personalised grading plans for higher education students, delivering precise and fair evaluations. This technology has enabled the development of customised learning trajectories, instantaneous feedback, virtual instructional platforms, and advanced evaluation tools like the ripple platform. It also enhances the educational experience through analysing learning objectives and providing immediate feedback. However, the effectiveness of AI-driven evaluations requires ongoing monitoring and review. As technology advances AI in education is expected to grow in providing innovative approaches to individualised learning and evaluation.

Based on the analysis of this study, we recommend the following:

- Comprehensive training programs for educators are essential to effectively integrate AI grading tools in to education. These programs should equip teachers with hands-on-skills and ongoing professional development opportunities. This will enable teachers to utilise AI tools in order to enhance the quality and efficiency of classroom assessment practices.
- User-centric design principles in AI grading platforms improve user experience, reduce learning curves, provide meaningful insights, and also enhance assessment effectiveness in educational settings.
- AI grading systems require continues evaluation and improvement, incorporating user feedback and addressing emerging challenges to ensure the effectiveness and relevance in assessment practices.
- AI grading algorithms require continuous monitoring and auditing to detect and mitigate biases, ensuring a fair assessment for all students and fostering an inclusive learning environment.
- Collaboration between educational institutions and EdTech developer is crucial for advancing AI grading algorithms. This allows for customization of educational objectives. Further, open standards promote interoperability, scalability and flexibility, enhancing the quality and efficiency of assessment practices in higher education.

REFERENCES

Afzaal, M., Nouri, J., Zia, A., Papapetrou, P., Fors, U., Wu, Y., Li, X., & Weegar, R. (2021). Explainable AI for data-driven feedback and intelligent action recommendations to support students self-regulation. *Frontiers in Artificial Intelligence*, *4*, 723447. doi:10.3389/frai.2021.723447 PMID:34870183

Ahuja, K., & Bala, I. (2021). Role of Artificial Intelligence and IoT in Next Generation Education System. *Intelligence of Things: AI-IoT Based Critical-Applications and Innovations*, 189-208.

Alamri, H., Lowell, V., Watson, W., & Watson, S. L. (2020). Using personalized learning as an instructional approach to motivate learners in online higher education: Learner self-determination and intrinsic motivation. *Journal of Research on Technology in Education*, *52*(3), 322–352.

Alias Rohini, S. G., & Mohanavel, S. (2022). Artificial Intelligence for Sustainable Pedagogical Development. In Applications of Artificial Intelligence, Big Data and Internet of Things in Sustainable Development (pp. 11-21). CRC Press.

Alordiah, C. O. (2023). Proliferation of Artificial Intelligence Tools: Adaptation Strategies in the Higher Education Sector. *Propellers Journal of Education*, *2*(1), 53–65.

Alqahtani, T., Badreldin, H. A., Alrashed, M., Alshaya, A. I., Alghamdi, S. S., bin Saleh, K., Alowais, S. A., Alshaya, O. A., Rahman, I., Al Yami, M. S., & Albekairy, A. M. (2023). The emergent role of artificial intelligence, natural learning processing, and large language models in higher education and research. *Research in Social & Administrative Pharmacy*, *19*(8), 1236–1242. doi:10.1016/j.sapharm.2023.05.016 PMID:37321925

An, D., Deng, H., Shen, C., Xu, Y., Zhong, L., & Deng, Y. (2023). Evaluation of virtual reality application in construction teaching: A comparative study of undergraduates. *Applied Sciences (Basel, Switzerland)*, *13*(10), 6170. doi:10.3390/app13106170

Ballesteros, D. M. (2019). Special Issue in Electrical and Telecommunications Engineering, and Computer Science. *Ciencia e Ingeniería Neogranadina*, *29*(2), 7–8. doi:10.18359/rcin.4162

Bates, T., Cobo, C., Mariño, O., & Wheeler, S. (2020). *Can artificial intelligence transform higher education?* (Vol. 17). Springer.

Bearman, M., Dawson, P., & Tai, J. (2020). Digitally mediated assessment in higher education: Ethical and social impacts. *Re-imagining university assessment in a digital world*, 23-36.

Benavides, L. M. C., Tamayo Arias, J. A., Arango Serna, M. D., Branch Bedoya, J. W., & Burgos, D. (2020). Digital transformation in higher education institutions: A systematic literature review. *Sensors (Basel)*, *20*(11), 3291. doi:10.3390/s20113291 PMID:32526998

Bujang, S. D. A., Selamat, A., Ibrahim, R., Krejcar, O., Herrera-Viedma, E., Fujita, H., & Ghani, N. A. M. (2021). Multiclass prediction model for student grade prediction using machine learning. *IEEE Access : Practical Innovations, Open Solutions*, *9*, 95608–95621.

Bulathwela, S., Pérez-Ortiz, M., Holloway, C., Cukurova, M., & Shawe-Taylor, J. (2024). Artificial Intelligence Alone Will Not Democratise Education: On Educational Inequality, Techno-Solutionism and Inclusive Tools. *Sustainability*, *16*(2), 781.

Bulten, W., Balkenhol, M., Belinga, J.-J. A., Brilhante, A., Çakır, A., Egevad, L., Eklund, M., Farré, X., Geronatsiou, K., & Molinié, V. (2021). Artificial intelligence assistance significantly improves Gleason grading of prostate biopsies by pathologists. *Modern Pathology*, *34*(3), 660–671.

Cantika, O., Syafrizal, S., & Evenddy, S. S. (n.d.). Enhancing Students' Reading Ability with Let's Read Asia Website at Eleventh Grade of SMK AL Fattah: A Classroom Action Research.

Chamorro-Atalaya, O., Arce-Santillan, D., Morales-Romero, G., Caycho-Salas, B., Guía-Altamirano, T., León-Velarde, C., & Rengifo-Tello, R. (2023). Evaluation of the functionality of the virtual platform in the teaching process: Analysis based on the usability factor. *Indonesian Journal of Electrical Engineering and Computer Science*, *29*(1), 583–590. doi:10.11591/ijeecs.v29.i1.pp583-590

Chan, C. K. Y., & Tsi, L. H. (2023). The AI Revolution in Education: Will AI Replace or Assist Teachers in Higher Education? *arXiv preprint arXiv:2305.01185*.

Chatterjee, S., & Bhattacharjee, K. K. (2020). Adoption of artificial intelligence in higher education: A quantitative analysis using structural equation modelling. *Education and Information Technologies*, *25*, 3443–3463.

Chen, L., Chen, P., & Lin, Z. (2020). Artificial intelligence in education: A review. *IEEE Access : Practical Innovations, Open Solutions*, *8*, 75264–75278. doi:10.1109/ACCESS.2020.2988510

Chen, X., Zou, D., Xie, H., Cheng, G., & Liu, C. (2022). Two decades of artificial intelligence in education. *Journal of Educational Technology & Society, 25*(1), 28–47.

Cheng, L., Umapathy, K., Rehman, M., Ritzhaupt, A., Antonyan, K., Shidfar, P., Nichols, J., Lee, M., & Abramowitz, B. (2023). Designing, developing, and validating a measure of undergraduate students' conceptions of artificial intelligence in education. *Journal of Interactive Learning Research, 34*(2), 275–311.

Conijn, R., Kahr, P., & Snijders, C. (2023). The effects of explanations in automated essay scoring systems on student trust and motivation. *Journal of Learning Analytics, 10*(1), 37–53.

Cooper, G. (2023). Examining science education in ChatGPT: An exploratory study of generative artificial intelligence. *Journal of Science Education and Technology, 32*(3), 444–452.

Dai, Y., Liu, A., & Lim, C. P. (2023). Reconceptualizing ChatGPT and generative AI as a student-driven innovation in higher education. *Procedia CIRP, 119*, 84–90.

Damuluri, S., Islam, K., Ahmadi, P., & Qureshi, N. S. (2020). Analyzing navigational data and predicting student grades using support vector machine. *Emerging Science Journal, 4*(4), 243–252.

Darvishi, A., Khosravi, H., Sadiq, S., & Gašević, D. (2022). Incorporating AI and learning analytics to build trustworthy peer assessment systems. *British Journal of Educational Technology, 53*(4), 844–875. doi:10.1111/bjet.13233

Dolezal, D., Roschger, C., Hahnenkamp, A., Mairinger, M., Zimmermann, D., Satek, A., Koppensteiner, G., & Motschnig, R. (2020). Educational Design Patterns for Student-Centered 21 st Century Learning in Technology-Enhanced Learning Environments. *International Conference on Interactive Collaborative Learning*

Ercikan, K., & McCaffrey, D. F. (2022). Optimizing implementation of artificial-intelligence-based automated scoring: An evidence centered design approach for designing assessments for AI-based scoring. *Journal of Educational Measurement, 59*(3), 272–287.

Farrokhnia, M., Banihashem, S. K., Noroozi, O., & Wals, A. (2023). A SWOT analysis of ChatGPT: Implications for educational practice and research. *Innovations in Education and Teaching International*, 1–15. doi:10.1080/14703297.2023.2195846

Ferrara, E. (2023). Fairness and bias in artificial intelligence: A brief survey of sources, impacts, and mitigation strategies. *Sci, 6*(1), 3.

García-Valcárcel, A., Rodríguez, A. I., & Mena Marcos, J. J. (2013). Educational innovation. *Proceedings of the First International Conference on Technological Ecosystem for Enhancing Multiculturality*

Gašević, D., Siemens, G., & Sadiq, S. (2023). *Empowering learners for the age of artificial intelligence* (Vol. 4). Elsevier.

Grassini, S. (2023). Shaping the future of education: Exploring the potential and consequences of AI and ChatGPT in educational settings. *Education Sciences, 13*(7), 692.

Greiner, CPeisl, T. CHöpfl, FBeese, O. (2023). Acceptance of AI in Semi-Structured Decision-Making Situations Applying the Four-Sides Model of Communication—An Empirical Analysis Focused on Higher Education. *Education Sciences, 13*(9), 865.

Guerrero-Roldán, A.-E., Rodríguez-González, M. E., Bañeres, D., Elasri-Ejjaberi, A., & Cortadas, P. (2021). Experiences in the use of an adaptive intelligent system to enhance online learners' performance: A case study in Economics and Business courses. *International Journal of Educational Technology in Higher Education, 18*, 1–27.

Gunawan, K., Kaniawati, I., & Setiawan, W. (2021). The responses to artificial intelligence in teacher integrated science learning training program. *Journal of Physics: Conference Series.*

Haenlein, MKaplan, A. (2019). A brief history of artificial intelligence: On the past, present, and future of artificial intelligence. *California Management Review, 61*(4), 5–14.

Halabi, O. (2020). Immersive virtual reality to enforce teaching in engineering education. *Multimedia Tools and Applications, 79*(3-4), 2987–3004. doi:10.1007/s11042-019-08214-8

Hall, E. E. (2023). *A User-Centered Design Approach to Evaluating the Usability of Automated Essay Scoring Systems.* Virginia Tech.

Huang, M. (2022). Research on C++ System Practice of Online Auxiliary Teaching Platform based on Trusted Data Analysis. *2022 International Conference on Inventive Computation Technologies (ICICT)*

Iglesias Pérez, M. C., Vidal-Puga, J., & Pino Juste, M. R. (2022). The role of self and peer assessment in Higher Education. *Studies in Higher Education, 47*(3), 683–692.

Islam, MMazlan, N. HAl Murshidi, GHoque, M. SKarthiga, SReza, M. (2023). UAE university students' experiences of virtual classroom learning during Covid 19. Smart Learning Environments, 10(1), 5.

Ivanov, S. (2023). The dark side of artificial intelligence in higher education. *Service Industries Journal*, *43*(15-16), 1055–1082.

Jayakumar, S., Sounderajah, V., Normahani, P., Harling, L., Markar, S. R., Ashrafian, H., & Darzi, A. (2022). Quality assessment standards in artificial intelligence diagnostic accuracy systematic reviews: A meta-research study. *NPJ Digital Medicine*, *5*(1), 11.

Johnson, M., Albizri, A., & Simsek, S. (2022). Artificial intelligence in healthcare operations to enhance treatment outcomes: A framework to predict lung cancer prognosis. *Annals of Operations Research*, *308*(1-2), 1–31. doi:10.1007/s10479-020-03872-6

Kamalov, F., Santandreu Calonge, D., & Gurrib, I. (2023). New era of artificial intelligence in education: Towards a sustainable multifaceted revolution. *Sustainability*, *15*(16), 12451.

Kaswan, K. S., Dhatterwal, J. S., & Ojha, R. P. (n.d.) AI in personalized learning. In *Advances in Technological Innovations in Higher Education* (pp. 103–117). CRC Press.

Khan, I., Ahmad, A. R., Jabeur, N., & Mahdi, M. N. (2021). An artificial intelligence approach to monitor student performance and devise preventive measures. *Smart Learning Environments*, *8*(1), 1–18.

Kim, J., Lee, H., & Cho, Y. H. (2022). Learning design to support student-AI collaboration: Perspectives of leading teachers for AI in education. *Education and Information Technologies*, *27*(5), 6069–6104.

Kumar, J. A., Bervell, B., & Osman, S. (2020). Google classroom: Insights from Malaysian higher education students' and instructors' experiences. *Education and Information Technologies*, *25*(5), 4175–4195.

Kumar, R. (2023). Faculty members' use of artificial intelligence to grade student papers: A case of implications. *International Journal for Educational Integrity*, *19*(1), 1–10.

Kuo, B.-C., Chang, F. T.-Y., & Lee, Y.-L. (2023). Trends and Issues of Digital Learning in Taiwan. *Trends and Issues of Promoting Digital Learning in High-Digital-Competitiveness Countries: Country Reports and International Comparison.*

Kuzminsky, J., Phillips, H., Sharif, H., Moran, C., Gleason, H. E., Topulos, S. P., Pitt, K., McNeil, L. K., McCoy, A. M., & Kesavadas, T. (2023). Reliability in performance assessment creates a potential application of artificial intelligence in veterinary education: evaluation of suturing skills at a single institution. *American journal of veterinary research, 1*(aop), 1-11.

Liu, L. T., Wang, S., Britton, T., & Abebe, R. (2023). Reimagining the machine learning life cycle to improve educational outcomes of students. *Proceedings of the National Academy of Sciences of the United States of America, 120*(9), e2204781120.

Miao, F., Holmes, W., Huang, R., & Zhang, H. (2021). *AI and education: A guidance for policymakers.* UNESCO Publishing.

Naseer, F., Khalid, M. U., Ayub, N., Rasool, A., Abbas, T., & Afzal, M. W. (2024). Automated Assessment and Feedback in Higher Education Using Generative AI. In Transforming Education With Generative AI: Prompt Engineering and Synthetic Content Creation (pp. 433-461). IGI Global.

Nazaretsky, T., Ariely, M., Cukurova, M., & Alexandron, G. (2022). Teachers' trust in AI-powered educational technology and a professional development program to improve it. *British Journal of Educational Technology, 53*(4), 914–931.

Nazaretsky, T., Bar, C., Walter, M., & Alexandron, G. (2022). Empowering teachers with AI: Co-designing a learning analytics tool for personalized instruction in the science classroom. *LAK22: 12th International Learning Analytics and Knowledge Conference*

Ng, W. C., Lim, W. Y. B., Ng, J. S., Xiong, Z., Niyato, D., & Miao, C. (2022). Unified resource allocation framework for the edge intelligence-enabled metaverse. *ICC 2022-IEEE International conference on Communications.*

Nguyen, A., Ngo, H. N., Hong, Y., Dang, B., & Nguyen, B.-P. T. (2023). Ethical principles for artificial intelligence in education. *Education and Information Technologies, 28*(4), 4221–4241.

Owan, V. J., Abang, K. B., Idika, D. O., Etta, E. O., & Bassey, B. A. (2023). Exploring the potential of artificial intelligence tools in educational measurement and assessment. *Eurasia Journal of Mathematics, Science and Technology Education, 19*(8), em2307.

Pitarch, C., Ribas, V., & Vellido, A. (2023). AI-Based Glioma Grading for a Trustworthy Diagnosis: An Analytical Pipeline for Improved Reliability. *Cancers (Basel)*, *15*(13), 3369.

Pursnani, V., Sermet, Y., Kurt, M., & Demir, I. (2023). Performance of ChatGPT on the US fundamentals of engineering exam: Comprehensive assessment of proficiency and potential implications for professional environmental engineering practice. *Computers and Education: Artificial Intelligence*, *5*, 100183.

Rawat, A. (n.d). Ethical Considerations in AI for Education: Addressing Privacy and Bias Concerns. *Education Unleashed: The AI Era*, 173.

Regan, P. M., & Jesse, J. (2019). Ethical challenges of edtech, big data and personalized learning: Twenty-first century student sorting and tracking. *Ethics and Information Technology*, *21*, 167–179.

Reidenberg, J. R., & Schaub, F. (2018). Achieving big data privacy in education. *Theory and Research in Education*, *16*(3), 263–279.

Remian, D. (2019). Augmenting education: ethical considerations for incorporating artificial intelligence in education.

Ruiz-Rojas, L. I., Acosta-Vargas, P., De-Moreta-Llovet, J., & Gonzalez-Rodriguez, M. (2023). Empowering education with generative artificial intelligence tools: Approach with an instructional design matrix. *Sustainability*, *15*(15), 11524.

Sapci, A. H., & Sapci, H. A. (2020). Artificial intelligence education and tools for medical and health informatics students: Systematic review. *JMIR Medical Education*, *6*(1), e19285.

Schmohl, T., Schelling, K., Go, S., Thaler, K. J., & Watanabe, A. (2022). Development, Implementation and Acceptance of an AI-based Tutoring System: A Research-Led Methodology. CSEDU (2).

Sharifuddin, N. S., & Hashim, H. (2019-2022). Benefits and Challenges in Implementing Artificial Intelligence in Education (AIED) in ESL Classroom. *Systematic Reviews*.

Shi, D., Wang, T., Xing, H., & Xu, H. (2020). A learning path recommendation model based on a multidimensional knowledge graph framework for e-learning. *Knowledge-Based Systems*, *195*, 105618.

Silva, M., Munk, D. D., & Bursuck, W. D. (2005). Grading adaptations for students with disabilities. *Intervention in School and Clinic*, *41*(2), 87–98. doi:10.1177/10534512050410020901

Slimi, Z., & Carballido, B. V. (2023). Navigating the Ethical Challenges of Artificial Intelligence in Higher Education: An Analysis of Seven Global AI Ethics Policies. *TEM Journal, 12*(2).

Southworth, J., Migliaccio, K., Glover, J., Reed, D., McCarty, C., Brendemuhl, J., & Thomas, A. (2023). Developing a model for AI Across the curriculum: Transforming the higher education landscape via innovation in AI literacy. *Computers and Education: Artificial Intelligence*, *4*, 100127. doi:10.1016/j.caeai.2023.100127

Srivastava, B., Rossi, F., Usmani, S., & Bernagozzi, M. (2020). Personalized chatbot trustworthiness ratings. *IEEE Transactions on Technology and Society*, *1*(4), 184–192.

Srivastava, R. (2020). Unlocking technology for language learning: A viability at the time of transition from traditional to online teaching and learning. Arab World English Journal (AWEJ) Proceedings of 2nd MEC TESOL Conference

Sullivan, M., Kelly, A., & McLaughlan, P. (2023). ChatGPT in higher education: Considerations for academic integrity and student learning.

Taylor, D. L., Yeung, M., & Bashet, A. (2021). Personalized and adaptive learning. *Innovative learning environments in STEM higher education: Opportunities, Challenges, and Looking Forward*, 17-34.

Timmons, A. C., Duong, J. B., Simo Fiallo, N., Lee, T., Vo, H. P. Q., Ahle, M. W., Comer, J. S., Brewer, L. C., Frazier, S. L., & Chaspari, T. (2023). A call to action on assessing and mitigating bias in artificial intelligence applications for mental health. *Perspectives on Psychological Science*, *18*(5), 1062–1096.

Vashishth, T. K., Sharma, V., Sharma, K. K., Kumar, B., Panwar, R., & Chaudhary, S. (2024). AI-Driven Learning Analytics for Personalized Feedback and Assessment in Higher Education. In *Using Traditional Design Methods to Enhance AI-Driven Decision Making* (pp. 206–230). IGI Global.

Wang, T., Lund, B. D., Marengo, A., Pagano, A., Mannuru, N. R., Teel, Z. A., & Pange, J. (2023). Exploring the Potential Impact of Artificial Intelligence (AI) on International Students in Higher Education: Generative AI, Chatbots, Analytics, and International Student Success. *Applied Sciences (Basel, Switzerland)*, *13*(11), 6716. doi:10.3390/app13116716

Williamson, B., Bayne, S., & Shay, S. (2020). *The datafication of teaching in Higher Education: critical issues and perspectives* (Vol. 25). Taylor & Francis.

Winstone, N. E., & Boud, D. (2022). The need to disentangle assessment and feedback in higher education. *Studies in Higher Education*, *47*(3), 656–667.

Yu, K., Guo, Z., Shen, Y., Wang, W., Lin, J. C.-W., & Sato, T. (2021). Secure artificial intelligence of things for implicit group recommendations. *IEEE Internet of Things Journal*, *9*(4), 2698–2707.

Zhai, X., Chu, X., Chai, C. S., Jong, M. S. Y., Istenic, A., Spector, M., Liu, J.-B., Yuan, J., & Li, Y. (2021). A Review of Artificial Intelligence (AI) in Education from 2010 to 2020. *Complexity*, *2021*, 1–18. doi:10.1155/2021/8812542

Chapter 5
Future Horizons:
Exploring Artificial Intelligence's Role in Shaping Research Landscapes

Nasser Al Harrasi
https://orcid.org/0000-0003-4456-0926
University of Technology and Applied Science, Muscat, Oman

Mohamed Salah El Din
https://orcid.org/0000-0002-9360-8589
Majan University College, Oman

ABSTRACT

This chapter explores the transformative impact of artificial intelligence (AI) on various research domains. The chapter highlights the leading role of AI research platforms in the development of AI in research practices. In addition, the chapter describes the fundamental concepts of AI powered tools such as generative artificial intelligence and large language models. The narrative extends to AI integration in modern research practices, spotlighting its use in hypothesis formulation, generation of research questions, and data analysis. AI's contributions to data analysis in many fields are explored, particularly in automating processes and generating insights. The discussion further explores several AI applications in various research domains such as RPA, Semantic Scholar, and DeepChem. However, potential bias and transparency are main challenges of AI-powered applications. Therefore, it is imperative to champion explainable AI and human-in-the-loop approaches to improve confidence. The chapter recommends further interdisciplinary collaboration between researchers and AI developers.

DOI: 10.4018/979-8-3693-2145-4.ch005

INTRODUCTION AND BACKGROUND

Artificial Intelligence (AI) is a transformative technology in various domains such as education, healthcare, and society. There is a significant progress has been noticed in development of AI in relation to its methods and AI powered tools (Nalepa & Stefanowski, 2020). Recently, AI research trend increased and provided insights into the impact of AI on various domains including economy and society from different perspectives which generated a solution for many challenges faced by governmental organizations, and companies (Han et al., 2020).

AI Applications are dominant in a multitude of fields, changing and revolutionizing the way we do things (Wirtz et al., 2018). In the medical field, AI is being leveraged for applications such as diagnosis, surgery, and combating diseases like COVID-19 (Shahnaz & Mukesh, 2022). AI competitions and platforms like Kaggle and Grand Challenge are driving AI-based research in medical imaging, highlighting its competitive and collaborative nature (Luitse et al., 2023). In addition, AI plays a significant role in supply chain management, social computing, and cloud computing, indicating its pervasive impact among diverse areas (Žigienė et al., 2020; Wang, 2021; Zheng & Wen, 2021). Furthermore, the deployment of AI is becoming crucial in finance and retail sector, which dominated by its broad spectrum of functionality (Wirtz et al., 2018; Rana et al., 2021), mainly with its ability to improve the Human-Computer Interaction (HCI) and user experience (Yang et al., 2020).

AI plays a prominent role in transforming teaching and learning by personalized and adaptive learning. Moreover, AI tools pioneering in its ability to structure the scientific literature review as well as an emerging technology for creating an adaptive computational system (Hinojo-Lucena et al., 2019). Machine learning algorithms which is part of AI have been identified as powerful tools for developing battery research cycle (Wu et al., 2023).

However, several challenges raised up while Implementing AI in research practices which need to be addressed for successful integration. These challenges highlighted and reported by several authors such as Wirtz et al., 2018; Gama et al., 2022; Lamberti et al., 2019; Petersson et al., 2022; Zhou et al., 2020; Borkowski, 2022; Bérubé et al., 2021; Nilsen et al., 2022; Ji et al., 2020; Huang, 2019. AI safety, system/data quality and integration, financial feasibility, specialization and expertise, staff skills, data structure, budgets, patient-centeredness, usability, ethical principles, material descriptors, data-related challenges, data quality, data sharing mechanisms, integrated AI systems, and patient acceptance are challenges identified recently which indicating the necessity of considering it while moving forward to AI Integration in research practices. Additionally, issues such as uncertainty and data dependency in AI are considered one of the unique challenges in AI implementation (Weber et al., 2022).

This chapter aim to provide a comprehensive discussion in AI deployment in research. Starting with understating the AI's system and its fundamental concepts. Then, moves into understanding AI in modern research practices, and delve into some AI's applications in various research areas. Then, the chapter address the challenges associated with applying AI in research, as well as highlighting the ethical consideration in using AI powered tool in research. Finally, the chapter concluded by anticipating the future trend of AI in research. Collectively, the chapter provides a comprehensive and updated impact of AI utilization in various fields of scientific research.

UNDERSTANDING AI'S SYSTEM

AI concepts include various aspect that are significant to develop and understand AI system. many authors emphasized and highlighted crucial concepts, such as assumptions underpinning dominant AI approaches (David & Alan, 2010), Evaluation of AI algorithms' performance (Kim et al., 2019), explainable (XAI) and role of AI implementation (Arrieta et al., 2020), and AI ethics guidelines in global landscape (Kazim & Koshiyama, 2021; Jobin & Ienca, 2019). Assumptions underpinning dominant AI approaches refers to the rules and criteria that construct the application of AI's system. Also, evaluating AI algorithms' performance is essential for examining the reliability and effectiveness of it in various area. Many research have focused on evaluating AI algorithms' performance of various AI's applications which provides valuable insights into the criteria and ways involved in the evaluation process (Qin et al. (2021); Römmele et al. (2022); Choi & Byeon (2021). Explainable (XAI) and role of AI implementation is a field of AI research as well as an important component of making AI decision-making process transparent and trustable across various areas (Tiwari, 2023). Additionally, the principles of using AI applications such as the General Data Protection Regulation's (GDPR) which is a legislation framework to address the collection, processing, and protection of personal information. GDPR introduced by the European Union (EU) which aim to support and emphasize the understanding of legal and ethics aspects of using personal information's in various sectors including AI applications (Becker et al., 2019; Mekovec & Peras, 2020; Artzt & Dung, 2022; Diamantopoulou et al., 2021).

Notably AI's concepts, generative artificial intelligence (GenAI) and large language models (LLMs) emerge as pivotal tools for liberating knowledge workers from difficult tasks, including ideas writing and literature review. GenAI includes a variety of machine learning methodologies like generative adversarial networks (GANs) and variational autoencoders (VAEs). It has the ability to generate new content depend on learned structure and patterns from provided data (Oermann

& Kondziolka, 2023). LLMs is a part of GenAI which demonstrate capabilities in tasks like text generation, contextual understanding, and language translation. These models focuses on natural language processing and generation such as OpenAI's GPT-3 (Oermann & Kondziolka, 2023; Hwang et al., 2021).

Nevertheless, Vertex AI's evaluating Text-to-Image Matching using Binary Image Selection (BISON) underscores its applicability in the analysis of scientific content. BISON refers to the process of evaluating text to image matching by using binary image selection (Hu et al., 2019) Moreover, the deployment of AI is discerned in the realm of academic article writing, where models such as ChatGPT-3 exhibit utility as auxiliary tools. The discernment of advantages and limitations in utilizing ChatGPT-3 for academic research paper composition forms a critical aspect of this narrative. The augmentation of research efficiency is a recurring theme, as AI, forced by natural language processing (NLP) models, facilitates rapid, error-free results in translation, digital assistance, sentiment analysis, and academic writing.

Furthermore, another main concept in the development and governance of AI is human centricity. Human centricity is an approach that consider human values, needs, and perspectives at the priority AI's system design, implementation, and governance. This approach is aiming to ensure that AI systems are aligned with human well-being (Sigfrids et al., 2023). Buabbas et al., (2022) and Bisdas et al., (2021) suggested that considering AI principles and terminology by students are crucial in shaping the future of AI in education as well as the technical concepts of AI such as classification, dimensions, categorization, machine/deep learning, and types of intelligence (Kear & Folkes, 2020).

Thus, Understanding AI fundamental concepts are crucial for development and implementation of AI in various fields including technical and ethical aspects. AI integration into various field such as research, education, medicine, art etc. are essential on determining outcomes quality of AI approaches as well as achieve responsible development, implementation, and governance of AI systems.

ROLE OF AI IN MODERN RESEARCH PRACTICES

Modern practices of research are changing rapidly, driven by the capabilities of AI powered tools. AI powered tools supports all stages of research process, from problem definition and hypothesis construction to data collection, analysis, interpretation, and publication. Ideally, AI reconstruct the process of knowledge production.

In the context of hypothesis formulation and research problem definition, Verma et al., (2021) argued that AI powered tools able to generate hypothesis and raise many research questions through the analysis of literature review, systematic reviews, conceptualization, thematic analysis, and content analysis. Furthermore, AI powered tools having the ability to identify the data patterns as well as suggest experimental parameters to enhance the research results accuracy and efficiency. There are many applications in academic article writing, with a focus on ChatGPT as supportive tool. This encourages to discover and open up many areas where it missed through traditional approaches. In addition, Natural language processing algorithms which is part of AI, empowered researcher for more scientific collaboration and communication. It supported researchers to have more access into scientific publication, identify the relevant research articles and researchers, extract and summarize the knowledge contributions from each publication (Clark et al., 2020; (Calderwood et al., 2023; Roozbahani et al., 2021; Pessoa et al., 2022). This emphasizes more international and global collaborations across various research fields and minimize communication and collaboration barriers.

In data analysis, AI powered tools can manage and analyze huge amount of data, exceeding human capabilities and digital technology as well as leading to significant development in many research fields such as medicine, public health, and precision medicine (Gao et al., 2020; Rivera et al., 2020; Lau & Staccini, 2019; Guo et al., 2021; Alrefaei et al., 2022; Oka et al., 2021; Van Belkon, 2020). For instance, research fields like social science, astronomy and genomics where depends on large and complex dataset. Zhao et al., (2020) emphasized the capabilities of AI algorithms in defining the hidden patterns, relationship, Predication, and variances by using machine learning and deep learning. These mechanisms led to discover many significant results such as Diez et al., (2020) uncovering dark matter distribution in the universe and Jumper et al., (2021) predicted protein folding in medicine. According to Jungwirth & Haluza, (2023), One of the most significant functions of AI in modern research practice is automate data analysis and generate new insights. Several researchers like Loh, (2018); Thomas et al., (2023). Li et al., (2020) argued that AI can revolutionize the role of doctors, change the academic publishing landscape, and even improve medical services though the ability of AI in automating the data analysis.

The use of AI in data analysis is not limited to healthcare only, research fields like supply chain risk management, social computing, and cloud computing are also influenced (Žigienė et al., 2020; Wang, 2021; Zheng & Wen, 2021). Also, academic libraries have been explored to reduce errors, emphasize smooth workforce and maximize resources output, especially in Caribbean academic libraries (Duncan, 2022). Human and AI collaboration in scientific discovery has been raised for designing effective system which combine both intelligence of Human and AI (Adesso, 2023). Moreover, Bogoviz et al., (2019) investigated the role of AI training in business production process in the context of Industry 4.0, which indicated the significant of diversifying the educational services.

In relation to interpretation of data analysis, AI-powered tools have automated and improved the process of interpreting research results from large and complex datasets (Roccapriore et al., 2022; Waldenmaier, 2023; Bak et al., 2021). Several studies examined the AI powered tools in interpreting the results, for example examining the automation of early disease diagnosis and management by Dumitrascu et al. (2022), Vall and Araya Bonmatí et al. (2022) emphasized the creation of a pan-European repository of health imaging data for the purpose of health imaging information interpretation, AI powered tool for complex geomatics data interpretations by Pierdicca & Paolanti (2022)

Generally, AI has interfered in all stages of Research process. AI ability is not limited to handle and analyze large data only, but also able to draft full research article starting from generating hypothesis and research question into provide insights and report the findings. The capability associated with AI powered tools force and direct researchers to gain the essential skills of adopting AI research tools in their research practices to cop up with vast changes in the world.

APPLICATIONS OF AI IN VARIOUS RESEARCH FIELDS

AI applications involved almost in everyday of our life, it is revolutionizing how researchers functioning research across various fields. It's capability in analyzing previous literature and large dataset, make predictions, identifying patterns encouraging to delve more to understand it and optimize its efficiency and accuracy. Table 1 summarize the applications of AI in various research fields.

There are many AI applications which are utilized in research process and having potential for growth and further innovation. Repetitive and time-consuming tasks in research process can be simplified and automated with the help of AI applications. Many tasks like data entry, data processing and cleaning, data analysis, result interpretation reports can be functioned by Robotic process automation (RPA) and this automation provides human resources for more strategic activities (Gartner, 2023). For example, Applications such as Semantic Scholar, Scite, Trinka and Grant Proposal Assistant are very effective for research planning and design. These applications aim to search and identify related literature review and analyze the research gap and key findings (Patra et al., 2020; Hannousse (2021); Sateli et al. (2017). In addition, AI-powered text analytics tools can analyze large volumes of scientific published researcher articles and books, define the research problem, identify research gaps, and generate new research question and hypotheses (Akter et al., 2016). Interestingly, create virtual environments by AI applications to simulate problem scenario with several solutions and findings (Obeid & Demirkan, 2020; Guegan et al., 2021).

Table 1. Summary of AI applications in various research fields

Research Field	AI Applications
Research Planning & Design	Semantic Scholar, Scite, Trinka, and Grant Proposal Assistant
Data Collection & Management	LabPlot, SciServer, Biomarker Discovery Platforms, and Environmental Sensor Networks
Data Analysis & Interpretation	DeepChem, AlphaFold, Rasa, and Tableau.
Management Decision-making	Machine Learning & Predictive Analytics, Natural Language Processing, and Sentiment Analysis.
Medical Research	Deep Learning Algorithms, and AI-driven Drug Development.
Astronomy	Telescope Data Analysis
Materials Science	Materials Discovery
Linguistics & History	Text Corpus Analysis

Source: Author made

Furthermore, applications like LabPlot, SciServer, Biomarker Discovery Platforms and Environmental Sensor Networks are supporting the process of data Collection and Management. These applications store, automate the data acquisition and analysis as well as sharing it for further collaborations Kwok and Wong (2015); Glatard et al. (2015); Zitnik et al. (2012); Akyildiz et al. (2015). For the Data Analysis and Interpretation, there are several applications such as DeepChem, AlphaFold, Rasa and Tableau which analyzed data for providing insightful interpretation and prediction Jumper et al. (2021); Rasa Technologies. (2023); Tableau Software. (2023)

Decision making in traditional management was rely on knowledge, skills, and experience of the decision maker. However, AI applications fostered with high-speed decision making and understanding customer needs and preferences by using tools such as machine learning, deep learning, natural language processing, sentiment analysis and predictive analytics to come up with an evidence-based decision (Chen et al., 2021). Akter et al., (2016) argued that AI applications can provide insights and recommendations for better utilization of resources, strategic planning, and management of risks. Furthermore, Bharadwaj et al., (2019) suggested that insights raised from AI applications can be used to develop targeted products, personalize marketing campaigns, and enhance customer satisfaction. For instance, several applications are available nowadays to predict consumer behavior and demand where retailers can optimize the inventory levels as well as banks can detect frauds and minimize financial losses with the help of AI applications (Cui et al., 2022).

In the field of medical research, AI is playing an important role in operating tasks for discovering diseases. This application relies on deep learning algorithms where it learned from large dataset of patient history and medical images (Liu et al., 2019). Furthermore, some AI models are participating in developing new drugs by analyzing biological data and simulating molecular interactions (Stokes et al., 2020). In astronomy also, researchers are adopting AI applications to analyze dataset from telescopes, discover hidden celestial objects and understanding galaxies (Groot et al., 2018). Ramprasad et al., 2016 reported in the field of materials science, that AI applications direct researchers toward creation of novel materials such as development of batteries and solar cells. Additionally, AI applications are involved in the fields like linguistics and history, where vast corpora of text are being analyzed and find out the hidden patterns in language use on historical events (Liu et al., 2017).

However, deployment of AI into research has numerous concerns. One of the main concerns is the potential for bias in AI applications, which can lead to inaccurate or discriminatory results (O'Neil, 2017). Additionally, Doshi-Velez & Kim, (2017) argued that AI applications may provide results without clear justifications which led to lack of transparency. Despite these concerns, AI applications has great potential in developing research applications. The next section discuss the challenges in implanting AI in research.

CHALLENGES IN IMPLEMENTING AI IN RESEARCH

AI has changed the research practices, which moved toward new era of producing knowledge. However, Integrating AI in research practices is faced with significant obstacles. Figure 1 shows the challenges in implementing AI in research.

One of the main challenges is the data training algorithms, where research data is often unstructured, messy and may led to unreliable results (Hutson, 2018). Gebru et al., (2019) suggested that adopting cleaning protocol of the data and conscious efforts are required to avoid perpetuating societal biases in research findings. Additionally, UNESCO, (2012) encouraged for more initiatives for open data and share standardized data practices to ensure quality and accessibility for the data across various disciplines. Moreover, data collection and privacy are pressing concerns where AI algorithms need data and research are reach with sensitive personal data. Researchers should ensure a balance between individual privacy and comprehensive datasets as well as data governance frameworks, informed consent processes and Robust anonymization techniques to ensure the ethical consideration in data collection and use (Mittelstadt, 2019).

Furthermore, Lack of transparency has been noticed in various AI models where many results dismantled without proper justifications. Gunning, (2017) argued that this challenge can increase the concerns associated with accountability, trust of research findings and explainability. To overcome this challange, Lipton, (2016) emphasized that researchers may incorporate Techniques such as explainable AI (XAI) and human-in-the-loop approaches to ensure the transparent of developed AI models. explainable AI (XAI) and human-in-the-loop approaches are supportive in bridge the gap between human understanding and output of the AI models as well as enhance the trust among researchers and AI.

Figure 1. Challenges in implementing AI in research
(Author)

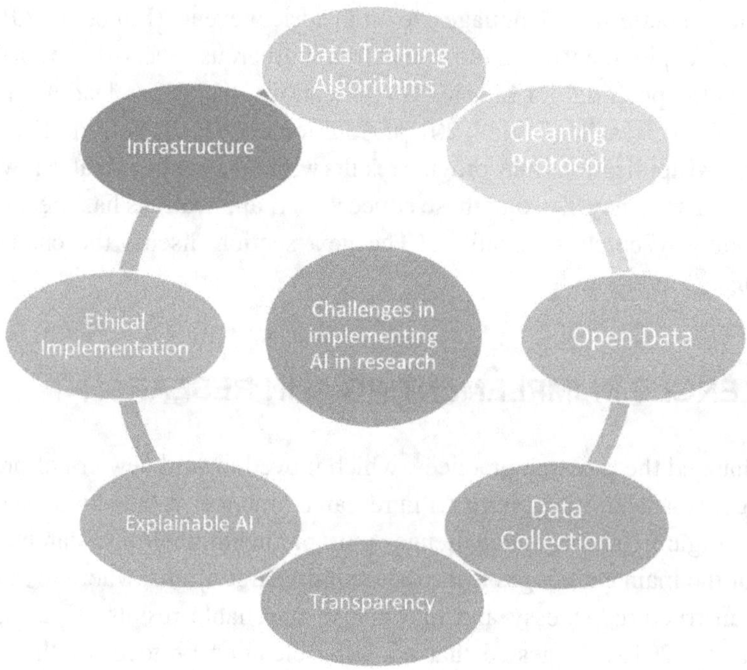

In additions, Ethical and responsible AI implementation are concerned challenges also where bias in training data may led to discrimination and inequalities in research outcomes (Eubanks, 2018). Also, the growth in process automation increased the chance of job displacement. Jobin et al., (2019) discussed the necessity of adopting ethical framework for the deployment of AI in all stages of research process. The ethical framework should promote transparency, fairness and accountability. Also, Misconduct is explored within the scientific fields with a focus on AI-generated knowledge. Fabrication of non-existent results and falsification of data are highlighted as key concerns, raising questions about the standards and expectations of authors and journal editors.

Finally, implementation of AI in research requires huge investment on infrastructure and accessibility. OECD, (2019) reported that AI application needs High-performance computing equipment and software and challenge researchers to have it. Currently, many researchers are accessing AI powered tools though Open-source software options and cloud-based computing platforms. Also, forming and developing interdisciplinary collaboration between AI application developers and researchers is crucial to find context-specific solutions for AI challenges in research.

Challenges always incurred in any changes and transformation. However, AI in research has potential for advancing scientific discovery. By considering model interpretability, data quality, ethical considerations and accessibility issues, researchers can develop and foster the quality of research output with AI integrations.

FUTURE PERSPECTIVES OF AI IN RESEARCH

AI has increasingly integrated into all stages of research landscape, offering transformative capabilities that promise breakthroughs across diverse fields. An attractive prospect of AI in research stands on in AI capability to revolutionize data analysis. AI powered tools provide its ability to handle large datasets with the power of identifying hidden patterns and connections unrecognized by human. This data-driven approach promises to push vast knowledge production across all research disciplines.

Furthermore, automation and optimization of research workflows has a potential in the future where the robots will carry out all research stages and experiments. This will allowing researchers to have more time for further innovations in research ideas and hypotheses formulating. Additionally, the ability of AI's applications in handling and managing deeper conceptual exploration and creative problem-solving. This will lead to Cutting-edge Insights. However, considering this future trend required an effort to overcome the inherent challenges such as data quality and accessibility as AI algorithms rely on input datasets. To overcome this challenges, Robust data governance frameworks, accessible data repositories, and efforts to avoid data bias are crucial for ensuring integrity and inclusivity of AI-powered research (Hutson, 2018).

The explainability of AI models pose another challenge. Operating as black boxes, these models often lack transparency, potentially eroding trust in research findings. Techniques like explainable AI (XAI) and human-in-the-loop approaches offer solutions, facilitating understanding and building trust in AI-driven research. Ethical implications also demand careful consideration. Job displacement due to AI automation necessitates reskilling programs for a smooth transition towards an AI-powered research ecosystem (Jobin et al., 2019). Societal impacts, such as biases in algorithms perpetuating inequalities, require proactive measures through public engagement, stakeholder consultations, and robust oversight mechanisms (Eubanks, 2018).

Investigating and addressing AI's challenges required a collaborative works and effort from researcher and AI's algorithms developers. Interdisciplinary discussions between AI experts, researchers, ethicists, and policymakers are required for the purpose of developing robust ethical frameworks and best practices in carrying out scientific research. Also, accelerate responsible AI development emphasize the necessity of having Open-source initiatives, knowledge-sharing platforms, and international collaboration to ensure the ethical considerations in scientific research process.

CONCLUSION

In conclusion, this chapter provides insights and exploration of Artificial Intelligence (AI) role in transforming the research practices. The transformative influence of AI is evident among different research area, including but not limited in healthcare, education, finance, and supply chain management.

Fundamental concepts of AI, such as assumptions in AI approaches, algorithm performance evaluation, and emerging tools like Generative Artificial Intelligence (GenAI) and Large Language Models (LLMs), are discussed in this chapter. Particularly LLMs like GPT-3, are discussed due to their ability to reduce the workload of researchers from complex tasks. The integration of AI into modern research practices discussed with an emphasize into its role in hypothesis and research question formulation and analyze the data. There is a potential of an advancement collaboration as AI fostering the global scientific communication.

The applications of AI in various research fields such as Robotic Process Automation (RPA) and Semantic Scholar and DeepChem, indicates the potential for AI growth in all research stages like planning, data collection, and data analysis. While acknowledging the concerns of bias and transparency challenges, the chapter emphasize the uses of Explainable AI (XAI) and human-in-the-loop approaches to improve the trust and accuracy of AI-generated results. Nevertheless, AI implementation challenges has been identified which includes data quality, ethical and privacy concerns. Also, there is a need for interdisciplinary collaboration including researchers and AI developers to overcome addressed challenges. The chapter encourage the need of developing ethical frameworks, open-source initiatives, and international collaboration to investigate the integration of AI in research responsibly.

The chapter highlighted the future of AI where the potencial of growing usage of AI application in all research stages. This including the focus on data-driven exploration, creative problem-solving, and responsible AI development. Furthermore, there is a potential that AI's applications can automate and optimize research lifecycle. This is allowing researchers to focus on innovation and hypothesis formulation. In essence, the chapter identified the need for a balanced approach by considering both challenges and potential growth of AI in research practice. The integration of AI can enhance the scientific discovery through ethical considerations, transparent practices, and collaborative efforts.

REFERENCES

AdessoG. (2023). Towards the ultimate brain: exploring scientific discovery with chatbot ai. https://doi.org/ doi:10.1002/aaai.12113

Akter, S., Uysal, M. O., & Mukhopadhyay, S. (2016). Big data in healthcare: Management challenges, opportunities, and future directions. *Business Horizons*, *59*(4), 365–374.

Akyildiz, I. F., Su, W., Sankarasubramaniam, Y., & Cayirci, E. (2015). Wireless sensor networks: A survey. *Computer Networks*, *54*(15), 2282–3034.

Alrefaei, A. F., Hawsawi, Y. M., Almaleki, D., Alafif, T., Alzahrani, F., & Bakhrebah, M. A. (2022). Genetic data sharing and artificial intelligence in the era of personalised medicine based on a cross-sectional analysis of the Saudi human genome program. *Scientific Reports*, *12*(1), 1405. Advance online publication. doi:10.1038/s41598-022-05296-7 PMID:35082362

Arrieta, A., Díaz-Rodríguez, N., Ser, J., Bennetot, A., Tabik, S., Barbado, A., ... Herrera, F. (2020). Explainable artificial intelligence (xai): Concepts, taxonomies, opportunities and challenges toward responsible AI. *Information Fusion*, *58*, 82–115. doi:10.1016/j.inffus.2019.12.012

Artzt, M., & Dung, T. V. (2022). Artificial intelligence and data protection: How to reconcile both areas from the European law perspective. *Vietnamese Journal of Legal Sciences*, *7*(2), 39–58. doi:10.2478/vjls-2022-0007

Bak, M. Y. S., Plavnick, J. B., Dueñas, A. D., Brodhead, M. T., Avendano, S. M., Wawrzonek, A. J., Weber, E., Dodson, S. N., & Oteto, N. (2021). The use of automated data collection in applied behaviour analytic research: A systematic review. *Behavior Analysis (Washington, D.C.)*, *21*(4), 376–405. doi:10.1037/bar0000228

Becker, R., Alper, P., Grouès, V., Munoz, S., Jarosz, Y., Lebioda, J., Rege, K., Trefois, C., Satagopam, V., & Schneider, R. (2019). Daisy: A data information system for accountability under the general data protection regulation. *GigaScience*, *8*(12), giz140. Advance online publication. doi:10.1093/gigascience/giz140 PMID:31800037

Bérubé, M., Giannelia, T., & Vial, G. (2021). Barriers to the implementation of AI in organisations: findings from a Delphi study.. doi:10.24251/HICSS.2021.805

Bharadwaj, A., Elangovan, A., & Balakrishnan, A. (2019). Artificial intelligence in marketing: The new frontier for creating value. *Journal of Service Management*, *30*(3), 455–472.

Bisdas, S., Topriceanu, C., Zakrzewska, Z., Irimia, A., Shakallis, L., Subhash, J., Casapu, M.-M., Leon-Rojas, J., Pinto dos Santos, D., Andrews, D. M., Zeicu, C., Bouhuwaish, A. M., Lestari, A. N., Abu-Ismail, L., Sadiq, A. S., Khamees, A., Mohammed, K. M. G., Williams, E., Omran, A. I., ... Ebrahim, E. (2021). Artificial intelligence in medicine: A multinational multi-centre survey on the medical and dental students' perception. *Frontiers in Public Health*, *9*, 795284. Advance online publication. doi:10.3389/fpubh.2021.795284 PMID:35004598

Bogoviz, A., Lobova, S., Karp, M., Vologdin, E., & Alekseev, A. (2019). Diversification of educational services in the conditions of Industry 4.0 based on training. On the Horizon the International Journal of Learning Futures, 27(3/4), 206-212. https://doi.org/ doi:10.1108/OTH-06-2019-0031

Borkowski, A. (2022). Establishing a hospital artificial intelligence committee to improve patient care. (39 (8)). https://doi.org/ doi:10.12788/fp.0299

BuabbasA.MiskinB.AyedA.AlnaqiA.ShehabA.SafarM. (2022). Investigating students' perceptions towards artificial intelligence in medical education. https://doi.org/ doi:10.21203/rs.3.rs-1805527/v1

Calderwood, J., Pedreschi, D., Craig, M. Ó., & Reid, D. G. (2023). *Reflecting on the importance of open communication and social capital for co-creating knowledge in Irish fisheries*. Frontiers in Marine Science., doi:10.3389/fmars.2022.1081616

Chen, H., Chiang, R. H., & Storey, V. C. (2021). Artificial intelligence and data analytics in marketing: Trends and prospects. *International Journal of Research in Marketing*, *38*(5), 659–679.

Choi, J., & Byeon, J. (2021). Key principles of clinical validation, device approval, and insurance coverage decisions of artificial intelligence. *Korean Journal of Radiology*, *22*(3), 442. doi:10.3348/kjr.2021.0048 PMID:33629545

Clark, K., Jha, M., & Murray, S. (2020). A survey of automatic summarisation for scientific literature. *ACM Transactions on Speech and Language Processing, 28*(4), 1–45.

Cooper, L., Holderness, D. K. Jr, Sorensen, T., & Wood, D. A. (2019). Robotic process automation in public accounting. *Accounting Horizons, 33*(4), 15–35. doi:10.2308/acch-52466

Costa, D. M. S., Mamede, H. S., & Silva, M. M. (2022). Robotic process automation (RPA) adoption: A systematic literature review. *Engineering Management in Production and Services, 14*(2), 1–12. doi:10.2478/emj-2022-0012

Cui, X., Xu, B., & Razzaq, S. A. (2022). *Artificial intelligence and its application in business management.* Management Science Letters.

David, L. and Alan, K. (2010). Artificial intelligence: foundations of computational agents. Choice Reviews Online, 48(04), 48-2130-48-2130. https://doi.org/doi:10.5860/CHOICE.48-2130

Diamantopoulou, V., Lambrinoudakis, C., King, J. R., & Gritzalis, S. (2021). Eu gdpr: toward a regulatory initiative for deploying a private digital era. Modern Socio-Technical Perspectives on Privacy, 427-448. https://doi.org/ doi:10.1007/978-3-030-82786-1_18

Diez, J., & .... (2020). Cosmological constraints from the DES Y3 galaxy shape catalogue. *Monthly Notices of the Royal Astronomical Society, 495*(3), 3208–3232.

Doshi-Velez, F., & Kim, B. (2017). Towards a rigorous science of interpretable machine learning. arXiv preprint arXiv:1702.08947.

Dumitrascu, O., Wang, Y., & Chen, J. (2022). Clinical machine learning modelling studies: Methodology and data reporting. *Journal of Neuro-Ophthalmology, 42*(2), 145–148. doi:10.1097/WNO.0000000000001605 PMID:35439230

Duncan, A. (2022). The intelligent academic library: A review of AI projects & and potential for Caribbean libraries. *Library Hi Tech News, 39*(5), 12–15. doi:10.1108/LHTN-01-2022-0014

Eubanks, V. (2018). *Automating inequality: How high-tech tools perpetuate bias.* John Wiley & Sons.

Eulerich, M., Pawlowski, J., Waddoups, N., & Wood, D. A. (2021). A framework for using robotic process automation for audit tasks*. *Contemporary Accounting Research, 39*(1), 691–720. doi:10.1111/1911-3846.12723

Gama, F., Tyskbo, D., Nygren, J., Barlow, J., Reed, J., & Svedberg, P. (2022). Implementation frameworks for artificial intelligence translation into health care practice: A scoping review. *Journal of Medical Internet Research, 24*(1), e32215. doi:10.2196/32215 PMID:35084349

Gao, S., He, L., Chen, Y., Li, D., & Lai, K. (2020). Public perception of artificial intelligence in medical care: Social media content analysis. *Journal of Medical Internet Research, 22*(7), e16649. doi:10.2196/16649 PMID:32673231

Gebru, T., Morgenstern, J., Blocher, B., Mitchell, M., & Barenholtz, E. (2019). Datasheets for datasets. arXiv preprint arXiv:1803.09010.

Glatard, T., Legrand, A., Loesek, V., Merlin, O., & Mouginot, F. (2015). SciServer: An open science platform for collaborative research. In *International Conference on Computational Science and Its Applications* (pp. 374-385). Springer, Cham.

Groot, P., Brinchmann, J., & Gieseke, F. (2018). Deep learning for cosmological surveys: Finding rare objects by anomaly detection. *Monthly Notices of the Royal Astronomical Society, 477*(4), 4967–4983.

Guegan, J., Brechet, C., & Nelson, J. (2021). Dreamlike and playful virtual environments to inspire children's divergent thinking. *Journal of Media Psychology, 33*(1), 28–38. doi:10.1027/1864-1105/a000279

Gunning, D. (2017). On the dark side of AI. arXiv preprint arXiv:1703.05057.

Guo, Y., Zhang, Y., Liu, T., Prosperi, M., Wang, F., Xu, H., ... Bian, J. (2021). The application of artificial intelligence and data integration in COVID-19 studies: A scoping review. *Journal of the American Medical Informatics Association : JAMIA, 28*(9), 2050–2067. doi:10.1093/jamia/ocab098 PMID:34151987

Han, C., Ling, C., & Ye, Y. (2020). Research on the influence of artificial intelligence on the economy and society. Destech Transactions on Engineering and Technology Research, (make). https://doi.org/ doi:10.12783/dtetr/mcaee2020/35030

Hannousse, A. (2021). Searching relevant papers for software engineering secondary studies: Semantic scholar coverage and identification role. *IET Software, 15*(1), 126–146. doi:10.1049/sfw2.12011

Hinojo-Lucena, F., Díaz, I., Cáceres-Reche, M., & Rodríguez, J. (2019). Artificial intelligence in higher education: A bibliometric study on its impact in the scientific literature. *Education Sciences, 9*(1), 51. doi:10.3390/educsci9010051

Hu, H., Misra, I., & Maaten, L. (2019). Evaluating text-to-image matching using binary image selection (bison).. https://doi.org/ doi:10.1109/ICCVW.2019.00237

Huang, C., Zhang, Z., Mao, B., & Yao, X. (2023). An overview of artificial intelligence ethics. *IEEE Transactions on Artificial Intelligence*, *4*(4), 799–819. doi:10.1109/TAI.2022.3194503

Hutson, M. (2018). *Big data in science: From hype to reality*. Routledge.

Hwang, D., Oh, H., & Lee, S. (2021). Asimov: A framework for simulation and optimisation of an embedded AI accelerator. *Micromachines*, *12*(7), 838. doi:10.3390/mi12070838 PMID:34357248

JiM.ChenX.GenchevG.XuT.WeiM.YuG. (2020). Status of ai-enabled clinical decision support systems clinical implementations in China. https://doi.org/ doi:10.21203/rs.2.22387/v1

Jobin, A., Ienca, M., & Vayanos, P. (2019). The ethics of artificial intelligence. *Nature*, *562*(7723), 288–293.

Jobin, A., Ienca, M., & Vayena, E. (2019). The global landscape of AI ethics guidelines. *Nature Machine Intelligence*, *1*(9), 389–399. doi:10.1038/s42256-019-0088-2

Jumper, J., Evans, R., Pritzel, A., Green, M. F., Figurn, V., Ronneberger, O., ... Senior, K. (2021). Highly accurate protein structure prediction with AlphaFold. *Nature*, *596*(7877), 587–594. doi:10.1038/s41586 021 03819 2 PMID:34265844

JungwirthD.HaluzaD. (2023). Feasibility study on utilisation of the artificial intelligence got-3 in public health. doi:10.20944/preprints202301.0521.v1

Kazim, E., & Koshiyama, A. (2021). A high-level overview of AI ethics. *Patterns (New York, N.Y.)*, *2*(9), 100314. doi:10.1016/j.patter.2021.100314 PMID:34553166

Kear, A., & Folkes, S. (2020). A solution to artificial intelligence's hypercomplex, cross-domain reality: The hierarchy of AI. *International Journal of Advanced Computer Science and Applications*, *11*(3). Advance online publication. doi:10.14569/IJACSA.2020.0110307

Kim, D., Jang, H., Kim, K., Shin, Y., & Park, S. (2019). Design characteristics of studies reporting the performance of artificial intelligence algorithms for diagnostic analysis of medical images: Results from recently published papers. *Korean Journal of Radiology*, *20*(3), 405. doi:10.3348/kjr.2019.0025 PMID:30799571

LabPlot:Kwok, H. Y., & Wong, P. K. (2015). LabPlot: A scientific graphing and data analysis software package. *Computer Applications in Science and Technology*, *7*(1), 35–43.

Lamberti, M., Wilkinson, M., Donzanti, B., Wohlhieter, G., Parikh, S., Wilkins, R., & Getz, K. (2019). A study on the application and use of artificial intelligence to support drug development. *Clinical Therapeutics*, *41*(8), 1414–1426. doi:10.1016/j.clinthera.2019.05.018 PMID:31248680

Lau, A., & Staccini, P. (2019). Artificial intelligence in health: New opportunities, challenges, and practical implications. *Yearbook of Medical Informatics*, *28*(01), 174–178. doi:10.1055/s-0039-1677935 PMID:31419829

Li, R., Yang, Y., Wu, S., Huang, K., Chen, W., Liu, Y., & Lin, H. (2020). Using artificial intelligence to improve medical services in China. *Annals of Translational Medicine*, *8*(11), 711–711. doi:10.21037/atm.2019.11.108 PMID:32617331

Lipton, Z. C. (2016). *The mythos of model interpretability. Why does AI matter? Essays on the societal consequences of artificial intelligence*. Princeton University Press.

Liu, X., Cheng, Y., Zheng, Q., Yang, H., Zhu, W., & Wu, M. (2019). Artificial intelligence in medical diagnosis: A review. *Engineering*, *5*(5), 1152–1159.

Liu, Y., Yang, F., Gomez, A., & Carbonell, J. (2017). Automated discovery of event sequences in text for historical analysis. In *Proceedings of the 2017 Conference on Empirical Methods in Natural Language Processing* (pp. 3048-3058).

Loh, E. (2018). Medicine and the rise of the robots: A qualitative review of recent advances of artificial intelligence in health. *BMJ Leader*, *2*(2), 59–63. doi:10.1136/leader-2018-000071

Luitse, D., Blanke, T., & Poell, T. (2023). *Ai competitions as infrastructures: examining power relations on kaggle and grand challenge in ai-driven medical imaging*. Aoir Selected Papers of Internet Research., doi:10.5210/spir.v2022i0.13044

Mekovec, R., & Peras, D. (2020). Implementing the general data protection regulation: The case of higher education institution. International Journal of E-Education, E-Business. *E-Management and E-Learning*, *10*(1), 104–113. doi:10.17706/ijeeee.2020.10.1.104-113

Mittelstadt, B. (2019). Principles for AI fairness. arXiv preprint arXiv:1901.09463.

Morandini, S., Fraboni, F., Angelis, M. D., Puzzo, G., Giusino, D., & Pietrantoni, L. (2023). The impact of artificial intelligence on workers' skills: upskilling and reskilling in organisations. Informing Science: The International Journal of an Emerging Transdiscipline, 26, 039-068. doi:10.28945/5078

Nalepa, G., & Stefanowski, J. (2020). Artificial intelligence research community and associations in Poland. *Foundations of Computing and Decision Sciences*, *45*(3), 159–177. doi:10.2478/fcds-2020-0009

Nilsen, P., Svedberg, P., Nygren, J., Frideros, M., Johansson, J., & Schueller, S. (2022). Accelerating the impact of artificial intelligence in mental healthcare through implementation science. *Implementation Research and Practice*, *3*, 263348952211120. doi:10.1177/26334895221112033 PMID:37091110

O'Neil, C. (2017). *Weapons of math destruction: How big data increases inequality and risks democracy*. Tim Duggan Books.

Obeid, S., & Demirkan, H. (2020). The influence of virtual reality on design process creativity in basic design studios. *Interactive Learning Environments*, *31*(4), 1841–1859. doi:10.1080/10494820.2020.1858116

OECD. (2019). Artificial intelligence in science. *Challenges*.

Oermann, E., & Kondziolka, D. (2023). On chatbots and generative artificial intelligence. *Neurosurgery*, *92*(4), 665–666. doi:10.1227/neu.0000000000002415 PMID:36779766

Oka, A., Ishimura, N., & Ishihara, S. (2021). A new dawn for the use of artificial intelligence in gastroenterology, hepatology and pancreatology. *Diagnostics (Basel)*, *11*(9), 1719. doi:10.3390/diagnostics11091719 PMID:34574060

Patra, B., Roberts, K., & Wu, H. (2020). A content-based dataset recommendation system for researchers—a case study on gene expression omnibus (geo) repository. Database, 2020. https://doi.org/ doi:10.1093/database/baaa064

Pessoa, G. J., Dias, T. M. R., Silva, T. H. P., & Laender, A. H. F. (2022). A geographic analysis of the interdisciplinary collaborations in the Brazilian scientific community. *Journal of the Brazilian Computer Society*, *28*(1), 1–12. doi:10.5753/jbcs.2022.2887

Petersson, L., Larsson, I., Nygren, J., Nilsen, P., Neher, M., Reed, J., Tyskbo, D., & Svedberg, P. (2022). Challenges to implementing artificial intelligence in healthcare: A qualitative interview study with healthcare leaders in Sweden. *BMC Health Services Research*, *22*(1), 850. Advance online publication. doi:10.1186/s12913-022-08215-8 PMID:35778736

Pierdicca, R., & Paolanti, M. (2022). Geoai: A review of artificial intelligence approaches for interpreting complex geomatics data. *Geoscientific Instrumentation, Methods and Data Systems*, *11*(1), 195–218. doi:10.5194/gi-11-195-2022

Qin, Z., Ahmed, S., Sarker, M., Paul, K., Adel, A., Naheyan, T., Barrett, R., Banu, S., & Creswell, J. (2021). Tuberculosis detection from chest x-rays for triaging in a high tuberculosis-burden setting: An evaluation of five artificial intelligence algorithms. *The Lancet. Digital Health*, *3*(9), e543–e554. doi:10.1016/S2589-7500(21)00116-3 PMID:34446265

Ramprasad, R., Pacholsky, A., & Wolverton, C. (2016). Automated exploration of the materials phase diagram using Density Functional Theory calculations. *Proceedings of the National Academy of Sciences of the United States of America*, *113*(47), 1.

Rana, J., Gaur, L., Singh, G., Awan, U., & Rasheed, M. (2021). Reinforcing customer journey through artificial intelligence: A review and research agenda. *International Journal of Emerging Markets*, *17*(7), 1738–1758. doi:10.1108/IJOEM-08-2021-1214

Rivera, S. C., Liu, X., Chan, A. W., Denniston, A. K., Calvert, M., Ashrafian, H., ... Yau, C. (2020). Guidelines for clinical trial protocols for artificial intelligence interventions: The spirit-ai extension. *The Lancet. Digital Health*, *2*(10), e549–e560. doi:10.1016/S2589-7500(20)30219-3 PMID:33328049

Roccapriore, K. M., Boebinger, M. G., Dyck, O., Ghosh, A., Unocic, R. R., Kalinin, S. V., & Ziatdinov, M. (2022). Probing electron beam-induced transformations on a single-defect level via automated scanning transmission electron microscopy. *ACS Nano*, *16*(10), 17116–17127. doi:10.1021/acsnano.2c07451 PMID:36206357

Römmele, C., Mendel, R., Barrett, C., Kiesl, H., Rauber, D., Rückert, T., Kraus, L., Heinkele, J., Dhillon, C., Grosser, B., Prinz, F., Wanzl, J., Fleischmann, C., Nagl, S., Schnoy, E., Schlottmann, J., Dellon, E. S., Messmann, H., Palm, C., & Ebigbo, A. (2022). An artificial intelligence algorithm is highly accurate for detecting endoscopic features of eosinophilic esophagitis. *Scientific Reports*, *12*(1), 11115. Advance online publication. doi:10.1038/s41598-022-14605-z PMID:35778456

Roozbahani, Z., Rezaeenour, J., Katanforoush, A., & Bidgoly, A. J. (2021). Personalisation of the collaborator recommendation system in multi-layer scientific social networks: A case study of researchgate. *Expert Systems: International Journal of Knowledge Engineering and Neural Networks*, *39*(5), e12932. Advance online publication. doi:10.1111/exsy.12932

Sandy, D. A., Ritchie, H., Adrianto, Z., & Gunardi, A. (2022). Robotic process automation in action: a use case in accounting task. Journal of Digital Innovation Studies, pp. 52–65. doi:10.24198/digits.v1i1.38534

Sateli, B., Löffler, F., König-Ries, B., & Witte, R. (2017). Scholarlens: Extracting competencies from research publications to automatically generate semantic user profiles. *PeerJ. Computer Science*, *3*, e121. doi:10.7717/peerj-cs.121

Shadravan, A., & Parsaei, H. (2023). *The paradigm shift from industry 4.0 implementation to industry 5.0 readiness.* AHFE International., doi:10.54941/ahfe1004296

Shahnaz, K., & Mukesh, D. (2022). The role of artificial intelligence in combat against COVID-19. *IJEAST*, *7*(4), 252–256. doi:10.33564/IJEAST.2022.v07i04.040

Sigfrids, A., Leikas, J., Salo-Pöntinen, H., & Koskimies, E. (2023). Human-centricity in AI governance: A systemic approach. *Frontiers in Artificial Intelligence*, *6*, 976887. doi:10.3389/frai.2023.976887 PMID:36872934

Tableau Software. (2023). *Tableau: Data visualisation software.* https://www.tableau.com/

Thomas, R., Bhosale, U., Shukla, K., & Kapadia, A. (2023). Impact and perceived value of the revolutionary advent of artificial intelligence in research and publishing among researchers: A survey-based descriptive study. *Science Editing*, *10*(1), 27–34. doi:10.6087/kcse.294

Tiwari, R. (2023). Explainable AI (xai) and its applications in building trust and understanding in AI decision-making. *International Journal of Scientific Research in Engineering and Management*, *07*(01). Advance online publication. doi:10.55041/IJSREM17592

Van Belkon, A. (2020). Speeding up to keep up: Exploring the use of AI in the research process. *AI & Society*, 1–17.

Verma, A., Sharma, Y., & Shekhar, S. (2021). *Artificial intelligence (AI) is used in qualitative research for theory development.* PhilArchive.

Waldenmaier, H. E., Gorre, E., Poltash, M. L., Gunawardena, H. P., Zhai, X. A., Li, J., Zhai, B., Beil, E. J., Terzo, J. C., Lawler, R., English, A. M., Bern, M., Mahan, A. D., Carlson, E., & Nanda, H. (2023). "lab of the future"—today: Fully automated system for high-throughput mass spectrometry analysis of biotherapeutics. *Journal of the American Society for Mass Spectrometry*, *34*(6), 1073–1085. doi:10.1021/jasms.3c00036 PMID:37186948

Weber, M., Engert, M., Schaffer, N., Weking, J., & Krcmar, H. (2022). Organisational capabilities for AI implementation—Coping with inscrutability and data dependency in AI. *Information Systems Frontiers*, *25*(4), 1549–1569. doi:10.1007/s10796-022-10297-y

Wirtz, B., Weyerer, J., & Geyer, C. (2018). Artificial intelligence and the public sector—Applications and challenges. *International Journal of Public Administration*, *42*(7), 596–615. doi:10.1080/01900692.2018.1498103

Wirtz, B., Weyerer, J., & Geyer, C. (2018). Artificial intelligence and the public sector—Applications and challenges. *International Journal of Public Administration*, *42*(7), 596–615. doi:10.1080/01900692.2018.1498103

Wu, Y., Hu, Q., Liang, H., Wang, A., Xu, H., Wang, L., & He, X. (2023). Electrostatic potential as a solvent descriptor enables rational electrolyte design for lithium batteries. *Advanced Energy Materials*, *13*(22), 2300259. Advance online publication. doi:10.1002/aenm.202300259

Yang, Q., Steinfeld, A., Rosé, C., & Zimmerman, J. (2020). *Re-examining whether, why, and how human-ai interaction is uniquely difficult to design*. doi:10.1145/3313831.3376301

Zhao, K., Cheng, M., & Guo, Y. (2020). Artificial intelligence in social and human sciences: An overview. *International Journal of Human-Computer Interaction*, *36*(8), 609–623.

Zheng, Y., & Wen, X. (2021). The application of artificial intelligence technology in cloud computing environment resources. *Journal of Web Engineering*. doi:10.13052/jwe1540-9589.2067

Zhou, J., Chen, F., Berry, A., Reed, M., Zhang, S., & Savage, S. (2020). *A survey on ethical principles of AI and implementations*. IEEE. doi:10.1109/SSCI47803.2020.9308437

Žigienė, G., Rybakovas, E., & Vaitkienė, R. (2020). Challenges in applying artificial intelligence for supply chain risk management. *International Journal of Economics and Business Administration*, *VIII*(4), 299–318. doi:10.35808/ijeba/589

Zitnik, M., Azuaje-Flores, L., Mac Jones, D., & Lengauer, T. (2012). Biomarker discovery platform: An R/Java framework for analysis of high-throughput proteomic data. *Journal of Proteome Research*, *11*(3), 1421–1432.

Chapter 6
AI-Driven Transformation in Higher Education:
New Frontiers in Administration and Management

Mohamed Salah El Din
https://orcid.org/0000-0002-9360-8589
Majan University College, Oman

Nasser Al Harrasi
https://orcid.org/0000-0003-4456-0926
University of Technology and Applied Science, Oman

ABSTRACT

The evolution of the higher education sector, especially during the COVID-19 pandemic, pinpointed the necessity for agility and innovation in performing the increased load in administrative duties. Artificial intelligence (AI) showed up as a prominent solution for higher education institutions (HEI). This chapter explores AI's potential in administrative functions like scheduling, library services, enrollment, and others, acknowledging the benefits and highlighting challenges such as stakeholder participation, lack of knowledge, privacy concerns, and budgetary limitations. It promotes a holistic, phased approach to AI integration, underscoring strong leadership, clear vision, and collaboration for successful adoption and enhancing educational quality.

DOI: 10.4018/979-8-3693-2145-4.ch006

INTRODUCTION AND BACKGROUND

Recently, the higher education sector has grown significantly. According to the United Nations Educational, Scientific and Cultural Organization's (UNESCO's) higher education global data report of 2022, there is a remarkable global upsurge in admissions in universities and colleges doubling to over 235 million in 2020 compared to the enrollments in the year 2000. Simultaneously, the number of Higher Education Institutions (HEIs), increased by 55% between 2006 and 2018 (UNESCO, 2022). This exponential growth, accompanied by the rising inclination towards the commercialization and privatization of HEIs' services, as reported by Chan (2016), Qureshi & Khawaja (2021) and Rakhimbekova et al. (2022), led to a notable rise in administrative workload (Yousefi & Abdullah, 2019). The increased workload is usually accompanied by high levels of stress for employees and depleted resources for organizations (Górak-Sosnowska & Piwowar-Sulej, 2023).

These escalating issues emphasize the necessity for developing innovative solutions to facilitate the complicated administrative tasks in higher education, while achieving efficiency. In this given context, Artificial Intelligence (AI) has shown up as a promising solution, shifting organizations towards automation, efficiency and data-driven operations (Chen et al., 2020). Incorporating AI in the management and administration of universities has a positive effect on the quality and accessibility of higher education (Sethi et al., 2021).

Furthermore, the advent of COVID-19 pandemic disrupted the higher education process, accelerating the shift towards automation and digital transformation, enabling HEIs to be more agile in the face of unforeseen disruption (Aristovnik et al., 2020; Biwer et al., 2021; Jakoet-Salie & Ramalobe, 2022; Orr et al., 2020; UNESCO, 2022). This rapid transformation has highlighted the significance of AI in enabling seamless administrative processes, while enhancing quality and reducing staff workloads (Slimi, 2021).

The concept of "Artificial Intelligence" (AI), first introduced by John McCarthy in 1956, has achieved noteworthy development and has become a fundamental component of technology innovation (Saraswat et al., 2022). AI refers to creating intelligent technologies that mimic human intelligence, including the ability to comprehend human language, identify themes and patterns, develop data-driven decisions, formulate strategies, respond to inquiries, cope with unique and developing circumstances, and carry out other cognitive functions generally performed by people (Naqvi, 2020; Saraswat et al., 2022). Nowadays, AI is prevailing in different sectors and industries (Suh & Ahn, 2022).

Within the educational landscape, HEIs started to realize the profound gains of employing AI in their operations, aiming to achieve a substantial competitive advantage (Hannan & Liu, 2021) and to evolve into smart universities (Furey &

Martin, 2019). Becoming a smart university can enhance service quality while minimizing operating expenses and increasing profitability (Fernández-Caramés & Fraga-Lamas, 2019). It is important to note that smart universities rely on other technologies, alongside with AI, including big data, blockchain, and the Internet of Things (IoT) (Phanichsiti et al., 2023). Jadrić et al. (2021) suggested that the transforming into smart organizations is now considered a crucial element affecting the perception and experience of students.

One remarkable example of AI's cutting-edge impact in educational institutions is the rise of generative AI tools, such as Open AI's ChatGPT and Google Gemini. According to Vasconcelos &dos Santos (2023), these tools are redefining processes and interactions for both educators and students, providing fresh and efficient approaches to managing tasks and educational material. However, these tools challenge the traditional educational process, as they introduce technical difficulties, privacy concerns, data security problems, and ethical issues (Mahligawati et al., 2023).

Most of the published studies have focused on the application of AI in education, with particular emphasis on curriculum development, assessment preparation, grading, lecturing, personalized learning, and other related areas (Hannan & Liu, 2021; Laato et al., 2023; A. K. Sharma et al., 2022; Toutain et al., 2023; Xia & Li, 2022). Nevertheless, the promise of AI encompasses much far greater potential, including applications in managerial responsibilities in HEIs. AI can automate and optimize administrative activities across different university functions and departments (Furey & Martin, 2019).

This chapter depends on the wealth of published literature on the uses of Artificial Intelligence (AI) to explore the potential of AI technologies in transforming the administration and management functions in Higher Education Institutions (HEIs), focusing on non-teaching areas such as resource allocation and scheduling, library, admission and enrollment, accounting, human resources management (HRM), procurement, facilities management and marketing.

RESEARCH OBJECTIVES

1. To understand the possible applications of AI tools in managerial and administrative functions in Higher Education Institutions (HEIs).
2. To investigate the challenges of AI integration in HEIs administration
3. To provide practical recommendations for integrating AI in academic administration and management.

RESEARCH METHODOLOGY

To achieve the objectives of the chapter, a thorough literature review was conducted. Snyder (2019) emphasized the importance of literature review as a research methodology. In this approach, researchers evaluate the available knowledge in a specific subject matter by collecting, synthesizing, and organizing related information. The information in this chapter was collected from relevant journal articles and reports. Authors used the keywords such as: Artificial Intelligence (AI) in management, AI in higher education administration, AI in administration, Ai in course scheduling, AI implementation challenges, AI best practices and AI integration roadmap. After collecting the secondary data, authors synthesized the information to provide valuable insights into the use of AI in managing HEIs. The following section includes a thorough examination of the available literature related to AI implementation in the administration and management of HEIs.

LITERATURE REVIEW

Resource Optimization and Scheduling With AI

Course scheduling in higher education, also known as The Timetabling Problem (TP)" or "University Class Scheduling Problem (UCSP)", is a complex and time-consuming process (Poole & Mackworth, 2017). It involves optimizing the organization's resources and satisfying students' needs by allocating modules to different rooms and timeslots constraints (Arratia-Martinez et al., 2021). This schedule should avoid duplication for both rooms and lecturers (K. Zhu & Li, 2021), and consider faculty specialization and student priorities (Pereira & Gomes Costa, 2016). The traditional approach in designing educational timetable is challenging and prone to errors, such as creating classroom conflicts, which necessitate the need for more efficient scheduling techniques that minimize human interference(Amariesta et al., 2022).

AI provides viable solutions for the abovementioned challenges by adopting a data-driven approach in developing efficient timetables (Zawacki-Richter et al., 2019; Kavade et al. 2023; Alansari 2022). This is achieved through prediction of the students' preferences and performances, which can be tackled with the use of the AI algorithms, including those in the Educational Data Mining (EDM). These algorithms enable institutions to make well-informed decisions on scheduling and classrooms allocation. Such an approach involves the use of large-scale datasets to determine the ideal schedule, considering the factors such as room sizes and course prerequisites, students' preferences, and university specific policies (Hernández-Blanco et al. 2019).

AI in Academic Libraries

Lately, the role of academic libraries has surpassed their traditional role of facilitating teaching, learning and research activities. It evolved into innovative digital centers (Peng et al., 2022; Walter & Lankes, 2015; Wheatley & Hervieux, 2020). Libraries are progressively employing AI, especially chatbots, aiming to improve user services (Ali et al., 2020; Cox, 2022; Research Planning and Review Committee, 2022; Siler, 2019; Subaveerapandiyan A, 2023). AI can act as "virtual assistants" or "virtual librarians", supporting in user navigation, cataloging, collection creation, straightforward reference requests and research support (Ali et al., 2020; Mckie & Narayan, 2019; Research Planning and Review Committee, 2022; Siler, 2019).

Nevertheless, the reality of AI-adoption in academic libraries remains far from its potential. Recent study reveals that only 5% of libraries are harnessing the power of AI, while 80% of them are still exploring its benefits (Prokop et al., 2021). Ethical issues and the requirement for balanced human-AI partnership are crucial for successful adoption (Librarian & Chakravarty, 2021; Mckie & Narayan, 2019; Tzachor et al., 2020). Notable examples of effective implementation include McMaster University, John Hopkins University, University of Pennsylvania, University of California, University of Rhode Island, Stanford University, and Massachusetts Institute of Technology (MIT), which have successfully incorporated AI into a range of library operations. These institutions focused on improving services delivered to their users including research support as a key application of AI in their libraries (Wheatley & Hervieux, 2020).

AI in Admission and Enrollment

The admissions process in HEIs is vital for sustaining diversity and equity within student cohorts (Kurysheva et al., 2019). AI applications, especially in chatbots and data analysis, have demonstrated the potential to expedite enrollment procedures, and reduce the increased load on admission teams, potentially leading to a stronger and diverse student body and demonstrating a tech-savvy university (Agarwal et al., 2022; Ahmad et al., 2022; Kumar & Raman, 2022; Kurysheva et al., 2019).

However, Murphy et al. (2021) and Winfield & Jirotka (2018) raise ethical concerns about data privacy, transparency, and prejudice, which indicates for proper moral governance to maintain system trustworthiness. Despite these limitations, the use of AI in handling high amounts of admission queries is demonstrated by Georgia State University's deployment of the "Pounce" system, a personal assistant dedicated to answering commonly asked inquiries from students. The system managed to address over 99% of the inquiries in a period of 5 months, while satisfying 80% of students with its performance (Klutka et al., 2020).

AI in Accounting

AI is reshaping the field of accounting, by improving productivity and accuracy (Askary et al., 2018; Hassan, 2021) and allowing for a smooth transition towards management accounting focused organization (Li et al., 2022; D. Zhu, 2020). Furthermore, AI address accounting-related ethical challenges (Kindzeka, 2023). According to Zadorozhnyi et al. (2023), AI chatbots simplify accounting tasks, from basic accounting data processing and automatically drafting tax documents to providing individualized, non-stop consultations on accounting matters, and ongoing training for new and current staff, thereby fostering a culture of continuous improvement. In addition, AI may take care of legal compliance and appraisals, turning accountants into interpreters, integrators, and communicators of information. Despite these benefits, there are major concerns about job placement which calls for moral oversight (Y. Tian & Zhang, 2022).

There is limited research on using AI in performing accounting tasks for HEIs. However, some studies are conducted showed that AI is helpful in handling vast amounts of data indifferent sectors such as business, healthcare and software development (Baviskar et al., 2021; Iqbal et al., 2022; Zhang et al., 2018). This could also apply to the case of universities' operations.

AI-Supported Human Resources Management

Plenty of studies have been conducted regarding the use of AI in HRM, mostly focusing on how it affects hiring, staff engagement and turnover, performance appraisal and staff turnover (Bubinger & Dinneen, 2021; Dasanayaka et al., 2021; X. Tian et al., 2022). AI technologies, notably in automating CV screening and candidate evaluation, have streamlined recruiting procedures, making them more efficient (Aydın & Turan, 2023; Hunkenschroer & Luetge, 2022). Additionally, technologies powered by AI such as chatbots and predictive analytics have improved decision-making in HR, aiding in talent mapping and decreasing repetitive administrative duties (Baakeel, 2020; Malik et al., 2022; G. Sharma, 2021; Venusamy et al., 2020).

Al Harrasi et. Al (2023) found that there are many AI-based chatbot tools that are used in all processes of recruitment and selection which are sourcing, screening, matching, and assessing of applicants. it helps organization with candidate-matching and hire the right candidate.AI enhances hiring as well as performance appraisals and staff training, thereby improving engagement and productivity (G. Sharma, 2021; Venusamy et al., 2020). Also, AI can facilitate decision-making and strategic HR planning (Fernández & Gallardo-Gallardo, 2020; Jain et al., 2023; Malik et al., 2022; Svitlana et al., 2022). On the other hand, the fast-paced transition towards AI in HRM raises concerns about bias and degree of transparency (Açıkgöz et al., 2020;

Aydın & Turan, 2023; Çalışkan et al., 2017; Köchling et al., 2022; Ore & Sposato, 2021; X. Tian et al., 2022). Consequently, efforts need to be made to control the ethical ramifications of AI, including possible biases in employee turnover analysis and performance evaluation (Lelli, 2022; Marín Díaz et al., 2023; Pillai, 2019).

AI in Procurement

HEIs depend on their procurement departments to efficiently acquire goods and services that are needed for smooth academic and administrative activities (Ning, 2023). AI applications support procurement in various ways, from locating suppliers and evaluating their performance to controlling costs, handling contracts, and mitigating supply risks. It is radically changing procurement by helping firms make well-informed decisions, improve procurement procedures, and lower costs by utilizing its capacity to analyze large datasets and forecast future trends (Chopra, 2019; Jahani et al., 2021; Modgil et al., 2021; Sai et al., 2022). Furthermore, AI can facilitate information sharing with suppliers, leading to efficiency and increased visibility in the supply chain (Jahani et al., 2021). Conversely, concerns on bias and fairness remain as vital challenges to AI adoption in procurement (Kazim & Koshiyama, 2021).

Facilities Management With AI

The success of HEIs depends on various factors, effective facilities management is one of them due to its immense impact on students' satisfaction and attraction (Abdullahi & Yusoff, 2019). Integrating AI into facilities management greatly boosts decision-making and efficiency. Applications include using predictive maintenance for proactive asset care, energy management, and space utilization (Marzouk & Zaher, 2020). AI pilot projects have been executed at MIT to lower energy consumption and emissions on campus. The program's main objective is to increase the efficiency of energy by utilizing AI-building controls to react in real time to a variety of condition (MIT, 2023).

AI in Marketing

Recently, marketing higher education services has changed dramatically, embracing a market-oriented mindset and digital transformation. HEIs are becoming significantly more marketized, as they target international markets (Williamson, 2020). Hence, Artificial Intelligence is instrumental in targeting and analyzing markets, creating personalized marketing campaigns, improving customer experiences (Ho & Chow, 2023; Huang & Rust, 2020) and reducing cost of marketing activities (K. Wang et al., 2023; Wu & Monfort, 2022; Yang et al., 2021). Moreover, AI proved effective in addressing and solving marketing issues, suggesting that it can assist marketing choices made in the higher education industry (Overgoor et al., 2019). HEIs has employed various tools to improve their marketing communication strategies, particularly social media (Dagumboy, 2022). Also, many functions in marketing process have been replaced by AI powered tools such as social media monitoring, digital marketing, web development, email marketing and search engine optimization (SEO) (Peyravi et al., 2020).

Challenges of AI Adoption in Administration

Although AI proved to be beneficial for different functions and departments in universities and colleges, there are plenty of challenges that need to be addressed properly.

1. ***Limited stakeholders' participation*** Despite AI's transformative potential, important stakeholders, particularly educators and administrators, have not always been sufficiently involved in the fast deployment of AI tools in higher education institutions. Lack of engagement can lead to confusion and unforeseen failure to achieve the expected goals (Hannan, 2021; Owan et al., 2023). This is even worsened by the existing disparity of AI literacy among these stakeholders. Effective communication is crucial to guarantee buy-in and commitment from relevant parties (Asatiani et al., 2021; Weber et al., 2022).
2. ***Lack of In-House Expertise*** The sophisticated nature of AI, alongside the scarcity in skilled staff and unwillingness of the organization to use AI applications, constitute profound obstacles in its adoption (Bérubé et al., 2021a; Jöhnk et al., 2020; Munz et al., 2023). Users of AI in HEIs, whether educators or support staff, need to have a minimum level of understanding of AI to be able to use it properly. This gap could be closed by hiring competent staff and investing in AI training programs (Ångström et al., 2023; Owan et al., 2023).
3. ***Cyber security and privacy*** AI systems are vulnerable to hacks that could trigger significant financial and data losses. While it is essential to maintain up-to-date cybersecurity solutions and solid AI security measures, emerging threats necessitate ongoing adaptation (Bérubé et al., 2021a; Jawaid, 2023; Plathottam et al., 2023). In the context of higher education, concerns about student data security and privacy are pressing, especially considering the sensitivity of students' data (Kamalov et al., 2021). Moreover, data access from AI third party providers poses new challenges (Rudolf & Grünbichler, 2023).

4. ***Ambiguity and bias*** AI mostly works as a black box. There is limited transparency with respect to the way AI takes decisions, which may lead to ambiguity and bias (Bérubé et al., 2021b; Enholm et al., 2021a; Owan et al., 2023). Large language models (LLMs) reflect their training data. This may result in unfair judgement and decisions (Owan et al., 2023). Sensitive decisions related to staff such as hiring, and performance appraisals should be clear from bias under all circumstances (Kaminski, 2022; Rodrigues, 2020).
5. ***Ethical and legal barriers*** The use of AI raises ethical concerns about data privacy, possible job displacement, and lack of transparency (Green, 2018; Owan et al., 2023; Taddeo & Floridi, 2018). In addition, there is a need to address legal issues such as accountability for AI-generated content and intellectual property rights (Rodrigues, 2020). These barriers highlight the need for a collaborative approach in devising ethical frameworks for AI adoption (Leimanis & Palkova, 2021; Rezwana & Maher, 2022; Zawacki-Richter et al., 2019b)
6. ***Merging AI tools with existing technologies*** HEIs have existing systems and technologies in place. Incorporating AI into these systems presents a significant challenge which requires appropriate planning and execution (Owan et al., 2023). Smooth integration of AI requires carefully modifying legacy systems (Brock & Wangenheim, 2019).
7. ***Financial considerations*** The substantial cost of developing, deploying and sustaining the AI systems including procuring technology and software, data processing and storage, and staff hiring and training presents a major challenge (Gao et al., 2023; Perret & Heitkamp, 2021; Rudolf & Grünbichler, 2023) especially with the current financial difficulties of HEIs (Owan et al., 2023). Nevertheless, this high investment is not risk-free, as its return on investment is not certain (Bérubé et al., 2021a).
8. ***Change Resistance*** The incorporation of artificial intelligence into operations necessitates adjustments to corporate procedures, in addition to a change in the current management, expertise, and skillset (Angelini et al., 2021; Rožman et al., 2022). AI adoption is further complicated by the resistance to change, often due to limited awareness and confusion and worried from job displacement (Ångström et al., 2023; Bérubé et al., 2021a; Owan et al., 2023; Rudolf & Grünbichler, 2023; Vorobeva et al., 2022). Proper change management plan is necessary to overcome this hindrance (Bérubé et al., 2021a).
9. ***Inadequate IT infrastructure*** Unleashing AI requires adequate IT infrastructure. Before moving towards AI integration, HEIs should make the floor ready by securing the required hardware, software, power supply, network coverage, and cloud services accessibility (Ångström et al., 2023; Bérubé et al., 2021a; Owan et al., 2023; Rudolf & Grünbichler, 2023).

10. ***Data availability and Quality*** Lack of high-quality data could be one of the main difficulties that face AI implementation (Budach et al., 2022; Enholm et al., 2021b; Rudolf & Grünbichler, 2023). High quality entails Data to be complete, accurate and relevant, objective, reliable, otherwise it may have a significant negative effect on the performance of the AI system (Bérubé et al., 2021a; Pagallo et al., 2022). Bérubé et al. (2021b) suggest the need for superior data management practices for AI integration.
11. ***Top management commitment and vision*** Effective AI integration requires significant degree of commitment from top-level management (Gao et al., 2023; Rudolf & Grünbichler, 2023). The pace of decision-making in implementing AI is greatly influenced by top management support (Rodrigues, 2020). This echoed by Bérubé et al. (2021a); Rudolf & Grünbichler (2023) who attested the vitality of possessing a strategic vision in selecting the appropriate AI initiative to enhance operations. Also, the role of top management includes setting appropriate AI strategies that facilitates its use (Herremans, 2021).
12. ***Limited awareness of AI potential*** The benefits of AI are still difficult to understand, especially by upper-level management. Insufficient understanding of the technological facets of artificial intelligence, including the approaches and models that may prove beneficial in a particular situation, hinders the advancement of AI adoption in businesses (Bérubé et al., 2021a).
13. ***Over-reliance on AI*** Despite the numerous advantages of AI, over-depending on it can lead to taking wrong decisions that affect operations and quality (Schemmer et al., 2022).

Best Practices in AI Adoption

The related literature review of integration AI in organizations administration identified the best practice where organization can benefit from it:

1. The technological side

Streamlined AI implementation necessitates careful planning for organization's technological capabilities, with an objective of adding value. This is made possible by better data management and accessibility, algorithms' quality, and most importantly, after identifying the appropriate AI tools (Ångström et al., 2023). Organizations should identify and assess their level of technological readiness and affordability of different AI systems (Martínez-Plumed et al., 2021).

2. Organizational strategies

A wholistic approach is required to manage and orchestrate AI transformation initiatives. This includes forming inter-departmental teams, assigning novel duties, and implementing oversight processes like budgetary and assessment standards.

Skilled companies concentrate on further developing AI evangelist positions to foster data-driven processes over the organization's borders (Ångström et al., 2023).

3. Cultural factors

After a thorough analysis of internal capacities (Martínez-Plumed et al., 2021). Organizations should focus on managing change and developing AI skills. Changing work patterns, encouraging staff growth in artificial intelligence, and conducting training courses and seminars are important tactics. AI is also advanced through proof-of-concept research and demonstrations (Ångström et al., 2023).

4. Stakeholder Considerations

It is imperative that HEIs acknowledge the different expectations and requirements of stakeholders, including employees. This may streamline the transition towards effective AI adoption, reducing resistance to change and gaining acceptance from all involved parties (Selenko et al., 2022).

5. Role of management and strategy

The success of AI deployment heavily relies on top-level management. This is usually reflected in the quality of decisions taken, appropriate infrastructure allocated for this transition, and coordinating AI initiatives with institutional goals. The speed and efficacy of AI implementation can be greatly impacted by a leadership team with the availability of clear vision (Kim, 2019; Rodrigues, 2020).

Steps of AI Implementation

The implementation of AI in HEIs requires a multi-stage approach based. The stages are shown in Figure 1.

Figure 1. Steps of AI implementation
(Authors)

1. ***Understanding*** The first step entails understanding the potential of AI and evaluation of the organization's current capabilities. This entails assessing the benefits and drawbacks of integrating AI while being aware of any possible hazards. In this stage, organizations should consider the pros and cons of AI integration and recognize the possible risks through market research or through

the efforts of R&D department, thereby identifying whether the organization needs new capabilities, or the available ones will be sufficient (Faggella & Bharadwaj, 2019; Reim et al., 2020).

2. ***Assessment*** This phase involves assessing the current business model and the organization's ecosystem. AI usually provides opportunities for innovation and business model modifications, which should be considered and addressed properly (Reim et al., 2020). Consequently, Organizations should select the best AI initiative that matches organizational resources and skills, while developing reasonable expectations and analysis for available supplier offerings (Faggella & Bharadwaj, 2019). In addition, it is important at this stage that organizations clearly set ethical and legal parameters for AI and data management (Brock & Wangenheim, 2019)
3. ***Building AI culture*** Organizations should make sure to get everyone on board. Staff acceptance is crucial for smooth deployment of AI. This could be done by showcasing the advantages of AI to all stakeholders, especially staff, in order to convince them with getting the needed knowhow and skillsets necessary for successful AI incorporation (Reim et al., 2020).
4. ***Incubation*** Developing the required capabilities, infrastructure and data collection tools needed to employ AI. It is imperative organizations digitize manual processes (Reim et al., 2020). This step includes training, setting success criteria and testing (Faggella & Bharadwaj, 2019).
5. ***Integration*** This phase focuses on the transition from incubation to implementation. AI maintenance teams should be assigned. The team should be knowledgeable and passionate about AI adoption (Faggella & Bharadwaj, 2019)

6. Expansion After implementing the AI system, organizations should constantly evaluate the business value and make the required changes aligning with the legal developments, new innovations in AI, and cybersecurity threats. Management support becomes even more important than previous stages as scaling usually encounters difficulties (Weber et al., 2022).

DISCUSSION

The use of Artificial Intelligence (AI) in Higher Education Institutions (HEIs) is not limited to teaching and learning, as it could include all aspects of administrative support duties, necessary for the viability of the educational process. Despite the transformative process of AI, there are major obstacles that could impede its deployment. The reviewed literature confirms that AI has the ability to boost efficiency, accuracy, customization, and creativity by incorporating it into a range of administrative functions in higher education, such as timetabling and resource scheduling, library and information centers services, student admissions, human resources, accounting, facilities management, procurement and marketing. However, AI integration is a multifaceted and complicated task. It requires steering through a complex array of organizational, cultural, technological, and ethical issues.

The literature emphasizes the ability of AI in facilitating timetabling and scheduling of courses, taking into consideration variables such as students' timetables, rooms' capacity, lecturers' specializations, and guiding policies. This could result in more accurate and efficient timetables, leading to more satisfied students, and reduced administrative load. Similarly, integrating AI in academic libraries provides valuable opportunities in responding to students' queries, supporting researchers, and recommending sources. Automating the admission and enrollment function in HEIs with the help of AI can streamline the process while considering diversity and inclusion. Also, AI supports the accounting team in HEIs by automating data processing, generating reports and providing real-time consultations. Moreover, AI- supported human resources operations relief employees from tedious and time-consuming tasks, allowing them to pay more attention to strategic initiatives. Given the competitive nature of the higher education sector, it is imperative for HEIs to reduce the costs associated with procurement and facilities management. AI applications have the capacity to promote sustainability and lower expenses without compromising on quality. Finally, AI can support marketing activities of HEIs. This could enhance student experience and optimize advertising campaigns.

However, the successful integration of AI in HEIs requires overcoming its key implementation obstacles. Low involvement of stakeholders in designing and implementing the AI system is a crucial challenge of the transformation. If left unresolved, it could lead to stakeholders' resistance to change. Moreover, issues of technical expertise including lack of internal talent and insufficient AI knowledge require HEIs to invest in staff hiring and training. It is important to pay close attention to the ethical issues related to bias in algorithms, confidentiality of data, intellectual property concerns and the possibility of job displacement from automation. To enable ethical AI creation and execution, HEIs need to set up clear ethical frameworks and data governance guidelines. Furthermore, the financial side of AI integration in HEIs is obvious, especially with their current financial difficulties and fierce market competition. There is a substantial cost associated with developing, implementing and maintaining AI systems. Consequently, before starting any AI project, a cost-benefit analysis should be done to make sure there will be a return on investment.

Organizations should not focus only on technology, when attempting to harness the AI capabilities. Instead, they should consider the big picture. HEIs should evaluate the technological readiness of AI adoption. Also, they could bridge the gap between theory and practice by promoting a data driven culture. Institutions should exert efforts to gain employees' acceptance and minimize opposition of AI deployment. This is facilitated by establishing a culture of trust, developing an appropriate skill development program, maintaining clear communication within the organization, and actively engaging stakeholders in the process. Moreover, successful AI implementation mandates strong leadership. This is crucial for formulating a clear vision for the entire transformation initiatives. In addition, leaders should align AI implementation projects with organizational strategic directions. At the same time, legal and ethical standards should be followed.

A phased approach is necessary to integrate AI in the administration and management of HEIs. First and foremost, these institutions need to be well informed about AI capabilities and limitations. Then, a complete revision of the organization model is required. This should be accompanied by developing a positive, supporting and AI friendly culture. Lastly, HEIs are required to accept the dynamic nature of AI implementation and become flexible regarding new legal requirements, technological progress, and cybersecurity risks in order to realize the potential of AI in transforming administrative and managerial functions.

CONCLUSION

The chapter conducted a comprehensive literature review to explore the revolutionary impact of Artificial Intelligence (AI) in reshaping and streamlining the way Higher Education Institutions (HEIs) perform their administrative and managerial activities. It has been shown that AI can automate tedious and time-consuming tasks, improve decision-making by depending on factual data, reduce workload, and significantly improve the quality of higher education services. While acknowledging its transformative abilities in this regard, its effective implementation depends on resolving pressing issues and barriers. This chapter necessitates adopting a forward-looking, holistic approach that takes into consideration everything from the availability of technical know-how and stakeholder buy-in to ethical issues and financial limitations. This approach, while endorsing the vitality of the technological side in the transformation process, should be human-centered, paying more attention to users of the AI system. HEIs should create knowledgeable and collaborative teams, invest in staff training, address ethical and legal concerns and carry out cost-benefit analysis. Furthermore, there is a need for continued research, collaboration and open communication among educational leaders, legislators, and AI experts. This collaborative approach is necessary to develop well-informed policies and innovative implementation strategies that overcome the challenges of AI while benefiting from its considerable potential.

REFERENCES

Abdullahi, I., & Yusoff, W. Z. W. (2019). *Influence of Facilities Performance on Student's Satisfaction in Northern Nigerian Universities*. Facilities. doi:10.1108/F-08-2017-0088

Açıkgöz, Y., Davison, K. H., Compagnone, M., & Laske, M. M. (2020). Justice Perceptions of Artificial Intelligence in Selection. *International Journal of Selection and Assessment*, *28*(4), 399–416. doi:10.1111/ijsa.12306

Agarwal, N., Kumar, S., Anand, S. K., Dharwal, M., & Vatsa, M. (2022). Artificial Intelligence and Higher Education Institutions. *Proceedings - 2022 International Conference on Smart and Sustainable Technologies in Energy and Power Sectors, SSTEPS 2022*, (pp. 185–187). IEEE. 10.1109/SSTEPS57475.2022.00055

Ahmad, S. F., Alam, M. M., Rahmat, M. K., Mubarik, M. S., & Hyder, S. I. (2022). Academic and Administrative Role of Artificial Intelligence in Education. In Sustainability (Switzerland), 14(3). MDPI. doi:10.3390/su14031101

Ali, M., Naeem, S., & Bhatti, R. (2020, September). Bin, & Bhatti, R. (2020). Artificial Intelligence Tools and Perspectives of University Librarians: An Overview. *Business Information Review*, *37*(3), 116–124. doi:10.1177/0266382120952016

Amariesta, T., Wardani, A. K., Adila, R. N., & Nurshiami, S. R. (2022). Implementation of Back Tracking Algorithm in the Scheduling of Mathematics Study Program Faculty of MIPA Unsoed. *Operations Research International Conference Series*. IEEE. 10.47194/orics.v3i3.129

Angelini, E., Wolf, A., Wijk, H., Brisby, H., & Baranto, A. (2021). The Impact of Implementing a Person-Centred Pain Management Intervention on Resistance to Change and Organizational Culture. *BMC Health Services Research*, *21*(1), 1323. doi:10.1186/s12913-021-06819-0 PMID:34895215

Ångström, R. C., Björn, M., Dahlander, L., Mähring, M., & Wallin, M. W. (2023). Getting AI Implementation Right: Insights from a Global Survey. *California Management Review*, *66*(1), 5–22. doi:10.1177/00081256231190430

Aristovnik, A., Keržič, D., Ravšelj, D., Tomaževič, N., & Umek, L. (2020). Impacts of the COVID-19 pandemic on life of higher education students: A global perspective. *Sustainability (Basel)*, *12*(20), 1–34. doi:10.3390/su12208438

Asatiani, A., Malo, P., Nagbøl, P. R., Penttinen, E., Rinta-Kahila, T., & Salovaara, A. (2021). Sociotechnical Envelopment of Artificial Intelligence: An Approach to Organizational Deployment of Inscrutable Artificial Intelligence Systems. *Journal of the Association for Information Systems*, *22*(2), 325–352. doi:10.17705/1jais.00664

Askary, S., Abu-Ghazaleh, N., & Tahat, Y. (2018). *Artificial Intelligence and Reliability of Accounting Information*. doi:10.1007/978-3-030-02131-3_28

Aydın, E., & Turan, M. (2023). An AI-Based Shortlisting Model for Sustainability of Human Resource Management. *Sustainability (Basel)*, *15*(3), 2737. doi:10.3390/su15032737

Baakeel, O. A. (2020). The Association Between the Effectiveness of Human Resource Management Functions and the Use of Artificial Intelligence. *International Journal of Advanced Trends in Computer Science and Engineering*. doi:10.30534/ijatcse/2020/9891.12020

Baviskar, D., Ahirrao, S., Potdar, V., & Kotecha, K. (2021). *Efficient Automated Processing of the Unstructured Documents Using Artificial Intelligence: A Systematic Literature Review and Future Directions*. IEEE. doi:10.1109/ACCESS.2021.3072900

Bérubé, M., Giannelia, T., & Vial, G. (2021). *Barriers to the Implementation of AI in Organizations: Findings from a Delphi Study*. doi:10.24251/HICSS.2021.805

Biwer, F., Wiradhany, W., & Egbrink, M. G. A. (2021, April 23). oude, Hospers, H. J., Wasenitz, S., Jansen, W., & Bruin, A. B. H. de. (2021). Changes and Adaptations: How University Students Self-Regulate Their Online Learning During the COVID-19 Pandemic. *Frontiers in Psychology*, *12*, 642593. doi:10.3389/fpsyg.2021.642593 PMID:33967903

Brock, J. K., & von Wangenheim, F. (2019). Demystifying AI: What Digital Transformation Leaders Can Teach You About Realistic Artificial Intelligence. *California Management Review*, *61*(4), 110–134. doi:10.1177/1536504219865226

Bubinger, H., & Dinneen, J. D. (2021). *Actionable Approaches to Promote Ethical AI in Libraries*. Algorithm Watch. https://inventory.algorithmwatch.org/

BudachL.FeuerpfeilM.IhdeN.NathansenA.NoackN.PatzlaffH.NaumannF. HarmouchH. (2022). *The Effects of Data Quality on Machine Learning Performance*. http://arxiv.org/abs/2207.14529

Çalışkan, A., Bryson, J. J., & Narayanan, A. (2017). Semantics Derived Automatically From Language Corpora Contain Human-Like Biases. *Science*, *356*(6334), 183–186. Advance online publication. doi:10.1126/science.aal4230 PMID:28408601

Chan, R. Y. (2016). *Understanding The Purpose Of Higher Education: An Analysis Of The Economic And Social Benefits For Completing A College Degree, 6*(5).

Chen, L., Chen, P., & Lin, Z. (2020). *Artificial Intelligence in Education: A Review*. IEEE Access. doi:10.1109/ACCESS.2020.2988510

Chopra, A. (2019). *AI in Supply & Procurement*. AICAI. . doi:10.1109/AICAI.2019.8701357

Cox, A. (2022). The rise of AI: Implications and applications of artificial intelligence in academic libraries (ACRL publications in librarianship, no. 78). *Journal of the Australian Library and Information Association, 71*(3), 300–302. doi:10.1080/24750158.2022.2103917

Dagumboy, E. (2022). ECD-IMC: An integrated marketing communications model for selected Philippine higher education institutions. [Indonesian Journal of Communications Studies]. *Jurnal Studi Komunikasi, 6*(3), 719–738. doi:10.25139/jsk.v6i3.4502

Dasanayaka, C. H., Abeykoon, C., Ranaweera, R. A. A. S., & Koswatte, I. (2021). The impact of the performance appraisal process on job satisfaction of the academic staff in higher educational institutions. *Education Sciences, 11*(10), 623. doi:10.3390/educsci11100623

Enholm, I. M., Papagiannidis, E., Mikalef, P., & Krogstie, J. (2021). Artificial Intelligence and Business Value: A Literature Review. *Information Systems Frontiers*. doi:10.1007/s10796-021-10186-w

Faggella, D., & Bharadwaj, R. (2019). *Getting Started with AI-Proven Best Practices for AI Adoption-for IT and Strategy Consultants Emerj Artificial Intelligence Research*.

Fernández, V., & Gallardo-Gallardo, E. (2020). Tackling the HR Digitalization Challenge: Key Factors and Barriers to HR Analytics Adoption. *Competitiveness Review an International Business Journal Incorporating Journal of Global Competitiveness*. doi:10.1108/CR-12-2019-0163

Fernández-Caramés, T. M., & Fraga-Lamas, P. (2019). Towards Next Generation Teaching, Learning, and Context-Aware Applications for Higher Education: A Review on Blockchain, IoT, Fog and Edge Computing Enabled Smart Campuses and Universities. *Applied Sciences (Basel, Switzerland), 9*(21), 4479. doi:10.3390/app9214479

Furey, H., & Martin, F. (2019). AI education matters. *AI Matters, 4*(4), 13–15. doi:10.1145/3299758.3299764

Gao, S., Low, S. P., & Lim, X. (2023). Prospects, Drivers of and Barriers to Artificial Intelligence Adoption In project Management. *Built Environment Project and Asset Management, 13*(5), 629–645. doi:10.1108/BEPAM-12-2022-0195

Górak-Sosnowska, K., & Piwowar-Sulej, K. (2023). *The Well-Being of Female Administrative Staff in Managerial Positions in Polish Higher Education Institutions*. Central European Management Journal., doi:10.1108/CEMJ-12-2021-0151

Green, B. P. (2018). Ethical reflections on artificial intelligence. *Scientia et Fides, 6*(2), 9–31. doi:10.12775/SetF.2018.015

Hannan, E. (2021). AI: New Source of Competitiveness in Higher Education. *Competitiveness Review an International Business Journal Incorporating Journal of Global Competitiveness*. doi:10.1108/CR-03-2021-0045

Hassan, S. A. A. (2021). The Impact of Artificial Intelligence on the Accounting Profession in the Tourism Sector in Egypt. *International Journal of Applied Research, 7*(6), 319–328. doi:10.22271/allresearch.2021.v7.i6e.8716

Hernández-Blanco, A., Herrera-Flores, B., Tomás, D., & Navarro-Colorado, B. (2019). A Systematic Review of Deep Learning Approaches to Educational Data Mining. *Complexity, 2019*, 1–22. doi:10.1155/2019/1306039

Herremans, D. (2021). *aiSTROM -- A roadmap for developing a successful AI strategy*. doi:10.1109/ACCESS.2021.3127548

Ho, S. P. S., & Chow, M. Y. C. (2023). The Role of Artificial Intelligence in Consumers' Brand Preference for Retail Banks in Hong Kong. *Journal of Financial Services Marketing*. doi:10.1057/s41264-022-00207-3

Huang, M. H., & Rust, R. T. (2020). A Strategic Framework for Artificial Intelligence in Marketing. *Journal of the Academy of Marketing Science*. doi:10.1007/s11747-020-00749-9

Hunkenschroer, A. L., & Luetge, C. (2022). Ethics of AI-Enabled Recruiting and Selection: A Review and Research Agenda. In Journal of Business Ethics, 178(4). Springer Science and Business Media B.V. doi:10.1007/s10551-022-05049-6

Iqbal, M. S., Abd-Alrazaq, A., & Househ, M. (2022). *Artificial Intelligence Solutions to Detect Fraud in Healthcare Settings: A Scoping Review*. doi:10.3233/SHTI220649

Jadrić, M., Ćukušić, M., & Mijač, T. (2021). Relating Smart Governance as a University Feature to Students' University Perceptions. *Journal of Information and Organizational Sciences, 45*(1), 1–20. doi:10.31341/jios.45.1.1

Jahani, N., Sepehri, A., Vandchali, H. R., & Tirkolaee, E. B. (2021). Application of industry 4.0 in the procurement processes of supply chains: A systematic literature review. *Sustainability (Basel)*, *13*(14), 7520. doi:10.3390/su13147520

Jain, E., Chopra, T., & Sharma, S. K. (2023). *Reinventing Human Resource Management in the Era of Artificial Intelligence*. doi:10.4108/eai.16-12-2022.2326241

Jakoet-Salie, A., & Ramalobe, K. (2022). *The Digitalization of Learning and Teaching Practices in Higher Education Institutions During the Covid-19 Pandemic*. Teaching Public Administration., doi:10.1177/01447394221092275

JawaidS. A. (2023). *Artificial Intelligence With Respect to Cyber Security*. https:// doi.org/ doi:10.20944/preprints202304.0923.v1

Jöhnk, J., Weißert, M., & Wyrtki, K. (2020). Ready or Not, AI Comes— An Interview Study of Organizational AI Readiness Factors. *Business & Information Systems Engineering*. doi:10.1007/s12599-020-00676-7

Kamalov, F., Thabtah, F., & Gurrib, I. (2021). *Autocorrelation for Time Series With Linear Trend*. IEEE. doi:10.1109/3ICT53449.2021.9581809

Kaminski, M. E. (2022). Regulating the Risks of AI. SSRN *Electronic Journal*. doi:10.2139/ssrn.4195066

Kazim, E., & Koshiyama, A. (2021). A High-Level Overview of AI Ethics. *Patterns (New York, N.Y.)*, *2*(9), 100314. Advance online publication. doi:10.1016/j.patter.2021.100314 PMID:34553166

Kim, J. (2019). Case Study About Efficient AI(Artificial Intelligence) Implementation Strategy. *International Journal of Advanced Research in Big Data Management System*. doi:10.21742/IJARBMS.2019.3.2.01

Kindzeka, K. C. (2023). Impact of Artificial Intelligence on Accounting, Auditing and Financial Reporting. *American Journal of Computing and Engineering*. doi:10.47672/ajce.1433

Köchling, A., Wehner, M. C., & Warkocz, J. (2022). Can I Show My Skills? Affective Responses to Artificial Intelligence in the Recruitment Process. *Review of Managerial Science*. doi:10.1007/s11846-021-00514-4

Kumar, V. V. R., & Raman, R. (2022). Artificial Intelligence (AI) as a computerized decision aid for selection of candidates in higher education. *2022 IEEE Integrated STEM Education Conference. ISEC*, *439–443*, 439–443. doi:10.1109/ISEC54952.2022.10025234

Kurysheva, A., van Rijen, H. V. M., & Dilaver, G. (2019). How Do Admission Committees Select? Do Applicants Know How They Select? Selection Criteria and Transparency at a Dutch University. *Tertiary Education and Management*, *25*(4), 367–388. Advance online publication. doi:10.1007/s11233-019-09050-z

Laato, S., Morschheuser, B., Hamari, J., & Bjorne, J. (2023). AI-Assisted Learning with ChatGPT and Large Language Models: Implications for Higher Education. *Proceedings - 2023 IEEE International Conference on Advanced Learning Technologies, ICALT 2023*, (pp. 226–230). IEEE. 10.1109/ICALT58122.2023.00072

Leimanis, A., & Palkova, K. (2021). Ethical Guidelines for Artificial Intelligence in Healthcare From the Sustainable Development Perspective. *European Journal of Sustainable Development*, *10*(1), 90. doi:10.14207/ejsd.2021.v10n1p90

LelliF. (2022). *On Exploring the Possibilities and the Limits of AI for an Interoperable and Empowering Industry 4.0*. doi:10.20944/preprints202202.0109.v1

Li, R., Wang, Y., & Zou, J. (2022). Research on the Transformation From Financial Accounting to Management Accounting Based on Drools Rule Engine. *Computational Intelligence and Neuroscience*, *2022*, 1–8. doi:10.1155/2022/9445776 PMID:35498191

Librarian, A., & Chakravarty, R. (2021). *Implementing Conversation al AI in Libraries: A practical approach Subhajit Panda*.

Mahligawati, F., Allanas, E., Butarbutar, M. H., & Nordin, N. A. N. (2023). Artificial Intelligence in Physics Education: A Comprehensive Literature Review. *Journal of Physics: Conference Series*, *2596*(1), 012080. doi:10.1088/1742-6596/2596/1/012080

Malik, A., Thevisuthan, P., & De Sliva, T. (2022). *Artificial Intelligence*. Employee Engagement, Experience, and HRM., doi:10.1007/978-3-030-90955-0_16

Marín Díaz, G., Galán Hernández, J. J., & Galdón Salvador, J. L. (2023). Analyzing Employee Attrition Using Explainable AI for Strategic HR Decision-Making. *Mathematics*, *11*(22), 4677. doi:10.3390/math11224677

Martínez-Plumed, F., Gómez, E., & Hernández-Orallo, J. (2021). Futures of artificial intelligence through technology readiness levels. *Telematics and Informatics*, *58*, 101525. doi:10.1016/j.tele.2020.101525

Marzouk, M., & Zaher, M. (2020). Artificial intelligence exploitation in facility management using deep learning. *Construction Innovation*, *20*(4), 609–624. doi:10.1108/CI-12-2019-0138

Mckie, I. A. S., & Narayan, B. (2019). Enhancing the Academic Library Experience with Chatbots: An Exploration of Research and Implications for Practice. *Journal of the Australian Library and Information Association*, *68*(3), 268–277. doi:10.1080/24750158.2019.1611694

MIT. (2023). AI pilot programs look to reduce energy use and emissions on MIT campus. *MIT News*. Massachusetts Institute of Technology. https://news.mit.edu/2023/ai-pilot-programs-look-reduce-energy-use-emissions-mit-campus-0908

Modgil, S., Singh, R., & Hannibal, C. (2021). Artificial Intelligence for Supply Chain Resilience: Learning From Covid-19. *International Journal of Logistics Management*. doi:10.1108/IJLM-02-2021-0094

Munz, P., Hennick, M., & Stewart, J. (2023). Maximizing AI Reliability Through Anticipatory Thinking and Model Risk Audits. *AI Magazine*, *44*(2), 173–184. doi:10.1002/aaai.12099

Murphy, K., Di Ruggiero, E., Upshur, R., Willison, D. J., Malhotra, N., Cai, J., Malhotra, N., Lui, V., & Gibson, J. L. (2021). Artificial Intelligence for Good Health: A Scoping Review of the Ethics Literature. *BMC Medical Ethics*, *22*(1), 14. Advance online publication. doi:10.1186/s12910-021-00577-8 PMID:33588803

Naqvi, A. (2020). What Is Artificial Intelligence? In *Artificial Intelligence for Audit, Forensic Accounting, and Valuation* (pp. 37–49).

Ning, Y.-Z. (2023). Factors Affecting the Cost Savings Rate of University Procurement. *Archives of Business Research*, *11*(5), 21–27. doi:10.14738/abr.115.14540

Ore, O., & Sposato, M. (2021). Opportunities and Risks of Artificial Intelligence in Recruitment and Selection. *The International Journal of Organizational Analysis*. doi:10.1108/IJOA-07-2020-2291

Orr, D., & Luebcke, M. Schmidt, J., Philipp, Ebner, M., Wannemacher, K., Ebner, M., & Dohmen, D. (2020). *Higher Education Landscape 2030 A Trend Analysis Based on the AHEAD International Horizon Scanning*. Springer. https://www.springer.com/series/8914

Overgoor, G., Chica, M., Rand, W., & Weishampel, A. (2019). Letting the Computers Take Over: Using AI to Solve Marketing Problems. *California Management Review*, *61*(4), 156–185. doi:10.1177/0008125619859318

Owan, V. J., Abang, K. B., Idika, D. O., Etta, E. O., & Bassey, B. A. (2023). Exploring the potential of artificial intelligence tools in educational measurement and assessment. In Eurasia Journal of Mathematics, Science and Technology Education, 19(8). Modestum LTD. doi:10.29333/ejmste/13428

Pagallo, U., Sciolla, J. C., & Durante, M. (2022). *The Environmental Challenges of AI in EU Law: Lessons Learned From the Artificial Intelligence Act (AIA) With Its Drawbacks*. Transforming Government People Process and Policy. doi:10.1108/TG-07-2021-0121

Peng, L., Wei, W., Gong, Y., & Jia, R. (2022). University Library Space Renovation Based on the User Learning Experience in Two Wuhan Universities. *International Journal of Environmental Research and Public Health*, *19*(16), 10395. doi:10.3390/ijerph191610395 PMID:36012030

Pereira, V., & Gomes Costa, H. (2016). Linear integer model for the course timetabling problem of a faculty in rio de janeiro. *Advances in Operations Research*, *2016*, 1–9. doi:10.1155/2016/7597062

Perret, J. K., & Heitkamp, M. (2021). On the Potentials of Artificial Intelligence in Marketing – The Case of Robotic Process Automation. *International Journal of Applied Research in Management and Economics*. doi:10.33422/ijarme.v4i4.768

Peyravi, B., Nekrošienė, J., & Lobanova, L. (2020). Revolutionised technologies for marketing: Theoretical review with focus on artificial intelligence. *Business: Theory and Practice*, *21*(2), 827–834. doi:10.3846/btp.2020.12313

Phanichsiti, S., Thamnita, O., & Thipphayasaeng, P. (2023). Internet of Things and Big Data for a Sustainable Smart University. *Journal of Higher Education Theory and Practice*, *23*(2).

Pillai, R. (2019). Technology and Talent Analytics for Talent Management – A Game Changer for Organizational Performance. *The International Journal of Organizational Analysis*. doi:10.1108/IJOA-01-2019-1634

Plathottam, S. J., Rzonca, A., Lakhnori, R., & Iloeje, C. O. (2023). A review of artificial intelligence applications in manufacturing operations. *Journal of Advanced Manufacturing and Processing*, *5*(3), e10159. doi:10.1002/amp2.10159

Poole, D., & Mackworth, A. K. (2017). *Artificial Intelligence* (2nd ed.). Cambridge University Press., doi:10.1017/9781108164085

Prokop, E., Han, X. Y., Papyan, V., Donoho, D., & Johnson, C. Jr. (2021). AI and the Digitized Photoarchive: Promoting Access and Discoverability. *Art Documentation: Journal of the Art Libraries Society of North America, 40*(1), 1–20. doi:10.1086/714604

Qureshi, F. H., & Khawaja, S. (2021). THE GROWTH OF PRIVATE HIGHER EDUCATION: AN OVERVIEW IN THE CONTEXT OF LIBERALISATION, PRIVATISATION AND MARKETISATION. *European Journal of Education Studies, 8*(9). doi:10.46827/ejes.v8i9.3896

Rakhimbekova, B., Seisebayeva, R., & Abdigaliyeva, G. (2022). *Higher Education in Kazakhstan: Global Trends and State Policy*. Farabi Journal of Social Sciences., doi:10.26577/FJSS.2022.v8.i2.01

Reim, W., Åström, J., & Eriksson, O. (2020). Implementation of Artificial Intelligence (AI): A Roadmap for Business Model Innovation. In AI (Switzerland) (Vol. 1, Issue 2). Multidisciplinary Digital Publishing Institute (MDPI). doi:10.3390/ai1020011

Research Planning and Review Committee. (2022). Top trends in academic libraries A review of the trends and issues. *College & Research Libraries News, 83*(2).

Rezwana, J., & Maher, M. Lou. (2022). *Identifying Ethical Issues in AI Partners in Human-Ai Co-Creation*. https://doi.org//arxiv.2204.07644 doi:10.48550

Rodrigues, R. (2020). Legal and human rights issues of AI: Gaps, challenges and vulnerabilities. *Journal of Responsible Technology, 4*, 100005. doi:10.1016/j.jrt.2020.100005

Rožman, M., Oreški, D., & Tominc, P. (2022). Integrating Artificial Intelligence Into a Talent Management Model to Increase the Work Engagement and Performance of Enterprises. *Frontiers in Psychology, 13*, 1014434. Advance online publication. doi:10.3389/fpsyg.2022.1014434 PMID:36506984

Rudolf, G., & Grünbichler, R. (2023). Implementation Barriers of Artificial Intelligence in Companies. *International Odyssey: Conference on Economics and Business*. IEEE. https://doi.org/10.22598/odyssey/2023.5

Sai, B., Thanigaivelu, S., Shivaani, N., Shyamala Babu, C. S., & Ramaa, A. (2022). Integration of Chatbots in the Procurement Stage of a Supply Chain. *6th IEEE International Conference on Computational System and Information Technology for Sustainable Solutions, CSITSS 2022*. IEEE. 10.1109/CSITSS57437.2022.10026367

Saraswat, D., Bhattacharya, P., Verma, A., Prasad, V. K., Tanwar, S., Sharma, G., Bokoro, P. N., & Sharma, R. (2022). *Explainable AI for Healthcare 5.0: Opportunities and Challenges*. IEEE. doi:10.1109/ACCESS.2022.3197671

Schemmer, M., Hemmer, P. H. J., Kühl, N., Benz, C., & Satzger, G. (2022). *Should I Follow AI-based Advice? Measuring Appropriate Reliance in Human-Ai Decision-Making*. https://doi.org//arxiv.2204.06916 doi:10.48550

Selenko, E., Bankins, S., Shoss, M. K., Warburton, J., & Restubog, S. L. D. (2022). Artificial Intelligence and the Future of Work: A Functional-Identity Perspective. *Current Directions in Psychological Science*, *31*(3), 272–279. doi:10.1177/09637214221091823

Sethi, K., Chauhan, S. S., & Jaiswal, V. (2021). *Artificial Intelligence in Higher Education*. Springer. doi:10.4018/978-1-7998-4763-2.ch001

Sharma, A. K., Pareta, A., Meena, J., & Sharma, R. (2022). A long term impact of artificial intelligence and robotics on higher education. *Proceedings - IEEE International Conference on Advances in Computing, Communication and Applied Informatics, ACCAI 2022*. IEEE. 10.1109/ACCAI53970.2022.9752633

Sharma, G. (2021). A literature review on application of Artificial Intelligence in Human Resource Management and its practices in current organizational scenario. *Proceedings of the 5th International Conference on I-SMAC (IoT in Social, Mobile, Analytics and Cloud), I-SMAC 2021*, (pp. 594–600). IEEE. 10.1109/I-SMAC52330.2021.9640954

Siler, E. (2019). Collection Development and Management for 21st Century Library Collections: An Introduction. *Technical Services Quarterly*, *36*(4), 426–427. doi:10.1080/07317131.2019.1664121

SlimiZ. (2021). *The Impact of AI Implementation in Higher Education on Educational Process Future: A Systematic Review*. https://doi.org/ doi:10.21203/rs.3.rs-1081043/v1

Snyder, H. (2019). Literature review as a research methodology: An overview and guidelines. *Journal of Business Research*, *104*, 333–339. https://doi.org/https://doi.org/10.1016/j.jbusres.2019.07.039. doi:10.1016/j.jbusres.2019.07.039

Subaveerapandiyan, A. (2023). *Application of Artificial Intelligence (AI) In Libraries and Its Impact on Library Operations Review*. https://digitalcommons.unl.edu/libphilprac

Suh, W., & Ahn, S. (2022). Development and Validation of a Scale Measuring Student Attitudes Toward Artificial Intelligence. *SAGE Open*, *12*(2). doi:10.1177/21582440221100463

Svitlana, T., Vasylyk, A., & Olga, B. (2022). Artificial Intelligence in HR: Practices and Prospects of the Spread in Ukraine. *The Eurasia Proceedings of Science Technology Engineering and Mathematics*. doi:10.55549/epstem.1176076

Taddeo, M., & Floridi, L. (2018). How AI can be a force for good. *Science*, *361*(6404), 751–752. doi:10.1126/science.aat5991 PMID:30139858

Tian, X., Pavur, R., Han, H., & Zhang, L. (2022). A Machine Learning-Based Human Resources Recruitment System for Business Process Management: Using LSA, BERT and SVM. *Business Process Management Journal*. doi:10.1108/BPMJ-08-2022-0389

Tian, Y., & Zhang, Y. (2022). Evaluation of Accounting Data of Water Company Based on Combination Model. *Scientific Programming*, *2022*, 1–9. doi:10.1155/2022/3373420

Toutain, O., Jabbouri, R., & Truong, Y. (2023). Artificial intelligence and the transformation of management education. *Management International*, *27*(2), 119–132. doi:10.59876/a-kthz-pbf0

Tzachor, A., Whittlestone, J., Sundaram, L., & hÉigeartaigh, S. (2020). Artificial intelligence in a crisis needs ethics with urgency. In *Nature Machine Intelligence*, *2*(7). Nature Research. doi:10.1038/s42256-020-0195-0

UNESCO. (2022). HIGHER EDUCATION GLOBAL. *Data Report*.

Vasconcelos, M. A. R., & dos Santos, R. P. (2023). Enhancing STEM learning with ChatGPT and Bing Chat as objects to think with: A case study. *Eurasia Journal of Mathematics, Science and Technology Education*, *19*(7), em2296. doi:10.29333/ejmste/13313

Venusamy, K., Krishnan Rajagopal, N., & Yousoof, M. (2020). A study of human resources development through chatbots using artificial intelligence. *Proceedings of the 3rd International Conference on Intelligent Sustainable Systems, ICISS 2020*, (pp. 94–99). IEEE. 10.1109/ICISS49785.2020.9315881

Vorobeva, D., El Fassi, Y., Pinto, D. C., Hildebrand, D., Herter, M. M., & Mattila, A. S. (2022). Thinking Skills Don't Protect Service Workers From Replacement by Artificial Intelligence. *Journal of Service Research*, *25*(4), 601–613. doi:10.1177/10946705221104312

Walter, S., & Lankes, R. D. (2015). The innovation agenda. In College and Research Libraries, 76(7). Association of College and Research Libraries. doi:10.5860/crl.76.7.854

Wang, K., Lu, L., Fang, J., Xing, Y., Tong, Z., & Wang, L. (2023). The Downside of Artificial Intelligence (AI) in Green Choices: How AI Recommender Systems Decrease Green Consumption. *MDE. Managerial and Decision Economics*, *44*(6), 3346–3353. doi:10.1002/mde.3882

Wang, Q. (2023). The Impact of COVID-19 on the Development of Online Education in Higher Education. *Journal of Education Humanities and Social Sciences*. doi:10.54097/ehss.v8i.4612

Weber, M., Engert, M., Schaffer, N., Weking, J., & Krcmar, H. (2022). Organizational Capabilities for AI Implementation—Coping With Inscrutability and Data Dependency in AI. *Information Systems Frontiers*. doi:10.1007/s10796-022-10297-y

Wheatley, A., & Hervieux, S. (2020). Artificial intelligence in academic libraries: An environmental scan. *Information Services & Use*, *39*(4), 347–356. doi:10.3233/ISU-190065

Williamson, B. (2020). Making Markets Through Digital Platforms: Pearson, Edu-Business, and the (E)valuation of Higher Education. *Critical Studies in Education*. doi:10.1080/17508487.2020.1737556

Winfield, A. F. T., & Jirotka, M. (2018). Ethical Governance Is Essential to Building Trust in Robotics and Artificial Intelligence Systems. *Philosophical Transactions. Series A, Mathematical, Physical, and Engineering Sciences*, *376*(2133), 20180085. doi:10.1098/rsta.2018.0085 PMID:30323000

Wu, C., & Monfort, A. (2022). Role of Artificial Intelligence in Marketing Strategies and Performance. *Psychology and Marketing*. doi:10.1002/mar.21737

Xia, X., & Li, X. (2022). Artificial Intelligence for Higher Education Development and Teaching Skills. *Wireless Communications and Mobile Computing*, *2022*, 1–10. doi:10.1155/2022/7614337

Yang, X., Hao-wen, L. I., Ni, L., & Li, T. (2021). Application of Artificial Intelligence in Precision Marketing. *Journal of Organizational and End User Computing*, *33*(4), 209–219. doi:10.4018/JOEUC.20210701.oa10

Yousefi, M., & Abdullah, A. G. K. (2019). The Impact of Organizational Stressors on Job Performance Among Academic Staff. *International Journal of Instruction*, *12*(3), 561–576. doi:10.29333/iji.2019.12334a

Zadorozhnyi, Z. M., Muravskyi, V., Pochynok, N., Muravskyi, V., Shevchuk, A., & Majda, M. (2023). Application of Chatbots with Artificial Intelligence in Accounting. *2023 13th International Conference on Advanced Computer Information Technologies, ACIT 2023 - Proceedings*, (pp. 196–200). IEEE. 10.1109/ACIT58437.2023.10275395

Zawacki-Richter, O., Marín, V. I., Bond, M., & Gouverneur, F. (2019). Systematic review of research on artificial intelligence applications in higher education – where are the educators? In International Journal of Educational Technology in Higher Education, 16(1). Springer Netherlands. doi:10.1186/s41239-019-0171-0

Zhang, Z., Zhou, X., Zhang, X., Wang, L., & Wang, P. (2018). A Model Based on Convolutional Neural Network for Online Transaction Fraud Detection. *Security and Communication Networks, 2018*, 1–9. doi:10.1155/2018/5680264

Zhu, D. (2020). *Research on the Transformation From Financial Accounting to Management Accounting in the Age of Artificial Intelligence*. Probe - Accounting Auditing and Taxation., doi:10.18686/aat.v2i2.1335

Zhu, K., Li, L. D., & Li, M. (2021). School Timetabling Optimisation Using Artificial Bee Colony Algorithm Based on a Virtual Searching Space Method. *Mathematics, 10*(1), 73. doi:10.3390/math10010073

Chapter 7
AI-Powered Teaching Plan:
Present and Post Evaluation

Janaki Sivakumar
https://orcid.org/0000-0003-0412-1515
Global College of Engineering and Technology, Oman

Khoula Al Harthy
Global College of Engineering and Technology, Oman

ABSTRACT

This chapter discusses AI-powered teaching and learning in Higher education. The main objective of this chapter is to examine the process of AI-powered teaching and Learning in Plan, Progress, and post-evaluation. Also, the chapter discusses major components involved in AI-powered teaching, the evolution of AI-powered learning, and various cutting-edge technologies used in teaching and learning major areas. Opportunities and challenges in incorporating AI-powered teaching have also been discussed. Case studies were analyzed to evaluate the power of AI-based teaching and learning. Implications of using AI in higher education in terms of psychology, social, cultural, and ethical aspects have been discussed in detail. Finally, this chapter also discusses recommendations to policymakers to navigate challenges

INTRODUCTION

The landscape of education is changing. Our educational system has undergone numerous changes as a result of the pandemic, including a greater dependence on technology and the use of remote and hybrid learning. Artificial intelligence then emerged, greatly improving the effectiveness and efficiency of our educational

DOI: 10.4018/979-8-3693-2145-4.ch007

system. Artificial intelligence (AI) refers to the development of computer systems capable of doing activities that would normally need human intelligence. These tasks include learning, thinking, problem-solving, vision, language comprehension, and even interacting with the environment (Creamer, 2012). AI technologies aim to simulate and replicate human cognitive abilities, allowing machines to adapt and improve over time.

In the rapidly evolving landscape of education, Artificial Intelligence (AI) is playing an increasingly prominent role in reshaping the way we teach and learn as in Figure 1.

Figure 1. AI in teaching
(Authors)

AI-powered teaching leverages advanced technologies to enhance the educational experience, making it more personalized, adaptive, and efficient (Picciano, 2017). This transformative approach holds the potential to revolutionize traditional teaching methods and address the diverse needs of students.

This book chapter mainly focuses on AI-powered teaching and Learning which includes, the History of AI in Teaching, Components of AI-powered teaching, the 3 P's (Plan, Progress, and Post evaluation) of AI-powered teaching and learning journey with its benefits, Challenges, and Opportunities, analyzing the impact in Higher Education through case studies, Particularly, the impact of AI in IT majors, implications of AI-powered teaching and learning such as Psychological, Social, Cultural and Ethical, Cutting edge technologies that support the future of AI-powered teaching, Recommendations to Policymakers to navigate the challenges and key areas to be concentrated in future of AI-powered teaching. All the above sections are reviewed, and evaluated, and in-depth information has been provided in line with the goals of this chapter.

EVOLUTION OF AI IN TEACHING: A COMPREHENSIVE HISTORICAL OVERVIEW

The integration of AI in teaching has witnessed transformative changes, influencing instructional methodologies, personalization, and educational accessibility. The term "artificial intelligence" was initially coined by John McCarthy at the Dartmouth Conference in 1956, which marked the beginning of AI in education. Early AI programs, such as the General Problem Solver, laid the groundwork for problem-solving approaches in education. Notable researchers during this period include Marvin Minsky, Allen Newell, and Herbert A. Simon (Casal-Otero et al., 2023).

The 1980s marked the emergence of expert systems and Intelligent Tutoring Systems (ITS). Expert systems aimed to replicate the decision-making processes of human experts, while ITS, exemplified by systems like the Geometry Tutor, introduced personalized instruction and feedback (Picciano, 2017). The late 1990s witnessed the growth of online education platforms, setting the stage for future AI applications. While not initially AI-driven, these platforms laid the groundwork for the integration of AI into educational technologies (Moore, 2007).

The 2010s saw a surge in the integration of AI into personalized learning platforms, with companies like Knewton and Dream Box utilizing AI to adapt content based on individual student needs. Massive Open Online Courses (MOOCs) gained prominence, incorporating AI for features such as automated grading and adaptive learning. Virtual classrooms and AI-powered chatbots became prevalent in the 2010s, providing students with interactive and automated support. These technologies aimed to enhance engagement and support students in real-time (Floridi et al., 2018).

Institutions started using predictive analytics and learning analytics, powered by AI, to identify at-risk students and provide timely interventions. AI-driven NLP technologies have been employed in language learning applications, offering more natural and interactive language instruction. AI has been used in assessments, including automated grading and the development of adaptive assessments that adjust difficulty based on student performance. As of the latest research, AI continues to advance in teaching applications, with a focus on natural language processing, emotion recognition, and augmented reality. Predictive analytics and learning analytics are increasingly used to identify at-risk students and provide timely interventions (Pratama et al., 2023). The below-listed Figure 2 describes current tools available to enhance AI-powered teaching in the evolution process.

Figure 2. Tools available for AI-powered education
(Authors)

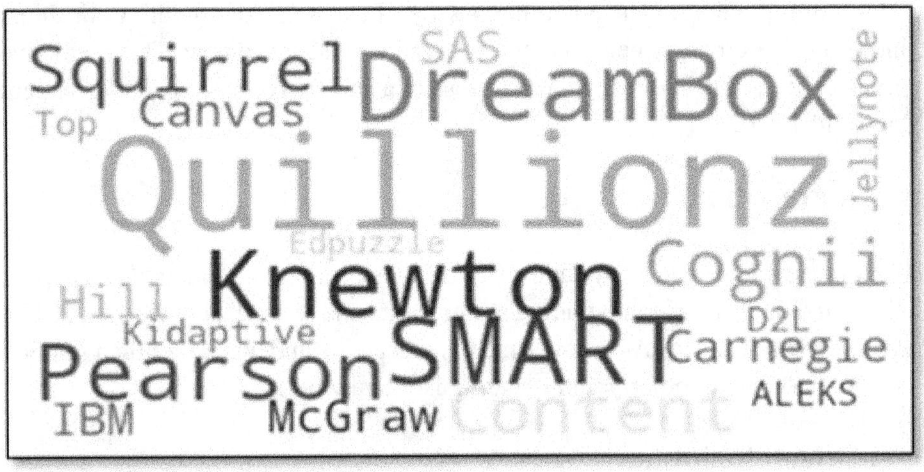

COMPONENTS OF AI-POWERED TEACHING

Since technology has been incorporated into classrooms around the globe, traditional teaching methods are changing. In recent years, the integration of AI in education has gained significant attention due to its potential to revolutionize traditional teaching methods. The incorporation of Artificial Intelligence (AI) has started to transform the way educators produce educational materials.

Adaptive Learning Systems

AI algorithms analyze student performance data to identify strengths and weaknesses, allowing for the adaptation of learning materials to individual needs (Peng et al., 2019). This personalized approach ensures that students receive content tailored to their proficiency levels, thereby maintaining their interest and engagement.

Intelligent Tutoring Systems

These systems use AI to provide immediate feedback and assistance to students, simulating one-on-one interactions with a tutor. By identifying and addressing misconceptions in real-time, intelligent tutoring systems keep students actively involved in the learning process (Manju G,2020).

Predictive Analytics

AI algorithms predict student outcomes based on historical data, enabling educators to intervene proactively when students are at risk of disengagement. This predictive approach allows for timely support and fosters a supportive learning environment (Manikandan, 2023).

Task Automation

AI learning systems can easily automate responsibilities like timetables, keeping track of attendance, and even grading assignments and tests (Tjahyadi et al., 2017). Automating these tasks gives more time to dedicate to students rather than grading papers or performing other pointless administrative work.

Data-Driven Insights

AI collects and analyzes massive volumes of data, providing educators with useful insights into student performance patterns (Bard, 2021). Using these insights, educators can improve their teaching practices to better suit the requirements of their students, resulting in more engaging and efficient learning.

A study conducted by Xie et al. (2019) demonstrated a significant increase in student engagement and academic performance when an AI-powered adaptive learning system was implemented in a high school mathematics class (Chiu et al., 2023). Smith and Johnson (2020) found that intelligent tutoring systems led to higher retention rates and increased engagement, particularly in STEM subjects, compared to traditional teaching methods (Liang et al., 2021).

A HOLISTIC JOURNEY THROUGH THE PLAN, PROGRESS, AND POST-EVALUATION PHASES OF AI-POWERED TEACHING AND LEARNING

A well-structured plan, continuous progress monitoring, and thorough post-evaluation are crucial for the effective blending of AI-based teaching methods in education. Successful AI integration begins with thoughtful planning by considering the following aspects: Curriculum alignment, Infrastructure, and Professional Development. The effective progress in terms of delivery of AI-powered teaching involves creating engaging and adaptive learning environments while presenting the curriculum to students (Chen et al., 2020). During curriculum delivery, personalized learning paths, collaborative discussions, and real-time feedback are considered as steppingstones of success. Monitoring and assessing the effectiveness of AI-powered teaching are critical for ongoing refinement in post evaluation stage (Saputra et al., 2023). These three stages are depicted in Figure 3.

Figure 3. Three Ps of AI-powered teaching and learning
(Authors)

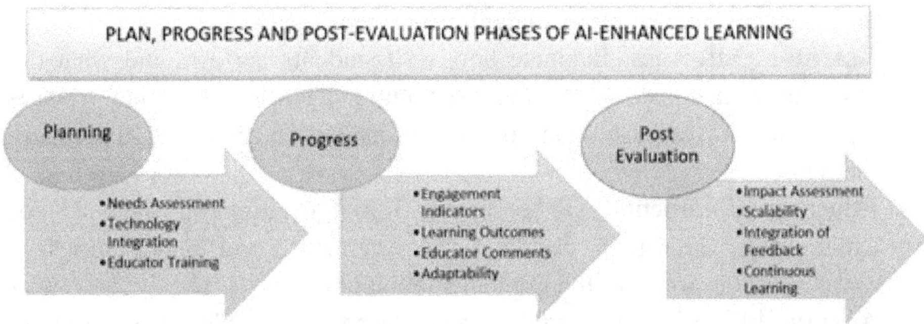

PLANNING

A strategy plan is needed to use artificial intelligence tools to improve the educational experience while implementing AI-based teaching (Chen et al., 2020). The following crucial components should be included in the plan:

- **Needs Assessment:** Determine the particular difficulties and needs in schooling that AI can help with. This includes awareness of the learning outcomes, topic areas, and the intended audience.
- **Technology Integration:** Provide a strong foundation for AI-based education by integrating analytics tools, Student learning management systems, and AI tools.
- **Curriculum Design:** Describe the process by which artificial intelligence will be included in the curriculum. Determine how AI can support traditional methods of teaching including adaptive testing, real-time feedback, and personalized learning.
- **Educator Training:** To introduce educators to AI technologies and methods and offer them extensive training programs. Tutorials on data analysis, planning lessons using AI, and adapting to new learning environments are included in the course.

PROGRESS

Tracking the execution of the strategy and assessing its effects on how students are taught and learned are necessary for AI-based education (Saputra et al., 2023). Important elements of a progress analysis consist of:

- **Engagement Indicators:** To determine areas for improvement and assess the degree of engagement, analyze data on the use of AI technologies, including the frequency and length of student interactions.
- **Learning Outcomes:** Evaluate how well students perform and what they have learned in comparison to more conventional teaching techniques. Assess the efficacy of AI-based solutions using qualitative as well as quantitative metrics.
- **Educator Comments:** Gather input from educators on their AI tool experiences. Determine obstacles, achievements, and opportunities for development to improve the implementation plan.
- **Adaptability:** Assess how well AI-based teaching strategies adjust to a range of subjects, academic levels, and learning preferences. Determine scalable strategies and best practices for wider implementation (Kabudi et al., 2021).

POST-EVALUATION

To ensure ongoing improvement and refine techniques, a post-evaluation phase follows the initial implementation (Bull et al., 2016). A post-evaluation's essential components include:

- **Impact Assessment:** Perform a thorough analysis of the general effects of AI-based instruction on the output, involvement, and satisfaction of students. Analyze long-term results about the initial predictions.
- **Scalability:** Find ways to expand the beneficial elements of AI integration to additional educational initiatives and establishments. Think about things like adaptability, infrastructural needs, and cost-effectiveness (Koedinger et al., 2013).
- **Integration of Feedback:** Future versions of the AI-based lesson plan should take into account input from educators, students, and other stakeholders. Resolve issues, improve tactics, and remain adaptable to the changing demands of education.
- **Continuous Learning:** Keep up with developments in AI technology and educational research to foster a culture of ongoing learning and development.

Revise the strategy and plan of action to take advantage of new opportunities and tackle fresh obstacles.

BENEFITS OF AI-POWERED TEACHING

To guarantee that every student is engaged and receives an education that is more tailored to their abilities and learning style. AI-powered teaching plans utilize advanced algorithms and data analytics to customize educational content, adapt to individual learning styles, and enhance overall student engagement. AI-powered lesson planning is intended to support, not replace a teacher.

a. Saves Time

Teachers spend a lot of time on routine duties that impede their ability to engage with pupils in the ways that like to. Since AI platforms automate duties for teachers, teachers can spend less time designing lessons or handling administrative tasks(Holmes et al.,2019). This can be a big time-saving tool. Teachers may spend less time on paperwork and more time getting to know their students and improving their learning experience by utilizing AI lesson planning tools.

b. Reachable

The accessibility of AI tools is one of their main benefits when used in the classroom. Regardless of a student's physical or mental capabilities, AI can suit their needs. It can help non-native English speakers, modify or convert information, help students with speech impairments, allow students with disabilities to interact with the content, and customize the content to meet the needs of every learner. All in all, its accessibility features guarantee a more inclusive learning environment for every student(Miao et al.,2021).

c. Boosts Involvement of Students

Using AI-powered lesson preparation tools will eliminate the need to constantly think of new ways to engage students (Bhardwaj et al., 2021). By customizing each student's learning experience to suit their unique interests and preferences, these tools can effectively increase student engagement. After it has some basic knowledge about each student, it can deliver engaging information, such as employing gaming components like leaderboards or badges to keep students motivated.

d. Produces Content Quickly

The capacity of AI systems to generate interesting educational content is a significant advantage. In addition to producing examinations, homework assignments, quizzes, and useful resources, it may also customize these items to meet the requirements and preferences of individual students and maintain alignment with the curriculum and learning objectives to make sure the course objectives are met. In the end, it can help by providing teachers with personalized educational resources that will improve students' education(Sheehy &Holliman,2017).

e. Personalized Learning

AI enables a tailored learning experience, accommodating diverse learning styles and preferences. This personalization enhances student engagement by catering to individual strengths and addressing specific challenges (Peng et al., 2019).

f. Real-time Feedback

Immediate feedback provided by AI systems helps students understand their progress, reinforcing positive behaviors and encouraging active participation. This timely feedback contributes to a more dynamic and engaging learning environment (Holmes et al.,2019).

g. Prompt Intervention

Using AI techniques to identify students suffering from a particular learning challenge or at risk of falling behind is another important aspect of early intervention. Artificial intelligence (AI)-powered solutions will employ algorithms to gather student data and then make recommendations about how best to support the learner, including suggesting certain resources or adjustments to make sure the learner can overcome obstacles (Lameras & Arnab, 2021).

CRUCIAL ASPECTS OF THE CHALLENGES AND OPPORTUNITIES OF AI-POWERED TEACHING

Integration of Artificial Intelligence (AI) in teaching holds tremendous potential for transforming education. AI-powered teaching holds great promise for revolutionizing education, but ensuring its effectiveness requires careful consideration.

Figure 4. Benefits of AI
(Authors)

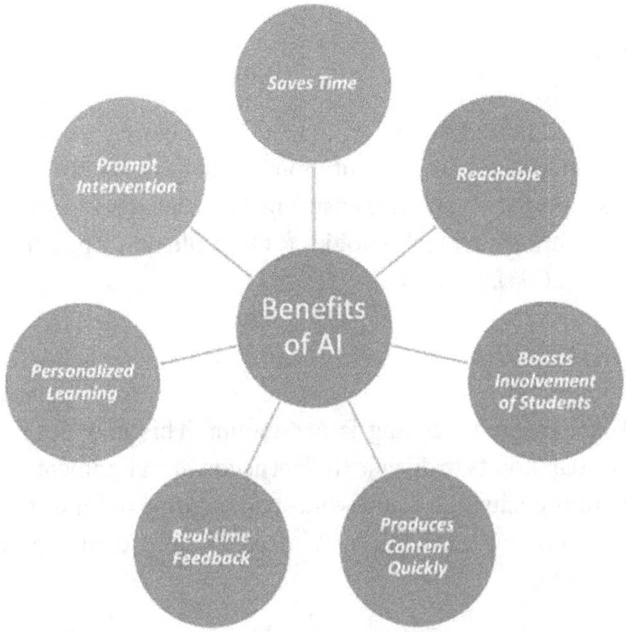

This topic critically examines the multifaceted crucial aspects that are shedding light on the challenges and opportunities of AI-powered teaching such as accessibility- accessible to all students, including those with diverse abilities, affordability- cost of implementing AI-powered teaching tools, achievability- ensuring successful integration of AI in teaching, and quality- accuracy of content delivery, adaptability to diverse student needs and alignment with educational needs (Su et al., 2023).

a) Accessibility

Ensuring that AI-powered teaching tools are accessible to all students, including those with diverse abilities, is essential. Universal Design for Learning (UDL) principles can be applied to create inclusive AI solutions that accommodate varied learning styles and needs (Moore, 2007).

b) Affordability

The cost of implementing AI-powered teaching tools can pose a barrier to widespread adoption, especially in resource-constrained environments. Policymakers and educators need to explore cost-effective solutions and sustainable funding models to make AI-enhanced education accessible (Lane, 2017).

c) Achievability

Achieving successful integration of AI in teaching requires overcoming resistance to change, both from educators and institutions. Professional development programs and continuous support are crucial for ensuring that teachers are adequately prepared and motivated to embrace AI technologies ("Oversold and Underused: Computers in the Classroom," 2004).

d) Quality

The quality of AI-powered teaching is paramount. This includes the accuracy of content delivery, adaptability to diverse student needs, and alignment with educational objectives. Rigorous evaluation frameworks and ongoing monitoring are necessary to maintain and improve the quality of AI-driven educational experiences (Felipe Redondo et al., 2015).

CASE STUDY ANALYSIS TO EVALUATE THE IMPACT OF AI-POWERED TEACHING AND LEARNING IN HIGHER EDUCATION

Case Study One: ChatGPT in education—A blessing or a curse? A qualitative study exploring early adopters' utilization and perceptions, November 2023 (Hadi Mogavi et al., 2024)

The study used APIs from Twitter Reddit, YouTube, and LinkedIn to collect data on ChatGPT usage in education. This study analyzes data from December 1st, 2022, to April 22nd, 2023, five months after the official public release of ChatGPT. It includes 6000 text samples comprising around 150,000 words. The results of the investigation are divided into two categories based on the research questions presented: (1) identifying the most common uses of ChatGPT in education, and (2) exploring various viewpoints on ChatGPT's utility in education by suggesting the rate with which a topic appears over the content evaluations. ChatGPT is most commonly used in higher education for content creation and editing, with 78.11% of recorded uses. The findings of this study revealed many intriguing opportunities for ChatGPT to assist learning, while also revealing major hazards associated with overreliance on the technology. These risks can inhibit critical thinking and creativity, limit profound comprehension of the subject matter, and promote laziness and inactivity.

This study offers advice for appropriate and effective incorporation of ChatGPT in educational settings.

Case Study-2 – A Student's Take on Challenges of AI-driven Grading in Higher Education, July 2022 (Cingillioglu et al., 2024)

In this study, interviews and surveys were done with teaching assistants to assess their perspectives regarding computerized grading. This research included both technical (such as computer science, industrial engineering, and management) and non-technical disciplines (such as communication science, philosophy of science, technology, and society). Throughout the investigation, it was fascinating to note that there was no discernible variation in perceptions and attitudes about different academic curricula. Technical studies may prefer this method for analyzing structured responses over creative ones, which are more common in non-technical investigations. During the research, it was discovered that human contribution is more valuable than artificial intelligence. The majority of respondents agreed that AI should only be used as a support tool, allowing the assessor to navigate the answer more easily, or having an AI review the assessors' work to ensure the fairness of the grades. Thus, it is clear that Teaching assistants should be involved in the grading process, given that a tool might serve several objectives. Currently, the best strategy to include AI in education is a hybrid one. According to the survey, this could help Teaching assistants validate their grades.

AI-POWERED COLLABORATIVE LEARNING

Online collaborative learning incorporates people who are geographically separate from one another but study together to solve issues, complete assignments, and gain real-world skills (Reeves et al., 2004).

To promote fruitful online collaborative learning, cognitive engagement, teamwork, and socially acknowledged supervision are essential (Nguyen et al., 2022). Collaborative knowledge construction has been utilized in higher education to enhance collaborative learning activities by allowing students to discuss, negotiate, and reflect on their ideas through interaction with others. To assist with this task, collaborative learning analytics tools have been developed for gathering and analyzing collaborative methods and outcome data to offer relevant feedback to enhance the quality of learning (Ouyang et al., 2024).

Computer-supported collaborative learning paradigms propose technology provides an integral workspace for discourse, reflection, and joint knowledge building. AI can significantly enhance Computer-supported collaborative learning environments and promote peer-to-peer interaction through various means:

a. **Personalized Recommendations:** AI algorithms can analyze learners' preferences, learning styles, and past interactions to recommend relevant resources, study groups, or peers with similar interests. This facilitates better collaboration by connecting learners with compatible partners.
b. **Adaptive Learning Platforms:** AI-powered adaptive learning platforms can dynamically adjust content difficulty and pacing based on individual performance, ensuring that learners receive personalized support. This fosters a supportive environment where peers can assist each other in overcoming learning challenges.
c. **Natural Language Processing (NLP):** NLP capabilities enable AI to facilitate communication between peers, allowing for real-time language translation, summarization of discussions, and sentiment analysis. This enhances collaboration by breaking down language barriers and promoting effective communication.
d. **Virtual Collaboration Tools:** AI-driven virtual collaboration tools, such as virtual reality (VR) environments and interactive simulations, enable learners to engage in immersive group activities regardless of geographical locations. These tools enhance peer-to-peer interaction by providing shared spaces for collaboration and exploration.
e. **Peer Assessment and Feedback:** AI-powered assessment tools can facilitate peer evaluation by providing structured feedback and evaluation criteria. This promotes active engagement among peers and encourages constructive feedback, fostering a culture of collaboration and continuous improvement.
f. **Content Curation and Creation:** AI algorithms can curate and generate educational content tailored to specific learning objectives and interests. By enabling learners to collaboratively create and share content, AI fosters peer-to-peer interaction and knowledge exchange within learning communities.
g. **Data Analytics for Collaboration:** AI-driven analytics tools can track learners' interactions within collaborative learning environments, providing insights into group dynamics, participation levels, and knowledge exchange patterns. Educators can use this data to identify areas for improvement and facilitate meaningful peer interactions.

A quantitative analysis study conducted by Han Kyul Kim (2024), confirms that ChatGPT reduces the level of active learning interactions between students, a critical component for successful collaborative learning, while a higher proportion of active learning interactions occur primarily between individual students and ChatGPT. A deeper look at ChatGPT's impact on the tangible outcomes of group brainstorming sessions remains an important path for future research (Silseth et al., 2024).

AI plays a crucial role in facilitating collaborative learning environments by providing personalized support, enhancing communication, and promoting peer-to-peer interaction, ultimately enriching the learning experience for all participants.

AI IN IT -IMPROVE SKILLS OF TEACHERS (SPECIALLY FOR CIT MAJORS)

Most of the researchers in this field (e.g.: Verma, Holmes, and NeSmith) agreed that adopting AI is improving teacher's skills, especially in the area of using technology. Hence, this section focuses on the most impacted areas and systems where adopting AI will make a real difference. Such as personalized professional development, resource aggregation, real-time feedback on teaching practices, facilitation of collaborative learning and enhanced student support.

Personalized Professional Development

AI nowadays simplifies the learning process by enabling the students to find the material and attempt the course by themselves. Muh. Putra. Al (2023) found in their investigation that currently, AI replaced standard self-study by utilizing AI tools and apps to help in personalized education. One of the techniques has been raised using AI platforms.

Resource Aggregation

Resource aggregation means a collection of data, tools, and information used by AI to enhance teaching materials creation and management. The AI tool will work in automated content curation which gathers all information and maps it with teaching objectives. Moreover, it can be used for a recommendation system which is similar to one that is used in e-commerce, but it will be to enhance staff and students learning experience. However, the main advantage of using AI in Resource aggregation is keeping the systems and content up to date This is particularly valuable in fast-evolving fields like science and technology, ensuring that learners and educators have access to the most current data and insights.

Real-Time Feedback on Teaching Practices

AI technology has extended its influence to providing real-time feedback on teaching practices, a development that holds the potential to revolutionize classroom instruction and professional development for educators. This utilization of AI allows for immediate insights and suggestions on teaching methods, enabling teachers to adapt and enhance their instructional strategies on the fly. AI-powered classroom observation tools use audio and video recordings to analyze teaching sessions. AI systems can track student engagement levels by analyzing their responses, participation, and attention during lessons. AI-powered virtual teaching assistants can provide real-time suggestions to teachers during lessons. For example, they can suggest when to introduce an interactive element or when to revisit a topic based on student responses and engagement levels.

THE SUCCESS OF HUMAN VS AI TEACHERS

This section will discuss the human Vs AI teachers and demonstrate the strengths and weaknesses of each style. The section will cover the efficacy of human versus AI teachers is multifaceted, delving into various aspects of education, pedagogy, and Impact on Student Engagement (Holmes & Tuomi, 2022) and Motivation as shown in below table 1.

Table 1. AI vs. human teachers (Authors)

	Human Teachers	AI Teachers
Pedagogy Efficacy	Adaptive Pedagogy Creative Problem-Solving Critical Thinking and Debate	Data-Driven Instruction Scalable Knowledge Delivery
Interpersonal Efficacy	Emotional and Social Learning Role Modeling	Limited Emotional Interaction Consistent Feedback Without Bias
Impact on Student Engagement and Motivation	Motivation and Engagement Adapting to Student Feedback	Engagement Through Technology Gamification and Interactive Learning

PSYCHOLOGICAL IMPLICATIONS OF USING AI IN HIGHER EDUCATION

With AI professionalism will be enhanced especially in the area of technical skills such as speeding up feedback, personalized learning, and providing a huge tutorial level. However, AI is impacting reverse-wise in psychological aspects. Key points that will be covered are maintaining human health, enhancing people's language learning, and detecting human emotions.

Human Health

Maintaining human health using AI through monitoring the teacher's stress and activity. Moreover, AI will help in reducing the workload and mental strain on educators. Additionally, the AI tools are used to give the teachers a notification regarding their physical health and activities.

Enhance Language Learning

AI-driven language learning platforms can provide personalized instruction, adapting to individual learning styles and proficiency levels. These platforms can offer diverse linguistic content, catering to a wide range of languages and dialects, thus supporting multicultural education.

Detect Human Emotions

AI can be also used to detect human emotion through different such as face recognition, voice analysis, and text analysis. Moreover, AI not only detects depressive symptoms but there is a possibility for early prediction as well.

These techniques can help in reducing the negative impacts of increasing machine interaction through e-learning systems. Some institutions used AI to create a treatment plan as well for the users. Higher education institutions, use AI to support special needs students, especially those who need additional mental support (Hickman & Petrin, 2020).

SOCIAL IMPLICATIONS OF USING AI IN HIGHER EDUCATION

Adopting AI in higher education had a great positive impact on social level. The new educational platforms with AI help foster the educational exchange within the universities internally, nationally, and globally education exchange. Additionally, AI customizes the learning materials which suit all culture's needs and perspectives. AI can be used to create more accessible learning materials for students in remote or underserved regions, helping to bridge the digital divide and promote educational equity, especially in the context of Language, Ethnicity, Socioeconomic Status, and Profession (LESP) (Chiappe & Rodríguez, 2017). AI can cater to the diverse learning needs of students, including those with disabilities, offering personalized rooms and support (Chiu et al., 2023).

ETHICAL IMPLICATIONS OF USING AI IN HIGHER EDUCATION

While incorporating artificial intelligence (AI) into education has great benefits, it also introduces obstacles and issues that must be addressed. This section highlights some of the main issues and concerns related to the ethical implications of using AI in education.

a) **Privacy and data security:** To create individualized learning experiences, AI collects and analyzes vast volumes of student data. This raise worries regarding the privacy and security of student data. Personal data security and compliance with data protection standards are critical (Chaudhary,2023) . Educational institutions and AI developers must put in place strong security procedures and processes to protect student privacy and prevent unwanted access to sensitive information.

b) **Ethical Considerations:** The use of AI technology in education raises ethical concerns, particularly with relation to the usage of student data and AI algorithm decision-making processes. There is a need to ensure that AI systems are transparent and accountable to ethical standards. Educators and governments must address issues of prejudice, fairness, and transparency in AI algorithms to guarantee that all children have equitable access to educational opportunities (Akhun & Greenhow,2021).

c) **Over-reliance on AI:** While AI can give specific educational experiences, there is a concern that it will be over-used, resulting in a passive learning experience for students. It is critical to create a balance between AI-powered instruction and personal connection. Human teachers play a critical role in giving advice, assistance, and tailored education that AI cannot mimic. Establishing a balance between AI and human education is critical for fostering relevant learning opportunities (Memarian & Doleck,2023).

d) **Skill Development and Adaptability:** As artificial intelligence (AI) technologies evolve, learners and teachers must develop the skills required for successful use and engagement with AI systems (Cargill,2004). To succeed in the AI-driven educational world, students must be able to think critically, solve problems, and communicate digitally. Additionally, educators prefer possibilities for professional growth to understand how to properly use artificial intelligence in their teaching techniques.

GUIDELINES TO POLICYMAKERS TO NAVIGATE ETHICAL CHALLENGES

AI ethics in higher education is becoming a growing concern as universities and colleges embrace and incorporate artificial intelligence into their activities and decision-making procedures. Educators and policymakers should leverage the full capabilities of AI technology to improve how students learn while protecting privacy, justice, and equality by addressing these concerns proactively and taking ethical and inclusive approaches to AI integration (Kaledio et al., 2024). Below are guidelines for policymakers can address a wide range of issues related to AI in higher education, such as fairness, accountability, transparency, safety, and human independence.

a) **Ethical Frameworks:** With the growing use of AI in Higher Education, it is critical to build ethical frameworks and norms that address issues such as data privacy, algorithmic bias, and transparency. Policymakers, educators, and developers of artificial intelligence should work together to build responsible AI practices that stress equity, responsibility, and transparency when designing and using artificial intelligence (AI) in education.
b) **Promote Collaboration Between AI and Educators**: AI should be considered as a tool to supplement and help educators, not to replace them. Collaboration between artificial intelligence and human instructors is critical for building effective learning environments. Educators should be given training and professional development opportunities to help them comprehend AI technology and incorporate it into their teaching practices in relevant ways.
c) **Address Diversity and Access Problems:** Steps should be taken to provide appropriate access to AI technologies for education. This involves ensuring that all students have equal access to infrastructure, gadgets, and high-quality AI-powered instructional tools, regardless of socioeconomic or geographic background. Closing the digital divide and ensuring inclusivity in AI integration would assist in avoiding exacerbating current educational inequities.
d) **Promote Digital Awareness and AI Skills:** As AI becomes more common in education, it is critical to provide students with digital literacy skills and an awareness of AI ideas. Students should learn to critically analyze and apply

AI-powered tools, as well as grasp the ethical implications of AI. They should also develop talents that complement AI technology, such as problem-solving, creativity, and flexibility.

e) **Continuous Research and Evaluation:** As AI technologies advance, it is critical to perform continuing investigations and assessments to better understand their impact on student learning experiences. Rigorous research should evaluate the efficacy of AI solutions, identify possibilities for enhancement, and support methods that are based on evidence. To guarantee that AI benefits all learners, this study should take into account a variety of student groups and educational environments (Kaledio et al., 2024).

AI-POWERED LEARNING-EMERGING TRENDS AND CUTTING-EDGE TECHNOLOGIES

In the field of AI in education, several emerging trends and cutting-edge technologies are shaping the future of learning. Below Table 2 showcases some key areas and examples of AI tools and platforms that correspond to each of the areas.

CHARTING THE PATH FORWARD: KEY FOCUS AREAS FOR THE FUTURE OF AI-POWERED LEARNING

AI-powered teaching holds tremendous potential for transforming education, but it is not without its challenges. Ethical concerns surround the use of AI in education, particularly regarding data privacy, security, and the potential for algorithmic bias. The collection and utilization of vast amounts of student data by AI systems raise concerns about data privacy and security. Safeguarding sensitive information and ensuring compliance with privacy regulations are essential considerations (Kaledio et al., 2024).

AI systems may inadvertently preserve and amplify existing biases present in their training data, leading to unfair and discriminatory outcomes. Despite the potential benefits, access to AI-powered educational tools is not universal. Educational institutions often encounter resistance to change from stakeholders, including teachers, students, and parents. This resistance can impede the successful adoption of AI technologies in teaching and learning environments (Alanoglu et al., 2021).

Table 2. Areas and tools in cutting edge AI technologies (Authors)

Areas of cutting-edge technologies	Description	examples of AI tools and platforms
Personalized Learning Pathways	AI algorithms are increasingly being utilized to design tailored educational paths based on each student's strengths, limitations, and academic style(Alamri et al.,2020). This movement tries to improve the learning experience by tailoring information, feedback, and pacing to individual learners	Knewton is an adaptive learning platform that employs artificial intelligence to create individualized educational experiences by monitoring student achievement data and modifying content as needed.
Adaptive Learning Systems	Adaptive learning systems continually analyze students' progress and dynamically change the level and substance of instructional materials. These systems may change in real time to fit each learner's specific needs, resulting in a more interesting and effective learning experience.	DreamBox Learning is a K-8 math application that employs artificial intelligence to change content and tempo based on student responses, thereby delivering tailored training to increase arithmetic performance.
Conversational AI chatbots	Chatbots and conversational AI interfaces are being integrated into educational systems to provide students with immediate assistance, answers to inquiries, and personalized support(Pappula & Allam,2023). These AI-powered solutions improve accessibility, efficiency, and interaction in educational settings.	Squirrel AI Learning is an AI-powered teaching platform that uses chatbots to provide students with immediate assistance, answers to queries, and individualized tutoring support.
Augmented and Virtual Reality (AR/VR)	These technologies are transforming education by offering immersive, interactive learning experiences. AI algorithms improve AR/VR experiences by personalizing information, measuring progress, and tailoring simulations to individual learners' needs.	Nearpod VR is an AR/VR educational platform that provides immersive learning experiences through virtual field trips, simulations, and interactive 3D models, all powered by AI algorithms for personalization and adaptability
Data Analytics and Learning Analytics	Data analytics solutions allow educators to evaluate enormous datasets created by students' interactions with educational content and platforms(Chen,2015). Educators can use this data to uncover learning trends, predict student success, and better personalize instruction.	Brightspace Insights is a learning analytics tool built within the Brightspace LMS (Learning Management System) that uses AI algorithms to evaluate student data and provide instructors with actionable insights to improve teaching and learning results.
AI for Content Creation and Curation	AI algorithms are increasingly being utilized to create educational content like quizzes, exercises, and instructional videos(The Impact of Content Curation for Learning,2016). AI-based content curation systems assist educators in discovering and recommending high-quality educational resources based on specific learning objectives and student needs.	Quillionz is an AI-powered content creation tool that creates quiz questions, summaries, and learning exercises from textual content, such as articles, textbooks, or lecture transcripts, to enhance individualized learning experiences.
Ethical and Responsible AI Use	As AI technologies become more widely used in education, there is a rising recognition of the importance of ethical and responsible AI use (Chan, 2022). Educators and politicians are looking into concerns like data privacy, algorithmic bias, and transparency to guarantee that AI applications in education promote fairness, diversity, and inclusion.	Fair learn is an open-source Python toolkit created by Microsoft Research that assists developers in assessing and mitigating algorithmic bias in AI systems, notably those used in educational applications, to promote fairness and equity.
Lifelong Learning and Continuous Skill Development	Microlearning tools enable people to learn and build new skills throughout their lives. These platforms provide tailored learning experiences that adapt to learners' evolving requirements and career aspirations (Fariani et al.,2022).	Coursera is an online learning platform that provides courses, specializations, and degrees from renowned colleges and institutions. It includes AI-driven features like personalized course suggestions, skill assessments, and adaptive learning pathways to encourage lifelong learning and skill development.

CONCLUSION

Upon the discussions in this chapter, the digital divide worsens limiting the reach of AI-based teaching methods. Ensuring inclusivity and accessibility for all students remains a significant challenge. Educators often face challenges in adapting to new AI technologies. AI-powered teaching tools may struggle to accommodate diverse learning styles and preferences. Customization remains a challenge, as AI systems need to adapt content and instruction for individual students with varying needs (Holmes & Tuomi, 2022). Insufficient training and professional development opportunities hinder the effective integration of AI tools into teaching practices. Teacher preparedness is crucial for maximizing the benefits of AI in education. There is a risk of over-relying on technology, neglecting the importance of human connections in the learning process. The overemphasis on AI may undermine the interpersonal aspects of education, including mentorship and social interaction. Transparency and clarity are critical aspects of sustainable AI development. Promote sustainable adoption of AI in higher education while optimizing benefits needs to be focused more on the future, Higher education stakeholders must employ AI effectively and fairly, by maximizing positive aspects while limiting risks.

REFERENCES

Akgun, S., & Greenhow, C. (2021, September 22). Artificial intelligence in education: Addressing ethical challenges in K-12 settings. *AI and Ethics*, *2*(3), 431–440. doi:10.1007/s43681-021-00096-7 PMID:34790956

Alamri, H. A., Watson, S., & Watson, W. (2020, July 31). Learning Technology Models that Support Personalization within Blended Learning Environments in Higher Education. *TechTrends*, *65*(1), 62–78. doi:10.1007/s11528-020-00530-3

Alanoglu, M., Aslan, S., & Karabatak, S. (2021, September 25). Do teachers' educational philosophies affect their digital literacy? The mediating effect of resistance to change. *Education and Information Technologies*, *27*(3), 3447–3466. doi:10.1007/s10639-021-10753-3 PMID:34602847

Bard, J. (2021). A Performance Comparison of Artificial Neural Networks and Spiking Neural Networks. SSRN *Electronic Journal*. doi:10.2139/ssrn.3814512

Bhardwaj, P., Gupta, P., Panwar, H., Siddiqui, M. K., Morales-Menendez, R., & Bhaik, A. (2021, July). Application of Deep Learning on Student Engagement in e-learning environments. *Computers & Electrical Engineering*, *93*, 107277. doi:10.1016/j.compeleceng.2021.107277 PMID:36567679

Bull, G., Thompson, A. D., Schmidt-Crawford, D., Garofalo, J., Hodges, C. B., Spector, J. M., Ferdig, R. E., Edyburn, D., & Kinshuk. (2016, September 2). Evaluating the Impact of Educational Technology. *Journal of Digital Learning in Teacher Education, 32*(4), 117–118. doi:10.1080/21532974.2016.1217052

Cargill, M. (2004, January). Transferable skills within research degrees: a collaborative genre-based approach to developing publication skills and its implications for research education. *Teaching in Higher Education, 9*(1), 83–98. doi:10.1080/1356251032000155858

Casal-Otero, L., Catala, A., Fernández-Morante, C., Taboada, M., Cebreiro, B., & Barro, S. (2023, April 19). AI literacy in K-12: A systematic literature review. *International Journal of STEM Education, 10*(1), 29. doi:10.1186/s40594-023-00418-7

Chan, A. (2022, April 4). GPT-3 and InstructGPT: Technological dystopianism, utopianism, and "Contextual" perspectives in AI ethics and industry. *AI and Ethics, 3*(1), 53–64. doi:10.1007/s43681-022-00148-6

Chaudhary, M. (2023, September 5). Exploring Ethical, Privacy, Security, and Societal Concerns in ChatGPT Implementation: Challenges and Solutions. [IJSR]. *International Journal of Science and Research (Raipur, India), 12*(9), 1054–1055. doi:10.21275/SR23905114533

Chen, L., Chen, P., & Lin, Z. (2020). Artificial Intelligence in Education: A Review. *IEEE Access : Practical Innovations, Open Solutions, 8*, 75264–75278. doi:10.1109/ACCESS.2020.2988510

ChiappeA.RodríguezL. P. (2017, June 26). Learning Analytics in 21st century education: a review. *Ensaio: Avaliação E Políticas Públicas Em Educação, 25*(97), 971–991. doi:10.1590/s0104-40362017002501211

Chiu, T. K., Xia, Q., Zhou, X., Chai, C. S., & Cheng, M. (2023). Systematic literature review on opportunities, challenges, and future research recommendations of artificial intelligence in education. *Computers and Education: Artificial Intelligence, 4*, 100118. doi:10.1016/j.caeai.2022.100118

Cingillioglu, I., Gal, U., & Prokhorov, A. (2024, March 26). AI-experiments in education: An AI-driven randomized controlled trial for higher education research. *Education and Information Technologies*. Advance online publication. doi:10.1007/s10639-024-12633-y

Creamer, D. B. (Ed.). (2012, December 6). Review of “The Future of Thinking: Learning Institutions in a Digital Age,” by Cathy N. Davidson and David Theo Goldberg (MIT Press, 2012). Journal of Religion, Media and Digital Culture, 1(1), 1–4. doi:10.1163/21659214-90000008

Fariani, R. I., Junus, K., & Santoso, H. B. (2022, November 17). A Systematic Literature Review on Personalised Learning in the Higher Education Context. *Technology. Knowledge and Learning*, *28*(2), 449–476. doi:10.1007/s10758-022-09628-4

Felipe Redondo, A. M., Nuñez Cárdenas, F. D. J., & Tomás Mariano, V. T. (2015, July 5). Reseña del NMC Horizon Report > Educación Superior 2015. *Ciencia Huasteca Boletín Científico De La Escuela Superior De Huejutla*, *3*(6). doi:10.29057/esh.v3i6.1128

Floridi, L., Cowls, J., Beltrametti, M., Chatila, R., Chazerand, P., Dignum, V., Luetge, C., Madelin, R., Pagallo, U., Rossi, F., Schafer, B., Valcke, P., & Vayena, E. (2018, November 26). AI4People—An Ethical Framework for a Good AI Society: Opportunities, Risks, Principles, and Recommendations. *Minds and Machines*, *28*(4), 689–707. doi:10.1007/s11023-018-9482-5 PMID:30930541

G, M. (2020, January 20). Rule-based Cognitive Modelling for Multimodal Intelligent Tutoring Systems. *International Journal of Psychosocial Rehabilitation, 24*(1), 1754–1760. https://doi.org/ doi:10.37200/IJPR/V24I1/PR200275

Hadi Mogavi, R., Deng, C., Juho Kim, J., Zhou, P., & Kwon, D., Y., Metwally, A., Tlili, A., Bassanelli, S., Bucchiarone, A., Gujar, S., Nacke, L. E., & Hui, P. (2024, January). ChatGPT in education: A blessing or a curse? A qualitative study exploring early adopters' utilization and perceptions. *Computers in Human Behavior: Artificial Humans*, *2*(1), 100027. doi:10.1016/j.chbah.2023.100027

Hickman, E., & Petrin, M. (2020). Trustworthy AI and Corporate Governance – The EU's Ethics Guidelines For Trustworthy Artificial Intelligence from a Company Law Perspective. SSRN *Electronic Journal*. doi:10.2139/ssrn.3607225

Holmes, W., Bialik, M., & Fadel, C. (2019, February 28). *Artificial Intelligence in Education*. http://books.google.ie/books?id=tzO7wgEACAAJ&dq=Artificial+Intelligence+in+Education:+A+Review&hl=&cd=1&source=gbs_api

Holmes, W., & Tuomi, I. (2022, October 30). State of the art and practice in AI in education. *European Journal of Education*, *57*(4), 542–570. doi:10.1111/ejed.12533

Kabudi, T., Pappas, I., & Olsen, D. H. (2021). AI-enabled adaptive learning systems: A systematic mapping of the literature. *Computers and Education: Artificial Intelligence*, *2*, 100017. doi:10.1016/j.caeai.2021.100017

Kaledio, P., Robert, A., & Frank, L. (2024). The Impact of Artificial Intelligence on Students' Learning Experience. SSRN *Electronic Journal*. https://doi.org/doi:10.2139/ssrn.4716747

Koedinger, K. R., Brunskill, E., Baker, R. S. J. D., McLaughlin, E. A., & Stamper, J. (2013, September). New Potentials for Data-Driven Intelligent Tutoring System Development and Optimization. *AI Magazine*, *34*(3), 27–41. doi:10.1609/aimag.v34i3.2484

Lameras, P., & Arnab, S. (2021, December 29). Power to the Teachers: An Exploratory Review on Artificial Intelligence in Education. *Information (Basel)*, *13*(1), 14. doi:10.3390/info13010014

Lane, A. (2017, November 20). Open Education and the Sustainable Development Goals: Making Change Happen. *Journal of Learning for Development*, *4*(3). doi:10.56059/jl4d.v4i3.266

Liang, J. C., Hwang, G. J., Chen, M. R. A., & Darmawansah, D. (2021, July 28). Roles and research foci of artificial intelligence in language education: An integrated bibliographic analysis and systematic review approach. *Interactive Learning Environments*, *31*(7), 4270–4296. doi:10.1080/10494820.2021.1958348

Manikandan, S. (2023, August). AI; A New Horizon of Promises & Challenges: 'Exploring the Impact of Artificial Intelligence (AI) in Mental Health Care'. *International Journal of Research Publication and Reviews*, *4*(8), 2038–2045. doi:10.55248/gengpi.4.823.51356

Memarian, B., & Doleck, T. (2023). Fairness, Accountability, Transparency, and Ethics (FATE) in Artificial Intelligence (AI) and higher education: A systematic review. *Computers and Education: Artificial Intelligence*, *5*, 100152. doi:10.1016/j.caeai.2023.100152

Miao, F., Holmes, W., Huang, R., & Zhang, H. (2021, April 8). *AI and education*. UNESCO Publishing. http://books.google.ie/books?id=yyE7EAAAQBAJ&printsec=frontcover&dq=Artificial+Intelligence+in+Education:+Promises+and+Implications+for+Teaching+and+Learning&hl=&cd=2&source=gbs_api

Moore, S. L. (2007, August 17). David H. Rose, Anne Meyer, Teaching Every Student in the Digital Age: Universal Design for Learning. *Educational Technology Research and Development*, *55*(5), 521–525. doi:10.1007/s11423-007-9056-3

Nguyen, A., Järvelä, S., Rosé, C., Järvenoja, H., & Malmberg, J. (2022, October 11). Examining socially shared regulation and shared physiological arousal events with multimodal learning analytics. *British Journal of Educational Technology, 54*(1), 293–312. doi:10.1111/bjet.13280

Ouyang, F., Zhang, L., Wu, M., & Jiao, P. (2024, June). Empowering collaborative knowledge construction through the implementation of a collaborative argument map tool. *The Internet and Higher Education*, *62*, 100946. doi:10.1016/j.iheduc.2024.100946

Oversold and Underused. (2004, May 1). Computers in the Classroom. *International Journal of Educational Management*, *18*(3), 205–206. doi:10.1108/09513540410527202

Pappula, S. R., & Allam, S. R. (2023, December 9). LLMs for Conversational AI: Enhancing Chatbots and Virtual Assistants. *International Journal of Research Publication and Reviews*, *4*(12), 1601–1611. doi:10.55248/gengpi.4.1223.123425

Peng, H., Ma, S., & Spector, J. M. (2019, September 18). Personalized adaptive learning: An emerging pedagogical approach enabled by a smart learning environment. *Smart Learning Environments*, *6*(1), 9. doi:10.1186/s40561-019-0089-y

Picciano, A. G. (2017, September 1). Theories and Frameworks for Online Education: Seeking an Integrated Model. *Online Learning : the Official Journal of the Online Learning Consortium*, *21*(3). doi:10.24059/olj.v21i3.1225

Pratama, M. P., Sampelolo, R., & Lura, H. (2023, August 10). REVOLUTIONIZING EDUCATION: HARNESSING THE POWER OF ARTIFICIAL INTELLIGENCE FOR PERSONALIZED LEARNING. *KLASIKAL : JOURNAL OF EDUCATION, LANGUAGE TEACHING AND SCIENCE*, *5*(2), 350–357. doi:10.52208/klasikal.v5i2.877

Ramazan, & Gizem. (n.d.). Investigation of student views on data privacy and ethical use of data in smart learning environments. *10th International İstanbul Scientific Research Congress, July 23-25, 2022*.

Reeves, T. C., Herrington, J., & Oliver, R. (2004, December). A development research agenda for online collaborative learning. *Educational Technology Research and Development*, *52*(4), 53–65. doi:10.1007/BF02504718

Saputra, I., Astuti, M., Sayuti, M., & Kusumastuti, D. (2023, August 30). Integration of Artificial Intelligence in Education: Opportunities, Challenges, Threats and Obstacles. A Literature Review. *Indonesian Journal of Computer Science*, *12*(4). Advance online publication. doi:10.33022/ijcs.v12i4.3266

Sheehy, K., & Holliman, A. (2017, December 13). *Education and New Technologies*. Routledge. http://books.google.ie/books?id=HilEDwAAQBAJ&printsec=frontcover&dq=Artificial+Intelligence+in+Education:+Promises+and+Implications+for+Teaching+and+Learning&hl=&cd=3&source=gbs_api

Silseth, K., Steier, R., & Arnseth, H. C. (2024, February 15). Exploring students' immersive VR experiences as resources for collaborative meaning making and learning. *International Journal of Computer-Supported Collaborative Learning*, *19*(1), 11–36. doi:10.1007/s11412-023-09413-0

Su, J., Ng, D. T. K., & Chu, S. K. W. (2023). Artificial Intelligence (AI) Literacy in Early Childhood Education: The Challenges and Opportunities. *Computers and Education: Artificial Intelligence*, *4*, 100124. doi:10.1016/j.caeai.2023.100124

The Impact of Content Curation for Personal / Informal Learning. (2016, January 5). The Impact of Content Curation for Personal / Informal Learning. *International Journal of Science and Research (Raipur, India)*, *5*(1), 1673–1676. doi:10.21275/v5i1.NOV153170

Tjahyadi, H., Budijono, Y. G., Lukas, S., & Krisnadi, D. (2017, October). Android Based Automated Scoring of Multiple-Choice Test. *International Journal of Machine Learning and Computing*, *7*(5), 110–113. doi:10.18178/ijmlc.2017.7.5.630

Zhang, K., & Aslan, A. B. (2021). AI technologies for education: Recent research & future directions. *Computers and Education: Artificial Intelligence*, *2*, 100025. doi:10.1016/j.caeai.2021.100025

ADDITIONAL READING

Chang, J. W., Yen, N., & Hung, J. C. (2021, November 8). *Frontier Computing*. Springer.

Groth, O., & Nitzberg, M. (2018, November 6). *The AI Generation*. Simon and Schuster.

Miao, F., Holmes, W., Huang, R., Zhang, H., & U. (2021, April 8). *AI and education*. UNESCO Publishing.

NeSmith, R. A. (2023, March 21). *How ChatGPT Will Change Education*. Applied Principles of Education & Learning.

Novais, P., Inglada, V. J., Hornos, M. J., Satoh, I., Carneiro, D., Carneiro, J., & Alonso, R. S. (2023, September 25). *Ambient Intelligence – Software and Applications – 14th International Symposium on Ambient Intelligence*. Springer Nature.

Panconesi, G., & Guida, M. (2021, February 19). *Handbook of Research on Teaching With Virtual Environments and AI*. IGI Global.

Raman, A., & Rathakrishnan, M. (2019, March 29). *Redesigning Higher Education Initiatives for Industry 4.0*. IGI Global.

Seldon, A., & Abidoye, O. (2018, April 30). *The Fourth Education Revolution*. Legend Press Ltd.

Verma, S., & Tomar, P. (2020, August 21). *Impact of AI Technologies on Teaching, Learning, and Research in Higher Education*. IGI Global.

Yu, S., & Lu, Y. (2021, November 29). *An Introduction to Artificial Intelligence in Education*. Springer Nature.

Chapter 8
Integrating AI in Higher Education:
Applications, Strategies, Ethical Considerations

Salim Bakhit Al Daraai
https://orcid.org/0000-0003-4136-2940
Muscat College, Oman

Mallak Al Maqrashi
Muscat College, Oman

Mohammed Al Zakwani
Muscat College, Oman

Zahir Al Shaikh
University of Technology and Applied Sciences, Muscat, Oman

ABSTRACT

This chapter provides a comprehensive overview of a study investigating the integration of artificial intelligence (AI) in higher education. The chapter examines various applications, strategies, and ethical considerations associated with this integration. It explores how AI technologies can automate tasks such as teaching, learning, and grading, enhancing the efficiency and accessibility of education. Additionally, the chapter investigates the potential benefits of AI in delivering personalised learning experiences, catering to diverse learning needs, and enhancing student engagement through intelligent tutoring systems and virtual environments. Furthermore, the chapter addresses ethical concerns related to AI, including issues concerning data privacy and algorithmic bias. It emphasises the importance of aligning AI applications with educational objectives. It highlights the necessity of providing teacher training and continuously improving AI implementation to ensure that these technologies complement, rather than replace, the human aspects of education.

DOI: 10.4018/979-8-3693-2145-4.ch008

INTRODUCTION

The new technologies and the processing capacity of newly created intelligent machines are intrinsically tied to the future of higher education. Artificial Intelligence (AI) has permeated every aspect of our lives, demonstrating the growing significance of technology (Singh & Hiran, 2022). In recent years, there has been a growing number of artificial intelligence-based educational applications developed. Higher education institutions' governance and internal architecture may change significantly due to the new opportunities and difficulties presented by artificial intelligence developments for teaching and learning. It is impossible to overestimate the significance of adaptive learning technologies systems (ALTS) and Artificial Intelligence (AI) in the classroom (Pardamean, Suparyanto, Cenggoro, Sudigyo, & Anugrahana, 2022).

The phrase artificial Intelligence (AI) evokes visions of massively parallel computers with the capacity to sense and adjust to their surroundings via sensors and other components (Górriz et al., 2020; Šumak, Brdnik, & Pušnik, 2021). Supercomputers with these characteristics can interact more with humans since they have human-like cognition and functionality. AI has been employed in movies in several ways, such as smart buildings that can regulate a room's music, temperature, and air quality based on how people feel (Zhang, Wu, & Calautit, 2022). The conventional meaning of artificial Intelligence, formerly limited to supercomputers, is now being used to embed computer systems in increasing educational circumstances. Examples include robots that, by combining AI, computers, and other supporting technology, can assist students in learning from the very beginning of their education, such as early childhood education. According to Timms, regular chores like pronunciation and punctuation are taught to kids by robots that adjust to their skill level. These robots operate in collaboration with teachers to help teach kids these skills. Multiple studies have shown that web-based and online education has changed over time. Gone are the days when students had to download online materials, study them, and turn in assignments to pass. Instead, students now have access to intelligent and adaptive web-based systems that adapt to their behaviour and that of their instructors to improve their overall learning experience. Education uses Artificial Intelligence to help with administration, instruction, and learning. This research aims to examine and comprehend Artificial Intelligence in education by concentrating on these three domains.

Automating Teaching and Learning

Numerous writers have examined the application of AI to Higher Education (HE), mostly emphasising how AI may enhance student learning possibilities and administrative processes (Pedro, Subosa, Rivas, & Valverde, 2019; Zawacki-Richter,

Marín, Bond, & Gouverneur, 2019). AI technologies have the potential to guarantee inclusive and egalitarian access to education. AI allows refugees, persons with impairments, and residents of remote areas to access appropriate learning pathways. Using robotics and holograms enables students with special needs to continue their education in times of emergency or crisis, such as the COVID-19 pandemic at the beginning of 2020 (Sousa et al., 2021). AI can potentially improve several areas, including smart content, personalised solutions for individuals with disabilities (such as the deaf or visually impaired), exponential scalability (e.g. through MOOCs), collaborative learning, and intelligent tools for cooperation (Sayers et al., 2021; Sousa et al., 2021). Computer-supported collaborative learning offers one of its most innovative features when learners are physically present in different places.

Automating Grading

Universities and colleges spend money on learning software platforms and course management systems like Pearson, McGraw-Hill, and Blackboard. However, this technology can be fully utilised with an equally sophisticated data mining system (Hannan & Liu, 2023). AI-powered automated grading can take the role of instructors' grading duties, freeing them up to concentrate on each student's unique needs. By increasing the worth of each student to the institution and enabling teachers to intervene sooner, an effective and customised evaluation system can boost retention rates for HEIs (Hannan & Liu, 2023).

Automated grading methods are common in the STEM fields, where quantitative data is used more frequently than qualitative data, such as literary essays. The AI assessment platform Gradescope is used by universities, including Purdue University, OR State University, and New York University, to grade advanced STEM coursework (Gundlach & Ward, 2021; Hannan & Liu, 2023). When a student answers a question differently than the proper response, Gradescope automatically combines comparable responses from the student. Instructors receive a brief data report to modify the programme best. Instructors can provide a customisable grading rubric to their AI software, saving them the time and effort to grade complex computer programming assignments. Through process automation in assignments, Pearson, a firm, has integrated cognitive computing technology into its digital courses through the Revel learning system, allowing teachers to concentrate on student outcomes (Hannan & Liu, 2023). AI's main function in higher education is to handle repetitive human duties, including grading so that the focus can be on high-quality instruction.

There has been criticism about AI's assessment of student homework, quizzes, and tests since it only partially grades non-STEM courses, such as writing tasks that do not have a right or incorrect answer. However, AI goes beyond this constraint at the University of Michigan, where the M-Write system was developed in 2016 to help instructors grade student papers using automated processing and an algorithm that recognises subpar writing in basic courses (Luckin, Cukurova, Kent, & du Boulay, 2022). This technique enables students to receive more individualised attention in large courses where teachers need more time to give one-on-one assessments. AI should be used in automatic grading for subjects other than STEM at universities that want to evaluate students at the same distinct level that they are taught. These evaluation methods show parents and students that the college is more committed to each student.

Offer Personal Feedback

Teachers' feedback usually focuses on three primary areas: the video's clarity, the voice actor's fluency, and the answer's connection to the issue. Consequently, we extract raw data from three modalities—image, audio, and text—given a question (q) and a video submission (Liu et al., 2020). A screenshot of the video, or image I, were captured as the signal of image modality when a student makes an oral presentation because visuals do not change much from start to finish. We isolate the sound from the video as soon as the audio signals a. Additionally, automated speech recognition (ASR) techniques are used to convert the audio into text—Figure. 1.

Figure 1. The figure provides an example of how the audio data is chosen to pass through the modality gate in the present decoding phases
(Liu, Liu, Wu, & Tang, 2020)

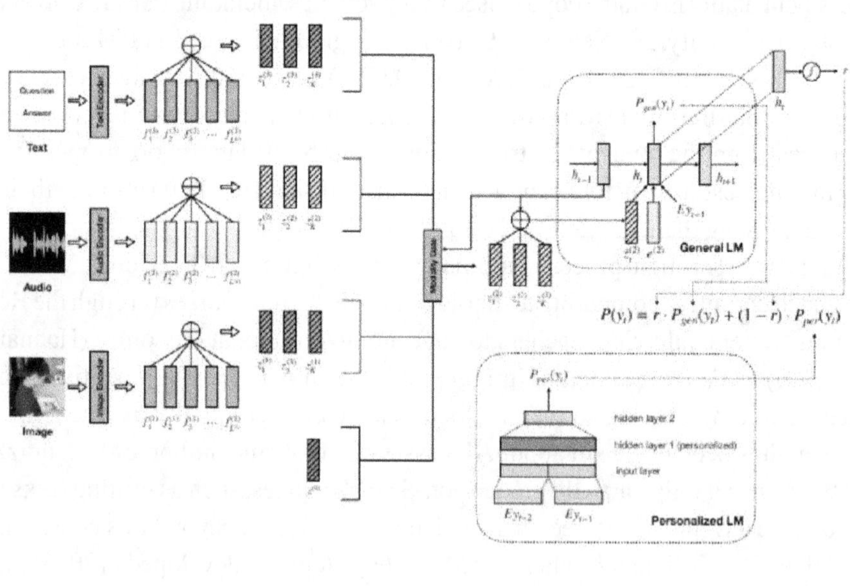

The ASR transcription (t) and the question's content (q) comprise the textual modality signals. The task of generating personalised multimodal feedback is formulated as follows. We aim to train a model to generate personalised feedback for teacher p given a set of the above multimodal inputs (i, a, t, q). The corpus where each instance contains an image i, a piece of audio a, a speech text t, a question text q, a teacher identifier p, and the corresponding feedback text y was written by that teacher (Liu, Liu, Wu, & Tang, 2020).

Intelligent Tutoring System

Artificial Intelligence (AI) disrupts the conventional classroom teaching paradigm by exposing novel approaches to provide individualised instruction to students that a human teacher cannot do (Schiff, 2021). Virtual culture, AI tutoring systems and chatbots are examples of cognitive engagement software that give teachers and students an academic edge. Students with disabilities and international students can be taught at HEIs without obstacles, thanks to automated language processing technologies.

VIRTUAL CULTURE

By attracting international students and providing them with international experiences, college campuses can increase the diversity of their student body. Virtual cultural experiences can be offered through cognitive classrooms, while chatbots on campus assist students in their mother tongue (Mageira et al., 2022). Azure Cognitive Services, developed by Microsoft, uses machine learning techniques to support automatic voice, image, and audio recognition (Salvaris, Dean, & Tok, 2018; Tajane, Dave, Jahagirdar, Ghadge, & Musale, 2018). This method translates subtitles during live classroom instruction and is available as a Microsoft PowerPoint plug-in. Speech recognition converts audio to text, records it automatically, transcribes it, and outputs an audio translation in the user's original tongue. With the help of this method, teachers may confidently instruct their disabled and international students who might struggle to keep up with the normal speed of instruction.

To provide students with an experiential learning opportunity, IBM and Rensselaer Polytechnic Institute (RPI) college collaborated in 2017 to introduce the Mandarin Project into Chinese language programmes (Chang et al., 2022; Divekar, 2020). Using virtual reality, an AI-powered assistant, and a cloud-based system, the technology turns a classroom into a 360-degree learning environment where students experience living in China (Agarwal et al., 2020; Hannan & Liu, 2021; Le, Van Le, Tromp, & Nguyen, 2018). In the first cognitive classroom, students may practise Mandarin by ordering takeaway or signing up for Tai Chi classes using a virtual reality simulation (Hannan & Liu, 2021). AI-powered non-traditional teaching goes beyond conventional lecture styles and enables students to apply what they have learned to practical settings. Watson's voice recognition capabilities help students speak more naturally by correcting vocabulary and pronunciation and evaluating pitch and tone as they exercise. With chatbots and virtual reality simulations, artificial Intelligence (AI) enables students to acquire a new language from an engaging cultural standpoint (Divekar, 2020; Hannan & Liu, 2021).

AI Tutoring Systems

In situations when instructors lack the one-on-one time to support challenging students, HEIs are adopting AI to deliver prompt assistance. Pearson partnered with IBM's Watson in 2016 to develop an AI tutoring platform to complement its learning software Revel, which can be integrated with course management systems like Blackboard or Canvas (George & Wooden, 2023; Hannan & Liu, 2023). Revel's Watson assists students with coursework through real-time questioning and communication with professors regarding specific tests (IBM, 2016). Currently restricted to individualised instruction in STEM (science, technology, engineering, and math) courses, AI personal assistants with machine learning capabilities can be developed to offer more precise feedback in qualitative assignments (Hannan & Liu, 2021).

Chatbots

Artificial Intelligence (AI) in the classroom is not intended to take the position of teachers; rather, it is intended to assist in closing the gap between students' education and learning. One way AI is being utilised as a teaching tool is through using chatbots as teaching assistants (TAs) in the classroom. In order to provide a remote AI-based education in computer science, Professor Ashok Goel of the Georgia Institute of Technology partnered with IBM's Watson to create the first AI Teaching Assistant (Hannan & Liu, 2021). Students should have been informed that Jill Watson was an AI chatbot during the platform's testing, highlighting the chatbot's capacity for interpersonal instruction (Hannan & Liu, 2021). In early 2019, the chatbot assisted students in in-person computer science and beginning biology courses. AI chatbots are capable of machine learning, which enables them to perform better over time. Jill Watson received training via Georgia Tech's online Q&A platform Piazza, loaded with 40,000 questions gleaned from two years of computer science course material. Higher education institutions (HEIs) looking for methods to enhance teaching without adding additional professors may consider investing in AI chatbots to give students access to special academic resources unavailable at other schools (Hannan & Liu, 2021).

Benefits of Using AI in Higher Education

Learning stems from personal experience, cognitive awareness, biases, beliefs, cultural background, and environment. According to Shemshack and Spector (2020), learning is a personalised experience that broadens one's knowledge, viewpoints, and practical abilities. While all students must follow the same learning sequences, not all have the same knowledge, interests, learning objectives, or needs, which is a major drawback of traditional teaching. Conventional educational materials urge students to adhere to learning steps to improve their academic standing (Fernandez-Antolin, del Río, & Gonzalez-Lezcano, 2021). Certain kids should not follow fixed learning patterns. The designers of modern educational courses pay special attention to developing personalised learning pathways that consider each student's needs, motivation, interests, behaviour patterns, and abilities (Elshani & Nuçi, 2021; Fernandez-Antolin et al., 2021).

A systematic approach to learning design known as "personalised learning" adjusts instruction to each learner's unique requirements, preferences, strengths, and objectives (Fariani, Junus, & Santoso, 2023; Kucirkova, Gerard, & Linn, 2021). It guarantees a broad selection of new subjects and skill development, which results in a full learning experience. With personalised learning, educators are responsible for empowering students to take charge of their education by helping them create and carry out learning objectives tailored to their individual needs and interests (Bishop et al., 2020; Tsai, Perrotta, & Gašević, 2020). According to Zlatarovet et al. (2021), individualised learning systems and strategies encourage pupils to learn and enhance their academic performance (Al Rawashdeh, Mohammed, Al Arab, Alara, & Al-Rawashdeh, 2021).

Students from various age groups, academic backgrounds, and socioeconomic backgrounds can improve their academic performance and learning experiences using artificial Intelligence (Jokhan, Chand, Singh, & Mamun, 2022). Technologies based on Artificial Intelligence (AI) are essential to the creation of customised learning paths. AI makes it possible to employ various teaching strategies that benefit every student, considering their learning challenges, skills, and areas of strength and weakness. Social and emotional learning abilities may be developed using advanced analytics and machine learning (Hidalgo, Gabaly, Morales-Alonso, & Urueña, 2020). New technologies allow teachers to create individualised learning routes and examine qualitative and quantitative data. Using an immersive virtual environment, Artificial Intelligence, data, analytics, and machine learning assist teachers in delivering instructional courses to pupils (Mao, 2022). This strategy aids in guaranteeing the calibre of online education and efficient instruction.

Artificial intelligence technologies assist teachers in creating a sophisticated learning environment. Education administration may become more inclusive, and learning can become more customised and flexible (Kauppi, Muukkonen, Suorsa, & Takala, 2020; Whalley, France, Park, Mauchline, & Welsh, 2021). Students can develop knowledge and abilities that are in demand in society with the aid of new learning settings. Customised learning is the cornerstone for successfully achieving the established goals when educational technologies are connected to other cutting-edge pedagogical approaches (Villegas-Ch & García-Ortiz, 2023). The potential of AIEd technologies for individualised teaching strategies is seen in Figure 2.

Figure 2. Technologies in personalised approaches to learning
(Tapalova & Zhiyenbayeva, 2022)

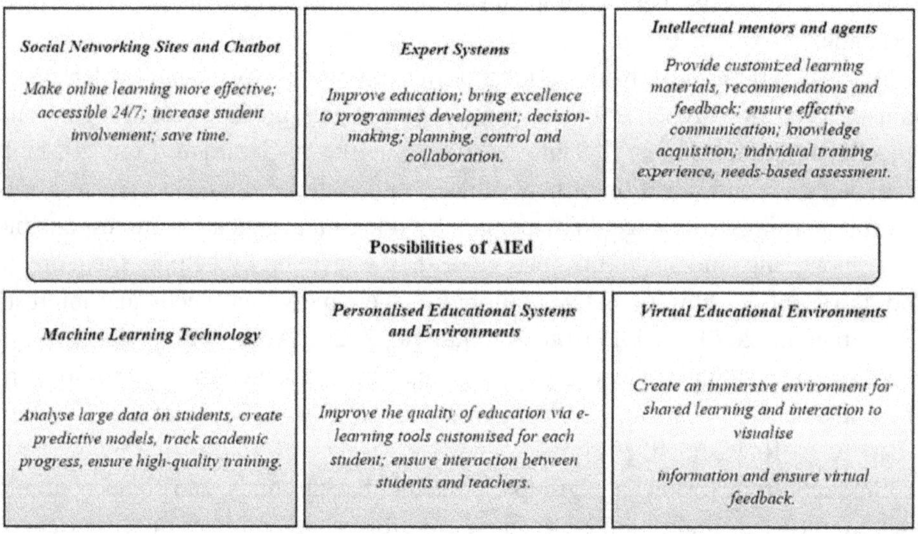

Artificial Intelligence in education technologies is useful for developing students' competencies. The new methods assist pupils in gaining information and abilities necessary for future challenges. Students apply and acquire new skills when they encounter strange or difficult circumstances. *Nanyang Technological University* is a Singaporean university that has studied virtual reality in medical teaching (Lee et al., 2022). Virtual reality technology enhances knowledge of medical topics (Barteit, Lanfermann, Bärnighausen, Neuhann, & Beiersmann, 2021; McGovern, Moreira, & Luna-Nevarez, 2020). A different study on digital education looked at the issue of online gamification for the growth of entrepreneurial abilities. The specially designed online game positively impacted students' acquisition of entrepreneurial abilities (Pardo-Garcia & Barac, 2020).

Natural language processing has led to deep and network learning advancements and increased technological capacity for large-scale data analysis (Lauriola, Lavelli, & Aiolli, 2022). These days, artificial Intelligence (AI) can assess psychological traits, choose an algorithm for raw data analysis, and use technology to detect stress, anxiety, and depression(Mentis, Lee, & Roussos, 2023). The Intelligent Computer-Assisted Language Acquisition (ICALL) system was created to use artificial Intelligence in language acquisition. Personalised teaching materials, machine translation tools, chatbots, artificial intelligence-based platforms and applications for language learning, intelligent learning systems, adaptive and intelligent systems for collaborative learning, and intelligent virtual reality are all part of the system (Patty, 2024; Weng & Chiu, 2023).

Challenges and Limitations of AI in Higher Education

For a considerable time, the complexity of human Intelligence was underestimated, particularly in the expert systems domain—managerial obstacles and technological limits still beset expert system development. Nevertheless, despite some setbacks, the future of expert systems is bright.

Negative Results

There are risks associated with using artificial Intelligence in higher education. The risk of unfavourable results is one (Chatterjee & Bhattacharjee, 2020). There will be unanticipated negative outcomes or the possibility of a backlash, even with the greatest intentions of people who create and utilise these systems. Various aspects need to be considered to prevent these negative consequences. The data these tools use is among the first to be considered. The data quality can vary; it can be antiquated and old, or it might come from a population subset that does not necessarily correspond with the students who are the target audience. AI learning systems, for instance, may not produce the same results or reflect the same accuracy for students in different regions of the nation when tested on students at a specific type of institution or university in California (Chan, 2023; Yu, Li, Fischer, Doroudi, & Xu, 2020). Likewise, an artificial intelligence system designed for Generation X students would be less effective for native digital learners (Hernandez-de-Menendez, Escobar Díaz, & Morales-Menendez, 2020; Pikhart & Klímová, 2020).

Implementation

Teachers and staff must know these systems' limits and advantages to use them properly (Rapanta, Botturi, Goodyear, Guàrdia, & Koole, 2020). Schools must also establish explicit procedures for staff members to follow when algorithmic evaluations or suggestions conflict with their professional judgment. They need explicit guidelines regarding when to follow or ignore computer-generated insights to avoid unfair inconsistencies (Minow, 2023).

Teaching Staff

There are no signs that AI-based apps in higher education are gaining traction, even if the educational technology sector is still producing new innovations (Alam & Mohanty, 2022). Their primary shortcoming is that, rather than addressing the concerns and problems that educators deal with daily, they advocate for novel approaches to teaching organisation that run counter to established customs (Yurkofsky, Peterson, Mehta, Horwitz-Willis, & Frumin, 2020), frequently needing more thorough assessments to back up the purported advantages of the novel approaches (Blanco-Elorrieta & Caramazza, 2021). It should be no surprise that teachers hear what vendors offer but may only embrace some of what is put forth. In this context, some nations have already created policies that aid the domestic educational technology sector's initiatives to foster innovation, bolster teacher demand qualification and empowerment mechanisms, and support their creative practices (Cole, 2023). Lastly, these policies investigate how artificial Intelligence (AI) can enhance the vibrant and more empirically based higher education learning environment.

Predictive algorithms can be used by platforms that offer learning analytics to assist teachers in identifying and foreseeing the learning challenges that students may encounter and then implementing tailored interventions to address those challenges (Mathrani, Susnjak, Ramaswami, & Barczak, 2021). Although predictive algorithms aid in the analysis and interpretation of data, learning analytics systems are not powerful because of these algorithms. Their relevance and use for teachers and students determine their effectiveness. Instantaneous data processing ought to yield instantaneous response, facilitating prompt pedagogical intervention and customised education (Siddiqui et al., 2023). Teachers need to take the lead role going forward.

Given that they are more accustomed to the needs of their pupils, managers and instructors should have enough authority to run their organisations and curricula (Hoq, 2020). Only when teachers and administrators are given the authority to oversee the provision of educational services at their institutions can automated testing support this autonomy. If not, using AI-driven technology will only cause confusion and contradicting outcomes, if not downright harmful.

Teachers will, therefore, continue to be at the forefront of higher education; those who argue that Artificial Intelligence (AI) can replace teachers are mistaken (Seldon, Abidoye, & Metcalf, 2020). Their arguments reduce university instruction to the completion of purely cognitive and routine tasks, disregard research that emphasises the value of a human tutor in assisting students with their learning and downplay the creative and socioemotional components of training beyond the simple transfer of knowledge. Furthermore, given their liberty above, university teachers will always determine how and when to use AI-enabled instruments. "Provide the support that teachers need – not the support that technologists or designers think they need" is the goal of the collaborative process that should accompany the creation of these AI-supported tools and their incorporation into higher education programmes (Pedró, 2020). Nevertheless, there are chances to automate many mundane and administrative duties that instructors now conduct, such as record-keeping and classification. By automating these kinds of chores, educators can free up more time to focus on the imaginative, compassionate, and motivating facets of teaching.

Teacher training is essential for educators to use educational data to enhance their teaching tactics and methods, which is necessary for the future generalisation of AI use in higher education institutions (Kuleto et al., 2021). The following new skills would also need to be assimilated by teachers for them to use AI-supported technologies effectively:

- Research and data analysis skills to interpret data provided by AI-based systems, interrogate data and give students feedback based on perceptions that emerge from the data.
- A clear understanding of how AI-supported systems can facilitate learning and the ability to make sound value judgements about new products and solutions offered to them in the classroom.
- A critical viewpoint on how artificial Intelligence (AI) and digital technologies impact people's lives, as well as innovative computer science and digital skill frameworks that help students comprehend AI's potential, risks, and power.

Therefore, these new talents should be considered in higher education institutions' teacher education programmes. However, educators need not just be ready to grasp the new technology opportunities that digital and AI education brings.

ETHICAL CONSIDERATION

The ethical consideration that emerges from the extensive gathering, creation, examination, and distribution of personal data about individuals warrants further attention when examining the potential of artificial Intelligence (Gerlick & Liozu, 2020; Richey Jr, Chowdhury, Davis-Sramek, Giannakis, & Dwivedi, 2023). Nonetheless, it should be highlighted that comprehending the moral ramifications of emerging technology is by no means a novel objective. What constitutes an ethical use of technology has been the central challenge for academics and practitioners trying to establish information ethics for the past thirty years. Many ethical issues can be discussed as follows:

- Entry to higher education. An increasing number of educational establishments are employing automatic learning algorithms to admit or dismiss pupils. Two possible issues arise: (1) A deficiency in clarity. Certain programmes find it difficult to justify the acceptance of some students while rejecting others. Is it fair that every pupil be entitled to comprehend those reasons? (2) unfair Discrimination. The results of training machine learning algorithms with a particular data set—students from a Western European nation, for example—might not be immediately transferable to students in other countries. When used in a different group, the original database may unfairly discriminate against that group due to its prejudice.
- Suggestions for personal data. Should the suggestions stem from automated learning grounded in a substantial dataset, they might not be appropriate for pupils of an alternative target audience. This issue is resolved if the recommendations are founded on each student's unique educational background.
- Accountability: What happens if the automated choices that direct pupils' learning are incorrect? In the end, who or what is accountable and responsible? Who is the platform's owner? The teacher that was assigned to you? The formula?
- Impact at work. What will happen to teachers' work if AI systems start automating more and more of the duties that they currently perform? Artificial intelligence (AI) systems can determine a student's starting competency level, assist her through the course's many phases by utilising both individual and collective Intelligence, automatically analyse exam results, and even recreate, to some extent, student-teacher interaction.
- Infrastructural Requirements:
    - Hardware and Software: Detailing the necessary computational resources, such as servers and cloud services, and software platforms needed for AI implementation (Slimi & Carballido, 2023). Network Infrastructure: Discussing the importance of robust internet connectivity and internal network infrastructure to support AI technologies. Learning

Management Systems (LMS): Exploring how AI can be integrated with existing LMS or require new platforms.

- Cost Considerations:
    - Initial Investment: Estimating the upfront costs associated with hardware, software, and training. Maintenance and Upgrades: Discussing the ongoing costs for maintenance, updates, and potential system upgrades. Cost Benefit Analysis: Providing a framework for institutions to assess the financial feasibility and long-term benefits of AI implementation (Remian, 2019).
- Resistance to Change:
    - Faculty and Staff: Addressing potential scepticism or resistance from faculty and staff, who may be concerned about job security, the effectiveness of AI, or the loss of personal touch in teaching. Cultural and Organizational Change Management: Offering strategies to manage change effectively, including stakeholder engagement, training programs, and phased implementation to ease the transition. Ethical and Privacy Concerns: Tackling concerns related to student data privacy, ethical use of AI, and ensuring transparency in AI-driven decisions (Abbas, 2023).
- Training and Professional Development:
    - Faculty Training: Highlighting the need for training programs to help faculty understand and leverage AI tools in their teaching. Staff Development: Discussing the importance of equipping administrative staff with the knowledge to support AI infrastructure and address student queries (Pedro et al., 2019).
- Student Engagement and Feedback:
    - Student Orientation: Creating programs to familiarize students with AI tools and their benefits for learning. Feedback Mechanisms: Establishing channels for student feedback on AI tools to continually improve their effectiveness and user experience (Zawacki-Richter et al., 2019).
- Pilot Programs and Phased Rollouts:
    - Testing and Evaluation: Recommending pilot programs to test AI implementations in controlled settings before a full rollout. Phased Implementation: Suggesting a phased approach to implementation, starting with noncritical areas to allow for learning and adjustments (Airaj, 2024; Nguyen, Ngo, Hong, Dang, & Nguyen, 2023).

FUTURE RESEARCH OF AI IN HIGHER EDUCATION

Personalised education entails reaching out to students wherever they are at any time, creating a feeling of community, and sending them tailored messages via the media they choose. A successful institution will see the experience of its students as a lifetime that starts with recruitment and admissions lasts the duration of their stay, and continues into their careers or graduate studies. Technology and data must collaborate across departments, including admissions, career services, health services, and inside the classroom, to stay linked during this lifelong journey. Institutions aiming to boost enrolment, engage students, and stay competitive in the higher education market must integrate every facet of the college system.

Currently impractical, customising a curriculum to each student's needs will become feasible using AI-powered devices. Using chatbots, predictive analytics, and process automation in various college system components is just the start of what lies ahead. In the future, a machine that uses computer vision technology will examine students' facial expressions to ascertain whether they have understood the material. Institutions may improve student and institutional success by gaining proactive insights and personalising the student experience at scale with a 360-degree perspective of each student. The instructor could change the pace of delivery to make the learning process more student-centred rather than instructor-centric.

Artificial Intelligence (AI) and machine learning developments have progressively enabled chatbots to transform into Intelligent Virtual Assistants (IVAs). A select few businesses employ IVAs enhanced with deep domain knowledge to comprehend their customers' intent and preferences completely, satisfy their needs, and gradually enhance performance by learning from each interaction. Although IVA is only used in a few HEIs, the Georgia Institute of Technology's AI Teaching Assistant looks into the day when technology would manage classes without human interaction. Professors would devote their efforts with the aid of IVA to developing a solid curriculum that AI can customise and evaluate further.

AI can enhance productivity not only in student-related areas but also in other areas of college campuses. However, more research must be done on applying AI in college administrative departments. Chatbots with round-the-clock assistance might manage any office, including the bursar's office and the health and counselling centre. Big data can be transformed into useful, actionable insights by moving college departments towards an automated, self-managing, and self-improving system.

CONCLUSION

In conclusion, the extensive exploration of Artificial intelligence (AI) in higher education underscores its transformative potential in automating teaching and learning, providing personalized feedback, and introducing intelligent tutoring systems. AI's capability to automate grading and offer tailored feedback presents an opportunity to enhance educational efficiency and efficacy, particularly in STEM fields. Intelligent tutoring systems, including AI chatbots and virtual culture initiatives, demonstrate the capacity to support diverse learning needs and facilitate immersive, interactive learning experiences. Despite these advancements, integrating AI in higher education has challenges, including ethical considerations, teacher training, and the importance of aligning AI applications with educational goals.

Moreover, the potential for AI to customize the educational experience holds promise for addressing individual student needs and learning styles, thereby fostering a more inclusive and effective learning environment. However, successful implementation necessitates careful consideration of ethical implications, particularly regarding data privacy and the potential for algorithmic bias. The future of AI in higher education hinges on balancing technological innovation with ethical responsibility, ensuring that AI serves as a tool to enhance, rather than replace, the human elements of teaching and learning.

To harness the full potential of AI in higher education, institutions must embrace a holistic approach that includes investing in teacher training, addressing ethical and privacy concerns, and fostering a culture of continuous improvement and innovation. By doing so, higher education can leverage AI to create more personalized, efficient, and inclusive learning experiences that prepare students for the challenges of the 21st century.

REFERENCES

Abbas, T. (2023). Ethical Implications of AI in Modern Education: Balancing Innovation and Responsibility. *Social Sciences Spectrum*, *2*(1), 51–57.

Agarwal, S., Punn, N. S., Sonbhadra, S. K., Tanveer, M., Nagabhushan, P., Pandian, K., & Saxena, P. (2020). Unleashing the power of disruptive and emerging technologies amid COVID-19: A detailed review. *arXiv preprint arXiv:2005.11507*.

Airaj, M. (2024). Ethical artificial intelligence for teaching-learning in higher education. *Education and Information Technologies*, 1–23. doi:10.1007/s10639-024-12545-x

Al Rawashdeh, A. Z., Mohammed, E. Y., Al Arab, A. R., Alara, M., Al-Rawashdeh, B., & Al-Rawashdeh, B. (2021). Advantages and disadvantages of using e-learning in university education: Analyzing students' perspectives. *Electronic Journal of e-Learning, 19*(3), 107–117. doi:10.34190/ejel.19.3.2168

Alam, A., & Mohanty, A. (2022). Business models, business strategies, and innovations in EdTech companies: integration of learning analytics and artificial intelligence in higher education. *Paper presented at the 2022 IEEE 6th Conference on Information and Communication Technology (CICT).* IEEE. 10.1109/CICT56698.2022.9997887

Barteit, S., Lanfermann, L., Bärnighausen, T., Neuhann, F., & Beiersmann, C. (2021). Augmented, mixed, and virtual reality-based head-mounted devices for medical education: Systematic review. *JMIR Serious Games, 9*(3), e29080. doi:10.2196/29080 PMID:34255668

Bishop, P. A., Downes, J. M., Netcoh, S., Farber, K., DeMink-Carthew, J., Brown, T., & Mark, R. (2020). Teacher roles in personalized learning environments. *The Elementary School Journal, 121*(2), 311–336. doi:10.1086/711079

Blanco-Elorrieta, E., & Caramazza, A. (2021). On the need for theoretically guided approaches to possible bilingual advantages: An evaluation of the potential loci in the language and executive control systems. *Neurobiology of Language (Cambridge, Mass.), 2*(4), 452–463. doi:10.1162/nol_a_00041 PMID:37214630

Chan, C. K. Y. (2023). A comprehensive AI policy education framework for university teaching and learning. *International Journal of Educational Technology in Higher Education, 20*(1), 38. doi:10.1186/s41239-023-00408-3

Chang, A., Chabot, S., Mathews, J., Briggs, S., Strzalkowski, T., Si, M., & Braasch, J. (2022). A spatially-aware companion system for language learning and foreign-language dialogue. *Paper presented at the Proceedings of the 24th International Congress on Acoustics (ICA).* IEEE.

Chatterjee, S., & Bhattacharjee, K. K. (2020). Adoption of artificial intelligence in higher education: A quantitative analysis using structural equation modelling. *Education and Information Technologies, 25*(5), 3443–3463. doi:10.1007/s10639-020-10159-7

Cole, L. (2023). Leadership, Education and Training for Youth in Contemporary African Union Programs. *Afrika Tanulmányok/Hungarian. Journal of African Studies, 17*(1), 69–102.

Divekar, R. R. (2020). *AI enabled foreign language immersion: Technology and method to acquire foreign languages with AI in immersive virtual worlds*. Rensselaer Polytechnic Institute.

Elshani, L., & Nuçi, K. P. (2021). Constructing a personalized learning path using genetic algorithms approach. *arXiv preprint arXiv:2104.11276*.

Fariani, R. I., Junus, K., & Santoso, H. B. (2023). A Systematic Literature Review on Personalised Learning in the Higher Education Context. *Technology. Knowledge and Learning*, *28*(2), 449–476. doi:10.1007/s10758-022-09628-4

Fernandez-Antolin, M.-M., del Río, J. M., & Gonzalez-Lezcano, R.-A. (2021). The use of gamification in higher technical education: Perception of university students on innovative teaching materials. *International Journal of Technology and Design Education*, *31*(5), 1019–1038. doi:10.1007/s10798-020-09583-0

George, B., & Wooden, O. (2023). Managing the strategic transformation of higher education through artificial intelligence. *Administrative Sciences*, *13*(9), 196. doi:10.3390/admsci13090196

Gerlick, J. A., & Liozu, S. M. (2020). Ethical and legal considerations of artificial intelligence and algorithmic decision-making in personalized pricing. *Journal of Revenue and Pricing Management*, *19*(2), 85–98. doi:10.1057/s41272-019-00225-2

Górriz, J. M., Ramírez, J., Ortíz, A., Martinez-Murcia, F. J., Segovia, F., Suckling, J., & Bologna, G. (2020). Artificial intelligence within the interplay between natural and artificial computation: Advances in data science, trends and applications. *Neurocomputing*, *410*, 237–270. doi:10.1016/j.neucom.2020.05.078

Gundlach, E., & Ward, M. D. (2021). The data mine: Enabling data science across the curriculum. *Journal of Statistics and Data Science Education*, *29*(sup1), S74-S82.

Hannan, E., & Liu, S. (2021). AI: New source of competitiveness in higher education. *Competitiveness Review*, *33*(2), 265–279. doi:10.1108/CR-03-2021-0045

Hannan, E., & Liu, S. (2023). AI: New source of competitiveness in higher education. *Competitiveness Review*, *33*(2), 265–279. doi:10.1108/CR-03-2021-0045

Hernandez-de-Menendez, M., Escobar Díaz, C. A., & Morales-Menendez, R. (2020). Educational experiences with Generation Z. [IJIDeM]. *International Journal on Interactive Design and Manufacturing*, *14*(3), 847–859. doi:10.1007/s12008-020-00674-9

Hidalgo, A., Gabaly, S., Morales-Alonso, G., & Urueña, A. (2020). The digital divide in light of sustainable development: An approach through advanced machine learning techniques. *Technological Forecasting and Social Change, 150*, 119754. doi:10.1016/j.techfore.2019.119754

Hoq, M. Z. (2020). E-Learning during the period of pandemic (COVID-19) in the kingdom of Saudi Arabia: An empirical study. *American Journal of Educational Research, 8*(7), 457–464.

Jokhan, A., Chand, A. A., Singh, V., & Mamun, K. A. (2022). Increased digital resource consumption in higher educational institutions and the artificial intelligence role in informing decisions related to student performance. *sustainability, 14*(4), 2377.

Kauppi, S., Muukkonen, H., Suorsa, T., & Takala, M. (2020). I still miss human contact, but this is more flexible—Paradoxes in virtual learning interaction and multidisciplinary collaboration. *British Journal of Educational Technology, 51*(4), 1101–1116. doi:10.1111/bjet.12929

Kucirkova, N., Gerard, L., & Linn, M. C. (2021). Designing personalised instruction: A research and design framework. *British Journal of Educational Technology, 52*(5), 1839–1861. doi:10.1111/bjet.13119

Kuleto, V., Ilić, M., Dumangiu, M., Ranković, M., Martins, O. M., Păun, D., & Mihoreanu, L. (2021). Exploring opportunities and challenges of artificial intelligence and machine learning in higher education institutions. *sustainability, 13*(18), 10424.

Lauriola, I., Lavelli, A., & Aiolli, F. (2022). An introduction to deep learning in natural language processing: Models, techniques, and tools. *Neurocomputing, 470*, 443–456. doi:10.1016/j.neucom.2021.05.103

Le, D.-N., Van Le, C., Tromp, J. G., & Nguyen, G. N. (2018). *Emerging technologies for health and medicine: virtual reality, augmented reality, artificial intelligence, internet of things, robotics, industry 4.0*.

Lee, T., Wen, Y., Chan, M., Azam, A., Looi, C. K., Taib, S., Ooi, C. H., Huang, L. H., Xie, Y., & Cai, Y. (2022). Investigation of virtual & augmented reality classroom learning environments in university STEM education. *Interactive Learning Environments*, 1–16. doi:10.1080/10494820.2022.2155838

Liu, H., Liu, Z., Wu, Z., & Tang, J. (2020). Personalized multimodal feedback generation in education. *arXiv preprint arXiv:2011.00192*. doi:10.18653/v1/2020.coling-main.166

Luckin, R., Cukurova, M., Kent, C., & du Boulay, B. (2022). Empowering educators to be AI-ready. *Computers and Education: Artificial Intelligence*, *3*, 100076.

Mageira, K., Pittou, D., Papasalouros, A., Kotis, K., Zangogianni, P., & Daradoumis, A. (2022). Educational AI chatbots for content and language integrated learning. *Applied Sciences (Basel, Switzerland)*, *12*(7), 3239. doi:10.3390/app12073239

Mao, W. (2022). Video analysis of intelligent teaching based on machine learning and virtual reality technology. *Neural Computing & Applications*, *34*(9), 6603–6614. doi:10.1007/s00521-021-06072-w

Mathrani, A., Susnjak, T., Ramaswami, G., & Barczak, A. (2021). Perspectives on the challenges of generalizability, transparency and ethics in predictive learning analytics. *Computers and Education Open*, *2*, 100060. doi:10.1016/j.caeo.2021.100060

McGovern, E., Moreira, G., & Luna-Nevarez, C. (2020). An application of virtual reality in education: Can this technology enhance the quality of students' learning experience? *Journal of Education for Business*, *95*(7), 490–496. doi:10.1080/08832323.2019.1703096

Mentis, A.-F. A., Lee, D., & Roussos, P. (2023). Applications of artificial intelligence−machine learning for detection of stress: A critical overview. *Molecular Psychiatry*, 1–13. doi:10.1038/s41380-023-02047-6 PMID:37020048

Minow, M. (2023). Equality, Equity, and Algorithms: Learning from Justice Rosalie Abella. *University of Toronto Law Journal*, *73*(Supplement 2), 163–178. doi:10.3138/utlj-2023-0064

Nguyen, A., Ngo, H. N., Hong, Y., Dang, B., & Nguyen, B.-P. T. (2023). Ethical principles for artificial intelligence in education. *Education and Information Technologies*, *28*(4), 4221–4241. doi:10.1007/s10639-022-11316-w PMID:36254344

Pardamean, B., Suparyanto, T., Cenggoro, T. W., Sudigyo, D., & Anugrahana, A. (2022). AI-based learning style prediction in online learning for primary education. *IEEE Access : Practical Innovations, Open Solutions*, *10*, 35725–35735. doi:10.1109/ACCESS.2022.3160177

Pardo-Garcia, C., & Barac, M. (2020). Promoting employability in higher education: A case study on boosting entrepreneurship skills. *sustainability, 12*(10), 4004.

Patty, J. (2024). The Use Of Ai In Language Learning: What You Need To Know. *Jurnal Review Pendidikan dan Pengajaran (JRPP), 7*(1), 642-654.

Pedró, F. (2020). Applications of Artificial Intelligence to higher education: Possibilities, evidence, and challenges. *IUL Research, 1*(1), 61–76. doi:10.57568/iulres.v1i1.43

Pedro, F., Subosa, M., Rivas, A., & Valverde, P. (2019). *Artificial intelligence in education: Challenges and opportunities for sustainable development.*

Pikhart, M., & Klímová, B. (2020). eLearning 4.0 as a sustainability strategy for generation Z language learners: Applied linguistics of second language acquisition in younger adults. *Societies (Basel, Switzerland), 10*(2), 38. doi:10.3390/soc10020038

Rapanta, C., Botturi, L., Goodyear, P., Guàrdia, L., & Koole, M. (2020). Online university teaching during and after the Covid-19 crisis: Refocusing teacher presence and learning activity. *Postdigital science and education, 2*, 923-945.

Remian, D. (2019). *Augmenting education: ethical considerations for incorporating artificial intelligence in education.*

Richey Jr, R. G., Chowdhury, S., Davis-Sramek, B., Giannakis, M., & Dwivedi, Y. K. (2023). *Artificial intelligence in logistics and supply chain management: A primer and roadmap for research.* Wiley Online Library.

Salvaris, M., Dean, D., & Tok, W. H. (2018). *Deep learning with azure. Building and Deploying Artificial Intelligence Solutions on Microsoft AI Platform.* Apress.

Sayers, D., Sousa-Silva, R., Höhn, S., Ahmedi, L., Allkivi-Metsoja, K., Anastasiou, D., & Catala, A. (2021). The Dawn of the Human-Machine Era: A forecast of new and emerging language technologies.

Schiff, D. (2021). Out of the laboratory and into the classroom: The future of artificial intelligence in education. *AI & Society, 36*(1), 331–348. doi:10.1007/s00146-020-01033-8 PMID:32836908

Seldon, A., Abidoye, O., & Metcalf, T. (2020). *The Fourth Education Revolution Reconsidered: Will Artificial Intelligence Enrich Or Diminish Humanity?* Legend Press Ltd.

Shemshack, A., & Spector, J. M. (2020). A systematic literature review of personalized learning terms. *Smart Learning Environments, 7*(1), 1–20. doi:10.1186/s40561-020-00140-9

Siddiqui, S. T., Sohail, M. M. A., Aftab, A., Sarfaraz, M., Alam, M. I., & Salim, A. (2023). Enhancing Efficiency and Empowering Institutions: Leveraging Wireless Sensor Devices, IoT Edge Computing, and Fog Computing in Educational Systems. *Paper presented at the 2023 7th International Conference on Computation System and Information Technology for Sustainable Solutions (CSITSS).* IEEE. 10.1109/CSITSS60515.2023.10334212

Singh, S. V., & Hiran, K. K. (2022). The Impact of AI on Teaching and Learning in Higher Education Technology. *Journal of Higher Education Theory and Practice, 12*(13).

Slimi, Z., & Carballido, B. V. (2023). Navigating the Ethical Challenges of Artificial Intelligence in Higher Education: An Analysis of Seven Global AI Ethics Policies. *TEM Journal, 12*(2).

Sousa, M., Dal Mas, F., Pesqueira, A., Lemos, C., Verde, J. M., & Cobianchi, L. (2021). The potential of AI in health higher education to increase the students' learning outcomes. *The potential of AI in health higher education to increase the students' learning outcomes,* (2), 488-497.

Šumak, B., Brdnik, S., & Pušnik, M. (2021). Sensors and artificial intelligence methods and algorithms for human–computer intelligent interaction: A systematic mapping study. *Sensors (Basel), 22*(1), 20. doi:10.3390/s22010020 PMID:35009562

Tajane, K., Dave, S., Jahagirdar, P., Ghadge, A., & Musale, A. (2018). AI based chat-bot using azure cognitive services. *Paper presented at the 2018 Fourth International Conference on Computing Communication Control and Automation (ICCUBEA).* IEEE. 10.1109/ICCUBEA.2018.8697737

Tapalova, O., & Zhiyenbayeva, N. (2022). Artificial Intelligence in Education: AIEd for Personalised Learning Pathways. *Electronic Journal of e-Learning, 20*(5), 639–653. doi:10.34190/ejel.20.5.2597

Tsai, Y.-S., Perrotta, C., & Gašević, D. (2020). Empowering learners with personalised learning approaches? Agency, equity and transparency in the context of learning analytics. *Assessment & Evaluation in Higher Education, 45*(4), 554–567. doi:10.1080/02602938.2019.1676396

Villegas-Ch, W., & García-Ortiz, J. (2023). Enhancing Learning Personalization in Educational Environments through Ontology-Based Knowledge Representation. *Computers, 12*(10), 199. doi:10.3390/computers12100199

Weng, X., & Chiu, T. K. (2023). Instructional design and learning outcomes of intelligent computer assisted language learning: Systematic review in the field. *Computers and Education: Artificial Intelligence*, 100117.

Whalley, B., France, D., Park, J., Mauchline, A., & Welsh, K. (2021). Towards flexible personalized learning and the future educational system in the fourth industrial revolution in the wake of Covid-19. *Higher Education Pedagogies*, *6*(1), 79–99. doi:10.1080/23752696.2021.1883458

Yu, R., Li, Q., Fischer, C., Doroudi, S., & Xu, D. (2020). Towards Accurate and Fair Prediction of College Success: Evaluating Different Sources of Student Data. *International educational data mining society*.

Yurkofsky, M. M., Peterson, A. J., Mehta, J. D., Horwitz-Willis, R., & Frumin, K. M. (2020). Research on continuous improvement: Exploring the complexities of managing educational change. *Review of Research in Education*, *44*(1), 403–433. doi:10.3102/0091732X20907363

Zawacki-Richter, O., Marín, V. I., Bond, M., & Gouverneur, F. (2019). Systematic review of research on artificial intelligence applications in higher education–where are the educators? *International Journal of Educational Technology in Higher Education*, *16*(1), 1–27. doi:10.1186/s41239-019-0171-0

Zhang, W., Wu, Y., & Calautit, J. K. (2022). A review on occupancy prediction through machine learning for enhancing energy efficiency, air quality and thermal comfort in the built environment. *Renewable & Sustainable Energy Reviews*, *167*, 112704. doi:10.1016/j.rser.2022.112704

ADDITIONAL READING

Alordiah, C. O. (2023). Proliferation of Artificial Intelligence Tools: Adaptation Strategies in the Higher Education Sector. *Propellers Journal of Education*, *2*(1), 53–65.

Cantú-Ortiz, F. J., Galeano Sánchez, N., Garrido, L., Terashima-Marin, H., & Brena, R. F. (2020). An artificial intelligence educational strategy for the digital Transformation. [IJIDeM]. *International Journal on Interactive Design and Manufacturing*, *14*(4), 1195–1209. doi:10.1007/s12008-020-00702-8

George, B., & Wooden, O. (2023). Managing the strategic Transformation of higher education through Artificial Intelligence. *Administrative Sciences*, *13*(9), 196. doi:10.3390/admsci13090196

Hutson, J., Jeevanjee, T., Vander Graaf, V., Lively, J., Weber, J., Weir, G., & Plate, D. (2022). Artificial Intelligence and the Disruption of Higher Education: Strategies for Integrations across Disciplines. *Creative Education, 13*(12), 3953–3980. doi:10.4236/ce.2022.1312253

Ocaña-Fernández, Y., Valenzuela-Fernández, L. A., & Garro-Aburto, L. L. (2019). Artificial Intelligence and Its Implications in Higher Education. *Journal of Educational Psychology-Propositos y Representaciones*, 7(2), 553–568.

KEY TERMS AND DEFINITIONS

Adaptive Learning Technologies: Refers to technology that, to improve a learner's performance through automated and instructor interventions, dynamically adapts to the kind or degree of course content based on the learner's skills or skill attainment.

Educational Applications: The educational application is software that makes virtual instruction possible and easier. It is not only for students but also for candidates, instructors, experts, online learning environments, and everyone looking to enhance their knowledge or abilities.

Educational Transformation: This refers to systemic changes in the prevailing educational model. Maintaining the core of the conventional teaching and learning process, together with its structure and organisation, separate from theories that support changes or renovations of specific model components.

Grading Automation: One tool intended to assist teachers or organisations in doing assessments more rapidly and efficiently is automated grading.

Personalised Feedback: In times of uncertainty and isolation, teachers might employ the tactic of personalised feedback to foster social connectivity among students.

Chapter 9
Navigating the Impact of AI Integration in Higher Education:
Ethical Frontiers

Dina Ahmed Mohamed Ghandour
https://orcid.org/0000-0003-0269-1872
Majan University College, Oman

ABSTRACT

Artificial intelligence has gained significant traction in various industries, including education, due to its potential to improve academic outcomes. However, the rapid advancement of technology raises concerns that educational discourse may lag behind in understanding its pros and cons. Thus, this chapter examines ethical considerations when incorporating AI into higher education institutions, with the aim to develop a conceptual framework to provide various stakeholders with precise guidelines.

INTRODUCTION

Technological advances and increased global connectivity have changed the world in many ways, including how we live economically, ecologically, and socially. The term "megatrend" describes the overall pattern of these changes. Haluza and Jungwirth (2023), revealed that for the foreseeable future, these megatrends will be around. Specifically, technology like ChatGPT from Open AI is a result of the exponential growth of Artificial Intelligence in the last few years. Technologically advanced

DOI: 10.4018/979-8-3693-2145-4.ch009

and potentially game-changing, the ChatGPT language model is shaking up the educational system. Responsible and ethical use of ChatGPT and other artificial intelligence tools is of the utmost importance, as its use in higher educational institutions continues to expand. In light of this, the current gold standard for chatbot technology is ChatGPT.

The speed and accuracy with which it generates high-quality text is one of the things that makes this chatbot unique. Despite widespread interest, some are concerned that it may alter the standards by which various disciplines assess student performance (Rudolph et al., 2023). The complex and multi-faceted nature of ChatGPT and other AI algorithms necessitates an all-encompassing and interdisciplinary approach to ensure its responsible and ethical use in educational settings. Academic investigations into AI in the classroom have lately focused on questions of responsibility and ethics. (Hamilton et al., 2020; Borenstein & Howard, 2021; Nguyen et al., 2022). Few studies have examined how problems such as bias, privacy, and the digital divide could be increased by AI. Thus, the importance of anticipating how AI will impact traditional classroom instruction has been emphasized by numerous scholars. Consequently, a number of researchers have stressed the need of interdisciplinary approaches to ensure the responsible and ethical use of AI in educational settings (Paulus & Langford, 2022; Hoppe et al., 2003; Carvalho et al., 2022).

In light of this, the objective of this chapter is to investigate the norms of ethical conduct for using AI in academic settings, all of which to develop a framework that incorporates ethical principles into AI-mediated education programs. To tackle the moral questions brought up by AI in the classroom, this framework will be helpful for policymakers, educators, students, and regulators. Within its eight parts, this chapter covers a vast array of areas, from outlining AI's ethical standards to creating a theoretical framework that accounts for the most important ethical concerns raised by AI in academic settings. Therefore, recommendations and future directions for ethical AI usage have been set forth for universities and their students.

LITERATURE REVIEW

AI's Impact on Students and Higher Education Institutions

Recently, there has been increased concern over the use of text-generative artificial intelligence (AI) in educational settings. Notable instances of this include Bing, ChatGPT, and Co-Pilot, the most recent addition to the Microsoft Office suite.

One of the primary worries is the potential for students to utilize generative AI tools to plagiarize or cheat on written assignments and tests (Chan, 2023). Concerning findings from an empirical study of university students revealed that nearly one-third had used artificial intelligence (AI) to some extent—such as essay-generating software—to finish assigned readings (Chan, 2023). Approximately one-third of the 1000 college students who took part in the survey in the United States admitted to using ChatGPT and other AI chatbots to complete written homework assignments. Notably, 60% of them said they relied on the program for more than half of their assignments. It's interesting to note that students have occasionally utilized ChatGPT and other generative AI tools for unethical purposes because of their ability to mimic human writing (Chan, 2023).

Interestingly, even though 75% of students think it is unethical to cheat, 30% of students still use these programs because they think their teachers are unaware that they are using them for that purpose. The survey also highlights a dilemma that some teachers are dealing with: should they advocate for ChatGPT's ban or incorporate it into their lesson plans. More importantly, 46% of students reported that their teachers or schools had already prohibited them from using the tool for homework. This led to discussions about stricter policies and sanctions to reduce the amount of academic misconduct cases involving AI (Chan, 2023).

There's also the concern that increasing the use of generative AI tools could deteriorate students' writing and critical thinking skills (Chan, 2023; Civil, 2023; Warschauer et al., 2023). According to academics, an over-reliance on automated tools may be harmful to the academic standards and learning outcomes of students (Chan & Lee, 2023; Korn & Kelly, 2023; Oliver, 2023; Zhai, 2022). Many academic institutions have taken the initiative to completely forbid the use of generative AI in their curricula in response to these concerns. Surprisingly, eight of the twenty-four prestigious UK Russell Group universities—including Cambridge and Oxford—have ruled that using AI bots for assignments is improper.

University plagiarism policies worldwide are also being updated as a result of concerns about academic integrity (Wood, 2023; Yau & Chan, 2023). In Australia, some universities are switching back to using paper exams and assessments (Cassidy, 2023; Cavendish, 2023). In spite of these reservations, advocates of generative AI believe that the technology has the power to transform education and improve learning environments for students. According to Kasneci et al. (2023) and Sinhaliz et al. (2023), generative AI may be able to assist students in identifying their areas of weakness and in developing their skills in an adaptive manner by providing them with tailored feedback and assistance. People are becoming increasingly excited and worried about the possible benefits and risks of artificial intelligence (AI) as it becomes more integrated into everyday life. Misuse or badly designed artificial intelligence applications could cause major societal and user-level disruptions (Fukuda-Parr & Gibbons, 2021).

Some worry that these technologies could make things worse, like more government authoritarianism, more data misuse, less personal agency, and more social injustice.

Fukuda-Parr and Gibbons (2021) note that such conflicts occur frequently in a wide variety of national and business settings.

Challenges to Stakeholders for Ethical AI Implementation

The possible threat that AI poses to more traditional methods of grading written work, like essays, is one of the main reasons it is not recommended to use it for writing task grading. Some teachers worry that because ChatGPT can produce appropriate text quickly, students will use the platform to outsource their work. This makes it more challenging to spot plagiarism cases, which worries some educators (Rudolph et al., 2023). This could, however, be the result of a resistance to changing the procedures used to assess students' learning. Written assignments are frequently faulted for being dull and useless in assessing students' knowledge and skill levels; nevertheless, this criticism might be the result of a resistance to changing the techniques employed to assess students' learning. Another thing that should worry people is that ChatGPT, which is essentially just a text-generating machine, cannot comprehend the information it produces or determine whether it is relevant or accurate.

Regulations that forbid its use may come from this, but it's also possible that ChatGPT technology will spread widely before establishments have a chance to change their guidelines. It would be more efficient to take a method that takes into account both the possible advantages and disadvantages of the platform and concentrates on fixing the problems that ChatGPT has caused. After a technological tool for education that has the potential to completely transform the field is released into the public domain, educators and legislators must address any issues that may arise from its use and come up with plans to replace ineffective teaching methods. One example of how crucial it is to adopt a responsible attitude when using technology in educational settings is the story of the Chinese schoolgirl who copied a ton of text using a machine.

METHODOLOGY

This study will adopt an analytical approach to synthesize the existing literature on the ethical use of AI in higher educational institutions. Based on this, a conceptual framework will be developed to gain insights, and recommendations as well as future directions for educators and learners will be provided.

ETHICAL POLICES FOR ARTIFICIAL INTELLIGENCE (AI) IN GENERAL

National policies are placing a greater emphasis on ethical issues in an attempt to encourage ethical AI management. Determining what is right or wrong is the main goal of these polices (Hogenhout, 2021, p. 11). Five core tenets were proposed by Floridi (2021) for the moral use of AI: beneficence, non-maleficence, autonomy, justice, and explicability. This framework serves as the foundation for many national AI policies that are currently being developed. Furthermore, Dexe and Franke (2020), found several implicit ethical principles after examining AI strategy documents from Nordic nations. Comparably, human-centric AI solutions and transparent, equitable AI usage in decision-making are given top priority in Singapore's official AI governance framework (IMDA & PDPC, 2020).

Organizations both domestically and abroad give ethics in AI policy top priority. In order to guide the ethical use of AI, UNESCO promotes human-centeredness and the adoption of human rights and values from the Universal Declaration of Human Rights (UDHR) (UNESCO, 2021b, 2023). Likewise, the European Union's AI strategy places a premium on ethics and employs a human-centered methodology, emphasizing adherence to laws, ethical congruence, and sociotechnical resilience to ensure reliable AI (Renda, 2020).

These policies' strong emphasis on ethics draws attention to the constraints that come with regulating AI applications. It is difficult to define ethical principles universally, which prevents some nations from developing comprehensive AI policies (Dexe & Franke, 2020). Furthermore, the widespread application of AI makes it more difficult to develop and implement policies in a variety of sectors (UNESCO, 2021b). As a result, model frameworks and ethical guidelines provide AI practitioners with directional guidance that they must adapt to different contexts (IMDA & PDPC, 2020).

In the future, national and international organizations will keep up their efforts to guarantee the responsible application of AI, concentrating on promoting dialogue and developing moral and legal guidelines (UNESCO, 2023). But these ideas remain mostly theoretical until they are applied to AI in the real world (Chatterjee, 2020). In order to properly manage AI practices in accordance with established legal and ethical guidelines, countries may eventually need to set up institutional support systems (Renda, 2020). Fundamental ethical guidelines for AI are compiled in Table 1 and are taken from various policies (IMDA & PDPC, 2020).

Table 1. Fundamental ethical code of conduct for AI

1. Accountability	Ensure AI actors are held responsible for the AI systems' functioning and adherence to ethical principles
2. Accuracy	Recognize and communicate sources of error and uncertainty in algorithms and data to inform mitigation procedures.
3. Auditability	Allow third parties to examine and review algorithm behavior through transparent information disclosure.
4. Explainability	Ensure that algorithmic decisions and underlying data can be explained in layman's terms.
5. Fairness	Prevent discriminatory impacts, include monitoring mechanisms, and consult diverse perspectives during system development.
6. Human Centricity & Well-being	Prioritize the well-being and needs of humans in AI development and implementation.
7.Human rights alignment	Ensure technologies do not violate internationally recognized human rights.
8. Inclusivity	Make AI accessible to everyone.
9. Progressiveness	Favor projects with significantly greater value than their alternatives.
10. Responsibility	Build trust through responsibility, accountability, and fairness, provide avenues for redress, and maintain records of design processes.
11. Robustness and Security	Ensure AI systems are safe, secure, and resistant to tampering or data compromise.
12. Sustainability	Favor implementations that provide long-lasting, Beneficial insights and can predict future behavior.

Source: IMDA & PDPC, 2020

ETHICS OF ARTIFICIAL INTELLIGENCE IN HIGHER EDUCATION

Artificial Intelligence (AI) in Higher Education: Ethical Applications

When using AI tools in educational settings, it is important to follow responsible and ethical practices to make sure that it is used in a way that is fair, safe, and considerate of students, teachers, and other stakeholders. Although there are many advantages to using artificial intelligence (AI) technology in educational settings like ChatGPT, there are also ethical and responsibility concerns that need to be considered.

The aforementioned Figure 1, provides an overview of the responsibilities and moral application of AI in the education sector. These obligations cover, among other things, respect for one's privacy, equity and nondiscrimination, and openness when using AI tools.

Figure 1. Responsible and ethical uses of AI in higher education
(Adapted from Mhlanga, D., 2023)

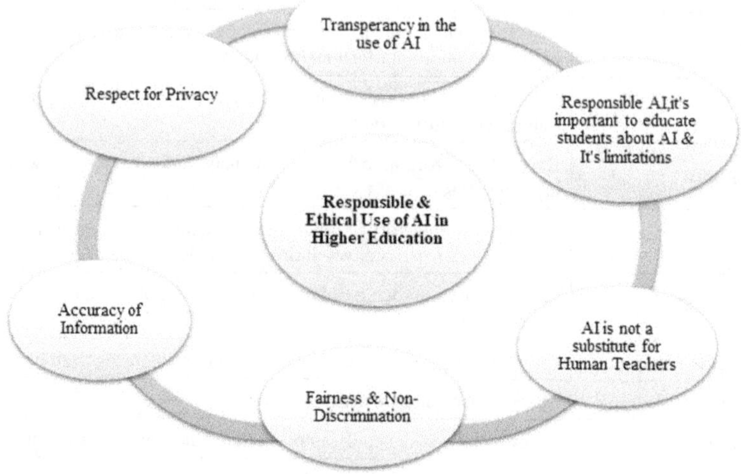

Adherence to Privacy

The privacy of user data protection is the first and most important concern. Students' personal information must be protected, and secured as AI tools is trained on vast amounts of data from the internet. Teachers should let their students know how GhatGPT and other AI tools will use and store their personal information before implementing them in the classroom. On top of that, students should know what security measures are in place to keep their data safe. Keeping users' personal information safe is a major concern for ChatGPT's educational use. Confidentiality of all parties participating in the educational process, including instructors, students, and others, must be guaranteed. Burger (2022) and Botha et al. (2017) note that businesses are required to protect individuals' private information by the General Data Protection Regulation (GDPR) of the European Union and the Children's Online Privacy Protection Act (COPPA) of the United States. Every one of these laws is identical in that it requires companies to take reasonable precautions to protect the personal information of various stakeholders. In light of this, all student information, grades, and test results gathered through artificial intelligence tools like ChatGPT in the classroom are part of this.

Loss of confidentiality could lead to serious legal and financial ramifications. More importantly, when students utilize ChatGPT in class, it is typically to share private information such as their grades, performance, and personal details. In order to keep the individuals' privacy intact, it is crucial to prevent the information from being accidentally or illegally used or disclosed. Myskja (2023) and Tartavulea et al. (2020), have also brought attention to the significance of trust in the learning process. If everyone participating in the educational process (students, teachers, and administrators) knows their information is kept confidential, they are more likely to be satisfied. But, trust is fragile, and when it is broken, it can have an adverse effect on the learning outcomes and user's satisfaction. It is essential that the creation and use of ChatGPT in educational settings adhere to ethical standards such as transparency, accountability, and informed consent.

Respecting people's right to privacy is an ethical necessity because it demonstrates that you care about people and their rights. For educational purposes, protecting user's privacy is of the utmost importance when using artificial intelligence tools like ChatGPT. Therefore, when it comes to educational technology, it is crucial to protect individuals' privacy, maintain their trust, and ensure the ethical use of AI tools. These three goals must be met in order for ChatGPT to be used ethically.

Accuracy of Information

It is critical to give accurate information when teaching scientific principles to avoid misunderstandings and misconceptions caused by incorrect knowledge. For example, if a student is taught that the world is flat, they will understand geography, astronomy, and any other relevant subjects taught alongside this topic incorrectly. Accurate knowledge is necessary for history lectures to effectively communicate the past's relevance to the present and its evolution.

A student's comprehension of the historical background of both South Africa and the United States would be lacking if they mistakenly believed that George Washington was the first president of France rather than the United States, or that Thabo Mbeki was the first African president to hold the office (Mhlanga, D., 2023). In the field of mathematics, precision is essential since it's necessary to comprehend mathematical ideas and solve problems (Al-Mutawah et al., 2019; Santia & Sutawidjadja). If an instructor tells a student that two plus four equals five, they will struggle to understand more complex mathematical concepts that depend on this basic knowledge. It is crucial to ensure that the data provided by ChatGPT and any other tool used in the teaching process is accurate as a result. It is imperative that educators and learners engage in critical thinking skills and verify information from reputable sources.

Nondiscrimination and Fairness

There is a risk of bias in AI systems, particularly with regard to the language they were taught.

Keep this in mind and use ChatGPT and other AI tools in the classroom wisely. Instructors need to exercise caution as well, especially if their students turn in assignments via ChatGPT. No ChatGPT user should be subjected to any form of bias, discrimination, or unfair treatment because of their gender, race, or socioeconomic status. It is forbidden to use any artificial intelligence algorithm, including ChatGPT, in a classroom without first making sure that it does not reinforce preexisting biases or discriminate against any students (Mhlanga, D., 2023).

Unfair and unequal treatment of students may result from these biases if they are not promptly recognized and addressed. To ensure that other AI systems are developed, tested, and put into use without bias, ongoing oversight is necessary. Consider ChatGPT's possible application in essay grading, for instance. According to Mhlanga (2023), the use of biased training data to train ChatGPT may make it unfair to grade essays by underrepresented groups.

This may result in a growing achievement gap and the marginalization of already excluded populations. Furthermore, there's a risk that bias, prejudice, and unfavorable misconceptions will be amplified and reinforced by ChatGPT and associated language models. If these models are used, this is possibly what will happen. Concerns exist that the use of ChatGPT in the classroom might produce unfair and discriminatory results. The training set may contain negative group stereotypes, which could be one explanation for this. According to Mhlanga (2023), this could cause problems for administrators, teachers, and students in the academic community. Therefore, the potential for bias and discrimination must be carefully considered before deploying ChatGPT and other AI systems in educational settings.

AI Cannot Replace Human Teachers

Artificial intelligence (AI) and machine learning are not a replacement for human teachers. It is better to think of it as an addition to in-person instruction rather than its replacement. Rather than using ChatGPT for everything, educators should use it to improve their methods and help students develop their analytical and critical thinking abilities. The use of ChatGPT and other forms of AI in educational settings has been the subject of recent discussions. It's crucial to remember that while ChatGPT can enhance learning environments in a variety of ways, it cannot replace human instructors. This can be attributed to a number of good reasons.

The human connection that occurs between a teacher and a student cannot be replaced by ChatGPT. The relationship that develops between an educator and their students is among the most significant features of education. Teachers can discover each student's needs, strengths, and weaknesses by developing relationships with them (Alam, 2022a; Attard & Holmes, 2020; Kim, 2020). But because ChatGPT is just a machine, it can't build a strong bond with its users, who are students. Along with disseminating knowledge, education should place a high value on the growth of interpersonal relationships. It is the teachers' primary duty to create a welcoming and inclusive learning environment for students from a variety of backgrounds.

Because ChatGPT is an AI language model, it lacks the emotional intelligence, empathy, and interpersonal skills of human teachers. This makes it difficult for ChatGPT to recognize each student's unique needs, to offer individualized support, and to establish a welcoming and engaging learning environment. It can't be said that ChatGPT is very creative or analytical.

To help each student in their classroom individually and provide guidance, instructors go through training to sharpen their critical and creative thinking skills. But unlike a human teacher, ChatGPT is constrained by the programming and algorithms that it uses, so it is unable to think critically or creatively. The field of education is dynamic and ever-evolving (Mhlanga, 2021, 2023, 2022a).

Human teachers are flexible enough to adjust to the ever-changing requirements of their pupils. Teachers are able to adapt their methods in response to feedback from their students and incorporate fresh concepts and techniques into their lessons. However, ChatGPT uses the data that it was trained on and cannot adapt its methodology to meet the needs of specific students or courses.Top of Form

Responsible AI, It's Important to Educate Students

Students must comprehend that artificial intelligence (AI) actually functions as a text-generating model and not as a sentient entity. Instructors should assist students in developing an enlightened and perceptive viewpoint concerning the application of artificial intelligence in academic environments, while simultaneously encouraging students to critically examine the outcomes produced by AI (Mhlanga, D., 2023). It is imperative that students understand AI's limitations prior to utilizing AI tools in the classroom for a number of additional reasons. Before proceeding, it is imperative that students comprehend that ChatGPT and other AI systems possess constraints and are vulnerable to biases. For example, GhatGPT may have contained biased, inaccurate, or misleading information because it was trained using an extensive amount of text from the internet. Students will be able to comprehend and critically assess data generated by artificial intelligence tools in the future, as well as differentiate between reliable and unreliable sources of information (Mhlanga, 2023). Second, and just as importantly, students need to be fully aware of the possible ethical and societal consequences of advancements in AI. It is possible to encourage bias and injustice, for instance, when using ChatGPT to grade essays or give students feedback. The following are some potential threats that ChatGPT may pose. Thus, it is the responsibility of each and every student to educate themselves about these issues and the various solutions. Mhlanga (2023), asserts that in an ever-evolving technological world, students must possess the ability to adapt and thrive.

Given the fast development and growing use of artificial intelligence (AI), it is important for students to have a good grasp of its principles, capabilities, and limitations (Alam, 2022c; Wong et al., 2020). As a result, individuals will be able to make well-informed choices regarding the integration of AI into their professional and personal lives. By making their students aware of the limitations of AI, teachers can help foster a more responsible and considerate attitude toward the relationship between humans and the technology. This action ensures that the community can have faith that the integration of AI will be implemented in an ethically sound, beneficial, and safe manner (Mhlanga, D., 2023).

Transparency in the Use of AI

Providing regular forums where instructors and students can discuss the responsible and ethical use of artificial intelligence is also essential, as is being open and honest about incorporating ChatGPT into classrooms. This type of discussion can be facilitated through workshops, online forums, or other frequent gatherings where participants can discuss the benefits and drawbacks of introducing AI into classrooms, and offer advice on how to do it responsibly and ethically (Mhlanga, D., 2023). Being transparent is the key when introducing AI tools into the classroom so that everyone involved (institution, students, and teachers) knows what it is and how it works. Before incorporating AI into the classroom, it is crucial for both teachers and students to have a good grasp of how systems like ChatGPT process data and generate responses. Both Mhlanga (2022b) and Rodgers et al. (2023), agree that following such a process will contribute to enhancing stakeholder's confidence with regard to ethical and responsible use of AI tools. Some examples of transparent AI implementation in the classroom include providing students with details about the data sources and algorithms used, as well as describing the processing and response generation processes performed by the technology (Mhlanga, D., 2023).

This information could potentially reach classrooms, instructors, and students through a number of different channels. The course catalog and student handbook are two examples of such channels. To further guarantee that all parties involved, including students and teachers, have access to the data and code behind artificial intelligence systems, universities should make their use of such systems the highest priority. As a result, open-source or transparent AI should be given top priority (Mhlanga, D., 2023).

A further example of CAI's transparent use in educational settings, is giving students a clear explanation of the possible biases and limitations of the technology used in the classroom. It's crucial to emphasize to students that ChatGPT and other related AI algorithms are only as objective as the data used to train them. Because the training data contains inherent biases, the system's output may be skewed. If students are aware of the limitations outlined here and how they apply to their coursework, they will be better equipped to evaluate and understand ChatGPT's outputs. When using ChatGPT and other AI systems in the classroom, transparency is essential because it informs students of what can be accomplished by the technology and motivates them to use it wisely and ethically. All of which, to ensure that the students are using AI tools intelligently and in a manner consistent with the values of the educational institution in which they are enrolled.

Finally, one must be aware of AI's impact on the instructions and the potential biases in order to use it in the classroom in an ethical and responsible manner. For instance, ChatGPT and other similar tools should be used in conjunction with teacher-led instruction to help students develop their critical thinking abilities when it comes to the integration of AI in higher educational institutions. Consequently, this will enhance safeguarding student data, being open about its use, and critically assessing its impact on education. In light of these, teachers should assist their students in developing complex, critical opinions about artificial intelligence (AI), even though ChatGPT and other AI technologies can enhance rather than replace traditional classroom instruction (Mhlanga, D., 2023).

Artificial Intelligence (AI) in Higher Education: Ethical Guidelines

The Stewardship and Governance Principle

The ethical principles that regulate AI in the classroom detail what the technology can and cannot do, as well as how to keep it safe and make sure it achieves its goals. The objective of this structure is to ensure that every single student receives the most out of their educational experience. In the context of artificial intelligence, governance refers to the process of creating and enforcing rules, regulations, and standards to ensure the right development, utilization, and administration of the info sphere (Floridi, 2018, p. 3).

The responsible management of AI development and implementation in academic institutions is known as AI stewardship, on the other hand. Modern ethical discussions have paid scant attention to stewardship and governance, despite their importance (Ashok et al., 2022). Building a framework is what governance is all about, while stewardship is about getting involved through things like developing transparency and capacity (Greer, 2018, p. 42).

The Principle of Governance and Stewardship in AI for Higher Education stresses the significance of looking at ethical issues from various angles, including interdisciplinary and multi-stakeholder viewpoints. Learning analytics, data ethics, computational ethics, human rights, and inclusivity are all part of this larger field (Andy Nguyen, et al., 2022). To create and implement trustworthy AI in higher education in an ethical manner while also optimizing its societal implications, it is necessary to combine hard and soft ethics from relevant domains.

The Transparency and Accountability Principle

The importance of being open and accountable when using data for AI in universities has been brought to light by data ethics (Larsson & Heintz, 2020). In order to enhance teaching and learning techniques, the use of AI tools in education has increased over time (Wang & Cheng, 2021). The data's transparency problem hasn't been handled yet, though. Cope & Kalantzis (2019) stressed the significance of this ethical principle for educators and students, noting that data visualization represents learner behavior and highlights the additional support that educators can provide.

It is critical to acknowledge that transparency includes knowing the type of data, the sources from which it is collected, the insights it offers, how it is used, and the processes that follow (Digital Curation Centre, 2020). Maintaining data ownership, accessibility, and explainability makes answering these questions possible. Transparency and fairness are inextricably linked to the idea of data ownership (Remian, 2019), raising concerns about who has access to students' personal information. Although data collectors usually receive consent, worries about possible privacy invasions still exist. An argument that supports the integrity of the reasons for collecting data points to the students as the rightful owners. Since they are the ones who provide the data, students have the inherent right to control and direct how the data is used to improve their educational experience (Holmes et al., 2021). Concurrently, given that learner interactions and performances are essentially recorded using structured learning systems provided by these educational institutions, there is a plausible argument regarding the rights of institutions to access and utilize student data (Andy Nguyen, et al., 2022).

In this sense, the concept of explainability in AI and data is closely linked to the transparency of the system and the data. In actuality, data ought to be able to explain specific predictions from a given human's technical point of view. The degree of explainability of AI systems is determined by the role of stakeholders and their technical proficiency. However, explainability of AI systems provides valuable insights into how these systems functioned and made informed decisions (Kazim & Koshiyama, 2021; UNESCO, 2019).

Several ethical guidelines, such as those set by the European Commission (2019), the European Parliament (2021), UNESCO (Miao et al., 2021), Beijing Consensus UNESCO (2019), and OECD (2021), highlight the significance of transparency in AI applications within higher education. The details of transparency, however, that are described in these reports and guidelines frequently diverge. For instance, the European Commission (2019) describes explicability and transparency as being closely related. This includes providing clarity on the components of an AI system, such as the data, the system, and the business model. On the other hand, the UNESCO 2020 Draft links adequate measures of responsibility and accountability to transparency (AHEG, 2020).

The idea of "responsible AI," which emphasizes the moral design, development, and application of AI systems to fairly empower stakeholders and society, is central to the accountability in AI in higher education. Although the phrase "responsible AI" has gained popularity, responsibility and accountability have hazy definitions (Jobin et al., 2019). However, in general, it means operating honorably and laying out precisely who is responsible and legally liable while considering the risks involved.

It is still debatable whether AI should be held to the same standards as humans or if humans should always be the only ones in charge of AI as technological artifacts. Furthermore, some AI policies support regulating AI in higher education to take sustainability and proportionality into account in addition to individual and organizational accountability (AHEG, 2020).

The Privacy Principle

One of the most crucial ethical considerations when incorporating AI into higher education is privacy. Privacy, defined as "the right to be left alone," heavily emphasizes the protection of personal information (Muller, 2020). In order to maximize learning opportunities, a lot of personal data is being generated, collected, and analyzed with the advent of the digital age in education, particularly with the application of AI and learning analytics (Tzimas & Demetriadis, 2021; Pardo & Siemens, 2014). However, privacy breaches and consent are concerns raised by the collection and use of personal data, particularly in the context of agent-based personalized education (Li, 2007).

Ethical conundrums could arise from the unauthorized use of learners' personal data, including their learning performance history, for future predictions (Miao et al., 2021). These worries are exacerbated by attendance tracking without consent and real-time facial expression recognition systems (Jian-Ming Sun et al., 2008; Pattnaik & Mohanty, 2020).

Security and Safety Principle

The main goal of most educational learning systems is to gather data from users in order to forecast their learning behaviors and performance. The risk of data corruption or manipulation by third parties or even cybercriminals is real, though (Andy Nguyen, et al., 2022).

In accordance with the Principle of Security, AI used in academic settings must undergo design and implementation procedures that guarantee the solution's robustness. This effectively protects sensitive information from cybercrimes, data breaches, and corruption threats, ensuring its security and privacy.

According to Bostrom and Yudkowsky (2014), one of the main requirements for maintaining the integrity of AI systems in universities is that they cannot be intentionally manipulated by outside forces. It is emphasized that AI systems must be able to withstand malicious actors' deliberate manipulation in order to identify algorithmic imperfections. Therefore, the overarching objective of guaranteeing strong data security is closely related to the preservation of data's incorruptible nature. This emphasizes the significance of safeguarding personal information of all stakeholders, such as students, teachers, and educational institutions, to avoid any possible abuse or breach.

In today's world of increasingly mainstreamed online education, protecting sensitive information should be a top priority. This can only be achieved if everyone takes an active role and learns to understand one another.

It is essential that AIED systems employ risk-management strategies throughout the design, development, and deployment phases, as highlighted by the Principle of Safety. Protecting users from accidental harm and reducing the risk of fatalities are the primary goals of this strategy.

Therefore, AI developers should be extremely careful when creating, training, pilot testing, and validating AI systems for security (Leslie, 2019). To maintain responsibility and robustness throughout the AI lifecycle, it is advised that multi-stakeholder groups, including product developers, government agencies, and educators, establish appropriate assessment, due diligence, and supervision processes (AHEG, 2020). This group should draft detailed regulations and ensure that all AI users, including educators, receive adequate training to operate the system in a safe manner.

Human-Centered AI Principle for Higher Education

Calvo et al. (2020) argue that the development and application of AI in higher education must uphold and enhance autonomy, since it is now recognized as a contemporary moral and political value. Miao et al. (2021) and UNESCO (2019) found that helping students reach their maximum potential is crucial.

Using a Human Lens to Understand AI in the Academic Setting: If our goal is to maintain and develop people's intellectual, social, and cultural abilities while simultaneously bolstering their independence, then artificial intelligence (AI) must find a home in universities.

It should also guarantee that employees have control over workflows enabled by AI. In order to ensure that AI in higher education is both learner- and human-centered, researchers, developers, and practitioners need to use an interdisciplinary approach to design negotiation-based adaptive learning systems that give priority to transversal competencies (European Parliament, 2021). Higher education should incorporate artificial intelligence (AI) to give students control over the type and frequency of support they receive, in addition to knowledge, metacognition, and self-regulation scaffolding (Chou et al., 2018; Daradoumis & Arguedas, 2020).

To create and incorporate suitable curricula into teaching methodologies, governments and educators must comprehend the AI literacy abilities necessary for human-machine collaboration. With students and teachers maintaining control and acting as the main stakeholders in the implementation process, humans and machines will work together to improve educational outcomes rather than trying to replace one another with AI (Bryson & Theodorou, 2019).

CONCEPTUAL FRAMEWORK FOR ETHICAL INTEGRATION OF AI IN HIGHER EDUCATION

Regular advancements in higher education are made possible by the creation of new laws and regulations or even by the incorporation of cutting-edge technology like Blockchain. Given this, artificial intelligence (AI) has the potential to drastically change a wide range of industries, including education. The key to using AI responsibly is to address ethical concerns. As a result, a conceptual framework outlining the ethical utilization of AI in higher educational institutions has been developed. This framework, which is depicted in Figure 2 below, aims to increase awareness of ethical issues among educators and students by taking into account a variety of ethical principles and considerations. All of which, to lessen the likelihood of unethical behavior and improper use of AI tools in higher education institutions.

By adopting this conceptual framework, universities can ensure that all students have equitable access to high-quality education while also fairly utilizing AI's transformative potential. This could improve how educators and students use AI tools in an ethical manner.

Figure 2. Framework for ethical AI integration in higher education
(Developed by Researcher)

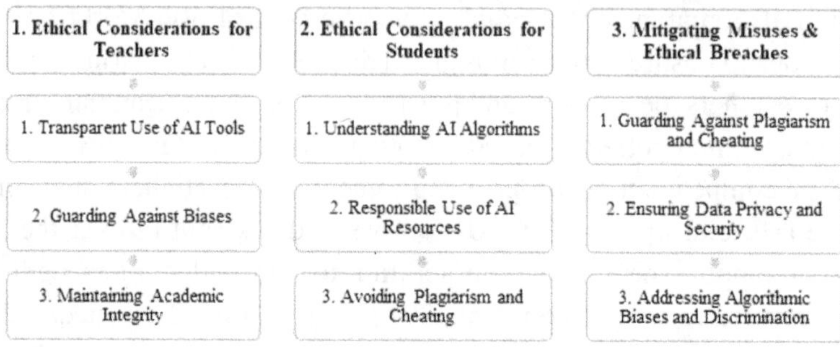

CONCLUSION AND RECOMMENDATIONS

Artificial intelligence (AI) has many potential advantages and disadvantages when applied to academic institutions. It is clear that universities should emphasize ethical concerns and promote responsible usage of ChatGPT and other AI technologies due to their extensive use in educational settings. By summarizing the existing literature, we can see how important it is for academic institutions to take a methodical and well-informed approach when integrating AI ethically. Consequently, key findings, recommendations, and a conceptual framework were produced.

Recommendations and Future Directions

Given the rapid and ongoing advancement of new AI applications, educators at all levels should closely monitor current and emerging uses in their institutions and actively contribute to the development of policy. Educators should proactively establish themselves as crucial contributors in the progress and implementation of emerging educational technology, rather than depending solely on the limited impact afforded to consumers of these technologies.

It is imperative to establish unambiguous and precise guidelines for policy and practice standards, which should be accompanied by regulatory safeguards to ensure the protection of student data. As implementation and effectiveness increase, it is essential to develop strategies that ensure access and fairness. If the efficacy of these approaches enhances, educators should contemplate redefining their responsibilities and instructional interventions to prioritize the implementation of novel and enhanced practices in the classroom.

This could entail prioritizing human interaction and promoting social learning. Further research should be undertaken in areas where the existing literature is insufficient. Additional research is required to explore the developmental and neurological impacts of technology interaction, especially among young children. If AI developers can devise systems that offer justifications for their decisions, more thorough and sophisticated survey techniques than those employed in this study could potentially reveal the soundness of the assumptions regarding AI discussed in this paper.

Moreover, these approaches have the potential to detect any deficiencies in comprehension and emphasize the need for improved education and cooperation between AI experts and education professionals. Phenomena such as bias, adherence to social norms, and the process of confirming information may become more apparent.

REFERENCES

ACOLA. (2019). The Effective and Ethical Development of Artificial Intelligence. In An opportunity to improve our wellbeing. UUID. papers3://publication/uuid/06B7168A-ED3A-4ECD-BAA7-2E4A17BBC439

Aheg, U. (2020). *First version of a draft text of a recommendation on the ethics of Artificial Intelligence.* SHS/BIO/AHEG-AI/2020/4.

Ashok, M., Madan, R., Joha, A., & Sivarajah, U. (2022). Ethical framework for Artificial Intelligence and Digital technologies. *International Journal of Information Management*, *62*, 102433. doi:10.1016/j.ijinfomgt.2021.102433

Berendt, B., Littlejohn, A., & Blakemore, M. (2020). AI in education: Learner choice and fundamental rights. *Learning, Media and Technology*, *45*(3), 312–324. doi:10.1080/17439884.2020.1786399

Borenstein, J., & Howard, A. (2021). Emerging challenges in AI and the need for AI ethics education. *AI and Ethics*, *1*(1), 61–65. doi:10.1007/s43681-020-00002-7 PMID:38624388

Bostrom, N., et, al. (2014). The ethics of artificial intelligence. In K. Frankish, & W. Ramsey (Eds.), *The Cambridge Handbook of Artificial Intelligence* (pp. 316–334). Cambridge University Press.

Bryson, J. J. (2019). How society can maintain human-centric artificial intelligence. In *Human-centered digitalization and services* (pp. 305–323). Springer.

Calvo, R. A., et, al. (2020). Supporting human autonomy in AI systems: A framework for ethical enquiry. In *Ethics of Digital Well-Being* (pp. 31–54). Springer.

Chan, C. K. et, al. (2023). *The AI generation gap: Are Gen Z students more interested in adopting generative AI such as ChatGPT in teaching and learning than their Gen X and Millennial Generation teachers?* arXiv preprint arXiv:2305.02878.

Chan, C. K. Y. (2023). A comprehensive AI policy education framework for university teaching and learning. *International Journal of Educational Technology in Higher Education*, *20*(1), 38. doi:10.1186/s41239-023-00408-3

Chatterjee, S. (2020). AI strategy of India: Policy framework, adoption challenges and actions for government. *Transforming Government*, *14*(5), 757–775. doi:10.1108/TG-05-2019-0031

Chou, C. Y., Lai, K. R., Chao, P.-Y., Tseng, S.-F., & Liao, T.-Y. (2018). A negotiation-based adaptive learning system for regulating help-seeking behaviors. *Computers & Education*, *126*, 115–128. doi:10.1016/j.compedu.2018.07.010

Civil, B. (2023). *ChatGPT can hinder students' critical thinking skills: Artificial intelligence is changing how students learn to write*. The Queen's Journal.

Corrin, L. et, al. (2019). *The Ethics of Learning Analytics in Australian Higher Education: A Discussion Paper.*

Daradoumis, T., et, al. (2020). Cultivating students' reflective learning in metacognitive activities through an affective pedagogical agent. *Journal of Educational Technology & Society*, *23*(2), 19–31.

Dexe, J., & Franke, U. (2020). Nordic lights? National AI policies for doing well by doing good. *Journal of Cyber Policy*, *5*(3), 332–349. doi:10.1080/23738871.2020.1856160

Digital Curation Centre, The University of Edinburgh. (2020). The Role of Data in AI: Report for the Data Governance Working Group of the Global Partnership of AI.

Dignum, V. (2018). Ethics in artificial intelligence: Introduction to the special issue. *Ethics and Information Technology*, *20*(1), 1–3. doi:10.1007/s10676-018-9450-z

European Commission (2019). *The European Commission's high-level expert group on artificial intelligence: Ethics guidelines for trustworthy AI.* EC.

European Parliament (2021). *Report on artificial intelligence in education, culture and the audiovisual sector (2020/2017(INI*)). IEEE.

Floridi, L. (2018). Soft Ethics and the Governance of the Digital. *Philosophy & Technology*, *31*(1), 1–8. doi:10.1007/s13347-018-0303-9 PMID:30322997

Floridi, L. (2021). A Unified Framework of Five Principles for AI in Society. In Ethics, Governance, and Policies in Artificial Intelligence, 144. Springer International Publishing AG. doi:10.1007/978-3-030-81907-1_2

Fukuda-Parr, S., & Gibbons, E. (2021). *Emerging Consensus on 'Ethical AI': Human.*

Garrett, N (2020). More than "If Time Allows" the role of ethics in AI education. In *Proceedings of the AAAI/ACM Conference on AI, Ethics, and Society* (pp. 272-278). IEEE.

Greer, S. L. (2018). *Organization and governance: Stewardship and governance in health systems. Health Care Systems and Policies*. Health Services Research. Springer.

Hagendorff, T. (2020). The ethics of AI ethics: An evaluation of guidelines. *Minds and Machines*, *30*(1), 99–120. doi:10.1007/s11023-020-09517-8

Hogenhout, L. (2021). *A framework for ethical AI at the United Nations*. arXiv preprint arXiv:2104.12547.

Holmes, W. (2021). Ethics of AI in education: Towards a community-wide framework. *International Journal of Artificial Intelligence in Education.*

IMDA & PDPC. (2020). *Model Artificial Intelligence Governance Framework*. IMDA & PDPC.

Jobin, A., et, al. (. (2019). Artificial Intelligence: The global landscape of ethics guidelines. *Nature Machine Intelligence*, *1*(9), 389–399. doi:10.1038/s42256-019-0088-2

Kazim, E., & Koshiyama, A. S. (2021). A high-level overview of AI ethics. *Patterns (New York, N.Y.)*, *2*(9), 100314. doi:10.1016/j.patter.2021.100314 PMID:34553166

Korn, J., & Kelly, S. (2023). *New York City public schools ban access to AI tool that could help students cheat*. CNN.

Larsson, S., & Heintz, F. (2020). Transparency in artificial intelligence. *Internet Policy Review*, *9*(2), 1–16. doi:10.14763/2020.2.1469

Leslie, D. (2019). *Understanding artificial intelligence ethics and safety: A guide for the responsible design and implementation of AI systems in the public sector.*

Li, W., et, al. (2021). Disparities in students' propensity to consent to learning analytics. *International Journal of Artificial Intelligence in Education.*

Li, X. (2007). Intelligent agent-supported online education. *Decision Sciences Journal of Innovative Education*, *5*(2), 311–331. doi:10.1111/j.1540-4609.2007.00143.x

Mhlanga, D. (2023). *Responsible Industry 4.0: A Framework for Human-Centered Artificial Intelligence*. Taylor & Francis. doi:10.4324/9781003393382

Miao, F., et, al. (2021). *AI and education: Guidance for policy-makers*. United Nations Educational, Scientific and Cultural Organization.

Müller, V. C. (2020). *Ethics of Artificial Intelligence and Robotics*.

Nigam, A., Pasricha, R., Singh, T., & Churi, P. (2021). A systematic review on ai-based proctoring systems: Past, present and future. *Education and Information Technologies, 26*(5), 6421–6445. doi:10.1007/s10639-021-10597-x PMID:34177348

Oliver, J. C., & McNeil, T. (2023). Undergraduate data science degrees emphasize computer science and statistics but fall short in ethics training and domain-specific context. *PeerJ. Computer Science, 7*, e441. doi:10.7717/peerj-cs.441 PMID:33834108

Palomares, I. (2021). *A panoramic view and swot analysis of artificial intelligence for achieving the sustainable development goals by 2030: progress and prospects*.

Pardo, A., & Siemens, G. (2014). Ethical and privacy principles for learning analytics. *British Journal of Educational Technology, 45*(3), 438–450. doi:10.1111/bjet.12152

Pattnaik, P. (2020). AI-Based Techniques for Real-Time Face Recognition-based Attendance System- A comparative Study. *2020 4th International Conference on Electronics, Communication and Aerospace Technology (ICECA),* (pp. 1034–1039). IEEE.

Remian, D. (2019). Augmenting Education: Ethical Considerations for Incorporating Artificial Intelligence in Education. Instructional Design Capstones Collection, 52. Rights Critique of Stakeholder Guidelines. *Global Policy, 12*(S6), 32–44.

Remian, D. (2019). *Augmenting education: Ethical considerations for incorporating artificial intelligence in education. ScholarWorks at UMass Boston*. University of Massachusetts Boston.

Renda, A. (2020). Europe: Toward a Policy Framework for Trustworthy AI. In M. D. Dubber, F. Pasquale, & S. Das (Eds.), *The Oxford Handbook of Ethics of AI* (pp. 650–666). Academic.

Schiff, D. (2022). Education for AI, not AI for Education: The Role of Education and Ethics in National AI Policy Strategies. *International Journal of Artificial Intelligence in Education, 32*(3), 527–563. doi:10.1007/s40593-021-00270-2

Sedenberg, E. (2016). *Recovering the history of informed consent for data science and internet industry research ethics*.

Sinhaliz, S., et,al. (2023). How ChatGPT Could Revolutionize Academia-The AI Chatbot Could Enhance Learning, But Also Creates Some Challenges. *IEEE Spectrum.*

Slimi, Z., et, al. (2023). Navigating the Ethical Challenges of Artificial Intelligence in Higher Education: An Analysis of Seven Global AI Ethics Policies. *TEM Journal, 12*(2).

Sullivan, M., et, al. (2023). ChatGPT in higher education: Considerations for academic integrity and student learning. *Journal of Applied Learning & Teaching*, *6*(1), 1–10.

Tzimas, D., & Demetriadis, S. (2021). Ethical issues in learning analytics: A review of the field. *Educational Technology Research and Development*, *69*(2), 1101–1133. doi:10.1007/s11423-021-09977-4

UNESCO. (2021). *Recommendation on the ethics of artificial intelligence*. UNESCO.

UNESCO (2023). *Ethics of Artificial Intelligence*. UNESCO.

Wang, T., & Cheng, E. C. K. (2021). An investigation of barriers to Hong Kong K-12 schools incorporating Artificial Intelligence in education. *Computers and Education: Artificial Intelligence*, *2*, 100031. doi:10.1016/j.caeai.2021.100031

Warschauer, M. (2023). *The affordances and contradictions of AI-generated text for second language writers*. SSRN.

Wood, P. (2023). Oxford and Cambridge ban AI language tool GPT-3 over fears of plagiarism. *inews.co.uk.*

Yau, C., & Chan, K. (2023). University of Hong Kong temporarily bans students from using ChatGPT, other AI-based tools for coursework. South China Morning Post, 17.

ZhaiX. (2022). ChatGPT user experience: Implications for education. Available at SSRN 4312418.

Chapter 10
Artificial Intelligence in Higher Education and Its Socioscientific Evaluation

Sema Cildir
Hacettepe University, Turkey

ABSTRACT

This chapter examines in detail the socioscientific (SS) dimensions of the widespread use of artificial intelligence (AI) in higher education. As a result, it was emphasized that the use of AI in higher education should be discussed as a topic with its features such as ethical and moral issues, complexity, and uncertainty issues. It is recommended that university administrations take urgent measures against the negativities that may occur in the near future both in higher education and in society, and to open the issue to discussion at the international level from the perspective of SS. In particular, determining the ethical and legal framework and setting standards as soon as possible is very important in order to minimize the negative effects of rapidly developing AI and to benefit from the advantages of its positive aspects without fear. Both students and academics should be informed about the conscious use of AI and the precautions to be taken against its negative effects. Thus, university administrations organizing trainings can solve the problems in the short term.

INTRODUCTION

Although the interaction between society and science has been ongoing since ancient times, its significance has increased notably since the 20th century. Science helps meet the needs of society, while society contributes to the advancement of science,

DOI: 10.4018/979-8-3693-2145-4.ch010

thus continuously enhancing each other. AI and its applications are products of this interaction over time. With the development of AI, societies have gained the opportunity to live in better conditions and more comfortably. For individuals whose living comfort increases gradually every day, AI has become indispensable (Tai, 2020). AI applications have become integrated into many different areas of our lives, including healthcare, defense industry, education, transportation, business, and communication (Baum, 2017; Goralski & Tan, 2020; Lee, 2020; Taeihagh, 2021, Tai, 2020). For example, in the healthcare sector, AI is widely applied from medical diagnostics to robotic surgeries, providing significant support to healthcare services (Jiang, et al., 2017; Rong, Mendez et al,, 2020). Education is also one of the areas affected by AI, and it has rapidly entered learning and teaching environments. Using AI in education saves time for teachers, students, and administrators, creating better learning environments by supporting teaching and learning settings (Arslan, 2020; Chen et al., 2020; Pokrivcakova, 2019; Qadir, 2023; Williamson, 2024). Smart homes, voice assistants, navigations, translation services, and other applications are examples of other AI applications commonly used in our daily lives.

The rapid rise of AI in almost every field has led to its increasing economic, social, and political significance, prompting stakeholders to take precautions (Cath et al., 2018). This is because while AI brings innovations and conveniences to our lives, it also possesses continuously increasing power, which is considered a risk for the future of societies. Carter (2020) has stated that the widespread adoption of AI benefits our daily lives and assists us, but when poorly managed and out of control, it also poses risks of harm. For example, Cheatham et.al (2019) listed privacy violations, discrimination and manipulation of political systems among the possible harms that AI can cause. Tredinnick & Laybats (2023) have pointed out the new challenges posed by artificial intelligence in terms of regulation, law, and professional practices, listing them as misinformation and fake content, privacy, data security and intellectual property, reinforcement of bias, malicious uses, and ethical issues. These potential risks create distrust in the use of artificial intelligence in societies. Therefore, it is important to encourage artificial intelligence developers to create applications that are both beneficial to society and make users feel safe. However, Baum (2017) in his study also expressed that guiding technology producers towards both safe and beneficial designs is not necessarily easy due to technical and social reasons. Despite the challenges, it has become a necessity to effectively manage the increasingly pervasive AI technologies in our lives to keep them under control. Thus, by taking measures, the lingering question marks regarding the place and future of artificial intelligence in society can be minimized as much as possible.

AI remains a controversial topic due to both its benefits and potential risks. Such controversial topics that create dilemmas within society are defined as SS issues. SS issues are grounded in scientific principles, inherently presenting a dilemma, and often debated under political and societal influences (Tekin et al., 2023). Levinson (2006) supported the notion that controversial issues arise when individuals in society hold different fundamental beliefs, understandings, and values about the relevant topic, and when the number of people representing a particular view increase. Examples of such controversial issues include nuclear power plants, cloning, surrogacy, genetically modified organisms, euthanasia, and others. These issues are debated at both local and global levels, with numerous studies found in the literature addressing these topics.

THE PURPOSE OF THE STUDY

This section aims to fill a gap in the literature by evaluating the impacts of AI in higher education from a SS perspective. To achieve this, the place of AI in higher education will be discussed along with its advantages and disadvantages. The scientific foundations that artificial intelligence should have as a SS issue, its ethical and moral dimensions, as well as the complexity and uncertainties inherent in its structure, will be evaluated.

AI in Higher Education

In contemporary education, the integration of educational technologies into higher education programs has become increasingly necessary. AI, a technology widely discussed and commonly used in various fields today, is one area that has been influencing higher education. AI technology can be utilized in higher education to enhance the quality of teaching processes. For example, it can be employed in various ways such as exams and exam evaluations, lesson planning, tracking students' academic achievements, and creating personalized course content for students. Particularly since 2022, AI has been frequently used by university students (Popenici, 2023; Chan, 2023). This trend aligns with the goal of higher education to produce technologically literate individuals, and it is encouraging to see university students using advanced technologies like AI. Similarly, it has been observed that academics have also begun to benefit from AI technologies in recent times. Yangyang (2023) noted in his study that Chinese professors frequently use AI in education to enhance both their teaching abilities and performance. This indicates that university professors are utilizing AI not only for conducting exams and evaluations but also to enhance the quality of teaching. By developing smarter strategies for using AI, university professors can lighten their workload and accelerate their academic research (Aithal & Aithal, 2023). However, both academics and students should be conscious and careful when using technological products like AI. This situation necessitates students and responsible course instructors to have more knowledge about AI and to keep their knowledge up to date.

The use of AI in higher education aims to make teaching and learning processes more effective. However, like in other areas of society, the use of AI in higher education is a topic that needs to be discussed from different perspectives. From the perspective of students and academics in higher education, if we consider the aspects in which AI could be beneficial, we can evaluate the topic under the following headings:

Identification of academic deficiencies and taking preventive measures. AI speeds up the process for course instructors in student assessments, exams, assignment checks, and grading (Weegar & Idestam-Almquist, 2023). Students quickly learn their grades with results obtained by AI in a short time (Landauer, 2003; Mao et al., 2024; Mizumoto & Eguchi, 2023). Additionally, through detailed result analysis, they identify the areas they are lacking in. AI assists course instructors in identifying students' academic deficiencies and taking preventive measures.

Impartial and consistent assessment. Impartiality, consistency, and fairness are important in student assessments. Various obstacles may hinder this (Burkholder, 2015; Chan & Hu, 2023). For example, when assessing, an academician may reflect their own values, beliefs, and biases in student evaluations. Or the psychological state of the academician during assessments may negatively affect exam or assignment evaluations. The fact that some students or a student is more active in the course than others may create the perception that they should get better grades in the evaluations. All of these can lead to the academician not being sufficiently objective. While students may be positively or negatively affected by this situation, since the given grades will not reflect the truth, the assessments lose their meaning. When AI conducts assessments, emotional effects stemming from the scorer are not present, so the results are expected to be much more reliable.

Personalized course content. Each student's learning pace and capacity vary due to their individual differences. Additionally, differences in prior knowledge levels among students can leave them at different learning levels at the end of the course. Therefore, with AI support, course content tailored to the student can minimize the level differences among students by starting from a level suitable for the student's learning pace and current knowledge level. Thus, personalized course content enhances students' learning experiences (Chaudhry & Kazım, 2022; Pokrivcakova, 2019). AI support can ensure full learning at the end of the learning process. It seems especially impractical for an academician to prepare and present individual course content for each student, especially in crowded classes. In this context, receiving AI support can create effective teaching environments for academics.

Compatibility with learning styles. When course content is designed to suit different learning styles, it can contribute to each student understanding the subject according to their own learning style (Chaudhry & Kazım, 2022). Thus, students can grasp the relevant topic more deeply through different learning styles. For an academician to provide this support to each student, a considerable amount of time and energy is required.

Different language options. Providing education in a language other than the mother tongue allows international students to learn the second language more quickly. It can also enable them to understand the relevant topic more quickly by choosing their native language.

Student tracking. In crowded groups, course instructors can receive support from AI in tracking students' attendance status and how effective they are in class or evaluating their academic progress. By evaluating small tasks, questions, and answers, students can be more effectively tracked.

Increased motivation. AI can provide rich content to increase students' motivation for the course (Chan & Hu, 2023). Thus, each student can choose course content tailored to their interests and curiosity. Students can repeat the activities they want as much as they want. Of course, academics can also enrich the course content with activities; however, the options for activities may be more limited, and the implementation time of these activities may be limited to the course duration.

Exact learning. In subjects where the student does not fully understand or has deficiencies, the topic can be retaught to the student by AI through different methods, examples, and activities. This approach can provide significant benefits for both teachers and students and ensure a more effective learning and teaching process.

Additional benefits of using AI in higher education can be added over time to those highlighted above. AI-supported university education provides many conveniences to administrators, academics, and students, and therefore its use is rapidly spreading. However, on the other hand, it may create obstacles in achieving the goals in different dimensions such as professional knowledge, skills, personal development and ethical behavior that are aimed to be acquired by students. In this context, examples of the disadvantages of using AI in higher education can be provided as follows.

Decrease in problem-solving and critical thinking skills. As students complete their course-related tasks such as assignments, research, or project preparation through AI, they may not develop problem-solving and critical thinking skills. Dependence on AI can diminish students' problem-solving and critical thinking skills over time (Chan, 2023). Additionally, it may dull their writing skills (Warschauer et al., 2023). In this case, they may grow up as individuals who struggle with problem-solving on their own, research, and accessing correct information. This contradicts the goals of higher education.

Decrease in decision-making skills. With the increasing use of AI, students and teachers may experience problems in individual decision-making and implementation over time. This can lead to a decrease in self-confidence over time, leading to a greater need for technological support. Over time, thinking and decision-making skills may weaken (Ahmad et al., 2023).

Weakening of student-teacher communication. Although the use of AI allows teachers to spend more time with students, the tendency of students to receive answers to their course-related questions from AI may weaken student-teacher communication (Guilherme, 2019).

Unethical use of AI tools. AI tools should be used in a way that supports learning. However, it is a matter of concern that students are using generative AI tools to cheat or plagiarize their assignments and exams (Chan, 2023). University administrations have begun to take measures against this, with some universities reverting to paper-based exam and assessment procedures (Cassidy, 2023; Chan, 2023; Cavendish, 2023). Misuse of AI can lead students to become lazy over time and habituate unethical behavior.

May hinder experiential learning. Activities and experiments conducted in virtual environments generated by AI may hinder students from acquiring manual skills. This can lead to serious problems in terms of professional competence. For example, in professions such as medicine and dentistry, students may need to use their sensory organs and experience by touch. Therefore, AI may not always be suitable in applied lessons and laboratory or workshop lessons, especially in the field of health.

Decrease in personal and social skills. While acquiring professional skills, it is also important to acquire personal and social skills. However, this will remain a significant deficiency in individually participatory learning environments organized only with AI. This can gradually reduce social intelligence and effective communication skills. This can confine these skills to virtual environments only.

Extra budget allocation by administrations. The rapid development of technology and software requires universities to keep applications like AI up to date. This will increase the dependence of school administrations on technology companies (Filgueiras, 2023). This may require regular purchases of new technologies and a significant allocation from the budget.

Discriminatory approach of AI. Certain parameters used in creating algorithms can cause AI to behave biasly and make evaluations towards a certain group. AI can make discriminatory evaluations based on a specific characteristic that the majority in the data possesses (age, gender, place of birth, etc.) (Popenici, 2023; Williams et al., 2020). This can lead to ethical issues.

Violation of the principle of equality in education. The university may not be able to provide equal opportunities for access to and use of technology to every student. This may result in a violation of the principle of equality in education.

Failure to protect data. Since internet-accessible environments are used for activities such as student tracking or exam evaluations, personal information and other important data can be seized by malicious individuals and used for different purposes. This can lead to serious security issues (Valle-Cruz et al., 2023).

The use of AI in university education, with the disadvantages listed above, is a controversial issue in terms of security, ethics, and professional development. Therefore, the risks posed by AI for the future of higher education will continue to raise questions in people's minds.

Examination of Artificial Intelligence in Higher Education as a Socio-Scientific Issue

Issues with a scientific basis and leaving the public in a dilemma are generally studied under the title of SS issues. When SS issues are addressed, they are examined from many different perspectives. Factors such as ethical and moral dimensions, scientific, economic, cultural, political, and environmental effects are taken into account. In this evaluation process, the balance and relationship between the benefits and possible harms of a subject to society are examined. Nuclear energy, cell phones and base stations, global climate change, gene therapy, insecticides, stem cell therapy, genetically modified foods, and many other topics are among the SS issues that create discussions in society (Albe, 2008; Rundgren & Rundgren, 2010; Sadler & Zeidler, 2005; Zeidler, Walker, Ackett, & Simmons, 2002). These issues are based on scientific foundations, but their existence creates a dilemma in society. SS issues can be addressed from local and national dimensions to a global scale. Because it is known that similar issues are problems and discussed in different regions of the world (Rundgren & Rundgren, 2010). Therefore, for the solution of global problems, there generally needs to be international awareness and readiness of other countries to discuss and decide on the issue.

Although the groups discussing SS issues have opposing views, the truths they defend are the truths brought by different perspectives, based on the benefit and harm relationship of the innovations offered by technology. One group may strongly argue that the subject is beneficial for society and therefore should be supported, while another group may propose and defend the opposite view. Since individuals in society have different life experiences, expectations from life, and levels of scientific literacy, the criteria they advocate for may vary. In fact, advocating for and discussing different ideas are actions that benefit society and lead it towards the most accurate ones.

Since SS issues entail uncertainty and complexity, they generally do not have definitive solutions. On the contrary, they may have multiple reasonable solutions (Özcan & Kaptan, 2020). Therefore, deciding on the most appropriate solution among them becomes important. Using reasoning skills when making decisions requires looking at events from both scientific and social perspectives. Evaluating the issue from multiple dimensions is not an easy process. Therefore, reasoning skills are important in solving SS problems and in the decision-making process individuals may encounter (Sağlam & Çoban, 2018; Zeidler et al., 2019). SS reasoning skills involve being able to see the issue from different perspectives, adopting a critical approach, conducting research on the subject, and ultimately solving complex problems (Sadler et al., 2007). These skills help individuals understand social issues more deeply and produce effective solutions.

The Socio-Scientific Sub-Dimensions of AI

The aim of the section is not to start a socio-scientific discussion. Nor is it to come to a decision like "whether AI should be used by students and academics in universities or not". The purpose here is to examine AI usage from a SS perspective, evaluating its controversial dimensions. It is to provide recommendations for the problems identified regarding the socio-scientific dimensions.

For a subject to be considered SS, it must first have a scientific basis, be important for society, contain ethical and moral dimensions, have a complex structure, and have uncertainties (Rundgren & Rundgren, 2010). It is certainly possible to expand these dimensions. Dimensions such as the military value of the specific area covered by the topic, its place in religion for that society, its economic value, its place in health, etc., can also become important. However, this chapter deals with the issue of AI in the field of education, especially in higher education. It is to discuss the dimensions that AI must provide to be considered a SS issue.

Scientific Foundations. AI technology has emerged with the advancement of computer science. However, its scientific foundations are not limited to computer science alone. It encompasses various disciplines such as mathematics, cognitive science, linguistics, neuroscience, and psychology (Chen et al., 2020; Devlin et al., 2018; Orrù et al., 2023). This is because AI has been developed to mimic the human mind in demonstrating problem-solving abilities. The problem-solving involved here is not simply solving a mathematical problem using predefined algorithms, as done by calculators or certain computer programs. It also entails demonstrating the main elements of cognitive science, including thinking, learning, language use, perception, and memory (Lieto et al., 2018). What distinguishes AI from conventional computer programs is precisely this aspect. The aim in developing AI is for it to be capable of solving any kind of problem that requires thinking and decision-making, much like how the human brain utilizes its intellect and intelligence. To be able to address problems accurately and comprehensively and make more informed decisions, it also requires the ability to learn. Artificial neural networks have been utilized to enhance AI's ability to make accurate decisions (Al-Surmi et al., 2022). The goal is to solve more complex problems involving classifying, processing, analyzing, and interpreting information using artificial neural networks (Dağ & Karamustafaoğlu, 2023). Self-improvement by constantly learning new things from data requires the use of techniques such as machine learning and deep learning. AI needs to learn because the more it learns about a subject, the more accurate its results will be.

Just like in the problem-solving steps formulated by Polya (1957) for the human brain, AI also comprehends incoming commands, evaluates data, quickly decides on the most accurate among possible solution paths, applies a solution strategy, and reaches a conclusion. However, AI is criticized because its outcomes are not always accurate; sometimes it provides unrealistic or misleading answers (Chattopadhyay, Sen, Gupta, et al., 2018). This is indeed a serious issue that prompts questioning the raison d'être of AI. In fact, the human brain also evaluates the correctness of the solution it reaches. In the evaluation stage, which is the last step in Polya's problem-solving process, the obtained result is pondered upon, and a decision is made regarding whether the possible outcomes have been reached based on the problem's subject and the available data. Either the problem-solving process is completed, or errors are sought by retracing steps back to the previous stages. At this stage, just like the human brain can make wrong decisions about the result, AI can also make mistakes by deciding that the presented outcome is correct.

As a result, AI is the product of a scientific process created by many disciplines working together and supports us in many areas of our lives. AI, which we also encounter in the educational dimension of higher education, is a subject based on scientific foundations and is a candidate for discussion as a SS issue.

The importance for the university community. Universities need to continuously renew themselves, be competitive, and frequently update their educational approaches to align with the era. They should be open to technological advancements and even contribute to these developments. The AI technologies that are increasingly being used in higher education have become significant for both students and academics. When utilized correctly, this technology has a facilitating and developmental characteristic for educational activities. It saves time and energy, which in turn creates an opportunity for more time to be allocated to scientific research at the university (Chen, et al., 2020). Improved educational quality translates to providing a well-educated workforce for society. Therefore, the use of AI is important for the university community. The subject of AI, with its scientific foundations, is also open to discussion from a socio-scientific perspective due to this feature.

The ethical and moral dimension. AI is a highly controversial issue in various areas of our lives such as health, economy, national security, education, and transportation. There are many positive effects of AI on society, such as simplifying daily life, leading to a more comfortable lifestyle for humanity, and benefiting from AI in situations that may endanger human beings. However, due to the unconscious use of AI or the malicious intent of individuals, there may be ethical and morally questionable outcomes that violate human rights.

In higher education, AI is used in enriching and planning course content, evaluating assignments, conducting exams and grading, language education, and many other different areas. Particularly in evaluating student performance and success in large groups, AI provides academics with time and speed (Chaudhry & Kazım, 2022). However, AI's decisions may be biased due to personal information such as race, gender, birthplace, etc., derived from its previous experiences and collected data (Nguyen et al., 2023; Williams et al., 2020). This could lead to unfair evaluations, posing ethical problems.

There may be students who maliciously use AI to cheat or have their assignments done (Chan, 2023). This situation also troubles the conscience of academics. Ultimately, no academician appreciates a student who succeeds by cheating in exams (Cavendish, 2023). Nor do they want a student to receive undeserved grades by having their assignments done by AI without any effort.

Ultimately, as long as these ethical issues persist, they will gradually affect the quality of education in higher education. Because over time, these problems can spread to other students, rendering assessment methods such as assignments, projects, and exams dysfunctional. Such erroneous behaviors can eventually become entrenched patterns of behavior. Moreover, the emergence of diplomated individuals who are actually undereducated and their assumption of roles and responsibilities in society over time will pose a separate ethical problem in the future.

Considering all these ethical issues, AI can be evaluated as a socio-scientific subject.

Dilemma and complexity. The issues that will be considered as SS topics have a complex structure. In other words, the issue has both benefits and harms for society, leaves individuals in society in a dilemma, and at the same time, it carries many problems such as ethical problems, political and religious problems. In solving such problems, the issue is considered in many dimensions at the same time and reasoning is used to make the healthiest decision.

The use of AI in higher education is complex enough. On the one hand, it is a great support for students and academics, but on the other hand, it is open to discussion due to ethical issues. On the one hand, there is an increasing use of this technology, but on the other hand, there is an unfair educational environment for those who have difficulty accessing this technology. Farrow (2022) concluded that the variations in application contexts complicate efforts to evaluate the impact of artificial intelligence on education as a whole. Moreover, the opacity and complexity of machine learning have hindered attempts to regulate it.

Considering all these factors, AI in higher education is worthy of consideration as a socio-scientific issue due to its complex and dilemma-inducing nature.

Uncertainty. The use of artificial intelligence in higher education brings about uncertainties for various reasons. It may create insecurity in data privacy, engage in discrimination, make biased decisions, commit errors, lack transparency, and be susceptible to malicious use, making its use in higher education controversial. All of these create uncertainties about the future. For instance, understanding the algorithms underlying AI applications is difficult, leading to negative impacts on transparency in higher education AI applications (Valle-Cruz et al., 2023). In addition, the risk of biased decision-making caused by artificial intelligence learning data creates uncertainty about the use of AI.

It can be asserted that the topic of AI, with its aforementioned dimensions, is an important scientific issue that needs to be discussed socio-scientifically in higher education. Its inclusion of science and technology, significance for university communities, creation of insecurity and uncertainties, ethical dimensions, and complex nature inducing dilemmas necessitate its socio-scientific discussion in universities.

DISCUSSION

A literature review on the use of AI in higher education now shows that it is much more advanced than simple computer software programs that only receive commands, process data, and convert them into output. AI has evolved into advanced technology products that learn, think, decide, and compete with human intelligence, which is evident from the recent trends. AI is a prime example of this. AI is an advanced product that thinks, decides, and learns from data instead of humans in many areas.

AI has already entered the lives of students and academics in higher education. However, AI, which is constantly expanding its technology and capabilities, also carries risks for the university community. For example, AI making decisions on our behalf may weaken our ability to think and decide over time. The disappearance of some professions and the emergence of new professions requiring new skills may also force higher education to constantly renew itself. Another issue is that students may use AI to cheat on their assignments or exams.

Cassidy (2023) has stated that many universities have announced changes, especially in exam application and evaluation systems, declaring that generating content with AI will be considered plagiarism. Such measures may seem like a short-term solution. However, the main issue that needs to be acknowledged is that we will encounter AI frequently in educational environments, as we encounter it in almost every field. At this stage, the most important thing to discuss is how AI will continue to be used in higher education. Therefore, it should be discussed from a socio-scientific perspective, and the most accurate decision should be made regarding its place in higher education. Understanding the potential advantages and disadvantages, as well as the dilemma and complex structure of AI under the title "AI in Higher Education," is crucial. With all these discussions, it is inevitable that both students and educators will embrace AI applications along with their advantages and disadvantages and transition to new educational models (Cóndor-Herrera et al., 2021).

CONCLUSION AND RECOMMENDATIONS

In summary, both students and academics need to be more thoroughly informed about the conscious use of AI and the measures to be taken against its negative effects. For this, university administrations making necessary regulations can provide short-term solutions to problems. Students should be encouraged to use this technology only for academic support. For this purpose, the importance of academic integrity should be emphasized to students, and they should be informed that they should avoid using such technological applications to cheat (King & ChatGPT, 2023). It is not correct behavior for a student to simply assign their task to AI without making any effort and to use the results given by it (which may be incorrect) as they are (Cavendish, 2023). Students who attempt to pass their courses by using AI in an uncontrolled manner face a great injustice, and they should be warned about the potential sanctions for this unethical behavior. The unethical use of AI by students undermines the ability of academics to ensure fairness among students (Cavendish, 2023). The widespread use of certain programs in online environments to cheat on exams and obtain grades that would not actually be achievable leads to academics continuing the course with misleading feedback. It should be noted that exams and assessments are not only for passing the class but also for academics to track the progress of their students, identify their weaknesses, and take measures accordingly.

The use of AI in higher education should be considered as a SS topic and evaluated academically, and international platforms for discussion should be prepared. Especially, the determination of ethical and legal frameworks in higher education, and the clarification of standards as soon as possible, are important. Measures to be taken regarding the long-term harm that uncontrolled developments in technology competition will cause to humanity should be decided on international platforms. University administrations coming together with AI manufacturers and taking all legal precautions as soon as possible will be more reassuring for users. Minimizing the negative effects of AI is crucial to comfortably benefit from its advantages.

REFERENCES

Ahmad, S. F., Han, H., Alam, M. M., Rehmat, M. K., Irshad, M., Arraño-Muñoz, M., & Ariza-Montes, A. (2023). Impact of artificial intelligence on human loss in decision making, laziness and safety in education. *Humanities & Social Sciences Communications*, *10*(1), 311. doi:10.1057/s41599-023-01787-8 PMID:37325188

Aithal, P. S., & Aithal, S. (2023). Optimizing the Use of Artificial Intelligence-Powered GPTs as Teaching and Research Assistants by Professors in Higher Education Institutions: A Study on Smart Utilization. International Journal of Management [IJMTS]. *Technology and Social Sciences*, *8*(4), 368–401. doi:10.47992/IJMTS.2581.6012.0326

Al-Surmi, A., Bashiri, M., & Koliousis, I. (2022). AI based decision making: Combining strategies to improve operational performance. *International Journal of Production Research*, *60*(14), 4464–4486. doi:10.1080/00207543.2021.1966540

Albe, V. (2008). Students' positions and considerations of scientific evidence about a controversial socioscientific issue. *Science & Education*, *17*(8-9), 805–827. doi:10.1007/s11191-007-9086-6

Arslan, K. (2020). Artificial Intelligence and Applications in Education. *Western Anatolia Journal of Educational Sciences*, *11*(1), 71–80.

Baum, S. D. (2017). On the promotion of safe and socially beneficial artificial intelligence. *AI & Society*, *32*(4), 543–551. doi:10.1007/s00146-016-0677-0

Burkholder, L. (2015). Impartial Grading Revisited. *Teaching Philosophy*, *38*(3), 261–272. doi:10.5840/teachphil201581136

Carter, D. (2020). Regulation and ethics in artificial intelligence and machine learning technologies: Where are we now? Who is responsible? Can the information professional play a role? *Business Information Review*, *37*(2), 60–68. doi:10.1177/0266382120923962

Cassidy, C. (2023). Universities to return to pen and paper exams after students caught using AI to write essays. *The Guardian*. https://www.theguardian.com/australia-news/2023/jan/10/universities-to-return-to-pen-and-paper-exams-after-stude nts-caught-using-ai-to-write-essays

Cath, C., Wachter, S., Mittelstadt, B., Taddeo, M., & Floridi, L. (2018). Artificial Intelligence and the 'Good Society': The US, EU, and UK approach. *Science and Engineering Ethics*, *24*, 505–528. doi:10.1007/s11948-017-9901-7 PMID:28353045

Cavendish, C. (2023). ChatGPT will force school exams out of the dark ages. *Financial Times*. https://www.ft.com/content/41243 doi:10.1186/s41239-023-00408-3

Chan, C. K. Y., & Hu, W. (2023). Students' voices on generative AI: Perceptions, benefits, and challenges in higher education. *International Journal of Educational Technology in Higher Education*, *20*(1), 43. doi:10.1186/s41239-023-00411-8

Chattopadhyay, M., Sen, R., & Gupta, S. (2018). A comprehensive review and meta-analysis on applications of machine learning techniques in intrusion detection. *AJIS. Australasian Journal of Information Systems*, *22*, 1–27. doi:10.3127/ajis.v22i0.1667

Chaudhry, M. A., & Kazım, E. (2022). Eğitimde Yapay Zeka (AIEd): Üst düzey bir akademik ve sektör notu 2021. *AI and Ethics*, *2*, 157–165. doi:10.1007/s43681-021-00074-z PMID:34790953

Cheatham, B., Javanmardian, K., & Samandari, H. (2019). Confronting the risks of artificial intelligence. *The McKinsey Quarterly*, *2*(38), 1–9.

Chen, L., Chen, P., & Lin, Z. (2020). Artificial Intelligence in Education: A Review. *IEEE Access : Practical Innovations, Open Solutions*, *8*, 75264–75278. doi:10.1109/ACCESS.2020.2988510

Chen, X., Xie, H., Zou, D., & Hwang, G. J. (2020). Application and theory gaps during the rise of artificial intelligence in education. *Computers and Education: Artificial Intelligence*, *1*, 100002. doi:10.1016/j.caeai.2020.100002

Cóndor-Herrera, O., Arias-Flores, H., Jadán-Guerrero, J., & Ramos-Galarza, C. (2021). Artificial Intelligence and Tomorrow's Education. In T. Z. Ahram, W. Karwowski, & J. Kalra (Eds.), *Advances in Artificial Intelligence, Software and Systems Engineering. AHFE 2021. Lecture Notes in Networks and Systems* (Vol. 271). Springer. doi:10.1007/978-3-030-80624-8_23

Dağ, M., & Karamustafaoğlu, O. (2023). Fen Lisesi Öğrencilerinin Öğrenme Stillerinin Çeşitli Değişkenlere Göre İncelenmesi. *Fen Bilimleri Öğretimi Dergisi*, *11*(1), 132–152. doi:10.56423/fbod.1264038

Devlin, J., Chang, M. W., Lee, K., & Toutanova, K. (2018). Bert: pre-training of deep bidirectional transformers for language understanding. arXiv preprint arXiv:1810.04805.

Dragoş, V., & Mih, D. (2015). Scientific Literacy in School. *Procedia: Social and Behavioral Sciences*, *209*, Pages167–172. doi:10.1016/j.sbspro.2015.11.273

Farrow, R. (2023). The possibilities and limits of XAI in education: A socio-technical perspective. *Learning, Media and Technology*, *48*(2), 266–279. doi:10.1080/17439884.2023.2185630

Filgueiras, F. (2023). Artificial intelligence and education governance. *Education, Citizenship and Social Justice*, *0*(0). doi:10.1177/17461979231160674

Goralski, M. A., & Tan, T. K. (2020). Artificial intelligence and sustainable development. *International Journal of Management Education*, *18*(1), 100330. doi:10.1016/j.ijme.2019.100330

Guilherme, A. (2019). AI and education: The importance of teacher and student relations. *AI & Society*, *34*(1), 47–54. doi:10.1007/s00146-017-0693-8

Jiang, F., Jiang, Y., Zhi, H., Dong, Y., Li, H., Ma, S., Wang, Y., Dong, Q., Shen, H., & Wang, Y. (2017). Artificial intelligence in healthcare: Past, present and future. *Stroke and Vascular Neurology*, *2*(4), 230–243. doi:10.1136/svn-2017-000101 PMID:29507784

Jufrida, J., Basuki, F. R., Kurniawan, W., Pangestu, M. D., & Fitaloka, O. (2019). Scientific literacy and science learning achievement at junior high school [IJERE]. *International Journal of Evaluation and Research in Education*, *8*(4), 630–636. doi:10.11591/ijere.v8i4.20312

King, M. R., & Chat, G. P. T. (2023). A conversation on artificial intelligence, chatbots, and plagiarism in higher education. *Cellular and Molecular Bioengineering*, *16*(1), 1–2. doi:10.1007/s12195-022-00754-8 PMID:36660590

Kolstø, S. D. (2001). Scientific literacy for citizenship: Tools for dealing with the science dimension of controversial socioscientific issues. *Science Education*, *85*(3), 291–310. doi:10.1002/sce.1011

Landauer, T. K. (2003). Automatic Essay Assessment, Assessment in Education: Principles. *Assessment in Education: Principles, Policy & Practice*, *10*(3), 295–308. doi:10.1080/0969594032000148154

Lee, R. S. T. (2020). Smart Education. In *Artificial Intelligence in Daily Life*. Springer. doi:10.1007/978-981-15-7695-9_11

Levinson, R. (2006). Towards a Theoretical Framework for Teaching Controversial Socio-scientific Issues. *International Journal of Science Education*, *28*(10), 1201–1224. doi:10.1080/09500690600560753

Lieto, A., Bhatt, M., Oltramari, A., & Vernon, D. (2018). The role of cognitive architectures in general artificial intelligence. *Cognitive Systems Research*, *48*, 1–3. doi:10.1016/j.cogsys.2017.08.003

Liu, X. (2009). Bilim okuryazarlığının ötesinde: Bilim ve halk. *Uluslararası Çevre ve Bilim Eğitimi Dergisi*, *4*(3), 301–311.

Mao, J., Chen, B., & Liu, J. C. (2024). Generative Artificial Intelligence in Education and Its Implications for Assessment. *TechTrends*, *68*(1), 58–66. doi:10.1007/s11528-023-00911-4

MizumotoA.EguchiM. (2023). Exploring the Potential of Using an Ai Language Model for Automated Essay Scoring. SSRN. https://ssrn.com/abstract=4373111 or doi:10.1016/j.rmal.2023.100050

Nguyen, A., Ngo, H. N., Hong, Y., Dang, B., & Nguyen, B. P. T. (2023). Ethical principles for artificial intelligence in education. *Education and Information Technologies*, *28*(4), 4221–4241. doi:10.1007/s10639-022-11316-w PMID:36254344

Orrù, G., Piarulli, A., Conversano, C., & Gemignani, A. (2023). Human-like problem-solving abilities in large language models using ChatGPT. *Frontiers in Artificial Intelligence*, *6*, 1199350. doi:10.3389/frai.2023.1199350 PMID:37293238

Özcan, C., & Kaptan, F. (2020). Investigation of the Studies on Socioscientific Issues between 2008-2017. *Journal of Muallim Rıfat Faculty of Education*, *2*(1), 16–36.

Pokrivcakova, S. (2019). Preparing teachers for the application of AI-powered technologies in foreign language education. *Journal of Language and Cultural Education*, *7*(3), 135–153. doi:10.2478/jolace-2019-0025

Polya, G. (1957). How to solve it: A new aspect of mathematical method. N.J.: Princeton.

Popenici, S. (2023). The critique of AI as a foundation for judicious use in higher education. *Journal of Applied Learning & Teaching, 6*(2). https://journals.sfu.ca/jalt/index.php/jalt/article/view/883/605

Qadir, J. (2023).Engineering Education in the Era of ChatGPT: Promise and Pitfalls of Generative AI for Education. *IEEE Global Engineering Education Conference (EDUCON)*. IEEE. 10.1109/EDUCON54358.2023.10125121

Rong, G., Mendez, A., Assi, E. B., Zhao, B., & Sawan, M. (2020). Artificial intelligence in healthcare: Review and prediction case studies. *Engineering (Beijing)*, *6*(3), 291–301. doi:10.1016/j.eng.2019.08.015

Rundgren, S. N. C., & Rundgren, C. J. (2010). SEE-SEP: From a separate to a holistic view of socioscientific issues. *Asia-Pacific Forum on Science Learning and Teaching*, *11*(1), 1.

Sadler, T. D., Barab, S., & Scott, B. (2007). What do students gain by engaging in socioscientific inquiry? *Research in Science Education*, *37*(4), 371–391. doi:10.1007/s11165-006-9030-9

Sadler, T. D., & Zeidler, D. L. (2005). The significance of content knowledge for informal reasoning regarding socioscientific issues: Applying genetics knowledge to genetic engineering issues. *Science Education*, *89*(1), 71–93. doi:10.1002/sce.20023

Sağlam, M. K., & Çoban, G. (2018). Fen bilimleri öğretmenleri ve öğretmen adaylarına yönelik akıl yürütme becerileri testi'nin geliştirilmesi. *Elementary Education*, *17*(3), 1496–1510. doi:10.17051/ilkonline.2018.466374

Taeihagh, A. (2021). Governance of artificial intelligence. *Policy and Society*, *40*(2), 137–157. doi:10.1080/14494035.2021.1928377

Tai, M. C.-T. (2020). The impact of artificial intelligence on human society and bioethics. *Tzu-Chi Medical Journal*, *32*(4), 339–343. doi:10.4103/tcmj.tcmj_71_20 PMID:33163378

Tekin, N., Oktay, K., & Özgül, K. (2023). Sosyobilimsel Konulara İlişkin Bir Projede Yetişen Fen Bilimleri Öğretmenlerinin Görüşlerinin İncelenmesi. *Science Insights Education Frontiers*, *14*(1), 2013–2037. doi:10.15354/sief.23.or089

Tredinnick, L., & Laybats, C. (2023). The dangers of generative artificial intelligence. *Business Information Review*, *40*(2), 46–48. doi:10.1177/02663821231183756

Valladares, L. (2021). Scientific Literacy and Social Transformation. *Science & Education*, *30*(3), 557–587. doi:10.1007/s11191-021-00205-2 PMID:33867683

Valle-Cruz, D., García-Contreras, R., & Gil-Garcia, J. R. (2023). Exploring the negative impacts of artificial intelligence in government: The dark side of intelligent algorithms and cognitive machines. *International Review of Administrative Sciences*, 00208523231187051. doi:10.1177/00208523231187051

WarschauerM.TsengW.YimS.WebsterT.JacobS.DuQ.TateT. (2023). The affordances and contradictions of AI- generated text for second language writers. doi:10.2139/ssrn.4404380

Weegar, R., & Idestam-Almquist, P. (2023). Reducing Workload in Short Answer Grading Using Machine Learning. *International Journal of Artificial Intelligence in Education*. doi:10.1007/s40593-022-00322-1

Williamson, B. (2024). Eğitimde Yapay Zekanın Sosyal Hayatı. *International Journal of Artificial Intelligence in Education, 34*, 97–104. doi:10.1007/s40593-023-00342-5

Xiufeng, L.,(2009). Beyond Science Literacy: Science and the Public. *International Journal of Environmental and Science Education, 4*(3), 301-311.

Yangyang, W. (2023). Teaching Ability, Performance and Professional Development Among Artificial Intelligence Chinese Professors. *Asia Pacific Journal of Management and Sustainable Development, 11*(1).

Zawacki-Richter, O., Marín, V. I., Bond, M., & Gouverneur, F. (2019). Systematic review of research on artificial intelligence applications in higher education – where are the educators? *International Journal of Educational Technology in Higher Education, 16*(1), 39. doi:10.1186/s41239-019-0171-0

Zeidler, D. L., Herman, B. C., & Sadler, T. D. (2019). New directions in socioscientific issues research. *Disciplinary and Interdisciplinary Science Education Research, 1*(11), 1–9. doi:10.1186/s43031-019-0008-7

ADDITIONAL READING

Ben-Horin, H., Kali, Y., & Tal, T. (2023). The Fifth Dimension in Socio-Scientific Reasoning: Promoting Decision-Making about Socio-Scientific Issues in a Community. *Sustainability (Basel), 15*(12), 9708. doi:10.3390/su15129708

Guilherme, A. (2019). AI and education: The importance of teacher and student relations. *AI & Society, 34*(1), 47–54. doi:10.1007/s00146-017-0693-8

Nguyen, A., Ngo, H. N., Hong, Y., Dang, B., & Nguyen, B.-P. T. (2023). Ethical principles for artificial intelligence in education. *Education and Information Technologies, 28*(4), 4221–4241. doi:10.1007/s10639-022-11316-w PMID:36254344

Pokrivcakova, S. (2019). Preparing teachers for the application of AI-powered technologies in foreign language education. *Journal of Language and Cultural Education, 7*(3), 135–153. doi:10.2478/jolace-2019-0025

Roll, I., & Wylie, R. (2016). Evolution and Revolution in Artificial Intelligence in Education. *International Journal of Artificial Intelligence in Education, 26*(2), 582–599. doi:10.1007/s40593-016-0110-3

Rudolph, J., Tan, S., & Tan, S. (2023). ChatGPT: Bullshit spewer or the end of traditional assessments in higher education? *Journal of Applied Learning and Teaching, 6*(1). Advance online publication. doi:10.37074/jalt.2023.6.1.9

Williams, M. L., Burnap, P., Javed, A., Liu, H., & Ozalp, S. (2020). Hate in the machine: Anti-Black and anti-Muslim social media posts as predictors of offline racially and religiously aggravated crime. *British Journal of Criminology*, *60*(1), 93–117. doi:10.1093/bjc/azz064

Wu, Y.-T., & Tsai, C.-C. (2007). High School Students' Informal Reasoning on a Socio-scientific Issue: Qualitative and quantitative analyses. *International Journal of Science Education*, *29*(9), 1163–1187. doi:10.1080/09500690601083375

KEY TERMS AND DEFINITIONS

Complexity: It refers to a situation where a topic involves multiple issues simultaneously, making finding a solution or making a decision extremely challenging.

Ethical Issues: These are problems created by situations and actions that do not comply with the general moral values and legal responsibilities in a particular topic.

Professional Development: It encompasses all kinds of professional knowledge and skills acquired as a result of education, usually obtained by individuals studying at university.

Reasoning Skills: It is a cognitive skill that includes the ability to solve complex problems, make correct decisions, and engage in critical thinking. Reasoning skills involve making accurate predictions and providing quick solutions to daily encountered problems.

Socio-Scientific Issues: These are scientific issues that create dilemmas, controversies, and complexities in society. Topics such as nuclear power plants, genetically modified foods, birth control, etc., are controversial issues in society in terms of health, ethics, religion, etc.

Uncertainty: It involves unspecified issues in the sub-dimensions of a topic. To find a solution to such a problem or make a decision, it is necessary to first identify what these uncertainties are.

University Community: A community consisting of students and academics, whose priority is to engage in scientific activities, sharing an environment called university.

Chapter 11
Strategies and Considerations of Implementing AI in Higher Education

Khoula Al Harthy
Global College of Engineering and Technology, Oman

Sulaiman Al Hasani
https://orcid.org/0000-0003-4194-3657
Global College of Engineering and Technology, Oman

ABSTRACT

AI and its tools and applications are continuing to reshape our world in general and the educational landscape in particular. This book chapter examines ways to improve teaching, learning, and administrative elements of higher education by integrating and implementing AI techniques. This chapter aims to provide insights into how higher education institutions can use AI's tools to enhance and enrich teaching and learning aspects as well as the administrative processes and procedures by taking strategic steps. Discuss the possible advantages, challenges, and ethical issues of various AI tools and applications as well as the tactics that can be used to achieve them. The chapter structure will be as complete strategy steps which are, investigation, analysis, evaluation, and recommendation.

DOI: 10.4018/979-8-3693-2145-4.ch011

INTRODUCTION

AI in Higher Education

Artificial intelligence (AI) has become a disruptive and transformative technology in several industries, including higher education, where its application and integration are changing pedagogical approaches, administrative procedures, and teaching and learning practices. AI's contribution to education was confined to computer-assisted instruction in the late 20th century, mostly handling and assisting mundane chores like scheduling and grading, despite the widespread belief that it has taken everyone by surprise. The introduction and development of advanced AI technologies, such as machine learning and natural language processing, has changed how technology is used in higher education and gathered enormous attention.

By the start of the 21st century, AI had advanced to cover intelligent tutoring systems, offering personalized feedback and guidance to students. Technologies like machine learning algorithms and natural language processing represented a significant shift from the conventional approach of traditional education to a new period of personalized and adaptive learning experiences. AI's ability to sift through and learn from extensive datasets has facilitated the creation of learning platforms that adjust to the individual needs of students, providing customized content and pathways that reflect their unique learning styles and progress.

The benefits of AI in higher education extend across multiple dimensions. Among the most noteworthy is the facilitation of personalized learning, where AI-driven platforms assess and adapt to each student's strengths, weaknesses, and preferences, thereby optimizing learning outcomes and maintaining high levels of engagement and motivation. AI has notably enhanced student engagement through gamified learning experiences, interactive content, and virtual reality simulations, making education more immersive. It has also created a more interactive and responsive learning environment, enabling students to receive instant feedback and support, which encourages a dynamic and participative educational experience. Technologies like intelligent tutoring systems and AI-assisted research tools offer a more individualized learning experience, addressing unique student needs. These tools help in pinpointing knowledge gaps and providing specific resources to bridge these gaps efficiently. Additionally, educators gain from AI's capacity to examine student behaviour and learning trends in order to modify their pedagogy for improved results. A more individualized learning experience is made possible by Intelligent Tutoring Systems (ITS), adaptable instructional systems that modify instructional tactics and activities to the unique needs and features of each student (Guo et al., 2021; Wang et al., 2023). ITS present an alternative approach to education, highlighting several key strengths and a number of limitations. Among their advantages, ITS can provide customized instructional strategies, accommodate a diverse range of subjects, and facilitate self-directed learning pace, as noted by Chan & Tsi (2023). However, ITS also faces significant challenges as they are complex to design, especially when it comes to accurately replicating the interactions found between students and human tutors. Additionally, their effectiveness is currently restrained by the limitations of existing AI technology, particularly in processing open-ended responses from learners. Through data analysis, organisation, and information provision, AI may oversee student learning. Personalised education is one of the major uses of AI in education. AI programmes examine student data to customise courses to each student's requirements, preferences, and learning preferences. Task difficulty is modified using adaptive learning technology in response to student performance. For instance, platforms like Coursera use AI to offer personalized course recommendations based on a user's learning history and preferences. Learning analytics tools can offer insights into students' interaction patterns, achievements, and learning goals (Crompton & Burke, 2023). With the advancement of language Natural Language Processing (NLP) technologies, language learning benefits from these personalized and tailored educational exercises allowing for real-time language translation and language practice tools. As an example of these tools is Duolingo's AI-driven platform which offers personalized language learning experiences.. With the above mentioned examples and cases where AI showed adaptability to individual learning styles, provision of customized content, and potential to enhance engagement and motivation (Chen, Lin, & Chen, 2020). There are the high development and maintenance costs, requires substantial data input for personalization.

AI technology can be applied to a variety of assessment and evaluation tasks, such as gauging student learning attitudes, tracking academic progress, and conducting online community assessments (Crompton & Burke, 2023). The learning process can be improved by these assistants by providing possibilities for self-testing, prompt answers, diagnostic inquiries, and personalised feedback (Chheang et al., 2023; Bull & Kharrufa, 2023; Wang et al., 2023; Schön et al., 2023; Yadlapally et al., 2023). Because AI can anticipate which students are at risk and when to intervene, academic achievement and retention rates are increased (Chang et al., 2022; Manhica et al., 2022).). This study shows the role of personalized learning platforms through their ability to adapt to the unique needs of each student, have been found to substantially boost student retention rates. By providing a more engaging and tailored learning experience, AI has the potential to mitigate common challenges associated with student engagement and continuity in their educational journey. Additional, there are an increasing use ofartificial intelligence (AI) to automatically evaluate emotional states and academic performance. For example, Zhang and Xu (2022) employed automatic assessment to improve the academic writing skills of Uyghur ethnic minority students in China (Zhang, Z., & Xu, L. 2022). Despite AI demonstrating significant capabilities in grading efficiency, offering immediate feedback, and utilizing predictive analytics to pinpoint students at risk (Hooda et al., 2022), its application in these areas is constrained by a lack of nuanced comprehension comparable to human graders and the possibility of bias in algorithmic evaluations. AI-powered predictive analytics can be used in Massive Open Online Courses (MOOCs) to predict students' future grades and identify students at risk of dropping out (Fu,Q et al., 2021). AI systems can provide automated, personalized feedback to students, tailored to their specific demographics, attributes, and academic status (Mousavi, A et al., 2021). The comprehensive study by Hooda et al. (2022) provided a rounded understanding on how AI-driven feedback mechanisms can significantly enhance student learning outcomes. When offering immediate and personalized feedback, the study shows that these systems notably improve students' academic performance, highlighting the potential of AI to transform traditional learning paradigms. Systems like Stat-Knowlab personalize students' learning and provide only educational activities that the student is ready to learn, monitoring the evolution of the learning process (de Chiusole et al., 2020). Tools such as exploratory learning environments with targeted visualizations can support classroom orchestration, providing teachers with valuable insights for decision-making (Mavrikis et al., 2019). AI technologies like the Artificial Intelligence-assisted Integrated Teaching–Learning Framework (AL-ITLF) can transform higher education into a more efficient, adaptable, and effective system. This approach utilizes techniques like Extreme Learning Machine (ELM) for evaluating student performance, leading to high accuracy and performance in educational outcomes (Chang et al., 2022). AI applications in Learning Management Systems (LMS), particularly Moodle, have been found effective in student performance assessment based on data analysis. Commonly used AI algorithms in this context include Random Forest, Neural Networks, and Support Vector Machine (Manhica et al., 2022). Tools that analyze student behavior and performance can predict learning outcomes and identify areas where students may need additional support, thereby enhancing teaching strategies (Alzahrani, 2023).

Additionally, repetitive tasks such as enrollment, scheduling, and handling student inquiries have been transformed by AI-driven chatbots and systems integrated with Virtual learning environments (VLEs) providing interactive and immersive learning experiences. For example, virtual assistants and chatbots, such as Georgia Tech's "Jill Watson," based on IBM's Watson, assist students by answering queries, providing resources, and offering guidance, thereby enhancing the learning experience (Goel, A.K & Polepeddil,L., 2018). This automation enhances and speeds operations, minimizes errors, and saves time, allowing staff to focus more on direct student interaction, knowledge creation, and quality assurance (Crompton & Burke, 2023). The challenges involved fine-tuning the AI to accurately understand and respond to student queries and ensuring the privacy and security of student data AI applications like facial expression recognition algorithms are being used for monitoring classroom status and achieving a balanced distribution of educational resources in higher education (Yao, G., 2022). Furthermore, the concept of a 'smart campus' is gaining traction, where AI is used to enhance campus management and operations. AI can optimize resource use, enhance security with intelligent surveillance systems, and improve campus facilities management through predictive maintenance. In the diverse higher education sector, there is a strong drive to adopt AI technologies such as Intelligent Tutoring Systems (ITS) and personalized learning platforms and they are increasingly recognized for their suitability in complementing traditional teaching methods, including lectures and seminars. These tools offer students the advantage of additional, tailor-made resources designed to meet their specific learning requirements. For remote and online educational formats, AI-enabled assessment tools and chatbots play a crucial role in providing necessary support and feedback, effectively bridging the gap created by the absence of in-person interactions. Moreover, within the scope of vocational training, AI proves invaluable by facilitating simulation-based learning environments. This is particularly relevant in specialized fields such as medicine, engineering, and information technology, where acquiring hands-on practical skills is of utmost importance.

This chapter aims to provide a comprehensive overview of AI's transformative impact on higher education. It shows the revolutionizing effects of AI on educational methodologies and administrative efficiencies, underlining the importance of embracing AI technologies. By addressing the challenges and strategizing for effective AI implementation, the chapter outlines a path forward for educational institutions to leverage AI's full potential. Through critical examination of ethical and social implications, the chapter advocates for responsible AI deployment, aiming to equip stakeholders with the insights needed for navigating the AI-driven higher educational landscape. The overarching goal is to ensure that higher education institutions can harness AI advancements to enhance the quality and accessibility of education.

Strategies for Effective AI Implementation

As AI tools and systems continue to expand and penetrate the higher education sector, it becomes crucial for higher education institutions to critically assess and formulate strategic approaches for the effective utilization and integration of these technologies. Higher education institutions that are not embracing this disruptive technology and are not taking it seriously could face significant difficulties in the road as the industry as a whole advance. Simões et al. (2022) conducted a systematic review to investigate future trends in digital transformation and AI across various sectors, including education. They identified key events related to the integration of AI technologies in educational settings, emphasizing the importance of preparing for future needs through strategic planning and the adoption of AI as a tool for value aggregation (Simões et al., 2022). The deployment of AI within higher education exceeds simple adoption of cutting-edge technological innovations; it necessitates a thoughtful transformation, backed by thorough strategic planning, adherence to ethical standards, the cultivation of talent, and a robust commitment to ongoing enhancement and innovation. Such strategic approaches facilitate effective and sustainable incorporation of AI into educational environments aiming to revolutionize teaching and learning methodologies and practice as well as administrative operations. Achieving effective integration of AI in higher education depends on a holistic strategy that prioritizes the personalization of learning experiences, the optimization of organizational processes, and the expansion of research capabilities. In this section, we will explore the steps needed to ensure holistic strategies for effective AI implementation in higher education as shown in Figure 1.

Figure 1. AI strategies for effective AI implementation

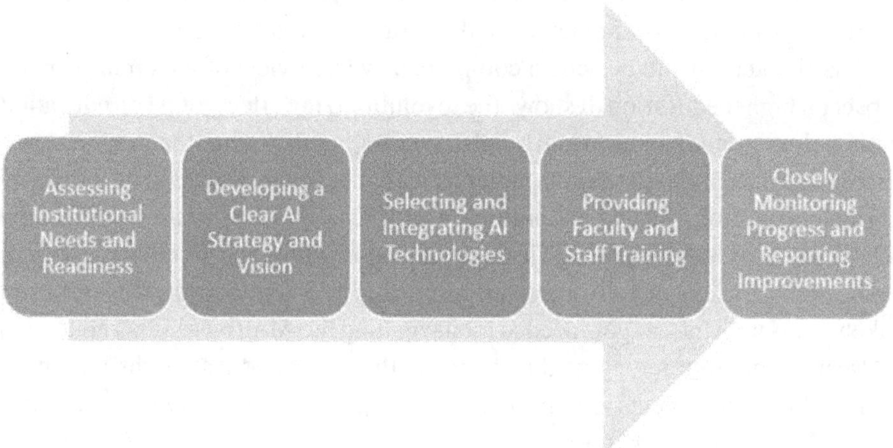

Assessing Institutional Needs and Readiness

The initial step in AI adoption is a comprehensive assessment of the institution's current capabilities and needs. This involves evaluating the existing technological infrastructure, understanding the specific educational objectives that AI is expected to fulfil, and assessing the readiness of the faculty and administrative staff to adopt new technologies. It is crucial to identify the gaps in current processes that AI can bridge and to set realistic expectations for the outcomes of AI integration as well as building and investing in the institutional capacity. Building institutional capacity for AI involves investing in the necessary infrastructure, such as high-speed internet and cloud computing services, and ensuring access to AI tools and platforms. Additionally, it requires developing the skills and knowledge of faculty, staff, and students through professional development and training programs focused on AI technologies and applications (Luckin et al., 2016). Data readiness is another critical factor in the successful implementation of AI and is part of the initial steps when defining the institutional AI strategy. George and Thomas (2019) address the integration of AI in human resources, emphasizing the importance of robust data governance and infrastructure. Without high-quality, accessible, and secure data, AI models cannot be developed or deployed effectively (George & Thomas, 2019).

Developing a Clear AI Strategy and Vision

After assessing needs and readiness, the next step is to develop a clear and coherent AI strategy that aligns with the institution's overall educational goals. This strategy should include specific objectives, timelines, resource allocation, and a vision for how AI will transform teaching, learning, and administrative processes. The vision should be shared with all stakeholders to ensure buy-in and to create a culture that is receptive to technological change. For institutions with existing digital transformation strategies, integrating AI requires thoughtful planning and adaptation. Herremans (2021) proposes the aiSTROM framework, which guides the creation of a successful AI strategy by addressing key areas such as data strategy, team composition, and continuous education of employees. This framework is instrumental for managers and lead developers in navigating the complexities of AI implementation (Herremans, 2021).

Selecting and Integrating AI Technologies

As there are a growing number of AI tools serving different purposes and with different functionalities, choosing the right AI technologies is key to any institution. This involves researching and selecting AI tools and solutions that are best suited to meet the institution's educational and administrative needs. Integration of these technologies should be done in a manner that minimally disrupts existing processes, with a focus on scalability and flexibility to adapt to future needs (Yathiraju, 2022). The build-or-buy decision presents a crucial crossroad for institutions, as they must choose between developing in-house AI capabilities or leveraging external partnerships. Perifanis and Kitsios (2023) discuss the challenges of adopting AI, pointing out that the decision hinges on factors like cost, expertise, and strategic importance. Building a team of AI experts or upskilling existing staff is crucial for the development of the necessary skills to drive AI initiatives forward (Perifanis & Kitsios, 2023).

Providing Faculty and Staff Training

One of the key challenges in AI implementation is ensuring that faculty and staff are adequately trained to utilize these new technologies. This training should not only cover the technical aspects of the AI tools but also include guidance on how to effectively incorporate AI into teaching methodologies and administrative processes. Continuous professional development and support are essential to enable staff to stay abreast of the rapidly evolving AI landscape.

Closely Monitoring Progress and Reporting Improvements

Once AI technologies are implemented, it is important to continuously monitor their performance and impact. This includes tracking metrics related to educational outcomes, student engagement, administrative efficiency, and overall user satisfaction. Regular reporting on these metrics will help in identifying areas for improvement and in making data-driven decisions for future AI initiatives. In some cases, pilot projects offer a pragmatic approach to testing AI solutions in controlled environments. Peretz-Andersson et al. (2021) examine the effects of bottom-up approaches in public sector AI transformation, advocating for pilot projects as a means to gather insights and make adjustments before wider deployment. This strategy aids in scaling AI solutions effectively, addressing challenges related to data management, infrastructure, and talent (Peretz-Andersson et al., 2021). Such an approach can be very beneficial in testing the tools in higher education institutions with vast data, stakeholders and operations. Equally, continuous monitoring, evaluation, and iteration are essential for ensuring that AI systems meet their intended objectives. Morandini et al. (2023) discuss the impact of AI on professional skills, emphasizing the need for organizations to adopt an iterative approach to AI implementation. This involves refining AI models and strategies based on feedback and performance data, ensuring that AI initiatives remain aligned with evolving workforce needs (Morandini et al., 2023).

Evaluating the Suitability of Different AI Technologies

This section focused in evaluating the suitability of different AI technologies in higher education, specially that adoption AI should be taken with proper consideration of different factors. Such as,

The integration of Artificial Intelligence (AI) into higher education presents a dynamic landscape of opportunities and challenges. With the potential to revolutionize learning and teaching methods, AI technologies must be adopted with a meticulous assessment of their alignment with the institution's goals, infrastructure compatibility, data handling practices, user engagement, evidence-based outcomes, and adherence to regulatory standards. This chapter delves into these critical factors, providing a comprehensive guide for educational institutions to evaluate the suitability of AI technologies for their specific needs. We are highlighting that in different points which are the educational goals, curriculum enhancements and infrastructure integration. In the following diagram discussion, the suitability of AI based on educational goals. The education goals and objectives are mainly focusing in utilizing AI in enhance learning within the institution. This will empower the institution reputation and education experiences. Examples of AI tool which can used to enhance educational aims and goals are the intelligence tutoring tool (ITT), natural language processing (NLP), educational data mining and analytics, virtual and augmented reality (AR, VR) and Chabot's. the below figure shoes the main factors of evaluating the suitability of different AI technologies in higher education.

Figure 2. Suitability of AI-based in educational goals

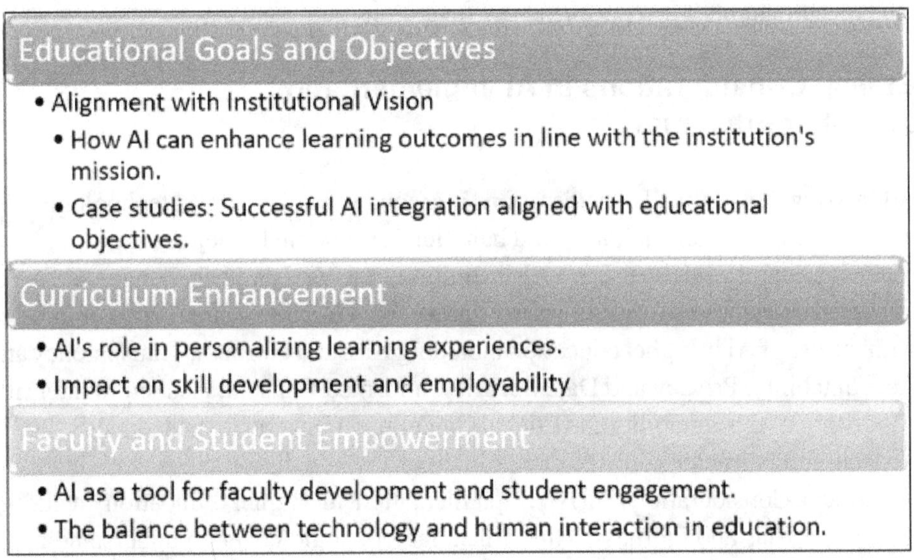

In the other hand, the suitability of AI can be measured by Infrastructure and Integration considering the different factors. Technological Readiness is one of the factors which before adopting AI technology in higher education, assessing current IT infrastructure for AI integration is an important action. This to ensure the compatibilities of current hardware and software to the proposed tools. Moreover, working in upgrading legacy systems and networks for optimal AI deployment. However, Integration with existing systems is an important factor which checking compatibility of AI solutions with current educational tools and following strategies for seamless integration of AI into existing workflows. To ensure all strategic process of al adoption working well, should consider user experience which include measuring the AI interfaces, educating stakeholders about AI capabilities and limitations and overcoming resistance and fostering a culture of innovation. Currently AI is integrated in every system and with any other technologies such as IoT and Blockchain. This to enhance the functionality, security and manageability of AI in different environments. For example, adopting AI with Blockchain technology in higher education is too add verification and validation level for the degree and documentations, to have tamper-proof and increase the trust within the system and data. Other example is adopting AI in IoT in higher educations, where AI can be used to analysing IoT devices data generated by IoT devices and predict the threats, action required such as maintenance and detect any unusual events in the classrooms, educational platforms and more.

The idea of integrating AI in Blockchain or IoT in educational sector is to enhance the educational platform performance, operations and security.

Ethical Considerations in AI Implementation in Higher Education

Addressing these ethical considerations is crucial to ensure that AI technologies are used in a responsible, equitable, and beneficial manner in higher education. Ethical frameworks and guidelines can help institutions navigate these challenges and make informed decisions about AI implementation. key ethical considerations associated with the use of AI in higher education including Bias and Fairness, Transparency and Accountability, Privacy and Data Security, Informed Consent, Academic Integrity, Algorithmic Accountability and Ethical Guidelines. (Ungerer, L. and Slade, S., 2022)

Bias and Fairness

Ethical Considerations in AI Implementation in Higher Education including measuring Bias and Fairness. This ethical factor should cover an understanding of AI bias through investigation of how biases can be embedded in AI systems and the Impact of biased AI on student outcomes and educational justice. Also, promoting fair AI practices strategies for identifying and mitigating biases in AI algorithms. Algorithm bias is an example of of AI bias and fairness which also referred to as algorithmic bias or AI bias. It is describes the unfair and biased results generated by algorithms used in artificial intelligence (AI) systems which can be intentionally or non-intentionally as noted by Suresh and Guttag (2020). It happens when AI systems show bias or favouritism toward particular groups or people based on factors like race, gender, age, ethnicity, socioeconomic status, or other protected characteristics" Rawar. A (2023).

Other type of AI Bias is Data Bias where using improper data, historical data or misunderstanding of program requirements and use irrelevant data will lead to data bias. Ferrer, X., et.al (2021) in their research stated that removing the security and validation of the input data through AI system will result in losing the accuracy of the results.

Suresh, H., & Guttag, J. (2021) in their research stated different possible solutions to mitigate the ethical consideration in using AI such as careful consideration during data collections, use reputated tools and test it first, "increasing openness and improving incentive structures". Where Ferrer, X., et.al (2021) suggests to us AI to detect the data Bias Or depan inknowledge-based.

Transparency and Accountability

Ensuring AI Transparency is an Importance factor which working of transparent AI processes in educational settings and apply approaches to making AI decisions understandable to users. This approach is raised security and privacy point of student data. The AI transparency is including many factors which need to be maintained such as data, algorithms, accountability, legal and regulation, standards and ethical. The following structure demonstrate the main consideration Transparency and Accountability factors in AI in higher education as stated summarized by Memarian, B., & Doleck, T. (2023).

Privacy and Data Security

Regarding Privacy and Data Security of AI in higher education, there are challenges of maintaining student privacy in AI applications. Moreover, Implementing robust data security measures. Pisica A et. Al (2023) stated that adopting AI has ethical challenges which reflect the lacking of managing data usage and following proper regulations during AI adoption process. Similarly, Rawar. A (2023) in book chapter highlights the importance of having principles of adopting AI to maintain data privacy and ethics. Murdoch, B. (2021) noted in his research that most challenges in AI is the requirements of processing big data where some institutions doe a collaborations of sharing their data to have training set suitable to their AI systems. This act as security privacy breaches of the personal information stored in these organizations. Moreover, this breaches of the privacy policies and regulations when data shared with third parties.

Sun, Y., et al (2020) in their paper which titles with . When machine learning meets privacy in 6G: A survey. They introduced several types of attacks can threat the data privacy in AI systems. Such as "Attackers can achieve (i) training data extraction, (ii) model extraction, and (iii) misprediction by changing dataset via active attack, or by passive attack which doesn't change dataset". However, these attacks can be defined as different levels as data in host, data-in network and data in transit. All of these level works to ensure data confidentiality, integrity and availability.

Figure 3. Transparency and accountability factors in AI

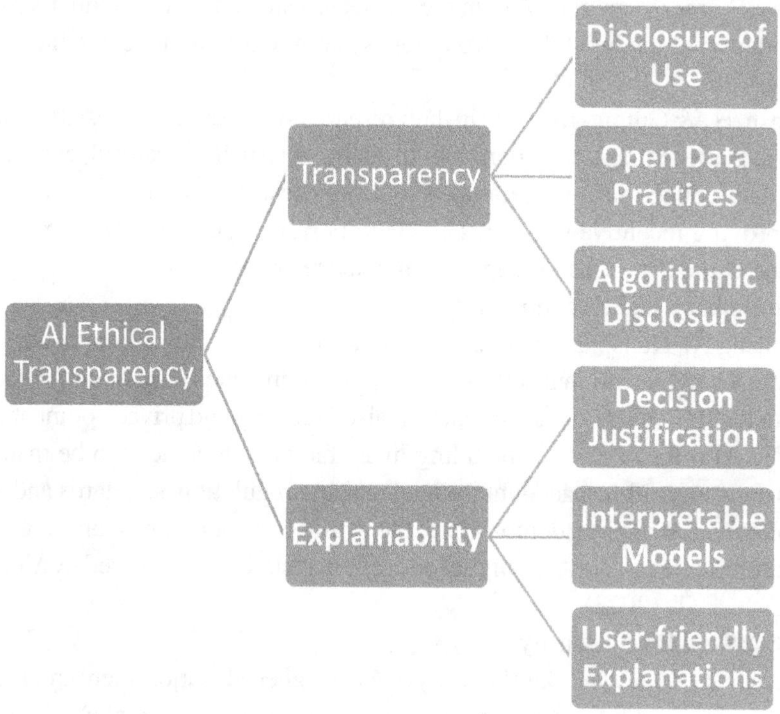

To control AI systems and ensure less security and privacy breaches are happening there are different countermeasures can be applied. For example, data encryptions, secure dataset storage and access control methods.

Academic Integrity

AI technology has been adopting in higher education to maintain the academic integrity. AI tools like plagiarism detectors or online proctoring software are widely used in higher education. The use of these tools raises consent issues, especially when students are required to agree to certain terms to participate in coursework. The balance between academic integrity and student privacy rights is a delicate one. AI and Academic Honesty is about the impact of AI on academic integrity and originality and Strategies for upholding academic standards in the AI era as noted by Kumar, R., Eaton, S. E., Mindzak, M., & Morrison, R. (2023). A case study from the University of New South Wales (UNSW) in Australia explores the use of AI-powered systems to detect plagiarism and enforce academic integrity. The challenge here was to balance privacy concerns with academic integrity needs and refine the AI system to minimize false positives detection of plagiarism. The deployment improved the detection of academic misconduct and heightened student awareness and understanding of academic integrity principles. This case emphasised AI's role in maintaining academic standards and the necessity for clear communication and policies regarding AI's application in educational contexts.

Social Impact of Using AI Technology

The advent of Artificial Intelligence (AI) in higher education presents a transformative opportunity. By leveraging AI, institutions can revolutionize educational practices, making them more inclusive, personalized, and aligned with the evolving needs of students and society. By implementing these strategies, higher education institutions can harness the power of AI to create a positive social impact, promote equitable access to education, and address the evolving needs of students and society as a whole. It's essential to consider the ethical, accessibility, and inclusivity aspects of AI implementations to ensure that the social impact is positive and far-reaching. This section of the chapter explores the strategies that higher education institutions can implement to harness the power of AI effectively, ensuring a positive and far-reaching social impact.

Accessible Education Through AI this can be done though Bridging the Digital Divide by letting AI offers a unique opportunity to bridge the digital divide in education. For Example, by providing AI-powered online learning platforms, including remote and underserved communities.

Assistive Technologies for Inclusivity where AI can play a pivotal role in creating inclusive learning environments. Tools like speech-to-text, personalized learning interfaces, and AI-assisted language translation can make education more accessible to students with disabilities and those who face language barriers. This will help in scaling education with AI-driven educational platforms means that quality education can be provided to a much larger number of students, overcoming the physical and logistical limitations of traditional classrooms.

Taking care of addressing educational challenges with AI is really important in any AI strategy adoption. Considering the enhancing academic Integrity where AI can help maintain high standards of academic integrity through tools that detect plagiarism and ensure fair assessment practices. This upholds the quality and credibility of higher education. Additionally, AI can act as supporting Faculty and Staff by providing AI tools for faculty and staff, enabling them to focus more on teaching and research.

In the other hand, there are negative social impact of adopting AI in higher education. Such as, job replacement where the technology will take role of the teachers and administrators in managing things. Privacy concerns are one of the social impacts where all data used within AI tool is stored in the application's database which puts the personal data in high risk to be exposed. Moreover, security risks and utilizing social media data in educations is high challenges which raised with AI usage.

Finally, it required to recognize the pros and Cons of AI tools in each of these environments and targeted users. As some tool not fully ethically allowed to the students which work in effecting their academic performance as noted by (Sethi, K., Sharma, A., Chauhan, S. and Jaiswal, V., 2020). Therefore, it is necessary to have a mitigation plan to maintain most of social impacts. For example, developing private AI tools to use within the organizations, ensuring that used AI systems are secure and accountable and applying the privacy roles to manage institutional and personal data security.

AI Adoption Strategy: Case Studies

Alam, A., & Mohanty, A. (2022) in their research, they run a study in over 18 educational institutions to measure the ability of AI adoption. The authors discussed the tools, solutions and barriers. Similarity, Al-Mughairi, H., & Bhaskar, P. (2024) used an interview with teachers to know the AI ChatGPT adoption in education in UTAS, Oman. The researchers shared the findings as utilising this tool improve the personalize learning among the students, time saving for self-learning and enhance the knowledge. However, the authors also noted the challenges related to data management and privacy. Similar research done by Wang, Y., Liu, C., & Tu, Y. F. (2021) in chaina, where students and teachers participated in research. This research considers case study of AI adoption strategy including benefits and limitations.

In Mohamed Hashim, M. A., Tlemsani, I., & Matthews, R. (2022) research they proposed a digital transformation module which focused insteps and phases the universities can adopt to have smooth digital transformation. AI is one of the concepts that discussed in the case with the impact of its implementations.

Quy, V. K et. Al (2023) is case study research investigation done in higher education in Vietnam. Their research focused in proposed AI-IoT adoption strategy for low-Middle economical countries. The research define the lacking of IT infrastructure is major challenge in the adoption process. Where Crompton, H., & Burke, D. (2023) run a study where participants from 31 countries over 7 continents participated. The study found that AI worked in enhancing the assessment quality, assessments conductions time, feedback time and personalized learning. Similarly, Alotaibi, N. S., & Alshehri, A. H. (2023) discussed in their research the prospects and challenges of applying AI-based learning in higher education institutions in Saudi Arabia. Additionally, we found Lubinga, S. N., Maramura, T. C., & Masiya, T. (2023) research who investigated the AI Adoption challenges in South African higher education institutions under 4th industrial revolution. Their funding's was four main points which are incompatibility with culture norms, digital skills gaps, global conflicts views and complexity of concepts.

Limitations and Challenges of Specific AI Technologies

AI includes hundreds of tools and methods, where each of them adding advantages but also it have limitations and challenges. Some of these challenges has been discussed in section 4 the ethical considerations such as data security and privacy, algorithms bias and transparency.

However, one of the challenges is adopting natural language processing (NLP) in higher educational platforms including set of challenges and limitation such as compatibilities with student's languages requirements, accuracy of the context and the content. Language algorithms bias of using certain style of writing.

Moreover, integrating chatbots with NLP algorithms to create student assistant is trending AI solution in higher education. This solution also contains limitations such as improper dataset which lead to generate irrelevant data. Hence, AI systems which work in NLP need for continues updates the datasets, terminologies and linguistics trends. Although, NLP is importance AI tool for educational institutions but it challenged to be implements to some universities or colleges because the high cost and resources requirements. Other limitation is regulations compliance, where current academic regulations are lacking the compatibility with AI factors such as data usability regulations. Also, lack of clear academic policies as stated by Michel-Villarreal, R et. Al (2023). However, Kohnke, L., Moorhouse, B. L., & Zou, D. (2023) investigate lunagusc challenges with NLP and AI in education in Hong Kong. Their research work in developing educational content and support teachers and students to intract through AI with the developed content.

It worth to note that challenges and limitations are many and different based on nature of AI adoption in higher education environments and not limited into the mentioned once in this section of this chapter.

CONCLUSION

The chapter outlined a strategy factors for educational institutions to leverage AI's full potential. Through critical examination of ethical and social implications, the chapter advocates for responsible AI deployment, aiming to equip stakeholders with the insights needed for navigating the AI-driven higher educational landscape. The chapter discussed the also the limitations and challenges in adoption AI in higher education where any institution should carefully study it before the real implementations. The chapter present some case studies and researches which proposed AI adoption strategies with highlighting strength, challenges. tools and limitations.

The chapter founds the main AI adoption strategy should have focused in running SWOT analysis first to define opportunities and threats. Moreover, reviewing and improving the IT regulations, IT infrastructure and social interaction with AI are the major strategic phased should be done during the AI adoption process.

REFERENCES

Al-Mughairi, H., & Bhaskar, P. (2024). Exploring the factors affecting the adoption AI techniques in higher education: insights from teachers' perspectives on ChatGPT. *Journal of Research in Innovative Teaching & Learning*.

Alam, A., & Mohanty, A. (2022, November). Business models, business strategies, and innovations in EdTech companies: integration of learning analytics and artificial intelligence in higher education. In *2022 IEEE 6th Conference on Information and Communication Technology (CICT)* (pp. 1-6). IEEE. 10.1109/CICT56698.2022.9997887

Alotaibi, N. S., & Alshehri, A. H. (2023). Prospers and obstacles in using artificial intelligence in Saudi Arabia higher education institutions—The potential of AI-based learning outcomes. *Sustainability (Basel)*, *15*(13), 10723. doi:10.3390/su151310723

Alqahtani, T., Badreldin, H. A., Alrashed, M., Alshaya, A. I., Alghamdi, S. S., bin Saleh, K., Alowais, S. A., Alshaya, O. A., Rahman, I., Al Yami, M. S., & Albekairy, A. M. (2023). The emergent role of artificial intelligence, natural learning processing, and large language models in higher education and research. *Research in Social & Administrative Pharmacy*, *19*(8), 1236–1242. doi:10.1016/j.sapharm.2023.05.016 PMID:37321925

Alzahrani, S. A., & Alqurashi, H. S. (2023). Using the flipped classroom model to improve Saudi EFL learners' English pronunciation. *Linguistics and Culture Review*, *7*(S1), 51–71. doi:10.21744/lingcure.v7nS1.2260

Bonsu, E. M., & Baffour-Koduah, D. (2023). From the consumers' side: Determining students' perception and intention to use ChatGPT in Ghanaian higher education. Journal of Education. *Society & Multiculturalism*, *4*(1), 1–29. doi:10.2478/jesm-2023-0001

Bull, C., & Kharrufa, A. (2023). *Generative AI Assistants in Software Development Education.*

Chan, C. K. Y. (2023). A comprehensive AI policy education framework for university teaching and learning. *International Journal of Educational Technology in Higher Education*, *20*(1), 38. doi:10.1186/s41239-023-00408-3

Chang, Q., Pan, X., Manikandan, N., & Ramesh, S. (2022). Artificial Intelligence Technologies for Teaching and Learning in Higher Education. *International Journal of Reliability Quality and Safety Engineering*, *29*(5), 2240006. doi:10.1142/S021853932240006X

Chheang, V., Marquez-Hernandez, R., Patel, M., Rajasekaran, D., Sharmin, S., Caulfield, G., Kiafar, B., Li, J., & Barmaki, R. (2023). *Towards Anatomy Education with Generative AI-based Virtual Assistants in Immersive Virtual Reality Environments.*

Crompton, H., & Burke, D. (2023). *Artificial Intelligence in Higher Education: A Systematic Review of the Literature from 2016 to 2022.*

Crompton, H., & Burke, D. (2023). Artificial intelligence in higher education: The state of the field. *International Journal of Educational Technology in Higher Education*, *20*(1), 22. doi:10.1186/s41239-023-00392-8

de Chiusole, D., Stefanutti, L., Anselmi, P., & Robusto, E. (2020). Stat-Knowlab. Assessment and learning of statistics with competence-based knowledge space theory. *International Journal of Artificial Intelligence in Education*, *30*(4), 668–700. doi:10.1007/s40593-020-00223-1

Dempere, J., Modugu, K., Hesham, A., & Ramasamy, L. K. (2023, September). The impact of ChatGPT on higher education. [). Frontiers.]. *Frontiers in Education*, *8*, 1206936. doi:10.3389/feduc.2023.1206936

Fernández, A., Gómez, B., Binjaku, K., & Meçe, E. K. (2023). Digital transformation initiatives in higher education institutions: A multivocal literature review. *Education and Information Technologies*, *28*(10), 12351–12382. doi:10.1007/s10639-022-11544-0 PMID:37361743

Ferrer, X., Van Nuenen, T., Such, J. M., Coté, M., & Criado, N. (2021). Bias and discrimination in AI: A cross-disciplinary perspective. *IEEE Technology and Society Magazine*, *40*(2), 72–80. doi:10.1109/MTS.2021.3056293

Fu, Q., Gao, Z., Zhou, J., & Zheng, Y. (2021). CLSA: A novel deep learning model for MOOC dropout prediction. *Computers & Electrical Engineering*, *94*, 107315. doi:10.1016/j.compeleceng.2021.107315

Gašević, D., Siemens, G., & Sadiq, S. (2023). Empowering learners for the age of artificial intelligence. *Computers and Education: Artificial Intelligence*, *4*, 100130.

George, B., & Wooden, O. (2023). Managing the strategic transformation of higher education through artificial intelligence. *Administrative Sciences*, *13*(9), 196. doi:10.3390/admsci13090196

George, G., & Thomas, M. R. (2019). *Integration of Artificial Intelligence in Human Resource*.

Goel, A. K., & Polepeddi, L. (2018). *Jill Watson. Learning engineering for online education: Theoretical contexts and design-based examples*. Routledge.

Guo, L., Wang, D., Gu, F., Li, Y., Wang, Y., & Zhou, R. (2021). *Evolution and trends in intelligent tutoring systems research: a multidisciplinary and scientometric view*.

Herremans, D. (2021*). aiSTROM - A roadmap for developing a successful AI strategy*.

Hutson, J., Jeevanjee, T., Vander Graaf, V., Lively, J., Weber, J., Weir, G., Arnone, K., Carnes, G., Vosevich, K., Plate, D., & Leary, M. (2022). Artificial Intelligence and the Disruption of Higher Education: Strategies for Integrations across Disciplines. *Creative Education*, *13*(12), 3953–3980. doi:10.4236/ce.2022.1312253

Kohnke, L., Moorhouse, B. L., & Zou, D. (2023). Exploring generative artificial intelligence preparedness among university language instructors: A case study. *Computers and Education: Artificial Intelligence*, *5*, 100156. doi:10.1016/j.caeai.2023.100156

Lubinga, S. N., Maramura, T. C., & Masiya, T. (2023). *Adoption of Fourth Industrial Revolution: challenges in South African higher education institutions*.

Luckin, R., Holmes, W., Griffiths, M., & Forcier, L. B. (2016). *Intelligence Unleashed: An argument for AI in Education*. Pearson Education.

Manhica, R., Santos, A., & Cravino, J. (2022). The use of artificial intelligence in learning management systems in the context of higher education: Systematic literature review. *2022 17th Iberian Conference on Information Systems and Technologies (CISTI),* (pp. 1-6). IEEE.

Martins, R. M., & Gresse Von Wangenheim, C. (2023). Findings on teaching machine learning in high school: A ten-year systematic literature review. *Informatics in Education*, *22*(3), 421–440.

Mavrikis, M., Geraniou, E., Gutierrez Santos, S., & Poulovassilis, A. (2019). Intelligent analysis and data visualisation for teacher assistance tools: The case of exploratory learning. *British Journal of Educational Technology*, *50*(6), 2920–2942. doi:10.1111/bjet.12876

McGrath, C., Pargman, T. C., Juth, N., & Palmgren, P. J. (2023). University teachers' perceptions of responsibility and artificial intelligence in higher education-An experimental philosophical study. *Computers and Education: Artificial Intelligence*, *4*, 100139. doi:10.1016/j.caeai.2023.100139

Memarian, B., & Doleck, T. (2023). Fairness, Accountability, Transparency, and Ethics (FATE) in Artificial Intelligence (AI), and higher education: A systematic review. *Computers and Education: Artificial Intelligence, 100152.*

Michel-Villarreal, R., Vilalta-Perdomo, E., Salinas-Navarro, D. E., Thierry-Aguilera, R., & Gerardou, F. S. (2023). Challenges and Opportunities of Generative AI for Higher Education as Explained by ChatGPT. *Education Sciences*, *13*(9), 856. doi:10.3390/educsci13090856

Mohamed Hashim, M. A., Tlemsani, I., & Matthews, R. (2022). Higher education strategy in digital transformation. *Education and Information Technologies*, *27*(3), 3171–3195. doi:10.1007/s10639-021-10739-1 PMID:34539217

Morandini, S., Fraboni, F., Puzzo, G., Giusino, D., Volpi, L., Brendel, H., & Pietrantoni, L. (2023). Examining the Nexus between Explainability of AI Systems and User's Trust: A Preliminary Scoping Review. *Proceedings*. Ceur. http://ceur-ws.org.

Mousavi, A., Schmidt, M., Squires, V., & Wilson, K. (2021). Assessing the effectiveness of student advice recommender agent (SARA): The case of automated personalized feedback. *International Journal of Artificial Intelligence in Education*, *31*(3), 603–621. doi:10.1007/s40593-020-00210-6

Murdoch, B. (2021). Privacy and artificial intelligence: Challenges for protecting health information in a new era. *BMC Medical Ethics*, *22*(1), 1–5. doi:10.1186/s12910-021-00687-3 PMID:34525993

Peretz-Andersson, E., Lavesson, N., Bifet, A., & Mikalef, P. (2021, June). AI Transformation in the Public Sector: Ongoing Research. In *2021 Swedish Artificial Intelligence Society Workshop (SAIS)* (pp. 1-4). IEEE. 10.1109/SAIS53221.2021.9483960

Perifanis, N. A., & Kitsios, F. (2023). Investigating the influence of artificial intelligence on business value in the digital era of strategy: A literature review. *Information (Basel)*, *14*(2), 85. doi:10.3390/info14020085

Pisica, A. I., Edu, T., Zaharia, R. M., & Zaharia, R. (2023). Implementing Artificial Intelligence in Higher Education: Pros and Cons from the Perspectives of Academics. *Societies (Basel, Switzerland)*, *13*(5), 118. doi:10.3390/soc13050118

Quy, V. K., Thanh, B. T., Chehri, A., Linh, D. M., & Tuan, D. A. (2023). AI and digital transformation in higher education: Vision and approach of a specific university in Vietnam. *Sustainability (Basel)*, *15*(14), 11093. doi:10.3390/su151411093

Sandu, N., & Gide, E. (2019, September). Adoption of AI-Chatbots to enhance student learning experience in higher education in India. In *2019 18th International Conference on Information Technology Based Higher Education and Training (ITHET)* (pp. 1-5). IEEE.

Schön, E.-M., Neumann, M., Hofmann-Stölting, C., Baeza-Yates, R., & Rauschenberger, M. (2023). How are AI assistants changing higher education?.

Sethi, K., Sharma, A., Chauhan, S., & Jaiswal, V. (2020). Impact of social and cultural challenges in education using AI. In *Revolutionizing Education in the Age of AI and Machine Learning* (pp. 130–151). IGI Global. doi:10.4018/978-1-5225-7793-5.ch007

Simões, R. V., Parreiras, M. V. C., Da Silva, A. C. C., Barbosa, C. E., de Lima, Y. O., & de Souza, J. M. (2022, October). Artificial intelligence and digital transformation: analyzing future trends. In *2022 IEEE International Conference on Systems, Man, and Cybernetics (SMC)* (pp. 1462-1467). IEEE. 10.1109/SMC53654.2022.9945429

Sullivan, M., Kelly, A., and McLaughlan, P. (2023). *ChatGPT in higher education: Considerations for academic integrity and student learning.*

Sun, Y., Liu, J., Wang, J., Cao, Y., & Kato, N. (2020). When machine learning meets privacy in 6G: A survey. *IEEE Communications Surveys and Tutorials*, *22*(4), 2694–2724. doi:10.1109/COMST.2020.3011561

Suresh, H., & Guttag, J. (2021, October). A framework for understanding sources of harm throughout the machine learning life cycle. In *Proceedings of the 1st ACM Conference on Equity and Access in Algorithms, Mechanisms, and Optimization* (pp. 1-9). 10.1145/3465416.3483305

Ungerer, L., & Slade, S. (2022). Ethical considerations of artificial intelligence in learning analytics in distance education contexts. In Learning Analytics in Open and Distributed Learning: Potential and Challenges (pp. 105-120). Springer Nature Singapore. doi:10.1007/978-981-19-0786-9_8

Wang, T., Vargas-Diaz, D., Brown, C., & Chen, Y. (2023). *Exploring the Role of AI Assistants in Computer Science Education: Methods*. Implications, and Instructor Perspectives.

Wang, Y., Liu, C., & Tu, Y. F. (2021). Factors affecting the adoption of AI-based applications in higher education. *Journal of Educational Technology & Society*, *24*(3), 116–129.

Yadlapally, D. K., Vasireddy, B., Marimganti, M., Chowdary, T., Karthikeyan, C., & Vignesh, T. (2023). *A Review on the Potential of AI Voice Assistants for Personalized and Adaptive Learning in Education.*

Yang, S., & Evans, C. (2019, November). Opportunities and challenges in using AI chatbots in higher education. In *Proceedings of the 2019 3rd International Conference on Education and E-Learning* (pp. 79-83). 10.1145/3371647.3371659

Yao, G. (2022). Application of higher education management in colleges and universities by deep learning. *Computational Intelligence and Neuroscience*, *2022*, 2022. doi:10.1155/2022/7295198 PMID:35990163

Yathiraju, N. (2022). Investigating the use of an Artificial Intelligence Model in an ERP Cloud-Based System. International Journal of Electrical. *Electronics and Computers*, *7*(2), 1–26.

Zembylas, M. (2023). A decolonial approach to AI in higher education teaching and learning: Strategies for undoing the ethics of digital neocolonialism. *Learning, Media and Technology*, *48*(1), 25–37. doi:10.1080/17439884.2021.2010094

Zhang, Z., & Xu, L. (2022). Student engagement with automated feedback on academic writing: A study on Uyghur ethnic minority students in China. *Journal of Multilingual and Multicultural Development*, 1–14. doi:10.1080/01434632.2022.2102175

Chapter 12
AI-Driven Innovation in Higher Education Marketing:
An Exploration of Oman's Academic Landscape

Ammar Abdulrahman AlBalushi
Majan University College, Oman

Ali Younis Al Bolushi
Majan University College, Oman

ABSTRACT

This book chapter systematically reviews AI's transformative impact on higher education marketing. It further explores the challenges of integrating AI within existing educational frameworks, emphasising the importance of AI literacy in curricula and addressing ethical considerations like data privacy and the balance between technology and human interaction. Moreover, it synthesises diverse literature to develop a framework for utilising AI in marketing, focusing on strategy, stakeholder experiences, and AI-driven initiatives. The research addresses AI integration challenges, AI literacy, and ethical concerns and aligns with Oman's Vision 2040 and digital strategies. It highlights the current state of AI in education and pinpoints gaps in existing literature, paving the way for future investigations within the Omani context. It emphasises strategic planning, campaign execution, and balancing technology with human aspects, offering insights for Oman's institutions to effectively utilise AI, highlighting current trends and future research directions in the Omani context.

DOI: 10.4018/979-8-3693-2145-4.ch012

INTRODUCTION

In the ever-changing world of higher education, the arrival of artificial intelligence (hereafter AI) jointly with technology has sparked the transformation of the traditional meeting point between academic administration, marketing, and technology. Analysis of different studies prompts higher education institutions to have a deeper understanding of AI's effective integration and impact on their operations. Consistent with the larger Vision 2040, Oman's National Digital Economy Program is simply a reflection of the change that is happening as it adopts AI and digital technology in its education sector. This chapter investigates the way AI's impact on higher education marketing redefines conventional methods with data-driven tactics and personalized student socialization.

Introducing AI in academic and administrative educational practices is not just a technological invasion but an attempt to nuances of student needs and behaviours. In line with Oman's ambitious digital transformation objectives, this strategic vision reiterates the aims of AI powered enhanced learning and administrative efficiencies (MTCIT 2021). AI enables educational organizations to personalize their marketing approaches via ChatGPT, machine learning, predictive analytics, student targeting, interactions, and engagement. Nevertheless, these technological progressions bring a critical problem of balance of automation and the human element in the marketing of educational institutions (Baidoo-Anu and Owusu-Ansah, 2023; Jain and Aggarwal, 2020).

Moreover, various studies show that AI is implemented at the operational management level in different higher education institutions (PWC, 2016). This is a direct outcome of government initiatives such as the National Digital Economy program, which focuses on utilising AI for operational efficiencies and increasing its applications to develop educational systems further. At an operational level, AI is increasingly used by administrators to optimise resource management systems, enhance student services, and influence student recruitment and retention, which highlights its importance in achieving higher institutional performance and reshaping the general traditional education landscape (Cihelkova et al., 2020; Zemanova, 2015). Therefore, reflecting these developments, the idea of this chapter stems from the potential role of AI in transforming higher education. More specifically, this chapter explores its application in Oman through the National Digital Strategy and other frameworks that may provide us with the

In Oman, precisely, this exploration coincides with the national digital strategy, signalling the role of AI in improving educational experiences and achieving institutional objectives in the digital era. Hence, this chapter offers reflective knowledge for academics, administrators and marketers alike to enable them to understand the evolving link between strategy development, emerging technologies, and human communication in the current times.

As we start this exploration, we will provide an overview of the utilisation of AI in higher education in general and Oman in particular through its Vision 2040 and Digital Economy Program and review any ethical issues linked with its innovative usage. Therefore, in its comprehensive review, the current chapter implies AI's transformative possibilities in higher education and emphasises the intelligent and flexible technology application in designing a more integrated, responsive, and comfortable learning environment (Carroll et al., 2009; Lancioni, 2013).

In conclusion, incorporating AI into higher education is the transition to a more progressive and adaptable educational model. The chapter aims to map it out by offering discussions and advice about how to optimise the power of AI in the best way to overcome the challenges and get the opportunities from AI in the constantly changing world of higher education.

In Oman, the convergence of traditional education with modern AI technologies, as the National Digital Economy Program promoted, is a primary part of this evolutionary path.

However, like in most other countries, this process in Oman is crucial, as the government attempts to unite its living cultural heritage with modern world developments and integrate its vivid cultural heritage with modern world tendencies. AI introduction in marketing in the higher education sector in Oman represents the move towards technology and strategic response to the changing behaviours of students, educators, and the entire academic community in Oman. This chapter discusses how AI technologies are changing marketing practices in Oman's educational organisations, giving details of strategic implementation, stakeholder experiences, and the general influence of these new methods.

Furthermore, this book chapter discusses the position of AI in higher education throughout the world in general and in Oman in particular. It lists the areas of literature that should be examined. It does so by creating a platform for further studies and discussions. The development of Oman as a state and the problems of the 21st century imply the relevance of AI use in higher education marketing. Ultimately, this chapter seeks to offer valuable recommendations for educational institutions in Oman to leverage AI in marketing more effectively.

LITERATURE REVIEW

Overview of AI in Higher Education Globally

Within the academic sector, the adaptation of AI is creative and dynamic as it is used for improving learning through building adaptive learning systems and automating manual administrative processes. Although these developments are expected to bring significant advantages, they also carry with them ethical issues and challenges that need to be addressed such as data privacy, the lack of ethical frameworks and the ambiguity on the level of transparency maintained within the AI algorithm systems (Klimova et al., 2023).

AI's potential ability to address and calculate large data sets for HEI's institutions has opened new doors for advancements in predictive analytics that allowed them to make data driven decisions that affect student success and institutional planning (Baker et al., 2019; Alshoaibi, 2015; Al Harthy, 2011). However, the perception and efficiency of these technologies may vary greatly depending on the student point of view. To develop successful AI applications for an effective educational experience, it is important to know students' responses towards AI-driven initiatives, their partiality to personalised learning, as well as doubts about data privacy (Williamson, 2024; Compton and Burke, 2023).

To fully capitalise on AI to enhance learning and administrative efficiency, educational institutions must involve students and faculty. Understanding students' perspectives towards AI-driven learning and resolving the issues of the faculty's adjustment are prerequisites for a more inclusive and efficient AI integration in higher education. This involvement can guarantee that AI tools will improve educational results and correspond to the academic community's demands and requirements (Kuleto et al., 2021).

AI's contribution to personalising the learning experience is a pivotal benefit of higher education. However, AI integration affects faculty and staff roles, leaving a need for professional development to work with these new technologies (Estrellado and Miranda, 2023). Consequently, there is a need for training programs that will provide educators with relevant knowledge and skills and administrative staff with the necessary competence to efficiently use AI tools, which will also address both obstacles and opportunities of AI in education.

AI-driven adaptive learning technologies customise learning material to individual student needs, considering various learning styles and rates. However, the effect of AI on academic and administrative roles should not be discounted. There is a significant demand for professional development and training programs that will help educators and staff stay up to date with the developments in AI technologies, that automate administrative tasks and provide new tools for content delivery, allowing them to fully exploit the potential of AI while addressing the problems arising from it (Estrellado and Miranda, 2023).

However, in this personalised approach, the human aspect is essential in making the learning environment inclusive and education accessible to a broader audience of students. AI's role in improving the learning journey is evident in its capacity to deliver personalised learning experiences that reflect every student's distinct learning path (Walczak and Cellary, 2023; Baker et al., 2019; Alshoaibi, 2015).

Administratively, AI has streamlined numerous routine tasks, from student admissions and scheduling to resource allocation. Yet, this technological push should be balanced with considerations of the human element in education, emphasising the need for cultural alignment, especially in places like Oman, where education practices are deeply rooted in cultural values (Al Matari et al., 2023).

AI-powered chatbots and virtual assistants offer instant responses to student questions, thus improving the student experience and saving administrative workloads. The influence of AI upon administrative efficacy exceeds mere task automation to strategic planning, crisis management and resource management, underpinning the overall institutional effectiveness (Al Matari et al., 2023; Alshoaibi, Kitsios, and Kamariotou, 2021; 2015; Al Harthy, 2011).

Emerging technologies in higher education, facilitated by AI and cloud computing, have enabled the university to sophisticate the network infrastructures to meet the need for change. This chapter highlights the need to embrace stakeholders' perspectives, including those of students, faculty, administrators, and policymakers when integrating AI into higher education marketing.

Furthermore, while integrating AI into higher education brings considerable advancements, it also poses problems connected to the legitimate use of technology, data privacy, and digital inequality. The disparity in access to AI technologies can worsen educational inequalities since only some people will have access to these tools and resources, ensuring everyone has access to such technologies (Walczak and Cellary, 2023). However, addressing these challenges demands joint efforts by all stakeholders to utilise AI's potential reasonably and efficiently.

AI insights are important in predictive diagnosis, providing solutions, and optimising experiences across wireless access, wired access, and SD-WAN domains (Alghaiti, 2023).

In the 21st century, HEI's are going through a digital transformation that demands advanced AI-based systems to explore a more adaptive learning environment and predictive analytics to enhance the student experience. AI's contribution to profiling and forecasting is substantial, mainly in engineering disciplines. For example, AI-powered predictive analytics provide educators with an understanding of how students learn so that they can adjust the methods and resources. This function is fundamental in the early detection of the learners' requirements, hence timely assistance to ensure they succeed in their learning process (Baidoo-Anu and Ansah, 2023; Zawacki-Richter et al., 2019).

However, introducing AI technologies in higher education brings its challenges. Data privacy and ethical considerations are among such concerns, as AI systems are sometimes required to interact with sensitive student data. It is essential to harmonise between accepting technological progress and maintaining the human communication element that underpins teaching and mentoring. Additionally, the digital divide in AI technologies should not be ignored as it may create unequal educational opportunities. Hence, fair and equitable access to AI tools and resources across the entire academic spectrum is crucial to preserving equality within the learning environment (Walczak and Cellary, 2023).

In conclusion, AI has a multifaceted role in global higher education, affecting areas like adaptive learning, predictive analytics, and automated administrative tasks. However, these progressions must be negotiated critically, holding ethical dimensions, the human element of education, and the social context of the use of such technologies in focus.

Higher Education in Oman and the Impact of AI

Oman's Vision 2040, under the guidance of His Majesty Sultan Haitham, places significant emphasis on harnessing advanced technologies, including AI, to revolutionise the economy, including the higher education sector (Oman Observer, 2023). The strategy aims to build an innovative, knowledge-based economy to ensure the education system is aligned to the world's best practice and the workforce is skilled in new technologies. This vision involves improving research capabilities and boosting international collaborations. AI implementation in educational practices in the country is anticipated to represent a revolutionary and advanced approach to enhancing the quality, accessibility, and relevance of higher education in Oman, which aligns with the Sultan's strategy of integrating top-notch technologies for national development. This vision aligns with the National Education Strategy 2040 and the National Digital Economy Program, which focus on modernising the curricula, investing in teacher training, and developing infrastructure to support the integration of AI and digital technologies in education. It emphasises the role played by AI in customising the education received, reinforcing the research, and raising administration efficacy. According to these national strategies, government bodies, educational institutions, and the private sector should collaborate to develop a forward-thinking and globally benchmarked AI-enabled education system that allows Oman to build its new knowledge-based economy. A specific focus is given to the development of student knowledge and skill set to satisfy the labour market needs, encourage uses of innovative technologies and achieve the best educational outcomes. Through integrating AI and the development of national digital strategies, the Omani government aims to strengthen its place in the new evolving world of academia and achieve its Vision 2040's general objectives (MTCIT, 2021).

The higher education sector of Oman is experiencing transformational changes, following the strategic objectives outlined in Vision 2040 and the National Education Strategy. Omani Higher education institutions are growing in number and witnessing an institutional cultural shift, with innovation, quality and international standards as the primary focus. They focus on STEM fields, research, and innovation per the national agenda to diversify the economy and embrace technological advancements.

In Oman's higher education landscape, AI integration represents strategic compliance with the national vision and educational objectives, as reflected in the initiatives of various HEIs. For example, Sultan Qaboos University has partnered with the Chinese organisation Star Vision to send the first Omani AI model into space. This project represents the university's determination to incorporate AI into its academic and research activities, promoting Oman's competence in AI and space technologies (Oxford Business Group, 2023, (Sultan Qaboos University, 2023).

Furthermore, AI is embedded into the teaching and learning process at A'Sharqiyah University in Oman to improve student engagement and performance (Al Matari et al., 2023). The International Maritime College Oman (IMCO) is one more case of AI dramatically influencing logistics studies, confirming its ability to be used in highly specialised educational areas (Alghaithi, et al., 2023).

Concerning the government investments in AI and Education, an 'action plan' to fast-track AI adoption is underway, Oman's Ministry of Transport, Communications and Information Technology is formulating an 'action plan' to accelerate AI adoption as part of the government's Digital Economy Programme. The plan introduces enhancing productivity in all sectors through AI, developing human capabilities in AI, speeding its adoption in services such as defence, healthcare and education, and ensuring just and ethical governance of AI and Advanced Technologies (Oman Observer, 2021).

However, despite all these transformational advantages and development, AI integration in higher education poses numerous challenges, including privacy of data, ethical AI use, but not limited to, digital divide, which remains crucial. While AI offers personalisation and efficiency, it raises privacy issues, unethical use, and the loss of human element in education. AI systems often need access to sensitive data, making robust protection measures essential. Protection measures must be extreme, as AI systems require access to sensitive data. The key to education is balancing technological innovation, ethical considerations, and human Interaction. The risks pointed out in recent research are the possibilities of AI-produced errors and content "hallucination", which may mislead if not verified correctly (Maleki et al., 2024; Monteith, 2023). There are also problems regarding authorship and originality, which is why tools that can differentiate between AI-generated and human-created content are needed (Liang et al., 2023).

Moreover, AI models can exhibit biases that depend on the fed training data, which could affect fairness and accuracy in educational settings (Ntoutsi et al., 2020). Other drawbacks include a lack of human interaction and understanding, creativity limitations, the number of questions and responses (Budler et al., 2023), and quality of data dependency (Brown et al., 2020). These restrictions accentuate the importance of balanced AI integration in the educational process, where human expertise and ethical aspects are the key. The more Oman becomes an integral part of AI in higher education, the more dealing with these issues using further research is paramount to fully realising AI's potential and the country's educational future.

Key Findings and Identification of Gaps in Literature

The findings of AI's role in higher education in Oman and GCC countries reflect important but imbalanced integration compared to other sectors like e-commerce and economics. For example, although the Abu Dhabi e-commerce sector shows rapid AI integration, with startups like swftbox raising significant funds for AI-powered delivery platforms, the same technological embracement is yet to be observed in the higher education sector (Oxford Business Group, 2023). Likewise, in the broader frame of the GCC, some countries adopted decentralised finance, cryptocurrencies, and other Web3 technologies. Whereas this type of action is in the finance sector, AI adoption in higher education is slow (Oxford Business Group, 2023). Similarly, in the broader context of the GCC, nations actively embrace decentralised finance and cryptocurrency, leveraging AI and other Web3 technologies. This proactive approach in sectors like finance contrasts with the slower pace of AI adoption in higher education (Oxford Business Group, 2023).

Moreover, the regional emphasis on technological advancements such as blockchain and AI in space activities highlights the gap in AI application in higher education. The significant economic opportunities presented by these technologies in other sectors underline the need for a more robust integration of AI in the educational landscape (Oxford Business Group, 2023). in Oman, despite agreements and collaborations aimed at enhancing digital skills and ICT infrastructure, there is a noticeable lag in the application of AI in higher education. Initiatives like the collaboration between Oman and Saudi Arabia for digital transformation and workforce development in areas like AI and programming have not yet translated into widespread AI adoption in educational settings (Oxford Business Group, 2023).

Lastly, Gulf CEOs identify technology and innovation as key drivers for corporate revenue growth, focusing on AI(Oxford Business Group, 2023). This enthusiasm for technological advancement has yet to be fully reflected in the higher education sector.

This gap in AI application between industries such as e-commerce, economics, and higher education in Oman highlights the need for a more concerted effort to integrate AI into the educational framework. The integration would involve embracing AI for administrative efficiency and personalised learning and aligning educational strategies with the rapid technological advancements observed in other sectors.

FROM THE LITERATURE STANDPOINT

limited research has focused on AI from a management perspective, particularly in areas such as information management (Chen and Siau, 2020), decision-making processes (Duan and Edwards, 2019), knowledge management (Lei and Wang, 2020), and skill development (Campi et al., 2020). This book chapter is unique in conducting a systematic review to investigate the link between artificial intelligence and organisational strategy in higher education, an area not thoroughly addressed in past research. If further research is needed, this method can explain how AI affects and merges with strategic planning and management in higher education institutions. In addition, the current literature points to the absence of extensive AI implementation models in Oman's higher education as one of the most evident gaps. This leaves a gap for future studies to develop culturally sensitive frameworks for using AI in the administrative processes of Omani higher education. Research of this kind could be a very important source of information for the integration of AI, and the focus would be on the challenges and successes of the Omani educational context. More importantly, research is required to investigate ways AI technologies can be modified to suit Oman's cultural and educational specificities, the government's graduate attributes, and long-term objectives.

Consequently, this research is expected to focus on the peculiar advantages and challenges of the educational environment in Oman and the GCC to develop a roadmap for AI deployment designed explicitly for the Omani educational sector. Additionally, there is a need for research that examines how AI technologies can be adapted to fit Oman's cultural and educational specifics, as well as the government's long-term goals for graduate attributes. This research should seek to understand the unique challenges and opportunities presented by the educational landscape in Oman and the broader GCC region, aiming to create a roadmap for AI implementation tailored to the Omani education sector's specific needs and cultural context.

A clear trend of increasing popularity of AI use in higher education worldwide is observed. In this regard, the GCC countries, especially Oman, present a unique area for research. Studying AI integration within this framework is crucial for creating powerful and culturally understandable AI-based educational practices. The demand is evident in the targeted research on how AI can be customised to address the unique needs and challenges of the higher education sector in Oman, focusing on ethical issues and cultural compatibility.

ROLE OF AI IN DIGITAL MARKETING IN EDUCATION

AI has significantly changed digital marketing in education, especially in the higher education sector. AI technologies are used increasingly for marketing strategy optimisation, thus, improving engagement and personalisation in education settings. Works such as those by Shanmugam et al. (2023) highlight the impact of AI on profitability and market potential through data-driven methods. The research demonstrates the relevance of AI in higher education, where providing the right messages to the right audience is essential in attracting and retaining students due to AI's capacity to analyse vast amounts of data and provide customised marketing solutions.

Moreover, AI use in education digital marketing goes beyond traditional approaches, allowing institutions to interact with prospects and current students more efficiently. For example, AI-powered chatbots are discussed in studies such as Rajendran et al. (2023), and they have started to play a significant part in delivering instant and customised communication, thus significantly enhancing student experience and involvement.

The synergistic effect of AL and digital marketing in higher education relates to the growing complexity of addressing a variety of student demographics and especially fits modern student digital behaviour. Illustrated in these studies, AI predictive analytics and machine learning enable more precise targeting and messaging, thus improving the efficiency and efficacy of marketing campaigns in the educational field.

This section will review two key areas where AI has considerable influence on the education domain. First, 'AI Applications in Digital Marketing' will cover how AI changes digital marketing approaches in education, emphasising improved student interaction, personalised communication, and effective targeting. Secondly, the 'Role of AI in Streamlining Administrative Processes in Education', will focus on how AI streamlines administrative activities and enhances operational effectiveness and overall management in educational institutions. The sub-sections are intended to give an in-depth overview of AI's transforming role in the marketing and administrative dimensions of the educational sector.

AI Applications in Digital Marketing

The influence of AI on digital marketing in education sector particularly higher education is largely transforming the way institution operate, particularly with regards to student engagement and development of marketing strategies. The ability of AI to create personalised content and targeted campaigns is reforming how marketing teams work and enhancing their outreach efforts. AI as a tool, enables creating the personalised marketing materials targeted specifically at various student segments (Shanmugam et al., 2023). This focused and targeted method is important in the current times where data is primarily is in a digital form. In addition, AI's skill in harvesting data, through data-mining techniques, is instrumental for decision makers to understand student demographics and inclinations. AI tools derived from processing large data sets provides the analysis of students' behaviors and needs that assists institution's management in developing marketing strategies that match students' expectations and market trends. Employing this data-driven approach will make educational institutions stay attractive and relevant for their target student markets (EL-MOFFOCK, 2023).

Moreover, according to the research carried out by Khatri (2021) on AI's capacity to develop targeted ads and automation of responses in different industries, AI also shows a lot of promise in improving social media management and Interaction in educational establishments. For example, AI tools like chatbots can help increase engagement on social media platforms by automating tasks like posting content and responding to inquiries. This automation strengthens the institutions' online presence and creates a feeling of community between students. This data-driven approach personalises customer experiences, significantly improves return on investment by customising customer experiences, and enhances the return on investment by making marketing campaigns more effective and solving security problems faster.

AI's impact extends to operational efficiency and profitability in the educational sector's marketing efforts. According to the research of Nair and Kumar (2021), technological innovations as a part of the integration process assist in the optimal use of resources and precision targeting. More specifically, the study states that AI reduces costs and enhances the effectiveness of marketing campaigns. This optimisation is vital in the competitive arena of higher education. Moreover, the study concludes that "*digitisation is of utmost importance where quality expects to meet the expectations of prompt delivery of educational services in the gamut of industry 4.0, imbibing the changes voluntarily*" (Nair and Kumar, 2021:5178).

Real-world applications of AI in digital marketing within education highlight its practical benefits, as seen in improved student recruitment and engagement. Camilleri's (2019) study indicates that global HEIs are moving towards marketisation of higher education to become less reliant on government scholarships, control, and intervention. This trend is also observed in Oman, where the government is currently the primary financier of the higher education system. The country's reliance on fluctuating oil revenues, especially with the significant downturn in the mid-1990s, has escalated costs due to increased enrollments in public educational institutions (Brandenburg in 2012). Such case studies offer valuable insights into the importance of marketing in higher education and the effective integration of AI in marketing strategies, demonstrating its potential to revolutionise how educational institutions connect with their audience.

Thilagavathy and Kumar's (2021) research shows AI's influence on digital marketing. AI enhances search experiences, including voice recognition and customer data analysis, which refines advertainment strategies and ensures that businesses can cater to the changing customer demand to remain competitive. In digital marketing, AI is widely used in social media and SEO analytics by machine learning and data mining methods. Marketing companies depend on such techniques as they are instrumental in analysing and improving web content, resulting in higher page ranking and better customer interaction. Moreover, AI is widely used in Pay-Per-Click (PPC) advertising and targeting specific segments in the market. For example, it assists companies to generate new content and recommendations for their customers based on their understanding of their web browsing history.

This comprehensive integration of AI into digital marketing represents a significant development towards more personalised, efficient, and data-driven marketing approaches that will define the future of customer engagement and the development of innovative business strategies. In summary, AI's integration into digital marketing represents an essential advancement in educational marketing, which provides personalised, efficient, and data-oriented strategies for Interaction with the student and institutional branding (Anca, 2023).

ROLE OF AI IN STREAMLINING ADMINISTRATIVE PROCESSES IN EDUCATION

The efficiency of administrative procedures in the dynamic context of higher education should not be underestimated. They are the backbone of the HEI's operations, ensuring a proper ecosystem for learning and research. As the world strides into the digital age, AI has become a revolutionary force that will change the administrative pattern of normal education. AI's's contribution in reforming administrative activities and functions lies in its ability to automate and optimise routine processes. This is manifested in various areas of education administration, ranging from student admissions and registration to resource management and financial planning.

For example, AI-enabled systems can quickly handle and analyse large numbers of applications to identify suitable candidates based on a defined criterion, paving the way for a more efficient admission process. The use of AI for these purposes significantly increases the speed of the process and provides a more subjective aspect of candidate selection (EL-MOFFOCK, 2023). Furthermore, AI demonstrates its effectiveness in data management and analysis. Educational institutions are known to handle vast amounts of data, including student records, academic performance metrics, and financial information. AI tools quickly process this data, delivering actionable insights that assist decision-making.

Another example is that AI can assist in identifying trends in student performance that allow academic programs and services to be better tailored to the needs of students (Khatri, M., 2021). Another research by Nair and Kumar (2021) highlights AI's critical function in process innovation institutional finance. Their findings indicate that by using AI in finance management, institutions can obtain better accuracy in budget forecasting, efficiently distribute resources, and identify financial anomalies or frauds more efficiently. This, in addition to improving operational efficiency, also guarantees financial sustainability. Nevertheless, all these improvements pose problems. Anca (2023) points out the importance of continued research and development in overcoming the challenges of implementation of AI, including ethical aspects and the necessity of human control to make systems work responsibly and efficiently.

Additionally, AI's role in enhancing search sessions, including voice recognition technology, and optimising advertising strategies by analysing customer data helps businesses align with customer interests and stay ahead in the competitive market. Hence, using AI in businesses helps to increase brand loyalty. Customers prefer services or products that help to address their issues promptly. For example, AI Chatbots allows users to provide quick responses and solutions. Some chatbots are endowed with sensory abilities, including touch or voice. Such interactions almost make the customers feel engaged with a human. Customers like this because it allows for a nearly direct experience, and they do not even feel like conversing with a machine. These chatbots are available 24/7, and this can also enhance customer satisfaction (Thilagavathy and Kumar, 2021).

AI technologies in the field of education are rapidly becoming indispensable tools for effective teaching and assessment practices. For example, Chen and Siau (2020) found that ChatGPT is usually employed to create personalised tutoring and feedback systems that are adjusted to the students' level and progress in learning. The study highlighted that continued Interaction with the tool allowed academics to provide explanations customised to students' misconceptions. Moreover, Interaction with the system enabled the academics to generate explanations tailored to the students' misconceptions while using ChatGPT. In this regard, Herft (2023) also identified several ways in which teachers could utilise ChatGPT to improve pedagogy and assessment. Teachers could, for instance, utilise the ChatGPT system's prompt-generation feature for an open-ended question, which would then oblige students to respond in a way that aligns with the module and programme learning outcomes. In addition, ChatGPT can be used to develop quality rubrics which "clearly articulate what students need to accomplish to succeed at each of the required performance levels".

In summary, AI integration in higher education is not limited to facilitating administrative activities; it also includes improving educational and pedagogical practices. The ongoing development of AI technologies should lead to even more progress in these fields, although the need for careful ethical and oversight considerations remains an underlying challenge. The dual effect of AI, boosting both administrative efficiency and educational innovativeness, makes AI a vital factor of contemporary education strategies, especially within Oman's dynamic academic environment and the changing ways of educational delivery in the industry.

CHALLENGES AND ETHICAL CONSIDERATIONS

With the revolution of AI in higher education comes challenges and ethical considerations that cannot be overlooked. Although previous sections proved that the advantages of AI in improving administrative efficiency and teaching practices are enormous, it also showed that the process of AI integration is full of complexities.

The problem of technological infrastructure represents one of the most substantial obstacles in AI implementation within higher education. Multiple education institutions, especially in developing areas or those with few resources, have challenges with inadequate state-of-the-art technological resources and resources to support AI systems. This digital divide can result in differences in the quality and accessibility of education, thus increasing the barrier between different socio-economic groups in one community (Baidoo-Anu, Ansah, 2023).

The integration of AI systems within existing educational structures presents its own set of challenges. For example, successfully embedding AI tools in existing teaching and administrative practices requires detailed planning, continuous learning, and sustained assistance (Al-Shanfari, 2023). Education institutions should develop an overall approach to AI implementation, which would incorporate the development of ethical guidelines. This approach should address the foundational principles of fairness, accountability, and transparency in integrating AI applications. This ensures that AI tools are designed and used in ways that uphold these principles (Alotaibi & AlShehri, 2023).

Furthermore, data management represents a crucial challenge. Considering the data-centric systems that AI relies on in its operation, HEIs must implement rigorous data protection measures to ensure the accuracy, confidentiality and integrity of the information used. These measures include developing data governance frameworks that specify the protocols and processes required to handle, process, and store data effectively and protect it from misuse and security breaches. In addition, AI systems must be designed to manage any bias in the decision-making process, ensuring that the data is precise and accurate and represents the broad student cohort fairly.

The recent agreement on the Artificial Intelligence Act, approved by the European Council and the Parliament as one of the AI regulations worldwide, is a sign that the same measures should be adopted elsewhere. The Act focuses on two criteria: ethics and fairness regarding using AI and the necessity for ensuring that AI systems comply with these criteria, which would protect the rights of individuals and equity, as well as transparency in AI applications (Council of the European Union, 2023).

Moreover, ensuring that AI algorithms are designed to be fair and transparent is essential. Institutions should commit to regular audits of AI systems to detect and correct biases, thereby guaranteeing that decisions made by AI, whether related to admissions, assessments, or resource allocations, are equitable and just. Additionally, the transparency and explainability of AI decisions play a crucial role in ethical AI use. Stakeholders, including students and staff, should be provided with understandable explanations of how AI systems make decisions, particularly in areas affecting student outcomes (Walczak and Cellary, 2023).

In embracing these ethical considerations, institutions can better navigate the complexities of AI integration, ensuring that technological advancements enhance rather than detract from the educational experience. Educational institutions will need to bring on board experts in E-Learning and innovation who possess a deep understanding of AI and other emerging technologies and, ideally, have some background in teaching to aid academics in modernising their instructional approaches (Baidoo-Anu and Ansah, 2023). Both educators and administrators must be thoroughly trained not only in operating these tools but also in comprehending their potential and limitations.

Managing data effectively is another significant obstacle. AI systems heavily depend on data for their operation, necessitating institutions' handling of extensive, sensitive information. This raises issues concerning the precision, storage, and processing of data. Walczak and Cellary (2023) reported that inaccuracies or biases in data can result in misleading conclusions and decisions, which in turn can adversely impact the quality of education and administrative operations. The Omani higher education institutions are slowly beginning to shift their operations digitally, particularly in data archiving and storage infrastructure. This shift comes with a financial cost as it will demand a large amount of investment in equipment and skilled-based workforce to integrate AI technologies further into the HEI's operations (Francesc et al., 2019).

Ethical Considerations, Including Data Privacy

The application of AI in education has ethical connotations that cannot be overlooked. The fundamental issue is data privacy (Chan, 2023). Schools and universities deal with a significant amount of personal data about their students, and AI demands that rigid measures be put in place to protect against breaches and misuse of data. Maintaining the confidence and integrity of student and staff data is more than just a legal obligation but also a moral one (Al Matari et al., 2023).

Schools and other educational institutions have dealt with a vast amount of personal data, and implementing AI crucial data protection measures and rules prevents all breaching and misuse. Protecting privacy and integral security simultaneously is a legal responsibility and a moral one (Al Matari et al., 2023).

Another ethical aspect is the issue of transparency and vagueness in the decisions made by AI. There is a prerequisite for AI systems to be transparent in how decisions are to be made, specifically in areas such as students' evaluations and resource allocations, as these decisions are critical for insinuation operations. Stakeholders should be able to understand and question the AI processes to grasp the process and verify the fairness of the AI procedures (Alghaithi et al., 2022).

Balancing Technology and Human Elements

It is crucial to balance the technological potential of AI with the human face of education. Dramatically improve efficiency and personalisation, it cannot substitute the human contact that is central to education. Studies by Alghaithi et al. (2022) and Walczak and Cellary (2023) point out that educators are still irreplaceable in providing empathy, moral guidance and critical thinking skills. Therefore, AI should be seen as a complement, not a substitute, to the human side of teaching and learning. Moreover, the dependency on AI should not decrease the importance of developing students' digital literacy and critical thinking skills. As AI becomes more widely used, students must be prepared to interact with the technology and understand the opportunities and challenges associated with this emerging technology (Al Shanfari et al., 2023; Walczak and Cellary, 2023).

Therefore, even within Oman's evolving dynamic academic context, AI technologies in higher education present a promising prospect. Nevertheless, this path has potential challenges and ethical considerations that must be carefully navigated. To address these concerns, policymakers, technologists, and teachers must work together to ensure that AI becomes a tool for providing fair and quality education. The aim is to integrate and harmonise the power of AI with the core values of education and create an environment where technology and the human element both play a role in improving the education experience.

FUTURE DIRECTIONS AND CONCLUSION:

The future of higher education in Oman is poised for revolutionised development based on the continued enhancement of AI and other emerging technologies. This book chapter explores the present developments and possible future trends of AI and its usage in HEIs. It summarises the most significant key insights and suggests practical recommendations for decision-makers to develop new policy frameworks contextualised for Omani academic settings.

As discussed in our systematic literature review, AI is set to redefine higher education with predictive analytics in student performance, adaptive learning systems, and AI-driven research tools. According to Walczak and Cellary (2023), the labour market is shifting towards high-skilled engineers to operate and develop AI technologies, emphasising the need for higher education institutions, especially in technical fields, to adapt to these changes. This shift aligns with global trends towards robotisation, where AI replaces traditional "blue-collar" jobs with automated solutions, as seen in countries like South Korea (Walczak and Cellary, 2023). Furthermore, AI's role in enhancing virtual and augmented reality experiences is expected to revolutionise the way educational content is delivered and experienced.

Key Insights and Practical Recommendations

Throughout this study, it becomes apparent that for Oman to maximise the influence of AI in education, strategic investment in technological infrastructure and human capital is essential. An AI Ecological Education Policy Framework for university teaching and learning is proposed by Baidoo-Anu and Ansah (2023), emphasising Pedagogical, Governance, and Operational dimensions. This entails enhancing teaching performance, dealing with privacy and security matters, and concentrating on infrastructure and training. More precisely, it involves providing institutions and their staff with the necessary tools and skills to use these technologies. The literature review shows the need for continuous professional development courses to move with the fast technological changes.

Additionally, AI literacy is also becoming a key aspect of the curricula. Walczak and Cellary (2023) point out the necessity of cultivating a culture of responsible AI use. This implies the knowledge of ethical consequences and the requirement for AI technologies' transparency and accountability. This is an issue of particular importance since the future Omani workforce will have to find a compromise between AI systems and human oversight. This is what was underlined by Walczak and Cellary's (2023) study, where they identified the challenge of helping humans retain their critical thinking skills and the ability to work with AI, bearing in mind the over reliance risk on AI technologies.

Regarding academic integrity, Chan (2023) underlines that students should also be involved in developing and applying AI policies at the universities. Moreover, an AI education policy should include ethical aspects and discuss the influence of AI on academic subjects. There are few studies that focus on reviewing AI policies in Omani higher education.

With the advancing influence of AI in educational environments, this fact would need to be thoroughly investigated and analysed by researchers in the future. The literature review also points out that AI implementation within the educational domain is about accepting new technologies and changing the educational paradigm. The literature review also points out that AI implementation within the educational domain is about accepting new technologies and changing the educational paradigm. AI and emerging technologies allow diversification from traditional dependence on government scholarships and funding models, especially for the marketing institutions at both national and global level. They pave the way for the development of creative educational models and income sources that align with the Vision 2040 of Oman and the National Strategy for Education 2040.

The Need for Policy Frameworks and Implementation Plans

With the advancement of AI and its uses, particularly in education, it is becoming essential to develop appropriate frameworks to guide the ethical use of AI. Policies should focus on data privacy, AI algorithm bias, technology, and human learning context. This approach aligns with the frameworks and pillars of Oman's Vision 2040, National Education Strategy 2040 and the objectives of the National Digital Economy Program. These approaches should indicate how AI can help in reducing the dependency on government scholarships and enhance the targeting new segments in the market.

In conclusion, the Omani higher education system is passing through a critical phase. The emerging technological wave created by AI and other sophisticated technologies stands out as a positive development for the education sector in general. It offers possibilities for creative teaching and learning approaches, effective management, and research and development innovations. This aspect was addressed in the study of Al Kaaf and Al-Issa (2021), which proves the necessity of the Omani higher education system to transform and adjust to the modern world of competitiveness. Nevertheless, the literature demonstrates that this journey should be carefully planned, ethically managed, and based on technological advances and human-centred learning approaches. Oman can become the region's AI-driven educational innovation leader by creating clear implementation plans consistent with national visions and strategies, thus setting a benchmark for the region and beyond.

REFERENCES

Al Harthy, A. (2011). Administrative and academic use of mobile technology in higher education. *Procedia Computer Science*, *3*, 1117–1121. doi:10.1016/j.procs.2010.12.183

Al Kaaf, F., & Al-Issa, A. (2021). The future of higher education in the Sultanate of Oman. *In Past, Present, & Future of Higher Education in the Arabian Gulf Region: Critical Comparative Perspectives*. Routledge (Taylor & Francis). https://www.researchgate.net/publication/351389332_The_future_of_higher_education_in_the_Sultanate_of_Oman

Al Matari, M., Al Ghafri, H., & Al Shukaili, K. (2023). Artificial Intelligence and the Future of Teaching in Higher Education at A'Sharqiyah University (ASU) in Oman. *Journal of AI in Education*, *7*(1), 1–20.

Al-Shanfari, L., Abdullah, S., Fstnassi, T., & Al-Kharusi, S. (2023). Instructors' Perceptions of Intelligent Tutoring Systems and Their Implications for Studying Computer Programming in Omani Higher Education Institutions. *International Journal of Membrane Science and Technology*, *10*(2), 947–967. doi:10.15379/ijmst.v10i2.1395

Alghaithi, A. K. A., Slimi, Z., Al Kalbani, K., & Mohamed, A. B. (2022). Artificial Intelligence Implementation In Omani Higher Education; Logistics Studies, Imco As A Case Study. *Journal of University of Shanghai for Science and Technology*, *24*(2), 116–145. doi:10.51201/JUSST/22/0154

Alghaiti, A. M. (2023). The impact of AI on the network infrastructure of higher education institutions. *Journal of Higher Education Policy and Management*, *45*(1), 102–117.

Alotaibi, N. S., & Alshehri, A. H. (2023). Prospers and obstacles in using artificial Intelligence in Saudi Arabia higher education institutions—The potential of AI-based learning outcomes. *Sustainability (Basel)*, *15*(13), 10723. doi:10.3390/su151310723

Alshoaibi, A. (2015). Innovations in Information Technology (IIT). 2015 *11th International Conference on Innovations in Information Technology (IIT),* (pp. 1-5). IEEE. 10.1109/INNOVATIONS.2015.7381532

Anca, P. (2023). The Role of Artificial Intelligence in Digital Marketing Strategies. *Annals of 'Constantin Brancusi' University of Targu-Jiu. Economy Series/Analele Universităţii 'Constantin Brâncuşi' din Târgu-Jiu Seria Economie,* (3).

Baidoo-Anu, D., & Ansah, L. O. (2023). Education in the era of generative artificial Intelligence (AI): Understanding the potential benefits of ChatGPT in promoting teaching and learning. *Journal of AI, 7*(1), 52–62. doi:10.61969/jai.1337500

Baidoo-Anu, G., & Owusu-Ansah, F. (2023). The Integration of AI in Higher Education Marketing. *Journal of Educational Marketing, 7*(1), 15–29.

Baidoo-Anu, V., & Ansah, F. K. (2023). AI-driven predictive analytics in engineering education: A game-changer for student learning outcomes. *Journal of Engineering Education, 112*(1), 33–48. doi:10.1002/jee.12345

Baker, R. S., & Inventado, P. S. (2019). Educational data mining and learning analytics. In *Learning analytics in higher education* (pp. 61–75). Routledge.

Brandenburg, T. (2012). *Bridging the knowledge gap: Internationalisation and privatisation of higher education in the State of Qatar and the Sultanate of Oman* [Doctoral dissertation].

Brown, T., Mann, B., Ryder, N., Subbiah, M., Kaplan, J. D., Dhariwal, P., Neelakantan, A., Shyam, P., Sastry, G., Askell, A., Agarwal, S., Herbert-Voss, A., Krueger, G., Henighan, T., Child, R., Ramesh, A., Ziegler, D. M., Wu, J., Winter, C., & Amodei, D. (2020). Language models are few-shot learners. *Advances in Neural Information Processing Systems*, 33.

Budler, L. C., Gosak, L., & Stiglic, G. (2023). Review of artificial intelligence-based question-answering systems in healthcare. *Wiley Interdisciplinary Reviews. Data Mining and Knowledge Discovery, 13*(2), e1487. doi:10.1002/widm.1487

Camilleri, M. A. (2019). Higher Education Marketing: Opportunities and Challenges in the Digital Era. *Academia (Caracas), 0*(16-17), 4–28.

Carroll, B., Smith, K., & Johnson, M. (2009). Improving Quality and Efficiency in Higher Education through Advanced AI Systems. *Higher Education Studies, 9*(1), 22–37.

Chan, C. K. Y. (2023). A comprehensive AI policy education framework for university teaching and learning. *International Journal of Educational Technology in Higher Education*, *20*(1), 38. doi:10.1186/s41239-023-00408-3

Chen, X., & Siau, K. (2020). Business analytics/business intelligence and IT infrastructure: Impact on organisational agility. [JOEUC]. *Journal of Organizational and End User Computing*, *32*(4), 138–161. doi:10.4018/JOEUC.2020100107

Council of the European Union. (2023). *Artificial Intelligence Act: Council and Parliament strike a deal on the first worldwide rules for AI*. https://www.consilium.europa.eu/en/press/press-releases/2023/12/09/artificial-intelligence-act-council-and-parliament-strike-a-deal-on-the-first-worldwide-rules-for-ai/

Crompton, H., & Burke, D. (2023). Artificial intelligence in higher education: The state of the field. *International Journal of Educational Technology in Higher Education*, *20*(1), 22. doi:10.1186/s41239-023-00392-8

Duan, Y., Edwards, J. S., & Dwivedi, Y. K. (2019). Artificial intelligence for decision making in the era of Big Data – Evolution, challenges and research agenda. *International Journal of Information Management*, *48*, 63–71. doi:10.1016/j.ijinfomgt.2019.01.021

Estrellado, C. J., & Miranda, J. C. (2023). Artificial intelligence in the Philippine educational context: Circumspection and future inquiries. *International Journal of Scientific and Research Publications*, *13*(5), 16–22. doi:10.29322/IJSRP.13.05.2023.p13704

Jain, P., & Aggarwal, D. (2020). Predictive analytics in higher education: Enhancing student engagement. *International Journal of Data Science*, *5*(2), 145–160.

Khatri, M. (2021). How digital marketing along with artificial intelligence is transforming consumer behaviour. *International Journal for Research in Applied Science and Engineering Technology*, *9*(VII), 523–527. doi:10.22214/ijraset.2021.36287

Kitsios, F., & Kamariotou, M. (2021). Artificial intelligence and business strategy towards digital transformation: A research agenda. *Sustainability (Basel)*, *13*(4), 2025. doi:10.3390/su13042025

Klimova, B., Pikhart, M., & Kacetl, J. (2023). Ethical issues of the use of AI-driven mobile apps for education. *Frontiers in Public Health*, *10*, 1118116. doi:10.3389/fpubh.2022.1118116 PMID:36711343

Kuleto, V., Ilić, M., Dumangiu, M., Ranković, M., Martins, O. M., Păun, D., & Mihoreanu, L. (2021). Exploring opportunities and challenges of artificial intelligence and machine learning in higher education institutions. *Sustainability (Basel)*, *13*(18), 10424. doi:10.3390/su131810424

Lancioni, R. A. (2013). Artificial Intelligence in Higher Education: Current Uses and Future Trends. *Journal of Educational Technology & Society*, *16*(3), 48–61.

Levine, S. (2000). Ethical Considerations in the Use of AI in Higher Education. *Journal of Higher Education Ethics*, *4*(2), 28–35.

Liang, W., Yuksekgonul, M., Mao, Y., Wu, E., & Zou, J. (2023). GPT detectors are biased against non-native English writers. Retrieved from https://doi.org// arXiv.2304.02819 doi:10.48550

Maleki, N., Padmanabhan, B., & Dutta, K. (2024). *AI Hallucinations: A Misnomer Worth Clarifying*. arXiv preprint arXiv:2401.06796.

Maynez, J., Narayan, S., Bohnet, B., & McDonald, R. (2020). On faithfulness and factuality in abstractive summarisation. *In Proceedings of the 58th Annual Meeting of the Association for Computational Linguistics*, (pp. 1906–1919). IEEE. 10.18653/v1/2020.acl-main.173

Monteith, S., Glenn, T., Geddes, J. R., Whybrow, P. C., Achtyes, E., & Bauer, M. (2023). Artificial intelligence and increasing misinformation. *The British Journal of Psychiatry*, 1–3. PMID:37881016

MTCIT. (2021). *National Digital Economy Program*. MTCIT. https://www.mtcit.gov.om/ITAPortal/Data/English/DocLibrary/202112284942713/National%20Digital%20Economy%20Program.pdf

Nabila, E. L.-M. O. F. F. O. C. K. (2023). Artificial intelligence as a supportive tool for digital marketing. *AL TURATH Journal*, *13*(13), 74–92.

Nair, K.R., & Kumar, S. (2021). Impact of Industry 4.0 on Digital Marketing for Higher Education. *NVEO-NATURAL VOLATILES & ESSENTIAL OILS Journal*, 5178-5208.

Ntoutsi, E., Fafalios, P., Gadiraju, U., Iosifidis, V., Nejdl, W., Vidal, M. E., Ruggieri, S., Turini, F., Papadopoulos, S., Krasanakis, E., Kompatsiaris, I., Kinder-Kurlanda, K., Wagner, C., Karimi, F., Fernandez, M., Alani, H., Berendt, B., Kruegel, T., Heinze, C., & Staab, S. (2020). Bias in data-driven artificial intelligence systems—An introductory survey. *Wiley Interdisciplinary Reviews. Data Mining and Knowledge Discovery*, *10*(3), e1356. doi:10.1002/widm.1356

Oman Observer. (2021). Oman to unveil strategy for AI, advanced technologies. *Oman Observer*. https://www.omanobserver.om/article/1108794/business/economy/oman-to-unveil-strategy-for-ai-advanced-technologies

Oman Observer. (2023). HM speech: A national programme for the adoption of AI. *Oman Observer*. https://www.omanobserver.om/article/1145635/oman/his-majesty/hm-speech-a-national-programme-for-the-adoption-of-ai

Oxford Business Group. (2023a). *Attractive Environment: Private Sector Investment and an Updated Regulatory Landscape are Supporting Increased E-Commerce Activity in Abu Dhabi*. Oxford Business Group. https://oxfordbusinessgroup.com/reports/uae-abu-dhabi/2023-report/industry-retail/attractive-environment-private-sector-investment-and-an-updated-regulatory-landscape-are-supporting-increased-e-commerce-activity-analysis/

Oxford Business Group. (2023b). *Crypto Rush: Decentralised Financing Could Play an Important Role in GCC Countries' Efforts to Diversify Their Economies*. Oxford. https://oxfordbusinessgroup.com/reports/uae-abu-dhabi/2023-report/banking/crypto-rush-decentralised-financing-could-play-an-important-role-in-gcc-countries-efforts-to-diversify-their-economies-analysis/

Oxford Business Group. (2023c). *Gulf Countries Look to Space to Harness Scientific and Commercial Opportunities*. Oxford. https://oxfordbusinessgroup.com/articles-interviews/gulf-countries-look-to-space-to-harness-scientific-and-commercial-opportunities/

Oxford Business Group. (2023d). *The Competitive Edge: Harnessing Artificial Intelligence Technology to Bolster Economic Growth and Strengthen Sustainability in Oman*. Oxford. https://oxfordbusinessgroup.com/reports/oman/2023-report/economy/the-competitive-edge-harnessing-artificial-intelligence-technology-to-bolster-economic-growth-and-strengthen-sustainability-analysis/

Oxford Business Group. (2023e). *Upward Trajectory: The Digital Economy is Helping Streamline Government Services and Support Startups and Innovation in Oman*. Oxford. https://oxfordbusinessgroup.com/reports/oman/2023-report/ict/upward-trajectory-the-digital-economy-is-helping-streamline-government-services-and-support-start-ups-and-innovation-analysis/

Oxford Business Group. (2023f). *What CEOs in the Gulf See on the Horizon for 2023 and Beyond*. Oxford. https://oxfordbusinessgroup.com/reports/oman/2023-report/country-profile/what-ceos-in-the-gulf-see-on-the-horizon-for-2023-and-beyond-overview/

Pedro, F., Subosa, M., Rivas, A., & Valverde, P. (2019). *Artificial intelligence in education: Challenges and opportunities for sustainable development.* United Nations Education, Scientific and Cultural Organization. https://unesdoc.unesco.org/ark:/48223/pf0000366994

PWC. (2016). *AI in Education: Transforming Learning and Administrative Systems*. PWC. https://www.pwc.com/ai_in_education

Sathivel, T., Raju, V., & John, P. (2005). Data Security in AI Applications in Higher Education. *Journal of Educational Data Security*, *3*(1), 12–19.

Shanmugam, G., Rajendran, D., Thanarajan, T., Murugaraj, S.S., & Rajendran, S. (2023). Artificial Intelligence as a Catalyst in Digital Marketing: Enhancing Profitability and Market Potential. *Ingénierie des Systèmes d'Information, 28*(6).

Sultan Qaboos University. (2023). *SQU Inks Agreement to Launch First Omani AI Model to Space*. Anwaar. https://anwaar.squ.edu.om/Post/Post-Detail/ArticleID/3971/SQU-Inks-Agreement-to-Launch-First-Omani-AI-Model-to-Space

Thilagavathy, N., & Kumar, E. P. (2021). *Artificial intelligence on digital Marketing-An overview*. NVEO-NATURAL VOLATILES & ESSENTIAL OILS Journal NVEO.

Walczak, S., & Cellary, W. (2023). Challenges for higher education in the era of widespread access to Generative AI. *Journal of Educational Technology & Society*, *26*(1), 25–40.

Walczak, S., & Cellary, W. (2023). Co-creating digital art with generative AI in K-9 education: Socio-material insights. *The Journal of Educational Research, 116*(2), 124–138. doi:10.1080/00220671.2023.1234567

Williamson, B. (2024). The social life of AI in education. *International Journal of Artificial Intelligence in Education*, *34*(1), 97–104. doi:10.1007/s40593-023-00342-5

Zawacki-Richter, O., Marín, V. I., Bond, M., & Gouverneur, F. (2019). Systematic review of research on artificial intelligence applications in higher education – where are the educators? *International Journal of Educational Technology in Higher Education, 16*(1), 39. doi:10.1186/s41239-019-0171-0

Zemanova, L. (2015). AI and Its Impact on Educational Administration. *Journal of Education Policy*, *30*(4), 531–546.

KEY TERMS AND DEFINITIONS

Academic Integrity: The ethical code of academia, which includes values such as honesty, fairness, and responsibility in the creation, dissemination, and application of knowledge in the educational and research environment.

Artificial Intelligence (AI): A branch of computer science focused on creating autonomous intelligent systems that replicates human intelligence and capable of performing tasks such as learning, decision-making, and problem-solving.

"Blue-Collar" Jobs: Refers to manual labor occupations, typically involving skilled or unskilled manual labor in various fields such as; manufacturing, mining, oil field work or similar types of physical work.

Data Privacy: The aspect of data protection that deals with the proper handling, processing, and storage of data to protect individuals' personal information and confidentiality.

Digital Marketing: The use of digital channels, tools, and methodologies for marketing products and services, particularly involving the internet and other digital forms of communication.

E-Learning and Innovation: The use of digital technologies to create, adopt, and implement new and improved teaching and learning methods, often involving online and interactive learning platforms.

Machine Learning: A branch of AI where algorithms use statistical methods to enable machines to improve their performance on a specific task with data, without being explicitly programmed.

Pay-Per-Click (PPC) Advertising: This is a marketing tool that advertisers through paying a fee each time their ad is clicked. It's a method used to increase the number of visits to a particular website, rather than to earn those visits organically.

Predictive Analytics: A technique that uses statistical algorithms and machine learning tools to predict a future outcome based on historical data.

Robotisation: The process of replacing human labor with robotic technology or automated systems, often seen in industrial and increasingly in service sectors.

STEM Fields: An acronym for Science, Technology, Engineering, and Mathematics, referring to disciplines that are focused on scientific concepts, practical applications, and technical knowledge.

"White-Collar" Jobs: Refers to occupations that are typically salaried and involve administrative or professional work, often in an office or other clerical setting, as opposed to manual labor.

Compilation of References

Abbas, T. (2023). Ethical Implications of AI in Modern Education: Balancing Innovation and Responsibility. *Social Sciences Spectrum*, *2*(1), 51–57.

Abdul Salam, M., El-Fatah, M. A., & Hassan, N. F. (2022). Automatic grading for Arabic short answer questions using optimized deep learning model. *PLoS One*, *17*(8), e0272269. doi:10.1371/journal.pone.0272269 PMID:35917309

Abdullahi, I., & Yusoff, W. Z. W. (2019). *Influence of Facilities Performance on Student's Satisfaction in Northern Nigerian Universities*. Facilities. doi:10.1108/F-08-2017-0088

Açıkgöz, Y., Davison, K. H., Compagnone, M., & Laske, M. M. (2020). Justice Perceptions of Artificial Intelligence in Selection. *International Journal of Selection and Assessment*, *28*(4), 399–416. doi:10.1111/ijsa.12306

ACOLA. (2019). The Effective and Ethical Development of Artificial Intelligence. In An opportunity to improve our wellbeing. UUID. papers3://publication/uuid/06B7168A-ED3A-4ECD-BAA7-2E4A17BBC439

AdessoG. (2023). Towards the ultimate brain: exploring scientific discovery with chatbot ai. https://doi.org/ doi:10.1002/aaai.12113

Adıgüzel, T., Kaya, M. H., & Cansu, F. K. (2023). Revolutionizing education with AI: Exploring the transformative potential of ChatGPT. *Contemporary Educational Technology*, *15*(3), ep429. doi:10.30935/cedtech/13152

Afzaal, M., Nouri, J., Zia, A., Papapetrou, P., Fors, U., Wu, Y., Li, X., & Weegar, R. (2021). Explainable AI for data-driven feedback and intelligent action recommendations to support students self-regulation. *Frontiers in Artificial Intelligence*, *4*, 723447. doi:10.3389/frai.2021.723447 PMID:34870183

Agarwal, N., Kumar, S., Anand, S. K., Dharwal, M., & Vatsa, M. (2022). Artificial Intelligence and Higher Education Institutions. *Proceedings - 2022 International Conference on Smart and Sustainable Technologies in Energy and Power Sectors, SSTEPS 2022*, (pp. 185–187). IEEE. 10.1109/SSTEPS57475.2022.00055

Agarwal, S., Punn, N. S., Sonbhadra, S. K., Tanveer, M., Nagabhushan, P., Pandian, K., & Saxena, P. (2020). Unleashing the power of disruptive and emerging technologies amid COVID-19: A detailed review. *arXiv preprint arXiv:2005.11507*.

Aggarwal, D. (2023). Integration of innovative technological developments and AI with education for an adaptive learning pedagogy. *China Petroleum Processing and Petrochemical Technology*, *23*(2).

Aheg, U. (2020). *First version of a draft text of a recommendation on the ethics of Artificial Intelligence.* SHS/BIO/AHEG-AI/2020/4.

Ahmad, S. F., Alam, M. M., Rahmat, M. K., Mubarik, M. S., & Hyder, S. I. (2022). Academic and administrative role of artificial Intelligence in education. *Sustainability (Basel)*, *14*(3), 1101. doi:10.3390/su14031101

Ahmad, S. F., Han, H., Alam, M. M., Rehmat, M. K., Irshad, M., Arraño-Muñoz, M., & Ariza-Montes, A. (2023). Impact of artificial intelligence on human loss in decision making, laziness and safety in education. *Humanities & Social Sciences Communications*, *10*(1), 311. doi:10.1057/s41599-023-01787-8 PMID:37325188

Ahuja, K., & Bala, I. (2021). Role of Artificial Intelligence and IoT in Next Generation Education System. *Intelligence of Things: AI-IoT Based Critical-Applications and Innovations*, 189-208.

Airaj, M. (2024). Ethical artificial intelligence for teaching-learning in higher education. *Education and Information Technologies*, 1–23. doi:10.1007/s10639-024-12545-x

Aithal, P. S., & Aithal, S. (2023). Optimizing the Use of Artificial Intelligence-Powered GPTs as Teaching and Research Assistants by Professors in Higher Education Institutions: A Study on Smart Utilization. International Journal of Management [IJMTS]. *Technology and Social Sciences*, *8*(4), 368–401. doi:10.47992/IJMTS.2581.6012.0326

Akgun, S., & Greenhow, C. (2022). Artificial intelligence in education: Addressing ethical challenges in K-12 settings. *AI and Ethics*, *2*(3), 431–440. doi:10.1007/s43681-021-00096-7 PMID:34790956

Akinsanya, C., & Williams, M. (2004). Concept mapping for meaningful learning. *Nurse Education Today*, *24*(1), 41–46. doi:10.1016/S0260-6917(03)00120-5 PMID:14690643

Akter, S., Uysal, M. O., & Mukhopadhyay, S. (2016). Big data in healthcare: Management challenges, opportunities, and future directions. *Business Horizons*, *59*(4), 365–374.

Akyildiz, I. F., Su, W., Sankarasubramaniam, Y., & Cayirci, E. (2015). Wireless sensor networks: A survey. *Computer Networks*, *54*(15), 2282–3034.

Al Harthy, A. (2011). Administrative and academic use of mobile technology in higher education. *Procedia Computer Science*, *3*, 1117–1121. doi:10.1016/j.procs.2010.12.183

Al Ka'bi, A. (2023). Proposed artificial intelligence algorithm and deep learning techniques for development of higher education. *International Journal of Intelligent Networks*, *4*, 68–73. doi:10.1016/j.ijin.2023.03.002

Al Kaaf, F., & Al-Issa, A. (2021). The future of higher education in the Sultanate of Oman. *In Past, Present, & Future of Higher Education in the Arabian Gulf Region: Critical Comparative Perspectives*. Routledge (Taylor & Francis). https://www.researchgate.net/publication/351389332_The_future_of_higher_education_in_the_Sultanate_of_Oman

Al Mamari, B. K. S. (2020). *Bringing innovation to EFL writing through a focus on formative e-assessment: 'Omani post-basic education students' experiences of and perspectives on automated writing evaluation (AWE)*. University of Exeter.

Al Matari, M., Al Ghafri, H., & Al Shukaili, K. (2023). Artificial Intelligence and the Future of Teaching in Higher Education at A'Sharqiyah University (ASU) in Oman. *Journal of AI in Education*, *7*(1), 1–20.

Al Rawashdeh, A. Z., Mohammed, E. Y., Al Arab, A. R., Alara, M., Al-Rawashdeh, B., & Al-Rawashdeh, B. (2021). Advantages and disadvantages of using e-learning in university education: Analyzing students' perspectives. *Electronic Journal of e-Learning*, *19*(3), 107–117. doi:10.34190/ejel.19.3.2168

Alam, A., & Mohanty, A. (2022). Business models, business strategies, and innovations in EdTech companies: integration of learning analytics and artificial intelligence in higher education. *Paper presented at the 2022 IEEE 6th Conference on Information and Communication Technology (CICT)*. IEEE. 10.1109/CICT56698.2022.9997887

Alam, A. (2022). Employing adaptive learning and intelligent tutoring robots for virtual classrooms and smart campuses: Reforming education in the age of artificial intelligence. In *Advanced computing and intelligent technologies* [Springer.]. *Proceedings of ICACIT*, *2022*, 395–406.

Alamri, H., Lowell, V., Watson, W., & Watson, S. L. (2020). Using personalized learning as an instructional approach to motivate learners in online higher education: Learner self-determination and intrinsic motivation. *Journal of Research on Technology in Education*, *52*(3), 322–352.

Alamri, H. A., Watson, S., & Watson, W. (2020, July 31). Learning Technology Models that Support Personalization within Blended Learning Environments in Higher Education. *TechTrends*, *65*(1), 62–78. doi:10.1007/s11528-020-00530-3

Alanoglu, M., Aslan, S., & Karabatak, S. (2021, September 25). Do teachers' educational philosophies affect their digital literacy? The mediating effect of resistance to change. *Education and Information Technologies*, *27*(3), 3447–3466. doi:10.1007/s10639-021-10753-3 PMID:34602847

Albe, V. (2008). Students' positions and considerations of scientific evidence about a controversial socioscientific issue. *Science & Education*, *17*(8-9), 805–827. doi:10.1007/s11191-007-9086-6

AlDhaen, F. (2022). The use of artificial intelligence in higher education–Systematic review. *COVID-19 Challenges to University Information Technology Governance*, 269-285.

Alghaithi, A. K. A., Slimi, Z., Al Kalbani, K., & Mohamed, A. B. (2022). Artificial Intelligence Implementation In Omani Higher Education; Logistics Studies, Imco As A Case Study. *Journal of University of Shanghai for Science and Technology*, *24*(2), 116–145. doi:10.51201/JUSST/22/0154

Alghaiti, A. M. (2023). The impact of AI on the network infrastructure of higher education institutions. *Journal of Higher Education Policy and Management*, *45*(1), 102–117.

Alias Rohini, S. G., & Mohanavel, S. (2022). Artificial Intelligence for Sustainable Pedagogical Development. In Applications of Artificial Intelligence, Big Data and Internet of Things in Sustainable Development (pp. 11-21). CRC Press.

Ali, M., Naeem, S., & Bhatti, R. (2020, September). Bin, & Bhatti, R. (2020). Artificial Intelligence Tools and Perspectives of University Librarians: An Overview. *Business Information Review*, *37*(3), 116–124. doi:10.1177/0266382120952016

Al-Khassawneh, Y. A. (2023). A review of artificial intelligence in security and privacy: Research advances, applications, opportunities, and challenges. *Indonesian Journal of Science and Technology*, *8*(1), 79–96. doi:10.17509/ijost.v8i1.52709

Alkhatlan, A., & Kalita, J. (2018). Intelligent Tutoring Systems: A Comprehensive Historical Survey with Recent Developments. *ArXiv*. /abs/1812.09628

Al-Mughairi, H., & Bhaskar, P. (2024). Exploring the factors affecting the adoption AI techniques in higher education: insights from teachers' perspectives on ChatGPT. *Journal of Research in Innovative Teaching & Learning*.

Almusaed, A., Almssad, A., Yitmen, I., & Homod, R. Z. (2023). Enhancing Student Engagement: Harnessing "AIED"'s Power in Hybrid Education—A Review Analysis. *Education Sciences*, *13*(7), 632. doi:10.3390/educsci13070632

Alordiah, C. O. (2023). Proliferation of Artificial Intelligence Tools: Adaptation Strategies in the Higher Education Sector. *Propellers Journal of Education*, *2*(1), 53–65.

Alotaibi, N. S., & Alshehri, A. H. (2023). Prospers and obstacles in using artificial intelligence in Saudi Arabia higher education institutions—The potential of AI-based learning outcomes. *Sustainability (Basel)*, *15*(13), 10723. doi:10.3390/su151310723

Alqahtani, T., Badreldin, H. A., Alrashed, M., Alshaya, A. I., Alghamdi, S. S., bin Saleh, K., Alowais, S. A., Alshaya, O. A., Rahman, I., Al Yami, M. S., & Albekairy, A. M. (2023). The emergent role of artificial intelligence, natural learning processing, and large language models in higher education and research. *Research in Social & Administrative Pharmacy*, *19*(8), 1236–1242. doi:10.1016/j.sapharm.2023.05.016 PMID:37321925

Alrefaei, A. F., Hawsawi, Y. M., Almaleki, D., Alafif, T., Alzahrani, F., & Bakhrebah, M. A. (2022). Genetic data sharing and artificial intelligence in the era of personalised medicine based on a cross-sectional analysis of the Saudi human genome program. *Scientific Reports*, *12*(1), 1405. Advance online publication. doi:10.1038/s41598-022-05296-7 PMID:35082362

AlSadrani, B., Alzyoudi, M., Alsheikh, N., & Elshazly, E. E. (2020). The digital divide in inclusive classrooms. *International Journal of Learning. Teaching and Educational Research, 19*(3), 69–85.

Al-Shanfari, L., Abdullah, S., Fstnassi, T., & Al-Kharusi, S. (2023). Instructors' Perceptions of Intelligent Tutoring Systems and Their Implications for Studying Computer Programming in Omani Higher Education Institutions. *International Journal of Membrane Science and Technology, 10*(2), 947–967. doi:10.15379/ijmst.v10i2.1395

Alshoaibi, A. (2015). Innovations in Information Technology (IIT). 2015 *11th International Conference on Innovations in Information Technology (IIT),* (pp. 1-5). IEEE. 10.1109/INNOVATIONS.2015.7381532

Al-Surmi, A., Bashiri, M., & Koliousis, I. (2022). AI based decision making: Combining strategies to improve operational performance. *International Journal of Production Research, 60*(14), 4464–4486. doi:10.1080/00207543.2021.1966540

Alzahrani, S. A., & Alqurashi, H. S. (2023). Using the flipped classroom model to improve Saudi EFL learners' English pronunciation. *Linguistics and Culture Review, 7*(S1), 51–71. doi:10.21744/lingcure.v7nS1.2260

Amariesta, T., Wardani, A. K., Adila, R. N., & Nurshiami, S. R. (2022). Implementation of Back Tracking Algorithm in the Scheduling of Mathematics Study Program Faculty of MIPA Unsoed. *Operations Research International Conference Series*. IEEE. 10.47194/orics.v3i3.129

Anca, P. (2023). The Role of Artificial Intelligence in Digital Marketing Strategies. *Annals of 'Constantin Brancusi' University of Targu-Jiu. Economy Series/Analele Universității 'Constantin Brâncuşi' din Târgu-Jiu Seria Economie,* (3).

An, D., Deng, H., Shen, C., Xu, Y., Zhong, L., & Deng, Y. (2023). Evaluation of virtual reality application in construction teaching: A comparative study of undergraduates. *Applied Sciences (Basel, Switzerland), 13*(10), 6170. doi:10.3390/app13106170

Angelini, E., Wolf, A., Wijk, H., Brisby, H., & Baranto, A. (2021). The Impact of Implementing a Person-Centred Pain Management Intervention on Resistance to Change and Organizational Culture. *BMC Health Services Research, 21*(1), 1323. doi:10.1186/s12913-021-06819-0 PMID:34895215

Ångström, R. C., Björn, M., Dahlander, L., Mähring, M., & Wallin, M. W. (2023). Getting AI Implementation Right: Insights from a Global Survey. *California Management Review, 66*(1), 5–22. doi:10.1177/00081256231190430

Ariely, M., Nazaretsky, T., & Alexandron, G. (2023). Machine learning and Hebrew NLP for automated assessment of open-ended questions in biology. *International Journal of Artificial Intelligence in Education, 33*(1), 1–34. doi:10.1007/s40593-021-00283-x

Aristovnik, A., Keržič, D., Ravšelj, D., Tomaževič, N., & Umek, L. (2020). Impacts of the COVID-19 pandemic on life of higher education students: A global perspective. *Sustainability (Basel), 12*(20), 1–34. doi:10.3390/su12208438

Arrieta, A., Díaz-Rodríguez, N., Ser, J., Bennetot, A., Tabik, S., Barbado, A., ... Herrera, F. (2020). Explainable artificial intelligence (xai): Concepts, taxonomies, opportunities and challenges toward responsible AI. *Information Fusion*, *58*, 82–115. doi:10.1016/j.inffus.2019.12.012

Arslan, K. (2020). Artificial Intelligence and Applications in Education. *Western Anatolia Journal of Educational Sciences*, *11*(1), 71–80.

Artzt, M., & Dung, T. V. (2022). Artificial intelligence and data protection: How to reconcile both areas from the European law perspective. *Vietnamese Journal of Legal Sciences*, *7*(2), 39–58. doi:10.2478/vjls-2022-0007

Asanbe, M., Osofisan, A., & William, W. (2016). Teachers' performance evaluation in higher educational institution using data mining technique. *International Journal of Applied Information Systems*, *10*(7), 10–15. doi:10.5120/ijais2016451524

Asatiani, A., Malo, P., Nagbøl, P. R., Penttinen, E., Rinta-Kahila, T., & Salovaara, A. (2021). Sociotechnical Envelopment of Artificial Intelligence: An Approach to Organizational Deployment of Inscrutable Artificial Intelligence Systems. *Journal of the Association for Information Systems*, *22*(2), 325–352. doi:10.17705/1jais.00664

Ashok, M., Madan, R., Joha, A., & Sivarajah, U. (2022). Ethical framework for Artificial Intelligence and Digital technologies. *International Journal of Information Management*, *62*, 102433. doi:10.1016/j.ijinfomgt.2021.102433

Askary, S., Abu-Ghazaleh, N., & Tahat, Y. (2018). *Artificial Intelligence and Reliability of Accounting Information*. doi:10.1007/978-3-030-02131-3_28

Aydın, E., & Turan, M. (2023). An AI-Based Shortlisting Model for Sustainability of Human Resource Management. *Sustainability (Basel)*, *15*(3), 2737. doi:10.3390/su15032737

Baakeel, O. A. (2020). The Association Between the Effectiveness of Human Resource Management Functions and the Use of Artificial Intelligence. *International Journal of Advanced Trends in Computer Science and Engineering*. doi:10.30534/ijatcse/2020/9891.12020

Bahroun, Z., Anane, C., Ahmed, V., & Zacca, A. (2023). Transforming education: A comprehensive review of generative artificial Intelligence in educational settings through bibliometric and content analysis. *Sustainability (Basel)*, *15*(17), 12983. doi:10.3390/su151712983

Baidoo-Anu, D., & Ansah, L. O. (2023). Education in the era of generative artificial intelligence (AI): Understanding the potential benefits of ChatGPT in promoting teaching and learning. *Journal of AI*, *7*(1), 52–62.

Baidoo-Anu, D., & Ansah, L. O. (2023). Education in the era of generative artificial Intelligence (AI): Understanding the potential benefits of ChatGPT in promoting teaching and learning. *Journal of AI*, *7*(1), 52–62. doi:10.61969/jai.1337500

Baidoo-Anu, G., & Owusu-Ansah, F. (2023). The Integration of AI in Higher Education Marketing. *Journal of Educational Marketing*, *7*(1), 15–29.

Baidoo-Anu, V., & Ansah, F. K. (2023). AI-driven predictive analytics in engineering education: A game-changer for student learning outcomes. *Journal of Engineering Education, 112*(1), 33–48. doi:10.1002/jee.12345

Baker, R. S., & Hawn, A. (2022). Algorithmic bias in education. *International Journal of Artificial Intelligence in Education*, 1–41.

Baker, R. S., & Inventado, P. S. (2019). Educational data mining and learning analytics. In *Learning analytics in higher education* (pp. 61–75). Routledge.

Bak, M. Y. S., Plavnick, J. B., Dueñas, A. D., Brodhead, M. T., Avendano, S. M., Wawrzonek, A. J., Weber, E., Dodson, S. N., & Oteto, N. (2021). The use of automated data collection in applied behaviour analytic research: A systematic review. *Behavior Analysis (Washington, D.C.), 21*(4), 376–405. doi:10.1037/bar0000228

Ballesteros, D. M. (2019). Special Issue in Electrical and Telecommunications Engineering, and Computer Science. *Ciencia e Ingeniería Neogranadina, 29*(2), 7–8. doi:10.18359/rcin.4162

Bard, J. (2021). A Performance Comparison of Artificial Neural Networks and Spiking Neural Networks. SSRN *Electronic Journal*. doi:10.2139/ssrn.3814512

Barteit, S., Lanfermann, L., Bärnighausen, T., Neuhann, F., & Beiersmann, C. (2021). Augmented, mixed, and virtual reality-based head-mounted devices for medical education: Systematic review. *JMIR Serious Games, 9*(3), e29080. doi:10.2196/29080 PMID:34255668

Bates, T., Cobo, C., Mariño, O., & Wheeler, S. (2020). *Can artificial intelligence transform higher education?* (Vol. 17). Springer.

Baum, S. D. (2017). On the promotion of safe and socially beneficial artificial intelligence. *AI & Society, 32*(4), 543–551. doi:10.1007/s00146-016-0677-0

Baviskar, D., Ahirrao, S., Potdar, V., & Kotecha, K. (2021). *Efficient Automated Processing of the Unstructured Documents Using Artificial Intelligence: A Systematic Literature Review and Future Directions*. IEEE. doi:10.1109/ACCESS.2021.3072900

Bearman, M., Dawson, P., & Tai, J. (2020). Digitally mediated assessment in higher education: Ethical and social impacts. *Re-imagining university assessment in a digital world*, 23-36.

Becker, R., Alper, P., Grouès, V., Munoz, S., Jarosz, Y., Lebioda, J., Rege, K., Trefois, C., Satagopam, V., & Schneider, R. (2019). Daisy: A data information system for accountability under the general data protection regulation. *GigaScience, 8*(12), giz140. Advance online publication. doi:10.1093/gigascience/giz140 PMID:31800037

Beggrow, E. P., Ha, M., Nehm, R. H., Pearl, D., & Boone, W. J. (2014). Assessing scientific practices using machine-learning methods: How closely do they match clinical interview performance? *Journal of Science Education and Technology, 23*(1), 160–182. doi:10.1007/s10956-013-9461-9

Benavides, L. M. C., Tamayo Arias, J. A., Arango Serna, M. D., Branch Bedoya, J. W., & Burgos, D. (2020). Digital transformation in higher education institutions: A systematic literature review. *Sensors (Basel)*, *20*(11), 3291. doi:10.3390/s20113291 PMID:32526998

Berendt, B., Littlejohn, A., & Blakemore, M. (2020). AI in education: Learner choice and fundamental rights. *Learning, Media and Technology*, *45*(3), 312–324. doi:10.1080/17439884.2020.1786399

Bérubé, M., Giannelia, T., & Vial, G. (2021). Barriers to the implementation of AI in organisations: findings from a Delphi study.. doi:10.24251/HICSS.2021.805

Bharadwaj, A., Elangovan, A., & Balakrishnan, A. (2019). Artificial intelligence in marketing: The new frontier for creating value. *Journal of Service Management*, *30*(3), 455–472.

Bhardwaj, P., Gupta, P., Panwar, H., Siddiqui, M. K., Morales-Menendez, R., & Bhaik, A. (2021, July). Application of Deep Learning on Student Engagement in e-learning environments. *Computers & Electrical Engineering*, *93*, 107277. doi:10.1016/j.compeleceng.2021.107277 PMID:36567679

Bhutani, A., & Sanaria, A. (2023). *The Past*. Present and Future of Artificial Intelligence.

Biggs, J. (1998). Assessment and classroom learning: A role for summative assessment? *Assessment in Education: Principles, Policy & Practice*, *5*(1), 103–110. doi:10.1080/0969595980050106

Biggs, J. (1999). What the student does: Teaching for enhanced learning. *Higher Education Research & Development*, *18*(1), 57–75. doi:10.1080/0729436990180105

Bisdas, S., Topriceanu, C., Zakrzewska, Z., Irimia, A., Shakallis, L., Subhash, J., Casapu, M.-M., Leon-Rojas, J., Pinto dos Santos, D., Andrews, D. M., Zeicu, C., Bouhuwaish, A. M., Lestari, A. N., Abu-Ismail, L., Sadiq, A. S., Khamees, A., Mohammed, K. M. G., Williams, E., Omran, A. I., ... Ebrahim, E. (2021). Artificial intelligence in medicine: A multinational multi-centre survey on the medical and dental students' perception. *Frontiers in Public Health*, *9*, 795284. Advance online publication. doi:10.3389/fpubh.2021.795284 PMID:35004598

Bishop, P. A., Downes, J. M., Netcoh, S., Farber, K., DeMink-Carthew, J., Brown, T., & Mark, R. (2020). Teacher roles in personalized learning environments. *The Elementary School Journal*, *121*(2), 311–336. doi:10.1086/711079

Biwer, F., Wiradhany, W., & Egbrink, M. G. A. (2021, April 23). oude, Hospers, H. J., Wasenitz, S., Jansen, W., & Bruin, A. B. H. de. (2021). Changes and Adaptations: How University Students Self-Regulate Their Online Learning During the COVID-19 Pandemic. *Frontiers in Psychology*, *12*, 642593. doi:10.3389/fpsyg.2021.642593 PMID:33967903

Blackboard Learn. (n.d.). Anthology. https://www.anthology.com/products/teaching-and-learning/learning-effectiveness/blackboard-learn

Black, P., Harrison, C., Lee, C., Marshall, B., & William, D. (2003). *Assessment for Learning – Putting It into Practice*. Open University Press.

Blanco-Elorrieta, E., & Caramazza, A. (2021). On the need for theoretically guided approaches to possible bilingual advantages: An evaluation of the potential loci in the language and executive control systems. *Neurobiology of Language (Cambridge, Mass.)*, *2*(4), 452–463. doi:10.1162/nol_a_00041 PMID:37214630

Bogoviz, A., Lobova, S., Karp, M., Vologdin, E., & Alekseev, A. (2019). Diversification of educational services in the conditions of Industry 4.0 based on training. On the Horizon the International Journal of Learning Futures, 27(3/4), 206-212. https://doi.org/ doi:10.1108/OTH-06-2019-0031

Bond, L. A. (2019). Norm-and criterion-referenced testing. *Practical Assessment, Research & Evaluation*, *5*(1), 2.

Bonsu, E. M., & Baffour-Koduah, D. (2023). From the consumers' side: Determining students' perception and intention to use ChatGPT in Ghanaian higher education. Journal of Education. *Society & Multiculturalism*, *4*(1), 1–29. doi:10.2478/jesm-2023-0001

Borenstein, J., & Howard, A. (2021). Emerging challenges in AI and the need for AI ethics education. *AI and Ethics*, *1*(1), 61–65. doi:10.1007/s43681-020-00002-7 PMID:38624388

Borkowski, A. (2022). Establishing a hospital artificial intelligence committee to improve patient care. (39 (8)). https://doi.org/ doi:10.12788/fp.0299

Bostrom, N., et, al. (2014). The ethics of artificial intelligence. In K. Frankish, & W. Ramsey (Eds.), *The Cambridge Handbook of Artificial Intelligence* (pp. 316–334). Cambridge University Press.

Boud, D. (2000). Sustainable assessment: Rethinking assessment for the learning society. *Studies in Continuing Education*, *22*(2), 151–167. doi:10.1080/713695728

Bozkurt, A., Karadeniz, A., Baneres, D., Guerrero-Roldán, A. E., & Rodríguez, M. E. (2021). Artificial intelligence and reflections from educational landscape: A review of AI Studies in half a century. *Sustainability (Basel)*, *13*(2), 800. doi:10.3390/su13020800

Brandenburg, T. (2012). *Bridging the knowledge gap: Internationalisation and privatisation of higher education in the State of Qatar and the Sultanate of Oman* [Doctoral dissertation].

Brindley, C., & Scoffield, S. (1998). Peer assessment in undergraduate programmes. *Teaching in Higher Education*, *3*(1), 79–90. doi:10.1080/1356215980030106

Brock, J. K., & von Wangenheim, F. (2019). Demystifying AI: What Digital Transformation Leaders Can Teach You About Realistic Artificial Intelligence. *California Management Review*, *61*(4), 110–134. doi:10.1177/1536504219865226

Brown, G. T. (2004). Teachers' conceptions of assessment: Implications for policy and professional development. *Assessment in Education: Principles, Policy & Practice*, *11*(3), 301–318. doi:10.1080/0969594042000304609

Brown, S., & Knight, P. (2012). *Assessing learners in higher education*. Routledge. doi:10.4324/9780203062036

Brown, T., Mann, B., Ryder, N., Subbiah, M., Kaplan, J. D., Dhariwal, P., Neelakantan, A., Shyam, P., Sastry, G., Askell, A., Agarwal, S., Herbert-Voss, A., Krueger, G., Henighan, T., Child, R., Ramesh, A., Ziegler, D. M., Wu, J., Winter, C., & Amodei, D. (2020). Language models are few-shot learners. *Advances in Neural Information Processing Systems*, 33.

Bryson, J. J. (2019). How society can maintain human-centric artificial intelligence. In *Human-centered digitalization and services* (pp. 305–323). Springer.

BuabbasA.MiskinB.AyedA.AlnaqiA.ShehabA.SafarM. (2022). Investigating students' perceptions towards artificial intelligence in medical education. https://doi.org/ doi:10.21203/rs.3.rs-1805527/v1

Bubinger, H., & Dinneen, J. D. (2021). *Actionable Approaches to Promote Ethical AI in Libraries*. Algorithm Watch. https://inventory.algorithmwatch.org/

BudachL.FeuerpfeilM.IhdeN.NathansenA.NoackN.PatzlaffH.NaumannF.HarmouchH. (2022). *The Effects of Data Quality on Machine Learning Performance*. http://arxiv.org/abs/2207.14529

Budler, L. C., Gosak, L., & Stiglic, G. (2023). Review of artificial intelligence-based question-answering systems in healthcare. *Wiley Interdisciplinary Reviews. Data Mining and Knowledge Discovery*, *13*(2), e1487. doi:10.1002/widm.1487

Bujang, S. D. A., Selamat, A., Ibrahim, R., Krejcar, O., Herrera-Viedma, E., Fujita, H., & Ghani, N. A. M. (2021). Multiclass prediction model for student grade prediction using machine learning. *IEEE Access : Practical Innovations, Open Solutions*, *9*, 95608–95621.

Bukie, O. F. (2014). Understanding technologies for e-assessment: A systematic review approach. *Journal of Emerging Trends in Computing and Information Sciences*, *5*(12), 936–947.

Bulathwela, S., Pérez-Ortiz, M., Holloway, C., Cukurova, M., & Shawe-Taylor, J. (2024). Artificial Intelligence Alone Will Not Democratise Education: On Educational Inequality, Techno-Solutionism and Inclusive Tools. *Sustainability*, *16*(2), 781.

Bulger, M. (2016). *Personalized learning: the conversations we're not having*. Data and Society Research Institute. https://datasociety.net/pubs/ecl/PersonalizedLearning_primer_2016.pdf

Bull, C., & Kharrufa, A. (2023). *Generative AI Assistants in Software Development Education*.

Bull, G., Thompson, A. D., Schmidt-Crawford, D., Garofalo, J., Hodges, C. B., Spector, J. M., Ferdig, R. E., Edyburn, D., & Kinshuk. (2016, September 2). Evaluating the Impact of Educational Technology. *Journal of Digital Learning in Teacher Education*, *32*(4), 117–118. doi:10.1080/21532974.2016.1217052

Bulten, W., Balkenhol, M., Belinga, J.-J. A., Brilhante, A., Çakır, A., Egevad, L., Eklund, M., Farré, X., Geronatsiou, K., & Molinié, V. (2021). Artificial intelligence assistance significantly improves Gleason grading of prostate biopsies by pathologists. *Modern Pathology*, *34*(3), 660–671.

Burkholder, L. (2015). Impartial Grading Revisited. *Teaching Philosophy*, *38*(3), 261–272. doi:10.5840/teachphil201581136

Buzzetto-More, N. A., & Alade, A. J. (2006). Best practices in e-assessment. *Journal of Information Technology Education, 5*(1), 251–269. doi:10.28945/246

Calderwood, J., Pedreschi, D., Craig, M. Ó., & Reid, D. G. (2023). *Reflecting on the importance of open communication and social capital for co-creating knowledge in Irish fisheries*. Frontiers in Marine Science., doi:10.3389/fmars.2022.1081616

Çalışkan, A., Bryson, J. J., & Narayanan, A. (2017). Semantics Derived Automatically From Language Corpora Contain Human-Like Biases. *Science, 356*(6334), 183–186. Advance online publication. doi:10.1126/science.aal4230 PMID:28408601

Calvo, R. A., et, al. (2020). Supporting human autonomy in AI systems: A framework for ethical enquiry. In *Ethics of Digital Well-Being* (pp. 31–54). Springer.

Camilleri, M. A. (2019). Higher Education Marketing: Opportunities and Challenges in the Digital Era. *Academia (Caracas), 0*(16-17), 4–28.

Cantika, O., Syafrizal, S., & Evenddy, S. S. (n.d.). Enhancing Students' Reading Ability with Let's Read Asia Website at Eleventh Grade of SMK AL Fattah: A Classroom Action Research.

Capterra: Reviews of Blackboard Learn . (n.d.). Capterra. https://www.capterra.com/p/14500/Blackboard-LMS-for-Business/reviews/

Capterra: Reviews of Digiexam. (n.d.). Capterra. https://www.capterra.com/p/161396/DigiExam/reviews/

Capterra: Reviews of Kahoot . (n.d.). Capterra. https://www.capterra.com/p/156399/Kahoot/reviews/

Cardona, M. A., Rodríguez, R. J., & Ishmael, K. (2023). *Artificial intelligence and the future of teaching and learning: Insights and recommendations*.

Cargill, M. (2004, January). Transferable skills within research degrees: a collaborative genre-based approach to developing publication skills and its implications for research education. *Teaching in Higher Education, 9*(1), 83–98. doi:10.1080/1356251032000155858

Caroline Hillier, U. o. G., Canada. (2022). Creating Computer Confidence: An Investigation into Current Privacy and Security Concerns of the Senior Demographic. [IJITE]. *International Journal of Innovative Trends in Engineering, 11*(3), 19–23.

Carroll, B., Smith, K., & Johnson, M. (2009). Improving Quality and Efficiency in Higher Education through Advanced AI Systems. *Higher Education Studies, 9*(1), 22–37.

Carter, D. (2020). Regulation and ethics in artificial intelligence and machine learning technologies: Where are we now? Who is responsible? Can the information professional play a role? *Business Information Review, 37*(2), 60–68. doi:10.1177/0266382120923962

Casal-Otero, L., Catala, A., Fernández-Morante, C., Taboada, M., Cebreiro, B., & Barro, S. (2023, April 19). AI literacy in K-12: A systematic literature review. *International Journal of STEM Education, 10*(1), 29. doi:10.1186/s40594-023-00418-7

Cassidy, C. (2023). Universities to return to pen and paper exams after students caught using AI to write essays. *The Guardian.* https://www.theguardian.com/australia-news/2023/jan/10/universities-to-return-to-pen-and-paper-exams-after-stude nts-caught-using-ai-to-write-essays

Cath, C., Wachter, S., Mittelstadt, B., Taddeo, M., & Floridi, L. (2018). Artificial Intelligence and the 'Good Society': The US, EU, and UK approach. *Science and Engineering Ethics, 24*, 505–528. doi:10.1007/s11948-017-9901-7 PMID:28353045

Celik, I. (2023). Towards Intelligent-TPACK: An empirical study on teachers' professional knowledge to ethically integrate artificial intelligence (AI)-based tools into education. *Computers in Human Behavior, 138*, 107468. doi:10.1016/j.chb.2022.107468

Celik, I., Dindar, M., Muukkonen, H., & Järvelä, S. (2022). The promises and challenges of artificial Intelligence for teachers: A systematic review of research. *TechTrends, 66*(4), 616–630. doi:10.1007/s11528-022-00715-y

Chamorro-Atalaya, O., Arce-Santillan, D., Morales-Romero, G., Caycho-Salas, B., Guía-Altamirano, T., León-Velarde, C., & Rengifo-Tello, R. (2023). Evaluation of the functionality of the virtual platform in the teaching process: Analysis based on the usability factor. *Indonesian Journal of Electrical Engineering and Computer Science, 29*(1), 583–590. doi:10.11591/ijeecs.v29.i1.pp583-590

Chan, C. K. et, al. (2023). *The AI generation gap: Are Gen Z students more interested in adopting generative AI such as ChatGPT in teaching and learning than their Gen X and Millennial Generation teachers?* arXiv preprint arXiv:2305.02878.

Chan, C. K. Y., & Tsi, L. H. (2023). The AI Revolution in Education: Will AI Replace or Assist Teachers in Higher Education? *arXiv preprint arXiv:2305.01185.*

Chan, R. Y. (2016). *Understanding The Purpose Of Higher Education: An Analysis Of The Economic And Social Benefits For Completing A College Degree, 6*(5).

Chan, A. (2022, April 4). GPT-3 and InstructGPT: Technological dystopianism, utopianism, and "Contextual" perspectives in AI ethics and industry. *AI and Ethics, 3*(1), 53–64. doi:10.1007/s43681-022-00148-6

Chan, C. K. Y. (2023). A comprehensive AI policy education framework for university teaching and learning. *International Journal of Educational Technology in Higher Education, 20*(1), 38. doi:10.1186/s41239-023-00408-3

Chan, C. K. Y., & Hu, W. (2023). Students' voices on generative AI: Perceptions, benefits, and challenges in higher education. *International Journal of Educational Technology in Higher Education, 20*(1), 43. doi:10.1186/s41239-023-00411-8

Chang, A., Chabot, S., Mathews, J., Briggs, S., Strzalkowski, T., Si, M., & Braasch, J. (2022). A spatially-aware companion system for language learning and foreign-language dialogue. *Paper presented at the Proceedings of the 24th International Congress on Acoustics (ICA)*. IEEE.

Chang, Q., Pan, X., Manikandan, N., & Ramesh, S. (2022). Artificial Intelligence Technologies for Teaching and Learning in Higher Education. *International Journal of Reliability Quality and Safety Engineering*, *29*(5), 2240006. doi:10.1142/S021853932240006X

Chan, K. S., & Zary, N. (2019). Applications and challenges of implementing artificial intelligence in medical education: Integrative review. *JMIR Medical Education*, *5*(1), e13930. doi:10.2196/13930 PMID:31199295

Chatterjee, S. (2020). AI strategy of India: Policy framework, adoption challenges and actions for government. *Transforming Government*, *14*(5), 757–775. doi:10.1108/TG-05-2019-0031

Chatterjee, S., & Bhattacharjee, K. K. (2020). Adoption of artificial intelligence in higher education: A quantitative analysis using structural equation modelling. *Education and Information Technologies*, *25*, 3443–3463.

Chattopadhyay, M., Sen, R., & Gupta, S. (2018). A comprehensive review and meta-analysis on applications of machine learning techniques in intrusion detection. *AJIS. Australasian Journal of Information Systems*, *22*, 1–27. doi:10.3127/ajis.v22i0.1667

Chaudhary, M. (2023, September 5). Exploring Ethical, Privacy, Security, and Societal Concerns in ChatGPT Implementation: Challenges and Solutions. [IJSR]. *International Journal of Science and Research (Raipur, India)*, *12*(9), 1054–1055. doi:10.21275/SR23905114533

Chaudhry, I. S., Sarwary, S. A. M., El Refae, G. A., & Chabchoub, H. (2023). Time to revisit existing student's performance evaluation approach in higher education sector in a new era of ChatGPT—A case study. *Cogent Education*, *10*(1), 2210461. doi:10.1080/2331186X.2023.2210461

Chaudhry, M. A., & Kazım, E. (2022). Eğitimde Yapay Zeka (AIEd): Üst düzey bir akademik ve sektör notu 2021. *AI and Ethics*, *2*, 157–165. doi:10.1007/s43681-021-00074-z PMID:34790953

Cheatham, B., Javanmardian, K., & Samandari, H. (2019). Confronting the risks of artificial intelligence. *The McKinsey Quarterly*, *2*(38), 1–9.

Cheng, L., Umapathy, K., Rehman, M., Ritzhaupt, A., Antonyan, K., Shidfar, P., ... Abramowitz, B. (2023). Designing, developing, and validating a measure of undergraduate students' conceptions of artificial Intelligence in education. *Journal of Interactive Learning Research*, *34*(2), 275–311.

Cheng, L., Umapathy, K., Rehman, M., Ritzhaupt, A., Antonyan, K., Shidfar, P., Nichols, J., Lee, M., & Abramowitz, B. (2023). Designing, developing, and validating a measure of undergraduate students' conceptions of artificial intelligence in education. *Journal of Interactive Learning Research*, *34*(2), 275–311.

Chen, H., Chiang, R. H., & Storey, V. C. (2021). Artificial intelligence and data analytics in marketing: Trends and prospects. *International Journal of Research in Marketing*, *38*(5), 659–679.

Chen, L., Chen, P., & Lin, Z. (2020). Artificial Intelligence in education: A review. *IEEE Access : Practical Innovations, Open Solutions*, *8*, 75264–75278. doi:10.1109/ACCESS.2020.2988510

Chen, X., & Siau, K. (2020). Business analytics/business intelligence and IT infrastructure: Impact on organisational agility. [JOEUC]. *Journal of Organizational and End User Computing*, *32*(4), 138–161. doi:10.4018/JOEUC.2020100107

Chen, X., Xie, H., Zou, D., & Hwang, G. J. (2020). Application and theory gaps during the rise of artificial intelligence in education. *Computers and Education: Artificial Intelligence*, *1*, 100002. doi:10.1016/j.caeai.2020.100002

Chen, X., Zou, D., Xie, H., Cheng, G., & Liu, C. (2022). Two decades of artificial intelligence in education. *Journal of Educational Technology & Society*, *25*(1), 28–47.

Chen, Y., Jensen, S., Albert, L. J., Gupta, S., & Lee, T. (2023). Artificial intelligence (AI) student assistants in the classroom: Designing chatbots to support student success. *Information Systems Frontiers*, *25*(1), 161–182. doi:10.1007/s10796-022-10291-4

Chen, Z., Zhang, J., Jiang, X., Hu, Z., Han, X., Xu, M., Savitha, V., & Vivekananda, G. (2020). Education 4.0 using artificial intelligence for students performance analysis. *Inteligencia Artificial*, *23*(66), 124–137.

Chheang, V., Marquez-Hernandez, R., Patel, M., Rajasekaran, D., Sharmin, S., Caulfield, G., Kiafar, B., Li, J., & Barmaki, R. (2023). *Towards Anatomy Education with Generative AI-based Virtual Assistants in Immersive Virtual Reality Environments.*

ChiappeA.RodríguezL. P. (2017, June 26). Learning Analytics in 21st century education: a review. *Ensaio: Avaliação E Políticas Públicas Em Educação, 25*(97), 971–991. doi:10.1590/s0104-40362017002501211

Chiu, T. K., Xia, Q., Zhou, X., Chai, C. S., & Cheng, M. (2023). Systematic literature review on opportunities, challenges, and future research recommendations of artificial intelligence in education. *Computers and Education: Artificial Intelligence*, *4*, 100118. doi:10.1016/j.caeai.2022.100118

Choi, J., & Byeon, J. (2021). Key principles of clinical validation, device approval, and insurance coverage decisions of artificial intelligence. *Korean Journal of Radiology*, *22*(3), 442. doi:10.3348/kjr.2021.0048 PMID:33629545

Chopra, A. (2019). *AI in Supply & Procurement.* AICAI. . doi:10.1109/AICAI.2019.8701357

Chou, C. Y., Lai, K. R., Chao, P.-Y., Tseng, S.-F., & Liao, T.-Y. (2018). A negotiation-based adaptive learning system for regulating help-seeking behaviors. *Computers & Education*, *126*, 115–128. doi:10.1016/j.compedu.2018.07.010

Cingillioglu, I., Gal, U., & Prokhorov, A. (2024, March 26). AI-experiments in education: An AI-driven randomized controlled trial for higher education research. *Education and Information Technologies.* Advance online publication. doi:10.1007/s10639-024-12633-y

Civil, B. (2023). *ChatGPT can hinder students' critical thinking skills: Artificial intelligence is changing how students learn to write*. The Queen's Journal.

Clark, I. (2012). Formative Assessment: Assessment Is for Self-Regulated Learning. *Educational Psychology Review*, *24*(2), 205–249. doi:10.1007/s10648-011-9191-6

Clark, K., Jha, M., & Murray, S. (2020). A survey of automatic summarisation for scientific literature. *ACM Transactions on Speech and Language Processing*, *28*(4), 1–45.

Cohen, M. S., Salas, E., & Riedel, S. L. (2002). Critical thinking: Challenges, possibilities, and purpose. *Contract No. DASW01-00-C-3010, March.*

Cole, L. (2023). Leadership, Education and Training for Youth in Contemporary African Union Programs. *Afrika Tanulmányok/Hungarian. Journal of African Studies*, *17*(1), 69–102.

Collis, B. (1989). Using information technology to create new educational situations. *Higher Education Policy*, *2*(4), 63–70. doi:10.1057/hep.1989.75

Cóndor-Herrera, O., Arias-Flores, H., Jadán-Guerrero, J., & Ramos-Galarza, C. (2021). Artificial Intelligence and Tomorrow's Education. In T. Z. Ahram, W. Karwowski, & J. Kalra (Eds.), *Advances in Artificial Intelligence, Software and Systems Engineering. AHFE 2021. Lecture Notes in Networks and Systems* (Vol. 271). Springer. doi:10.1007/978-3-030-80624-8_23

Conijn, R., Kahr, P., & Snijders, C. (2023). The effects of explanations in automated essay scoring systems on student trust and motivation. *Journal of Learning Analytics*, *10*(1), 37–53.

Cook, C., Jones, J., & Al-Twal, A. (2022). Validity and fairness of utilising student evaluation of teaching (SET) as a primary performance measure. *Journal of Further and Higher Education*, *46*(2), 172–184. doi:10.1080/0309877X.2021.1895093

Cook, G. (2010). *Translation in language teaching: An argument for reassessment.* Oxford University Press.

Cooper, G. (2023). Examining science education in ChatGPT: An exploratory study of generative artificial intelligence. *Journal of Science Education and Technology*, *32*(3), 444–452.

Cooper, L., Holderness, D. K. Jr, Sorensen, T., & Wood, D. A. (2019). Robotic process automation in public accounting. *Accounting Horizons*, *33*(4), 15–35. doi:10.2308/acch-52466

Cope, B., & Kalantzis, M. (2016). Big data comes to school: Implications for learning, assessment, and research. *AERA Open*, *2*(2). doi:10.1177/2332858416641907

Cope, B., Kalantzis, M., & Searsmith, D. (2021). Artificial intelligence for education: Knowledge and its assessment in AI-enabled learning ecologies. *Educational Philosophy and Theory*, *53*(12), 1229–1245. doi:10.1080/00131857.2020.1728732

Corrin, L. et, al. (2019). *The Ethics of Learning Analytics in Australian Higher Education: A Discussion Paper.*

Costa, D. M. S., Mamede, H. S., & Silva, M. M. (2022). Robotic process automation (RPA) adoption: A systematic literature review. *Engineering Management in Production and Services*, *14*(2), 1–12. doi:10.2478/emj-2022-0012

Council of the European Union. (2023). *Artificial Intelligence Act: Council and Parliament strike a deal on the first worldwide rules for AI.* https://www.consilium.europa.eu/en/press/press-releases/2023/12/09/artificial-intelligence-act-council-and-parliament-strike-a-deal-on-the-first-worldwide-rules-for-ai/

Cox, A. (2022). The rise of AI: Implications and applications of artificial intelligence in academic libraries (ACRL publications in librarianship, no. 78). *Journal of the Australian Library and Information Association*, *71*(3), 300–302. doi:10.1080/24750158.2022.2103917

Creamer, D. B. (Ed.). (2012, December 6). Review of "The Future of Thinking: Learning Institutions in a Digital Age," by Cathy N. Davidson and David Theo Goldberg (MIT Press, 2012). Journal of Religion, Media and Digital Culture, 1(1), 1–4. doi:10.1163/21659214-90000008

Crompton, H., & Burke, D. (2023). *Artificial Intelligence in Higher Education: A Systematic Review of the Literature from 2016 to 2022.*

Crompton, H., & Burke, D. (2023). Artificial intelligence in higher education: The state of the field. *International Journal of Educational Technology in Higher Education*, *20*(1), 22. doi:10.1186/s41239-023-00392-8

Cui, X., Xu, B., & Razzaq, S. A. (2022). *Artificial intelligence and its application in business management*. Management Science Letters.

Cukurova, M., Miao, X., & Brooker, R. (2023). Adoption of Adaptive Learning Platforms in Schools: Unveiling Factors Influencing Teachers Engagement. *arXiv preprint arXiv:2304.00903*.

Dabingaya, M. (2022). Analyzing the Effectiveness of AI-Powered Adaptive Learning Platforms in Mathematics Education. *Interdisciplinary Journal Papier Human Review*, *3*(1), 1–7. doi:10.47667/ijphr.v3i1.226

Dağ, M., & Karamustafaoğlu, O. (2023). Fen Lisesi Öğrencilerinin Öğrenme Stillerinin Çeşitli Değişkenlere Göre İncelenmesi. *Fen Bilimleri Öğretimi Dergisi*, *11*(1), 132–152. doi:10.56423/fbod.1264038

Dagumboy, E. (2022). ECD-IMC: An integrated marketing communications model for selected Philippine higher education institutions. [Indonesian Journal of Communications Studies]. *Jurnal Studi Komunikasi*, *6*(3), 719–738. doi:10.25139/jsk.v6i3.4502

Dai, Y., Liu, A., & Lim, C. P. (2023). Reconceptualizing ChatGPT and generative AI as a student-driven innovation in higher education. *Procedia CIRP*, *119*, 84–90.

Damuluri, S., Islam, K., Ahmadi, P., & Qureshi, N. S. (2020). Analyzing navigational data and predicting student grades using support vector machine. *Emerging Science Journal*, *4*(4), 243–252.

Daradoumis, T., et, al. (2020). Cultivating students' reflective learning in metacognitive activities through an affective pedagogical agent. *Journal of Educational Technology & Society, 23*(2), 19–31.

Darvishi, A., Khosravi, H., Abdi, S., Sadiq, S., & Gašević, D. (2022). Incorporating training, self-monitoring and AI-assistance to improve peer feedback quality. Proceedings of the Ninth ACM Conference on Learning@ Scale, Darvishi, A., Khosravi, H., Sadiq, S., & Gašević, D. (2022). Incorporating AI and learning analytics to build trustworthy peer assessment systems. *British Journal of Educational Technology, 53*(4), 844–875. doi:10.1111/bjet.13233

Dasanayaka, C. H., Abeykoon, C., Ranaweera, R. A. A. S., & Koswatte, I. (2021). The impact of the performance appraisal process on job satisfaction of the academic staff in higher educational institutions. *Education Sciences, 11*(10), 623. doi:10.3390/educsci11100623

David, L. and Alan, K. (2010). Artificial intelligence: foundations of computational agents. Choice Reviews Online, 48(04), 48-2130-48-2130. https://doi.org/ doi:10.5860/CHOICE.48-2130

de Chiusole, D., Stefanutti, L., Anselmi, P., & Robusto, E. (2020). Stat-Knowlab. Assessment and learning of statistics with competence-based knowledge space theory. *International Journal of Artificial Intelligence in Education, 30*(4), 668–700. doi:10.1007/s40593-020-00223-1

De Gagne, J. C. (2023). Values clarification exercises to prepare nursing students for artificial intelligence integration. *International Journal of Environmental Research and Public Health, 20*(14), 6409. doi:10.3390/ijerph20146409 PMID:37510641

Deeva, G., Bogdanova, D., Serral, E., Snoeck, M., & De Weerdt, J. (2021). A review of automated feedback systems for learners: Classification framework, challenges and opportunities. *Computers & Education, 162*, 104094. doi:10.1016/j.compedu.2020.104094

Dempere, J., Modugu, K., Hesham, A., & Ramasamy, L. K. (2023, September). The impact of ChatGPT on higher education. [). Frontiers.]. *Frontiers in Education, 8*, 1206936. doi:10.3389/feduc.2023.1206936

Devlin, J., Chang, M. W., Lee, K., & Toutanova, K. (2018). Bert: pre-training of deep bidirectional transformers for language understanding. arXiv preprint arXiv:1810.04805.

Dexe, J., & Franke, U. (2020). Nordic lights? National AI policies for doing well by doing good. *Journal of Cyber Policy, 5*(3), 332–349. doi:10.1080/23738871.2020.1856160

Dhirani, L. L., Mukhtiar, N., Chowdhry, B. S., & Newe, T. (2023). Ethical dilemmas and privacy issues in emerging technologies: A review. *Sensors (Basel), 23*(3), 1151. doi:10.3390/s23031151 PMID:36772190

Diamantopoulou, V., Lambrinoudakis, C., King, J. R., & Gritzalis, S. (2021). Eu gdpr: toward a regulatory initiative for deploying a private digital era. Modern Socio-Technical Perspectives on Privacy, 427-448. https://doi.org/ doi:10.1007/978-3-030-82786-1_18

Diez, J., & … . (2020). Cosmological constraints from the DES Y3 galaxy shape catalogue. *Monthly Notices of the Royal Astronomical Society, 495*(3), 3208–3232.

Digiexam . (n.d.). DigiExam. https://www.digiexam.com/

Digital Curation Centre, The University of Edinburgh. (2020). The Role of Data in AI: Report for the Data Governance Working Group of the Global Partnership of AI.

Dignum, V. (2018). Ethics in artificial intelligence: Introduction to the special issue. *Ethics and Information Technology*, *20*(1), 1–3. doi:10.1007/s10676-018-9450-z

Divekar, R. R. (2020). *AI enabled foreign language immersion: Technology and method to acquire foreign languages with AI in immersive virtual worlds*. Rensselaer Polytechnic Institute.

Do Quyen, N. T., & Khairani, A. Z. (2017). Reviewing the challenges of implementing formative assessment in Asia: The need for a professional development program. *Journal of Social Science Studies*, *4*(1), 160–177. doi:10.5296/jsss.v4i1.9728

Dolezal, D., Roschger, C., Hahnenkamp, A., Mairinger, M., Zimmermann, D., Satek, A., Koppensteiner, G., & Motschnig, R. (2020). Educational Design Patterns for Student-Centered 21 st Century Learning in Technology-Enhanced Learning Environments. *International Conference on Interactive Collaborative Learning*

Doshi-Velez, F., & Kim, B. (2017). Towards a rigorous science of interpretable machine learning. arXiv preprint arXiv:1702.08947.

Drachsler, H., & Greller, W. (2016, April). Privacy and analytics: it's a DELICATE issue a checklist for trusted learning analytics. In *Proceedings of the sixth international conference on learning analytics & knowledge* (pp. 89-98). 10.1145/2883851.2883893

Dragoş, V., & Mih, D. (2015). Scientific Literacy in School. *Procedia: Social and Behavioral Sciences*, *209*, Pages167–172. doi:10.1016/j.sbspro.2015.11.273

Drugova, E. (2023). Learning analytics driven improvements in learning design in Higher Education: A systematic literature review [Preprint]. *Journal of Computer Assisted Learning*. Advance online publication. doi:10.1111/jcal.12894

Duan, Y., Edwards, J. S., & Dwivedi, Y. K. (2019). Artificial intelligence for decision making in the era of Big Data – Evolution, challenges and research agenda. *International Journal of Information Management*, *48*, 63–71. doi:10.1016/j.ijinfomgt.2019.01.021

Dumitrascu, O., Wang, Y., & Chen, J. (2022). Clinical machine learning modelling studies: Methodology and data reporting. *Journal of Neuro-Ophthalmology*, *42*(2), 145–148. doi:10.1097/WNO.0000000000001605 PMID:35439230

Duncan, A. (2022). The intelligent academic library: A review of AI projects & and potential for Caribbean libraries. *Library Hi Tech News*, *39*(5), 12–15. doi:10.1108/LHTN-01-2022-0014

Earle, R. S. (2002). The integration of instructional technology into public education: Promises and challenges. *Educational Technology*, *42*(1), 5–13.

Ellis, E. (2022). The potential of artificial intelligence in assessment feedback. *Times Higher Education.* https://www.timeshighereducation.com/campus/potential-artificial-intelligence-assessment-feedback

Elsayed, S., & Cakir, D. (2023). Implementation of Assessment and Feedback in Higher Education. *Acta Pedagogia Asiana*, *2*(1), 34–42. doi:10.53623/apga.v2i1.170

Elshani, L., & Nuçi, K. P. (2021). Constructing a personalized learning path using genetic algorithms approach. *arXiv preprint arXiv:2104.11276.*

Enholm, I. M., Papagiannidis, E., Mikalef, P., & Krogstie, J. (2021). Artificial Intelligence and Business Value: A Literature Review. *Information Systems Frontiers*. doi:10.1007/s10796-021-10186-w

Ercikan, K., & McCaffrey, D. F. (2022). Optimizing implementation of artificial-intelligence-based automated scoring: An evidence centered design approach for designing assessments for AI-based scoring. *Journal of Educational Measurement*, *59*(3), 272–287.

Estrellado, C. J., & Miranda, J. C. (2023). Artificial intelligence in the Philippine educational context: Circumspection and future inquiries. *International Journal of Scientific and Research Publications*, *13*(5), 16–22. doi:10.29322/IJSRP.13.05.2023.p13704

Eubanks, V. (2018). *Automating inequality: How high-tech tools perpetuate bias*. John Wiley & Sons.

Eulerich, M., Pawlowski, J., Waddoups, N., & Wood, D. A. (2021). A framework for using robotic process automation for audit tasks*. *Contemporary Accounting Research*, *39*(1), 691–720. doi:10.1111/1911-3846.12723

European Commission (2019). *The European Commission's high-level expert group on artificial intelligence: Ethics guidelines for trustworthy AI.* EC.

European Parliament (2021). *Report on artificial intelligence in education, culture and the audiovisual sector (2020/2017(INI))*. IEEE.

Evans, D. J., Zeun, P., & Stanier, R. A. (2014). Motivating student learning using a formative assessment journey. *Journal of Anatomy*, *224*(3), 296–303. doi:10.1111/joa.12117 PMID:24111930

Faggella, D., & Bharadwaj, R. (2019). *Getting Started with AI-Proven Best Practices for AI Adoption-for IT and Strategy Consultants Emerj Artificial Intelligence Research.*

Fariani, R. I., Junus, K., & Santoso, H. B. (2022, November 17). A Systematic Literature Review on Personalised Learning in the Higher Education Context. *Technology. Knowledge and Learning*, *28*(2), 449–476. doi:10.1007/s10758-022-09628-4

Farrokhnia, M., Banihashem, S. K., Noroozi, O., & Wals, A. (2023). A SWOT analysis of ChatGPT: Implications for educational practice and research. *Innovations in Education and Teaching International*, 1–15. doi:10.1080/14703297.2023.2195846

Farrow, R. (2023). The possibilities and limits of XAI in education: A socio-technical perspective. *Learning, Media and Technology*, *48*(2), 266–279. doi:10.1080/17439884.2023.2185630

Federspiel, F., Mitchell, R., Asokan, A., Umana, C., & McCoy, D. (2023). Threats by artificial Intelligence to human health and human existence. *BMJ Global Health*, *8*(5), e010435. doi:10.1136/bmjgh-2022-010435 PMID:37160371

Felipe Redondo, A. M., Nuñez Cárdenas, F. D. J., & Tomás Mariano, V. T. (2015, July 5). Reseña del NMC Horizon Report > Educación Superior 2015. *Ciencia Huasteca Boletín Científico De La Escuela Superior De Huejutla*, *3*(6). doi:10.29057/esh.v3i6.1128

Fernández, V., & Gallardo-Gallardo, E. (2020). Tackling the HR Digitalization Challenge: Key Factors and Barriers to HR Analytics Adoption. *Competitiveness Review an International Business Journal Incorporating Journal of Global Competitiveness*. doi:10.1108/CR-12-2019-0163

Fernández, A., Gómez, B., Binjaku, K., & Meçe, E. K. (2023). Digital transformation initiatives in higher education institutions: A multivocal literature review. *Education and Information Technologies*, *28*(10), 12351–12382. doi:10.1007/s10639-022-11544-0 PMID:37361743

Fernandez-Antolin, M.-M., del Río, J. M., & Gonzalez-Lezcano, R.-A. (2021). The use of gamification in higher technical education: Perception of university students on innovative teaching materials. *International Journal of Technology and Design Education*, *31*(5), 1019–1038. doi:10.1007/s10798-020-09583-0

Fernández-Caramés, T. M., & Fraga-Lamas, P. (2019). Towards Next Generation Teaching, Learning, and Context-Aware Applications for Higher Education: A Review on Blockchain, IoT, Fog and Edge Computing Enabled Smart Campuses and Universities. *Applied Sciences (Basel, Switzerland)*, *9*(21), 4479. doi:10.3390/app9214479

Ferrara, E. (2023). Fairness and bias in artificial intelligence: A brief survey of sources, impacts, and mitigation strategies. *Sci*, *6*(1), 3.

Ferrer, X., Van Nuenen, T., Such, J. M., Coté, M., & Criado, N. (2021). Bias and discrimination in AI: A cross-disciplinary perspective. *IEEE Technology and Society Magazine*, *40*(2), 72–80. doi:10.1109/MTS.2021.3056293

Filgueiras, F. (2023). Artificial intelligence and education governance. *Education, Citizenship and Social Justice*, *0*(0). doi:10.1177/17461979231160674

Fitria, T. N. (2021). Artificial Intelligence (AI) In Education: Using AI Tools for Teaching and Learning Process. In Prosiding Seminar Nasional & Call for Paper STIE AAS, 4(1), 134-147.

Floridi, L. (2021). A Unified Framework of Five Principles for AI in Society. In Ethics, Governance, and Policies in Artificial Intelligence, 144. Springer International Publishing AG. doi:10.1007/978-3-030-81907-1_2

Floridi, L. (2018). Soft Ethics and the Governance of the Digital. *Philosophy & Technology*, *31*(1), 1–8. doi:10.1007/s13347-018-0303-9 PMID:30322997

Floridi, L., Cowls, J., Beltrametti, M., Chatila, R., Chazerand, P., Dignum, V., Luetge, C., Madelin, R., Pagallo, U., Rossi, F., Schafer, B., Valcke, P., & Vayena, E. (2018, November 26). AI4People—An Ethical Framework for a Good AI Society: Opportunities, Risks, Principles, and Recommendations. *Minds and Machines*, *28*(4), 689–707. doi:10.1007/s11023-018-9482-5 PMID:30930541

Fujimoto, T. (2022). Reproduction of humanness based on eXtended intelligence: Concept of artificial personality and its mechanism. *International Journal of Computational Systems Engineering*, *7*(1), 30–40. doi:10.1504/IJCSYSE.2022.131034

Fukuda-Parr, S., & Gibbons, E. (2021). *Emerging Consensus on 'Ethical AI': Human.*

Fu, Q., Gao, Z., Zhou, J., & Zheng, Y. (2021). CLSA: A novel deep learning model for MOOC dropout prediction. *Computers & Electrical Engineering*, *94*, 107315. doi:10.1016/j.compeleceng.2021.107315

Furey, H., & Martin, F. (2019). AI education matters. *AI Matters*, *4*(4), 13–15. doi:10.1145/3299758.3299764

G, M. (2020, January 20). Rule-based Cognitive Modelling for Multimodal Intelligent Tutoring Systems. *International Journal of Psychosocial Rehabilitation, 24*(1), 1754–1760. https://doi.org/ doi:10.37200/IJPR/V24I1/PR200275

Gama, F., Tyskbo, D., Nygren, J., Barlow, J., Reed, J., & Svedberg, P. (2022). Implementation frameworks for artificial intelligence translation into health care practice: A scoping review. *Journal of Medical Internet Research*, *24*(1), e32215. doi:10.2196/32215 PMID:35084349

Gao, R., Merzdorf, H. E., Anwar, S., Hipwell, M. C., & Srinivasa, A. (2024). Automatic assessment of text-based responses in post-secondary education: A systematic review. *Computers and Education: Artificial Intelligence*, 100206.

Gao, S., He, L., Chen, Y., Li, D., & Lai, K. (2020). Public perception of artificial intelligence in medical care: Social media content analysis. *Journal of Medical Internet Research*, *22*(7), e16649. doi:10.2196/16649 PMID:32673231

Gao, S., Low, S. P., & Lim, X. (2023). Prospects, Drivers of and Barriers to Artificial Intelligence Adoption In project Management. *Built Environment Project and Asset Management*, *13*(5), 629–645. doi:10.1108/BEPAM-12-2022-0195

García-Pérez, D., Fraile, J., & Panadero, E. (2021). Learning strategies and self-regulation in context: How higher education students approach different courses, assessments, and challenges. *European Journal of Psychology of Education*, *36*(2), 533–550. doi:10.1007/s10212-020-00488-z

García-Valcárcel, A., Rodríguez, A. I., & Mena Marcos, J. J. (2013). Educational innovation. *Proceedings of the First International Conference on Technological Ecosystem for Enhancing Multiculturality*

Gardner, J., O'Leary, M., & Yuan, L. (2021). Artificial intelligence in educational assessment: 'Breakthrough? Or buncombe and ballyhoo?'. *Journal of Computer Assisted Learning*, *37*(5), 1207–1216. doi:10.1111/jcal.12577

Garrett, N (2020). More than "If Time Allows" the role of ethics in AI education. In *Proceedings of the AAAI/ACM Conference on AI, Ethics, and Society* (pp. 272-278). IEEE.

Gašević, D., Siemens, G., & Sadiq, S. (2023). *Empowering learners for the age of artificial intelligence* (Vol. 4). Elsevier.

Gašević, D., Siemens, G., & Sadiq, S. (2023). Empowering learners for the age of artificial intelligence. *Computers and Education: Artificial Intelligence*, *4*, 100130.

Gebru, T., Morgenstern, J., Blocher, B., Mitchell, M., & Barenholtz, E. (2019). Datasheets for datasets. arXiv preprint arXiv:1803.09010.

Gedrimiene, E., Celik, I., Kaasila, A., Mäkitalo, K., & Muukkonen, H. (2024). Artificial intelligence (AI)-enhanced learning analytics (LA) for supporting career decisions: Advantages and challenges from user perspective. *Education and Information Technologies*, *29*(1), 297–322. doi:10.1007/s10639-023-12277-4

George, G., & Thomas, M. R. (2019). *Integration of Artificial Intelligence in Human Resource*.

George, B., & Wooden, O. (2023). Managing the strategic transformation of higher education through artificial Intelligence. *Administrative Sciences*, *13*(9), 196. doi:10.3390/admsci13090196

Gerlick, J. A., & Liozu, S. M. (2020). Ethical and legal considerations of artificial intelligence and algorithmic decision-making in personalized pricing. *Journal of Revenue and Pricing Management*, *19*(2), 85–98. doi:10.1057/s41272-019-00225-2

Ghelani, D. (2022). *A review on student automatic grading system D.*

Gima Lee, Y. J. L., Hee-jeong Kim. (2023). *Analysis of adaptive learning in Korea's AI mathematics learning platforms.* Korean School Mathematics Society. doi:10.30807/ksms.2023.26.3.004

Glatard, T., Legrand, A., Loesek, V., Merlin, O., & Mouginot, F. (2015). SciServer: An open science platform for collaborative research. In *International Conference on Computational Science and Its Applications* (pp. 374-385). Springer, Cham.

Gligorea, I., Cioca, M., Oancea, R., Gorski, A. T., Gorski, H., & Tudorache, P. (2023). Adaptive Learning Using Artificial Intelligence in e-Learning: A Literature Review. *Education Sciences*, *13*(12), 1216. doi:10.3390/educsci13121216

Goel, A. K., & Polepeddi, L. (2018). *Jill Watson. Learning engineering for online education: Theoretical contexts and design-based examples*. Routledge.

González-Calatayud, V., Prendes-Espinosa, P., & Roig-Vila, R. (2021). Artificial intelligence for student assessment: A systematic review. *Applied Sciences (Basel, Switzerland)*, *11*(12), 5467. doi:10.3390/app11125467

González-Carrillo, C. D., Restrepo-Calle, F., Ramírez-Echeverry, J. J., & González, F. A. (2021). Automatic grading tool for jupyter notebooks in artificial intelligence courses. *Sustainability (Basel), 13*(21), 12050. doi:10.3390/su132112050

Górak-Sosnowska, K., & Piwowar-Sulej, K. (2023). *The Well-Being of Female Administrative Staff in Managerial Positions in Polish Higher Education Institutions*. Central European Management Journal., doi:10.1108/CEMJ-12-2021-0151

Goralski, M. A., & Tan, T. K. (2020). Artificial intelligence and sustainable development. *International Journal of Management Education, 18*(1), 100330. doi:10.1016/j.ijme.2019.100330

Górriz, J. M., Ramírez, J., Ortíz, A., Martinez-Murcia, F. J., Segovia, F., Suckling, J., & Bologna, G. (2020). Artificial intelligence within the interplay between natural and artificial computation: Advances in data science, trends and applications. *Neurocomputing, 410*, 237–270. doi:10.1016/j.neucom.2020.05.078

Gour, A. (2020). AI-based Natural Language Processing (NLP) Systems. *Journal of Algebraic Statistics, 11*(1), 48–58.

Gradescope . (n.d.). Gradescope. https://www.gradescope.com/

Graesser, A. C., Hu, X., & Sottilare, R. (2018). Intelligent tutoring systems. In *International Handbook of the Learning Sciences* (pp. 246–255). Routledge. doi:10.4324/9781315617572-24

Grassini, S. (2023). Shaping the future of education: Exploring the potential and consequences of AI and ChatGPT in educational settings. *Education Sciences, 13*(7), 692.

Green, B. P. (2018). Ethical reflections on artificial intelligence. *Scientia et Fides, 6*(2), 9–31. doi:10.12775/SetF.2018.015

Greer, S. L. (2018). *Organization and governance: Stewardship and governance in health systems. Health Care Systems and Policies*. Health Services Research. Springer.

Greiner, CPeisl, T. CHöpfl, FBeese, O. (2023). Acceptance of AI in Semi-Structured Decision-Making Situations Applying the Four-Sides Model of Communication—An Empirical Analysis Focused on Higher Education. *Education Sciences, 13*(9), 865.

Grenander, M., Belfer, R., Kochmar, E., Serban, I. V., St-Hilaire, F., & Cheung, J. C. (2021, May). Deep discourse analysis for generating personalized feedback in intelligent tutor systems. *Proceedings of the AAAI Conference on Artificial Intelligence, 35*(17), 15534–15544. doi:10.1609/aaai.v35i17.17829

Groot, P., Brinchmann, J., & Gieseke, F. (2018). Deep learning for cosmological surveys: Finding rare objects by anomaly detection. *Monthly Notices of the Royal Astronomical Society, 477*(4), 4967–4983.

Guangul, F. M., Suhail, A. H., Khalit, M. I., & Khidhir, B. A. (2020). Challenges of remote assessment in higher education in the context of COVID-19: A case study of Middle East College. *Educational Assessment, Evaluation and Accountability*, *32*(4), 519–535. doi:10.1007/s11092-020-09340-w PMID:33101539

Guegan, J., Brechet, C., & Nelson, J. (2021). Dreamlike and playful virtual environments to inspire children's divergent thinking. *Journal of Media Psychology*, *33*(1), 28–38. doi:10.1027/1864-1105/a000279

Guerrero-Roldán, A.-E., Rodríguez-González, M. E., Bañeres, D., Elasri-Ejjaberi, A., & Cortadas, P. (2021). Experiences in the use of an adaptive intelligent system to enhance online learners' performance: A case study in Economics and Business courses. *International Journal of Educational Technology in Higher Education*, *18*, 1–27.

Guilherme, A. (2019). AI and education: The importance of teacher and student relations. *AI & Society*, *34*(1), 47–54. doi:10.1007/s00146-017-0693-8

Gunawan, K., Kaniawati, I., & Setiawan, W. (2021). The responses to artificial intelligence in teacher integrated science learning training program. *Journal of Physics: Conference Series*.

Gundlach, E., & Ward, M. D. (2021). The data mine: Enabling data science across the curriculum. *Journal of Statistics and Data Science Education*, *29*(sup1), S74-S82.

Gunning, D. (2017). On the dark side of AI. arXiv preprint arXiv:1703.05057.

Guo, L., Wang, D., Gu, F., Li, Y., Wang, Y., & Zhou, R. (2021). *Evolution and trends in intelligent tutoring systems research: a multidisciplinary and scientometric view*.

Guo, Y., Zhang, Y., Liu, T., Prosperi, M., Wang, F., Xu, H., ... Bian, J. (2021). The application of artificial intelligence and data integration in COVID-19 studies: A scoping review. *Journal of the American Medical Informatics Association : JAMIA*, *28*(9), 2050–2067. doi:10.1093/jamia/ocab098 PMID:34151987

Hadi Mogavi, R., Deng, C., Juho Kim, J., Zhou, P., & Kwon, D., Y., Metwally, A., Tlili, A., Bassanelli, S., Bucchiarone, A., Gujar, S., Nacke, L. E., & Hui, P. (2024, January). ChatGPT in education: A blessing or a curse? A qualitative study exploring early adopters' utilization and perceptions. *Computers in Human Behavior: Artificial Humans*, *2*(1), 100027. doi:10.1016/j.chbah.2023.100027

Haenlein, MKaplan, A. (2019). A brief history of artificial intelligence: On the past, present, and future of artificial intelligence. *California Management Review*, *61*(4), 5–14.

Hagendorff, T. (2020). The ethics of AI ethics: An evaluation of guidelines. *Minds and Machines*, *30*(1), 99–120. doi:10.1007/s11023-020-09517-8

Hahn, M. G., Navarro, S. M. B., Valentín, L. D. L. F., & Burgos, D. (2021). A systematic review of the effects of automatic scoring and automatic feedback in educational settings. *IEEE Access : Practical Innovations, Open Solutions*, *9*, 108190–108198. doi:10.1109/ACCESS.2021.3100890

Halabi, O. (2020). Immersive virtual reality to enforce teaching in engineering education. *Multimedia Tools and Applications*, *79*(3-4), 2987–3004. doi:10.1007/s11042-019-08214-8

Halagatti, M., Gadag, S., Mahantshetti, S., Hiremath, C. V., Tharkude, D., & Banakar, V. (2023). Artificial Intelligence: The New Tool of Disruption in Educational Performance Assessment. In Smart Analytics, Artificial Intelligence and Sustainable Performance Management in a Global Digitalised Economy (pp. 261-287). Emerald Publishing Limited.

Haleem, A., Javaid, M., & Singh, R. P. (2022). An era of ChatGPT as a significant futuristic support tool: A study on features, abilities, and challenges. *BenchCouncil transactions on benchmarks, standards and evaluations, 2*(4), 100089.

Hall, E. E. (2023). *A User-Centered Design Approach to Evaluating the Usability of Automated Essay Scoring Systems.* Virginia Tech.

Han, C., Ling, C., & Ye, Y. (2020). Research on the influence of artificial intelligence on the economy and society. Destech Transactions on Engineering and Technology Research, (make). https://doi.org/ doi:10.12783/dtetr/mcaee2020/35030

Han, C., & Lu, X. (2023). Can automated machine translation evaluation metrics be used to assess students' interpretation in the language learning classroom? *Computer Assisted Language Learning*, *36*(5-6), 1064–1087. doi:10.1080/09588221.2021.1968915

Han, C., Xiao, R., & Su, W. (2021). Assessing the fidelity of consecutive interpreting. Interpreting. *Interpreting*, *23*(2), 245–268. doi:10.1075/intp.00058.han

Hannan, E., & Liu, S. (2023). AI: New source of competitiveness in higher education. *Competitiveness Review*, *33*(2), 265–279. doi:10.1108/CR-03-2021-0045

Hannousse, A. (2021). Searching relevant papers for software engineering secondary studies: Semantic scholar coverage and identification role. *IET Software*, *15*(1), 126–146. doi:10.1049/sfw2.12011

Hanrahan, S. J., & Isaacs, G. (2001). Assessing self-and peer-assessment: The students' views. *Higher Education Research & Development*, *20*(1), 53–70. doi:10.1080/07294360123776

Hargreaves, E. (2005). Assessment for learning? Thinking outside the (black) box. *Cambridge Journal of Education*, *35*(2), 213–224. doi:10.1080/03057640500146880

Harry, A. (2023). Revolutionizing Healthcare: The transformative role of artificial intelligence in the health sector. *BULLET: Jurnal Multidisiplin Ilmu*, *2*(2), 326–335.

Hasan, R., Palaniappan, S., Mahmood, S., Abbas, A., Sarker, K. U., & Sattar, M. U. (2020). Predicting student performance in higher educational institutions using video learning analytics and data mining techniques. *Applied Sciences (Basel, Switzerland)*, *10*(11), 3894. doi:10.3390/app10113894

Hassan, S. A. A. (2021). The Impact of Artificial Intelligence on the Accounting Profession in the Tourism Sector in Egypt. *International Journal of Applied Research, 7*(6), 319–328. doi:10.22271/allresearch.2021.v7.i6e.8716

Heil, J., & Ifenthaler, D. (2023). Online Assessment in Higher Education: A Systematic Review. *Online Learning : the Official Journal of the Online Learning Consortium, 27*(1), 187–218. doi:10.24059/olj.v27i1.3398

Helm, J. M., Swiergosz, A. M., Haeberle, H. S., Karnuta, J. M., Schaffer, J. L., Krebs, V. E., Spitzer, A. I., & Ramkumar, P. N. (2020). Machine learning and artificial intelligence: Definitions, applications, and future directions. *Current Reviews in Musculoskeletal Medicine, 13*, 69–76.

Hernández-Blanco, A., Herrera-Flores, B., Tomás, D., & Navarro-Colorado, B. (2019). A Systematic Review of Deep Learning Approaches to Educational Data Mining. *Complexity, 2019*, 1–22. doi:10.1155/2019/1306039

Hernandez-de-Menendez, M., Escobar Díaz, C. A., & Morales-Menendez, R. (2020). Educational experiences with Generation Z. [IJIDeM]. *International Journal on Interactive Design and Manufacturing, 14*(3), 847–859. doi:10.1007/s12008-020-00674-9

Herremans, D. (2021*). aiSTROM - A roadmap for developing a successful AI strategy.*

Herremans, D. (2021). *aiSTROM -- A roadmap for developing a successful AI strategy*. doi:10.1109/ACCESS.2021.3127548

Hickman, E., & Petrin, M. (2020). Trustworthy AI and Corporate Governance – The EU's Ethics Guidelines For Trustworthy Artificial Intelligence from a Company Law Perspective. SSRN *Electronic Journal*. doi:10.2139/ssrn.3607225

Hidalgo, A., Gabaly, S., Morales-Alonso, G., & Urueña, A. (2020). The digital divide in light of sustainable development: An approach through advanced machine learning techniques. *Technological Forecasting and Social Change, 150*, 119754. doi:10.1016/j.techfore.2019.119754

Hinojo-Lucena, F., Díaz, I., Cáceres-Reche, M., & Rodríguez, J. (2019). Artificial intelligence in higher education: A bibliometric study on its impact in the scientific literature. *Education Sciences, 9*(1), 51. doi:10.3390/educsci9010051

Hogenhout, L. (2021). *A framework for ethical AI at the United Nations*. arXiv preprint arXiv:2104.12547.

Holmes, W., Bialik, M., & Fadel, C. (2019, February 28). *Artificial Intelligence in Education*. http://books.google.ie/books?id=tzO7wgEACAAJ&dq=Artificial+Intelligence+in+Education:+A+Review&hl=&cd=1&source=gbs_api

Holmes, W., Porayska-Pomsta, K., Holstein, K., Sutherland, E., Baker, T., Shum, S. B., Santos, O. C., Rodrigo, M. T., Cukurova, M., Bittencourt, I. I., & Koedinger, K. R. (2022). Ethics of AI in education: Towards a community-wide framework. *International Journal of Artificial Intelligence in Education, 32*(3), 1–23. doi:10.1007/s40593-021-00239-1

Holmes, W., & Tuomi, I. (2022, October 30). State of the art and practice in AI in education. *European Journal of Education*, *57*(4), 542–570. doi:10.1111/ejed.12533

Hooda, M., Rana, C., Dahiya, O., Rizwan, A., & Hossain, M. S. (2022). Artificial intelligence for assessment and feedback to enhance student success in higher education. *Mathematical Problems in Engineering*, *2022*, 2022. doi:10.1155/2022/5215722

Hopfenbeck, T. N., Zhang, Z., Sun, S., Robertson, P., & McGrane, J. A. (2023). Challenges and opportunities for classroom-based formative assessment and AI: A perspective article. []. Frontiers.]. *Frontiers in Education*, *8*, 1270700. doi:10.3389/feduc.2023.1270700

Hoq, M. Z. (2020). E-Learning during the period of pandemic (COVID-19) in the kingdom of Saudi Arabia: An empirical study. *American Journal of Educational Research*, *8*(7), 457–464.

Ho, S. P. S., & Chow, M. Y. C. (2023). The Role of Artificial Intelligence in Consumers' Brand Preference for Retail Banks in Hong Kong. *Journal of Financial Services Marketing*. doi:10.1057/s41264-022-00207-3

Hoti, A. H., Zenuni, X., Hamiti, M., & Ajdari, J. (2023, June). Student performance prediction using AI and ML: state of the art. In *2023 12th Mediterranean Conference on Embedded Computing (MECO)* (pp. 1-6). IEEE. 10.1109/MECO58584.2023.10154933

Hourani, H., Hammad, A., & Lafi, M. (2019). The impact of artificial intelligence on software testing. *2019 IEEE Jordan International Joint Conference on Electrical Engineering and Information Technology (JEEIT)*. IEEE.

Hu, H., Misra, I., & Maaten, L. (2019). Evaluating text-to-image matching using binary image selection (bison).. https://doi.org/ doi:10.1109/ICCVW.2019.00237

Huang, J., Saleh, S., & Liu, Y. (2021). A review on artificial intelligence in education. *Academic Journal of Interdisciplinary Studies, 10*(3).

Huang, A. Y., Lu, O. H., & Yang, S. J. (2023). Effects of artificial Intelligence–Enabled personalized recommendations on learners' learning engagement, motivation, and outcomes in a flipped classroom. *Computers & Education*, *194*, 104684. doi:10.1016/j.compedu.2022.104684

Huang, C., Zhang, Z., Mao, B., & Yao, X. (2023). An overview of artificial intelligence ethics. *IEEE Transactions on Artificial Intelligence*, *4*(4), 799–819. doi:10.1109/TAI.2022.3194503

Huang, L. (2023). Ethics of artificial intelligence in education: Student privacy and data protection. *Science Insights Education Frontiers*, *16*(2), 2577–2587. doi:10.15354/sief.23.re202

Huang, M. (2022). Research on C++ System Practice of Online Auxiliary Teaching Platform based on Trusted Data Analysis. *2022 International Conference on Inventive Computation Technologies (ICICT)*

Huang, M. H., & Rust, R. T. (2020). A Strategic Framework for Artificial Intelligence in Marketing. *Journal of the Academy of Marketing Science*. doi:10.1007/s11747-020-00749-9

Humble, N., & Mozelius, P. (2022). Discover. *Artificial Intelligence.*

Hunkenschroer, A. L., & Luetge, C. (2022). Ethics of AI-Enabled Recruiting and Selection: A Review and Research Agenda. In Journal of Business Ethics, 178(4). Springer Science and Business Media B.V. doi:10.1007/s10551-022-05049-6

Husain, N. (2023). Educational Renaissance: Unleashing the Potential of Interdisciplinary AI Integration. *Journal of Environmental Science and Technology*, *2*(1), 159–166.

Hutson, J., Jeevanjee, T., Vander Graaf, V., Lively, J., Weber, J., Weir, G., Arnone, K., Carnes, G., Vosevich, K., Plate, D., & Leary, M. (2022). Artificial Intelligence and the Disruption of Higher Education: Strategies for Integrations across Disciplines. *Creative Education*, *13*(12), 3953–3980. doi:10.4236/ce.2022.1312253

Hutson, M. (2018). *Big data in science: From hype to reality*. Routledge.

Hwang, D., Oh, H., & Lee, S. (2021). Asimov: A framework for simulation and optimisation of an embedded AI accelerator. *Micromachines*, *12*(7), 838. doi:10.3390/mi12070838 PMID:34357248

Ifenthaler, D. (2022). Automated essay scoring systems. In *Handbook of open, distance and digital education* (pp. 1–15). Springer. doi:10.1007/978-981-19-0351-9_59-1

Ifenthaler, D., & Yau, J. Y.-K. (2020). Utilising learning analytics to support study success in higher education: A systematic review. *Educational Technology Research and Development*, *68*(4), 1961–1990. doi:10.1007/s11423-020-09788-z

Iglesias Pérez, M. C., Vidal-Puga, J., & Pino Juste, M. R. (2022). The role of self and peer assessment in Higher Education. *Studies in Higher Education*, *47*(3), 683–692. doi:10.1080/03075079.2020.1783526

IMDA & PDPC. (2020). *Model Artificial Intelligence Governance Framework*. IMDA & PDPC.

Indriasari, T. D., Luxton-Reilly, A., & Denny, P. (2020). Gamification of student peer review in education: A systematic literature review. *Education and Information Technologies*, *25*(6), 5205–5234. doi:10.1007/s10639-020-10228-x

Iqbal, M. S., Abd-Alrazaq, A., & Househ, M. (2022). *Artificial Intelligence Solutions to Detect Fraud in Healthcare Settings: A Scoping Review*. doi:10.3233/SHTI220649

Islam, MMazlan, N. HAl Murshidi, GHoque, M. SKarthiga, SReza, M. (2023). UAE university students' experiences of virtual classroom learning during Covid 19. Smart Learning Environments, 10(1), 5.

Ismail, F. (2023). Artificial Intelligence in higher education. A protocol paper for a Systematic Literature Review. *Journal of Applied Learning and Teaching*, *6*(2), 56–63. doi:10.37074/jalt.2023.6.2.34

Ismail, S. M., Rahul, D., Patra, I., & Rezvani, E. (2022). Formative vs. summative assessment: Impacts on academic motivation, attitude toward learning, test anxiety, and self-regulation skill. *Language Testing in Asia*, *12*(1), 40. doi:10.1186/s40468-022-00191-4

Israel, M. J., & Amer, A. (2023). Rethinking data infrastructure and its ethical implications in the face of automated digital content generation. *AI and Ethics*, *3*(2), 427–439. doi:10.1007/s43681-022-00169-1

Ivanov, S. (2023). The dark side of artificial intelligence in higher education. *Service Industries Journal*, *43*(15-16), 1055–1082.

Jadrić, M., Ćukušić, M., & Mijač, T. (2021). Relating Smart Governance as a University Feature to Students' University Perceptions. *Journal of Information and Organizational Sciences*, *45*(1), 1–20. doi:10.31341/jios.45.1.1

Jahani, N., Sepehri, A., Vandchali, H. R., & Tirkolaee, E. B. (2021). Application of industry 4.0 in the procurement processes of supply chains: A systematic literature review. *Sustainability (Basel)*, *13*(14), 7520. doi:10.3390/su13147520

Jain, E., Chopra, T., & Sharma, S. K. (2023). *Reinventing Human Resource Management in the Era of Artificial Intelligence*. doi:10.4108/eai.16-12-2022.2326241

Jain, G. P., Gurupur, V. P., Schroeder, J. L., & Faulkenberry, E. D. (2014). Artificial intelligence-based student learning evaluation: A concept map-based approach for analyzing a student's understanding of a topic. *IEEE Transactions on Learning Technologies*, *7*(3), 267–279. doi:10.1109/TLT.2014.2330297

Jain, P., & Aggarwal, D. (2020). Predictive analytics in higher education: Enhancing student engagement. *International Journal of Data Science*, *5*(2), 145–160.

Jakoet-Salie, A., & Ramalobe, K. (2022). *The Digitalization of Learning and Teaching Practices in Higher Education Institutions During the Covid-19 Pandemic*. Teaching Public Administration., doi:10.1177/01447394221092275

Jansen, R. S., van Leeuwen, A., Janssen, J., Conijn, R., & Kester, L. (2020). Supporting learners' self-regulated learning in Massive Open Online Courses. *Computers & Education*, *146*, 103771. doi:10.1016/j.compedu.2019.103771

JawaidS. A. (2023). *Artificial Intelligence With Respect to Cyber Security*. https://doi.org/doi:10.20944/preprints202304.0923.v1

Jayakumar, S., Sounderajah, V., Normahani, P., Harling, L., Markar, S. R., Ashrafian, H., & Darzi, A. (2022). Quality assessment standards in artificial intelligence diagnostic accuracy systematic reviews: A meta-research study. *NPJ Digital Medicine*, *5*(1), 11.

Jiang, F., Jiang, Y., Zhi, H., Dong, Y., Li, H., Ma, S., Wang, Y., Dong, Q., Shen, H., & Wang, Y. (2017). Artificial intelligence in healthcare: Past, present and future. *Stroke and Vascular Neurology*, *2*(4), 230–243. doi:10.1136/svn-2017-000101 PMID:29507784

JiM.ChenX.GenchevG.XuT.WeiM.YuG. (2020). Status of ai-enabled clinical decision support systems clinical implementations in China. https://doi.org/ doi:10.21203/rs.2.22387/v1

Jobin, A., Ienca, M., & Vayanos, P. (2019). The ethics of artificial intelligence. *Nature*, *562*(7723), 288–293.

Jobin, A., Ienca, M., & Vayena, E. (2019). The global landscape of AI ethics guidelines. *Nature Machine Intelligence*, *1*(9), 389–399. doi:10.1038/s42256-019-0088-2

Jöhnk, J., Weißert, M., & Wyrtki, K. (2020). Ready or Not, AI Comes— An Interview Study of Organizational AI Readiness Factors. *Business & Information Systems Engineering*. doi:10.1007/s12599-020-00676-7

Johnson, M., Albizri, A., & Simsek, S. (2022). Artificial intelligence in healthcare operations to enhance treatment outcomes: A framework to predict lung cancer prognosis. *Annals of Operations Research*, *308*(1-2), 1–31. doi:10.1007/s10479-020-03872-6

Jokhan, A., Chand, A. A., Singh, V., & Mamun, K. A. (2022). Increased digital resource consumption in higher educational institutions and the artificial intelligence role in informing decisions related to student performance. *sustainability, 14*(4), 2377.

Jopp, R. (2020). A case study of a technology enhanced learning initiative that supports authentic assessment. *Teaching in Higher Education*, *25*(8), 942–958. doi:10.1080/13562517.2019.1613637

Jufrida, J., Basuki, F. R., Kurniawan, W., Pangestu, M. D., & Fitaloka, O. (2019). Scientific literacy and science learning achievement at junior high school [IJERE]. *International Journal of Evaluation and Research in Education*, *8*(4), 630–636. doi:10.11591/ijere.v8i4.20312

Juma, Z. R. (2015). *Exploring the development of biological literacy in Tanzanian junior secondary school students*. Open Access Te Herenga Waka-Victoria University of Wellington.

Jumper, J., Evans, R., Pritzel, A., Green, M. F., Figurn, V., Ronneberger, O., ... Senior, K. (2021). Highly accurate protein structure prediction with AlphaFold. *Nature*, *596*(7877), 587–594. doi:10.1038/s41586-021-03819-2 PMID:34265844

JungwirthD.HaluzaD. (2023). Feasibility study on utilisation of the artificial intelligence got-3 in public health. doi:10.20944/preprints202301.0521.v1

Jurāne-Brēmane, A. (2023). Digital assessment in technology-enriched education: Thematic review. *Education Sciences*, *13*(5), 522. doi:10.3390/educsci13050522

Kabudi, T., Pappas, I., & Olsen, D. H. (2021). AI-enabled adaptive learning systems: A systematic mapping of the literature. *Computers and Education: Artificial Intelligence*, *2*, 100017. doi:10.1016/j.caeai.2021.100017

Kahoot: Kahoot! for schools Assessment. (n.d.). Kahoot. https://kahoot.com/schools/assessment/

Kaledio, P., Robert, A., & Frank, L. (2024). The Impact of Artificial Intelligence on Students' Learning Experience. SSRN *Electronic Journal*. https://doi.org/ doi:10.2139/ssrn.4716747

Kamalov, F., & Gurrib, I. (2023). A new era of artificial intelligence in education: A multifaceted revolution. *arXiv preprint arXiv:2305.18303*.

Kamalov, F., Thabtah, F., & Gurrib, I. (2021). *Autocorrelation for Time Series With Linear Trend*. IEEE. doi:10.1109/3ICT53449.2021.9581809

Kamalov, F., Santandreu Calonge, D., & Gurrib, I. (2023). New era of artificial intelligence in education: Towards a sustainable multifaceted revolution. *Sustainability (Basel)*, *15*(16), 12451. doi:10.3390/su151612451

Kamalov, F., Santandreu Calonge, D., & Gurrib, I. (2023). New era of artificial intelligence in education: Towards a sustainable multifaceted revolution. *Sustainability*, *15*(16), 12451.

Kaminski, M. E. (2022). Regulating the Risks of AI. SSRN *Electronic Journal*. doi:10.2139/ssrn.4195066

Kamruzzaman, M., Alanazi, S., Alruwaili, M., Alshammari, N., Elaiwat, S., Abu-Zanona, M., Innab, N., Mohammad Elzaghmouri, B., & Ahmed Alanazi, B. (2023). AI-and IoT-Assisted Sustainable Education Systems during Pandemics, such as COVID-19, for Smart Cities. *Sustainability (Basel)*, *15*(10), 8354. doi:10.3390/su15108354

Karadağ, N. (2023). The impact of artificial intelligence on online assessment: A preliminary review. *Journal of Educational Technology and Online Learning*, *6*(4), 822–837. doi:10.31681/jetol.1351548

Kasneci, E., Seßler, K., Küchemann, S., Bannert, M., Dementieva, D., Fischer, F., Gasser, U., Groh, G., Günnemann, S., Hüllermeier, E., Krusche, S., Kutyniok, G., Michaeli, T., Nerdel, C., Pfeffer, J., Poquet, O., Sailer, M., Schmidt, A., Seidel, T., & Kasneci, G. (2023). ChatGPT for good? On opportunities and challenges of large language models for education. *Learning and Individual Differences*, *103*, 102274. doi:10.1016/j.lindif.2023.102274

Kaswan, K. S., Dhatterwal, J. S., & Ojha, R. P. (n.d.) AI in personalized learning. In *Advances in Technological Innovations in Higher Education* (pp. 103–117). CRC Press.

Katz, O., Presil, D., Cohen, L., Nachmani, R., Kirshner, N., Hoch, Y., Lev, T., Hadad, A., Hewitt, R. J., & Owens, D. R. (2022). Evaluation of a new neural network classifier for diabetic retinopathy. *Journal of Diabetes Science and Technology*, *16*(6), 1401–1409. doi:10.1177/19322968211042665 PMID:34549633

Kauppi, S., Muukkonen, H., Suorsa, T., & Takala, M. (2020). I still miss human contact, but this is more flexible—Paradoxes in virtual learning interaction and multidisciplinary collaboration. *British Journal of Educational Technology*, *51*(4), 1101–1116. doi:10.1111/bjet.12929

Kazim, E., & Koshiyama, A. (2021). A high-level overview of AI ethics. *Patterns (New York, N.Y.)*, *2*(9), 100314. doi:10.1016/j.patter.2021.100314 PMID:34553166

Kear, A., & Folkes, S. (2020). A solution to artificial intelligence's hypercomplex, cross-domain reality: The hierarchy of AI. *International Journal of Advanced Computer Science and Applications*, *11*(3). Advance online publication. doi:10.14569/IJACSA.2020.0110307

Kelly, S. M. (2023). *Teachers are adapting to concerns about a powerful new AI tool*. CNN. https://edition.cnn.com/2023/01/19/tech/chatgpt-teachers-adjusting/index.html

Khan, I., Ahmad, A. R., Jabeur, N., & Mahdi, M. N. (2021). An artificial intelligence approach to monitor student performance and devise preventive measures. *Smart Learning Environments*, *8*(1), 1–18.

Khatri, M. (2021). How digital marketing along with artificial intelligence is transforming consumer behaviour. *International Journal for Research in Applied Science and Engineering Technology*, *9*(VII), 523–527. doi:10.22214/ijraset.2021.36287

Khosravi, H., Shum, S. B., Chen, G., Conati, C., Tsai, Y.-S., Kay, J., Knight, S., Martinez-Maldonado, R., Sadiq, S., & Gašević, D. (2022). Explainable artificial intelligence in education. *Computers and Education: Artificial Intelligence*, *3*, 100074.

Kibble, J. D. (2017). Best practices in summative assessment. *Advances in Physiology Education*, *41*(1), 110–119. doi:10.1152/advan.00116.2016 PMID:28188198

Kiennert, C., Rocher, P.-O., Ivanova, M., Rozeva, A., Durcheva, M., & Garcia-Alfaro, J. (2017). Security challenges in e-assessment and technical solutions. *Paper presented at the 2017 21st International Conference Information Visualisation (IV)*. IEEE. 10.1109/iV.2017.70

Kim, J. (2019). Case Study About Efficient AI(Artificial Intelligence) Implementation Strategy. *International Journal of Advanced Research in Big Data Management System*. doi:10.21742/IJARBMS.2019.3.2.01

Kim, D., Jang, H., Kim, K., Shin, Y., & Park, S. (2019). Design characteristics of studies reporting the performance of artificial intelligence algorithms for diagnostic analysis of medical images: Results from recently published papers. *Korean Journal of Radiology*, *20*(3), 405. doi:10.3348/kjr.2019.0025 PMID:30799571

Kim, J., Lee, H., & Cho, Y. H. (2022). Learning design to support student-AI collaboration: Perspectives of leading teachers for AI in education. *Education and Information Technologies*, *27*(5), 6069–6104.

Kindzeka, K. C. (2023). Impact of Artificial Intelligence on Accounting, Auditing and Financial Reporting. *American Journal of Computing and Engineering*. doi:10.47672/ajce.1433

King, M. R., & Chat, G. P. T. (2023). A conversation on artificial intelligence, chatbots, and plagiarism in higher education. *Cellular and Molecular Bioengineering*, *16*(1), 1–2. doi:10.1007/s12195-022-00754-8 PMID:36660590

Kitsios, F., & Kamariotou, M. (2021). Artificial intelligence and business strategy towards digital transformation: A research agenda. *Sustainability (Basel)*, *13*(4), 2025. doi:10.3390/su13042025

Klimova, B., Pikhart, M., & Kacetl, J. (2023). Ethical issues of the use of AI-driven mobile apps for education. *Frontiers in Public Health*, *10*, 1118116. doi:10.3389/fpubh.2022.1118116 PMID:36711343

Knight, P. T. (2002). Summative assessment in higher education: Practices in disarray. *Studies in Higher Education*, *27*(3), 275–286. doi:10.1080/03075070220000662

Köchling, A., Wehner, M. C., & Warkocz, J. (2022). Can I Show My Skills? Affective Responses to Artificial Intelligence in the Recruitment Process. *Review of Managerial Science*. doi:10.1007/s11846-021-00514-4

Kochmar, E., Vu, D. D., Belfer, R., Gupta, V., Serban, I. V., & Pineau, J. (2020). Automated personalized feedback improves learning gains in an intelligent tutoring system. In *Artificial Intelligence in Education: 21st International Conference, AIED 2020, Ifrane, Morocco, July 6–10, 2020* [Springer International Publishing.]. *Proceedings*, *21*(Part II), 140–146.

Koedinger, K. R., Brunskill, E., Baker, R. S. J. D., McLaughlin, E. A., & Stamper, J. (2013, September). New Potentials for Data-Driven Intelligent Tutoring System Development and Optimization. *AI Magazine*, *34*(3), 27–41. doi:10.1609/aimag.v34i3.2484

Kohnke, L., Moorhouse, B. L., & Zou, D. (2023). Exploring generative artificial intelligence preparedness among university language instructors: A case study. *Computers and Education: Artificial Intelligence*, *5*, 100156. doi:10.1016/j.caeai.2023.100156

Kolstø, S. D. (2001). Scientific literacy for citizenship: Tools for dealing with the science dimension of controversial socioscientific issues. *Science Education*, *85*(3), 291–310. doi:10.1002/sce.1011

Korn, J., & Kelly, S. (2023). *New York City public schools ban access to AI tool that could help students cheat*. CNN.

Kucirkova, N., Gerard, L., & Linn, M. C. (2021). Designing personalised instruction: A research and design framework. *British Journal of Educational Technology*, *52*(5), 1839–1861. doi:10.1111/bjet.13119

Kuleto, V., Ilić, M., Dumangiu, M., Ranković, M., Martins, O. M., Păun, D., & Mihoreanu, L. (2021). Exploring opportunities and challenges of artificial intelligence and machine learning in higher education institutions. *sustainability, 13*(18), 10424.

Kuleto, V., Ilić, M., Dumangiu, M., Ranković, M., Martins, O. M., Păun, D., & Mihoreanu, L. (2021). Exploring opportunities and challenges of artificial intelligence and machine learning in higher education institutions. *Sustainability (Basel)*, *13*(18), 10424. doi:10.3390/su131810424

Kumar, A., Krishnamurthi, R., Bhatia, S., Kaushik, K., Ahuja, N. J., Nayyar, A., & Masud, M. (2021). Blended learning tools and practices: A comprehensive analysis. *IEEE Access : Practical Innovations, Open Solutions*, *9*, 85151–85197. doi:10.1109/ACCESS.2021.3085844

Kumar, J. A., Bervell, B., & Osman, S. (2020). Google classroom: Insights from Malaysian higher education students' and instructors' experiences. *Education and Information Technologies*, *25*(5), 4175–4195.

Kumar, R. (2023). Faculty members' use of artificial intelligence to grade student papers: A case of implications. *International Journal for Educational Integrity*, *19*(1), 1–10.

Kumar, V. V. R., & Raman, R. (2022). Artificial Intelligence (AI) as a computerized decision aid for selection of candidates in higher education. *2022 IEEE Integrated STEM Education Conference. ISEC, 439–443*, 439–443. doi:10.1109/ISEC54952.2022.10025234

Kundi, B., El Morr, C., Gorman, R., & Dua, E. (2023). Artificial Intelligence and Bias: A scoping review. *AI & Society*, 199–215.

Kuo, B.-C., Chang, F. T.-Y., & Lee, Y.-L. (2023). Trends and Issues of Digital Learning in Taiwan. *Trends and Issues of Promoting Digital Learning in High-Digital-Competitiveness Countries: Country Reports and International Comparison.*

Kurysheva, A., van Rijen, H. V. M., & Dilaver, G. (2019). How Do Admission Committees Select? Do Applicants Know How They Select? Selection Criteria and Transparency at a Dutch University. *Tertiary Education and Management*, *25*(4), 367–388. Advance online publication. doi:10.1007/s11233-019-09050-z

Kuzminsky, J., Phillips, H., Sharif, H., Moran, C., Gleason, H. E., Topulos, S. P., Pitt, K., McNeil, L. K., McCoy, A. M., & Kesavadas, T. (2023). Reliability in performance assessment creates a potential application of artificial intelligence in veterinary education: evaluation of suturing skills at a single institution. *American journal of veterinary research, 1*(aop), 1-11.

Laato, S., Morschheuser, B., Hamari, J., & Bjorne, J. (2023). AI-Assisted Learning with ChatGPT and Large Language Models: Implications for Higher Education. *Proceedings - 2023 IEEE International Conference on Advanced Learning Technologies, ICALT 2023*, (pp. 226–230). IEEE. 10.1109/ICALT58122.2023.00072

Labadze, L., Grigolia, M., & Machaidze, L. (2023). Role of AI chatbots in education: Systematic literature review. *International Journal of Educational Technology in Higher Education*, *20*(1), 56. doi:10.1186/s41239-023-00426-1

LabPlot: Kwok, H. Y., & Wong, P. K. (2015). LabPlot: A scientific graphing and data analysis software package. *Computer Applications in Science and Technology*, *7*(1), 35–43.

Lai, T., Xie, C., Ruan, M., Wang, Z., Lu, H., & Fu, S. (2023). Influence of artificial intelligence in education on adolescents' social adaptability: The mediatory role of social support. *PLoS One*, *18*(3), e0283170. doi:10.1371/journal.pone.0283170 PMID:36930593

Lamberti, M., Wilkinson, M., Donzanti, B., Wohlhieter, G., Parikh, S., Wilkins, R., & Getz, K. (2019). A study on the application and use of artificial intelligence to support drug development. *Clinical Therapeutics*, *41*(8), 1414–1426. doi:10.1016/j.clinthera.2019.05.018 PMID:31248680

Lameras, P., & Arnab, S. (2021, December 29). Power to the Teachers: An Exploratory Review on Artificial Intelligence in Education. *Information (Basel)*, *13*(1), 14. doi:10.3390/info13010014

Lancioni, R. A. (2013). Artificial Intelligence in Higher Education: Current Uses and Future Trends. *Journal of Educational Technology & Society*, *16*(3), 48–61.

Landauer, T. K. (2003). Automatic Essay Assessment, Assessment in Education: Principles. *Assessment in Education: Principles, Policy & Practice*, *10*(3), 295–308. doi:10.1080/0969594032000148154

Lane, A. (2017, November 20). Open Education and the Sustainable Development Goals: Making Change Happen. *Journal of Learning for Development*, *4*(3). doi:10.56059/jl4d.v4i3.266

Larsson, S., & Heintz, F. (2020). Transparency in artificial intelligence. *Internet Policy Review*, *9*(2), 1–16. doi:10.14763/2020.2.1469

Lau, A., & Staccini, P. (2019). Artificial intelligence in health: New opportunities, challenges, and practical implications. *Yearbook of Medical Informatics*, *28*(01), 174–178. doi:10.1055/s-0039-1677935 PMID:31419829

Lauriola, I., Lavelli, A., & Aiolli, F. (2022). An introduction to deep learning in natural language processing: Models, techniques, and tools. *Neurocomputing*, *470*, 443–456. doi:10.1016/j.neucom.2021.05.103

Le, D.-N., Van Le, C., Tromp, J. G., & Nguyen, G. N. (2018). *Emerging technologies for health and medicine: virtual reality, augmented reality, artificial intelligence, internet of things, robotics, industry 4.0*.

Lee, H. (2023). The rise of ChatGPT: Exploring its potential in medical education. *Anatomical Sciences Education*, ase.2270. doi:10.1002/ase.2270 PMID:36916887

Lee, R. S. T. (2020). Smart Education. In *Artificial Intelligence in Daily Life*. Springer. doi:10.1007/978-981-15-7695-9_11

Lee, T., Wen, Y., Chan, M., Azam, A., Looi, C. K., Taib, S., Ooi, C. H., Huang, L. H., Xie, Y., & Cai, Y. (2022). Investigation of virtual & augmented reality classroom learning environments in university STEM education. *Interactive Learning Environments*, 1–16. doi:10.1080/10494820.2022.2155838

Leimanis, A., & Palkova, K. (2021). Ethical Guidelines for Artificial Intelligence in Healthcare From the Sustainable Development Perspective. *European Journal of Sustainable Development*, *10*(1), 90. doi:10.14207/ejsd.2021.v10n1p90

LelliF. (2022). *On Exploring the Possibilities and the Limits of AI for an Interoperable and Empowering Industry 4.0*. doi:10.20944/preprints202202.0109.v1

Leslie, D. (2019). *Understanding artificial intelligence ethics and safety: A guide for the responsible design and implementation of AI systems in the public sector*.

Levine, S. (2000). Ethical Considerations in the Use of AI in Higher Education. *Journal of Higher Education Ethics*, *4*(2), 28–35.

Levinson, R. (2006). Towards a Theoretical Framework for Teaching Controversial Socio-scientific Issues. *International Journal of Science Education*, *28*(10), 1201–1224. doi:10.1080/09500690600560753

Lew, M. D., Alwis, W. A. M., & Schmidt, H. G. (2010). Accuracy of students' self-assessment and their beliefs about its utility. *Assessment & Evaluation in Higher Education*, *35*(2), 135–156. doi:10.1080/02602930802687737

Liang, J. C., Hwang, G. J., Chen, M. R. A., & Darmawansah, D. (2021, July 28). Roles and research foci of artificial intelligence in language education: An integrated bibliographic analysis and systematic review approach. *Interactive Learning Environments*, *31*(7), 4270–4296. doi:10.1080/10494820.2021.1958348

Librarian, A., & Chakravarty, R. (2021). *Implementing Conversation al AI in Libraries: A practical approach Subhajit Panda.*

Lieto, A., Bhatt, M., Oltramari, A., & Vernon, D. (2018). The role of cognitive architectures in general artificial intelligence. *Cognitive Systems Research*, *48*, 1–3. doi:10.1016/j.cogsys.2017.08.003

Lim, S. M., & Rodger, S. (2010). Use of formative assessment to enhance learning. *Focus on Health Professional Education: A Multi-disciplinary Journal, 12*(2), 30-33.

Lin, C. C., Huang, A. Y., & Lu, O. H. (2023). Artificial intelligence in intelligent tutoring systems toward sustainable education: A systematic review. *Smart Learning Environments*, *10*(1), 41. doi:10.1186/s40561-023-00260-y

Lipton, Z. C. (2016). *The mythos of model interpretability. Why does AI matter? Essays on the societal consequences of artificial intelligence*. Princeton University Press.

Li, R., Wang, Y., & Zou, J. (2022). Research on the Transformation From Financial Accounting to Management Accounting Based on Drools Rule Engine. *Computational Intelligence and Neuroscience*, *2022*, 1–8. doi:10.1155/2022/9445776 PMID:35498191

Li, R., Yang, Y., Wu, S., Huang, K., Chen, W., Liu, Y., & Lin, H. (2020). Using artificial intelligence to improve medical services in China. *Annals of Translational Medicine*, *8*(11), 711–711. doi:10.21037/atm.2019.11.108 PMID:32617331

Liu, H., Liu, Z., Wu, Z., & Tang, J. (2020). Personalized multimodal feedback generation in education. *arXiv preprint arXiv:2011.00192*. doi:10.18653/v1/2020.coling-main.166

Liu, C., Hou, J., Tu, Y.-F., Wang, Y., & Hwang, G.-J. (2023). Incorporating a reflective thinking promoting mechanism into artificial intelligence-supported English writing environments. *Interactive Learning Environments*, *31*(9), 5614–5632. doi:10.1080/10494820.2021.2012812

Liu, L. T., Wang, S., Britton, T., & Abebe, R. (2023). Reimagining the machine learning life cycle to improve educational outcomes of students. *Proceedings of the National Academy of Sciences of the United States of America*, *120*(9), e2204781120.

Liu, X. (2009). Bilim okuryazarlığının ötesinde: Bilim ve halk. *Uluslararası Çevre ve Bilim Eğitimi Dergisi*, *4*(3), 301–311.

Liu, X., Cheng, Y., Zheng, Q., Yang, H., Zhu, W., & Wu, M. (2019). Artificial intelligence in medical diagnosis: A review. *Engineering*, *5*(5), 1152–1159.

Liu, Y., Yang, F., Gomez, A., & Carbonell, J. (2017). Automated discovery of event sequences in text for historical analysis. In *Proceedings of the 2017 Conference on Empirical Methods in Natural Language Processing* (pp. 3048-3058).

Li, W., et, al. (2021). Disparities in students' propensity to consent to learning analytics. *International Journal of Artificial Intelligence in Education.*

Li, X. (2007). Intelligent agent-supported online education. *Decision Sciences Journal of Innovative Education, 5*(2), 311–331. doi:10.1111/j.1540-4609.2007.00143.x

Lo, C. K. (2023). What is the impact of ChatGPT on education? A rapid review of the literature. *Education Sciences, 13*(4), 410. doi:10.3390/educsci13040410

Loh, E. (2018). Medicine and the rise of the robots: A qualitative review of recent advances of artificial intelligence in health. *BMJ Leader, 2*(2), 59–63. doi:10.1136/leader-2018-000071

Lok, B., McNaught, C., & Young, K. (2016). Criterion-referenced and norm-referenced assessments: Compatibility and complementarity. *Assessment & Evaluation in Higher Education, 41*(3), 450–465. doi:10.1080/02602938.2015.1022136

Luan, H., Geczy, P., Lai, H., & Li, P. (2020). Challenges and future directions of big data and artificial intelligence in education. *Frontiers in Psychology, 11*, 580820. doi:10.3389/fpsyg.2020.580820 PMID:33192896

Lubinga, S. N., Maramura, T. C., & Masiya, T. (2023). *Adoption of Fourth Industrial Revolution: challenges in South African higher education institutions.*

Luckin, R., Cukurova, M., Kent, C., & du Boulay, B. (2022). Empowering educators to be AI-ready. *Computers and Education: Artificial Intelligence, 3*, 100076.

Luckin, R., Holmes, W., Griffiths, M., & Forcier, L. B. (2016). *Intelligence Unleashed: An argument for AI in Education.* Pearson Education.

Ludwig, S., Mayer, C., Hansen, C., Eilers, K., & Brandt, S. (2021). Automated essay scoring using transformer models. *Psych, 3*(4), 897–915. doi:10.3390/psych3040056

Luitse, D., Blanke, T., & Poell, T. (2023). *Ai competitions as infrastructures: examining power relations on kaggle and grand challenge in ai-driven medical imaging.* Aoir Selected Papers of Internet Research., doi:10.5210/spir.v2022i0.13044

Lukasenko, R., Anohina-Naumeca, A., Vilkelis, M., & Grundspenkis, J. (2010). Feedback in the concept map based intelligent knowledge assessment system. *Rigas Tehniskas Universitates Zinatniskie Raksti, 43*(1), 17. doi:10.2478/v10143-010-0020-z

Luo, Q. Z. (2023). The Influence of AI-Powered Adaptive Learning Platforms on Student Performance in Chinese Classrooms. *Journal of Education, 6*(3), 1–12. doi:10.53819/81018102t4181

Luthfiyyah, R., Aisyah, A., & Sulistyo, G. H. (2021). Technology-enhanced formative assessment in higher education: A voice from Indonesian EFL teachers. *EduLite: Journal of English Education. Literature and Culture*, *6*(1), 42–54.

Lynch, L. (2024) *Ai in education: Introduction.* Britannica. https://britannicaeducation.com/blog/ai-in-education/

Mageira, K., Pittou, D., Papasalouros, A., Kotis, K., Zangogianni, P., & Daradoumis, A. (2022). Educational AI chatbots for content and language integrated learning. *Applied Sciences (Basel, Switzerland)*, *12*(7), 3239. doi:10.3390/app12073239

Maghsudi, S., Lan, A., Xu, J., & van Der Schaar, M. (2021). Personalized education in the artificial intelligence era: What to expect next. *IEEE Signal Processing Magazine*, *38*(3), 37–50. doi:10.1109/MSP.2021.3055032

Magnisalis, I., Demetriadis, S., & Karakostas, A. (2011). Adaptive and Intelligent Systems for Collaborative Learning Support: A Review of the Field. *IEEE Transactions on Learning Technologies*, *4*(1), 5–20. doi:10.1109/TLT.2011.2

Mahligawati, F., Allanas, E., Butarbutar, M. H., & Nordin, N. A. N. (2023). Artificial Intelligence in Physics Education: A Comprehensive Literature Review. *Journal of Physics: Conference Series*, *2596*(1), 012080. doi:10.1088/1742-6596/2596/1/012080

Maleki, N., Padmanabhan, B., & Dutta, K. (2024). *AI Hallucinations: A Misnomer Worth Clarifying*. arXiv preprint arXiv:2401.06796.

Malik, A., Thevisuthan, P., & De Sliva, T. (2022). *Artificial Intelligence*. Employee Engagement, Experience, and HRM., doi:10.1007/978-3-030-90955-0_16

Manhica, R., Santos, A., & Cravino, J. (2022). The use of artificial intelligence in learning management systems in the context of higher education: Systematic literature review. *2022 17th Iberian Conference on Information Systems and Technologies (CISTI)*, (pp. 1-6). IEEE.

Manikandan, S. (2023, August). AI; A New Horizon of Promises & Challenges: 'Exploring the Impact of Artificial Intelligence (AI) in Mental Health Care'. *International Journal of Research Publication and Reviews*, *4*(8), 2038–2045. doi:10.55248/gengpi.4.823.51356

Manoharan, S. (2016). Personalized assessment as a means to mitigate plagiarism. *IEEE Transactions on Education*, *60*(2), 112–119. doi:10.1109/TE.2016.2604210

Mao, J., Chen, B., & Liu, J. C. (2024). Generative Artificial Intelligence in Education and Its Implications for Assessment. *TechTrends*, *68*(1), 58–66. doi:10.1007/s11528-023-00911-4

Mao, W. (2022). Video analysis of intelligent teaching based on machine learning and virtual reality technology. *Neural Computing & Applications*, *34*(9), 6603–6614. doi:10.1007/s00521-021-06072-w

Marín Díaz, G., Galán Hernández, J. J., & Galdón Salvador, J. L. (2023). Analyzing Employee Attrition Using Explainable AI for Strategic HR Decision-Making. *Mathematics*, *11*(22), 4677. doi:10.3390/math11224677

Marks, I. (2014). Formative (classroom) assessment techniques. *Acta Educationis Generalis*, *4*(1), 46–50.

Marriott, P. (2009). Students' evaluation of the use of online summative assessment on an undergraduate financial accounting module. *British Journal of Educational Technology*, *40*(2), 237–254. doi:10.1111/j.1467-8535.2008.00924.x

Martínez-Plumed, F., Gómez, E., & Hernández-Orallo, J. (2021). Futures of artificial intelligence through technology readiness levels. *Telematics and Informatics*, *58*, 101525. doi:10.1016/j.tele.2020.101525

Martins, R. M., & Gresse Von Wangenheim, C. (2023). Findings on teaching machine learning in high school: A ten-year systematic literature review. *Informatics in Education*, *22*(3), 421–440.

Marzouk, M., & Zaher, M. (2020). Artificial intelligence exploitation in facility management using deep learning. *Construction Innovation*, *20*(4), 609–624. doi:10.1108/CI-12-2019-0138

Mathrani, A., Susnjak, T., Ramaswami, G., & Barczak, A. (2021). Perspectives on the challenges of generalizability, transparency and ethics in predictive learning analytics. *Computers and Education Open*, *2*, 100060. doi:10.1016/j.caeo.2021.100060

Mavrikis, M., Geraniou, E., Gutierrez Santos, S., & Poulovassilis, A. (2019). Intelligent analysis and data visualisation for teacher assistance tools: The case of exploratory learning. *British Journal of Educational Technology*, *50*(6), 2920–2942. doi:10.1111/bjet.12876

Ma, X., & Jiang, C. (2023). On the Ethical Risks of Artificial Intelligence Applications in Education and Its Avoidance Strategies. *Journal of Education. Humanities and Social Sciences*, *14*, 354–359.

May, M., & George, S. (2011). Privacy Concerns in E-learning: Is UsingTracking System a Threat? *International Journal of Information and Education Technology (IJIET)*, *1*(1), 1–8. doi:10.7763/IJIET.2011.V1.1

Maynez, J., Narayan, S., Bohnet, B., & McDonald, R. (2020). On faithfulness and factuality in abstractive summarisation. *In Proceedings of the 58th Annual Meeting of the Association for Computational Linguistics*, (pp. 1906–1919). IEEE. 10.18653/v1/2020.acl-main.173

McGovern, E., Moreira, G., & Luna-Nevarez, C. (2020). An application of virtual reality in education: Can this technology enhance the quality of students' learning experience? *Journal of Education for Business*, *95*(7), 490–496. doi:10.1080/08832323.2019.1703096

McGrath, C., Pargman, T. C., Juth, N., & Palmgren, P. J. (2023). University teachers' perceptions of responsibility and artificial intelligence in higher education-An experimental philosophical study. *Computers and Education: Artificial Intelligence*, *4*, 100139. doi:10.1016/j.caeai.2023.100139

Mckie, I. A. S., & Narayan, B. (2019). Enhancing the Academic Library Experience with Chatbots: An Exploration of Research and Implications for Practice. *Journal of the Australian Library and Information Association*, *68*(3), 268–277. doi:10.1080/24750158.2019.1611694

McLaren, B. M., Scheuer, O., & Mikšátko, J. (2010). Supporting collaborative learning and e-discussions using artificial intelligence techniques. *International Journal of Artificial Intelligence in Education*, *20*(1), 1–46.

Mehrabi, N., Morstatter, F., Saxena, N., Lerman, K., & Galstyan, A. (2021). A survey on bias and fairness in machine learning. *ACM Computing Surveys*, *54*(6), 1–35. doi:10.1145/3457607

Mekonen, Y. K., & Fitiavana, R. A. (2021). Assessment of Learning Outcomes in Higher Education: Review of literature. *Assessment of Learning Outcomes in Higher Education: Review of Literature*, *71*(1), 8–8. doi:10.47119/IJRP100711220211766

Mekovec, R., & Peras, D. (2020). Implementing the general data protection regulation: The case of higher education institution. International Journal of E-Education, E-Business. *E-Management and E-Learning*, *10*(1), 104–113. doi:10.17706/ijeeee.2020.10.1.104-113

Memarian, B., & Doleck, T. (2023). Fairness, Accountability, Transparency, and Ethics (FATE) in Artificial Intelligence (AI), and higher education: A systematic review. *Computers and Education: Artificial Intelligence, 100152*.

Memarian, B., & Doleck, T. (2023). Fairness, Accountability, Transparency, and Ethics (FATE) in Artificial Intelligence (AI) and higher education: A systematic review. *Computers and Education: Artificial Intelligence*, *5*, 100152. doi:10.1016/j.caeai.2023.100152

Mentis, A.-F. A., Lee, D., & Roussos, P. (2023). Applications of artificial intelligence− machine learning for detection of stress: A critical overview. *Molecular Psychiatry*, 1–13. doi:10.1038/s41380-023-02047-6 PMID:37020048

Merenda, M., Porcaro, C., & Iero, D. (2020). Edge machine learning for ai-enabled iot devices: A review. *Sensors (Basel)*, *20*(9), 2533. doi:10.3390/s20092533 PMID:32365645

Messer, M., Brown, N. C., Kölling, M., & Shi, M. (2024). Automated grading and feedback tools for programming education: A systematic review. *ACM Transactions on Computing Education*, *24*(1), 1–43. doi:10.1145/3636515

Mhlanga, D. (2023). *Responsible Industry 4.0: A Framework for Human-Centered Artificial Intelligence*. Taylor & Francis. doi:10.4324/9781003393382

Miao, F., et, al. (2021). *AI and education: Guidance for policy-makers*. United Nations Educational, Scientific and Cultural Organization.

Miao, F., Holmes, W., Huang, R., & Zhang, H. (2021, April 8). *AI and education*. UNESCO Publishing. http://books.google.ie/books?id=yyE7EAAAQBAJ&printsec=frontcover&dq=Artificial+Intelligence+in+Education:+Promises+and+Implications+for+Teaching+and+Learning&hl=&cd=2&source=gbs_api

Miao, F., Holmes, W., Huang, R., & Zhang, H. (2021). *AI and education: A guidance for policymakers*. UNESCO Publishing.

Michel-Villarreal, R., Vilalta-Perdomo, E., Salinas-Navarro, D. E., Thierry-Aguilera, R., & Gerardou, F. S. (2023). Challenges and Opportunities of Generative AI for Higher Education as Explained by ChatGPT. *Education Sciences, 13*(9), 856. doi:10.3390/educsci13090856

Minow, M. (2023). Equality, Equity, and Algorithms: Learning from Justice Rosalie Abella. *University of Toronto Law Journal, 73*(Supplement 2), 163–178. doi:10.3138/utlj-2023-0064

Mishra, S., & Tyagi, A. K. (2022). The role of machine learning techniques in internet of things-based cloud applications. *Artificial intelligence-based internet of things systems*, 105-135.

MIT. (2023). AI pilot programs look to reduce energy use and emissions on MIT campus. *MIT News*. Massachusetts Institute of Technology. https://news.mit.edu/2023/ai-pilot-programs-look-reduce-energy-use-emissions-mit-campus-0908

Mittelstadt, B. (2019). Principles for AI fairness. arXiv preprint arXiv:1901.09463.

Mizumoto, A., & Eguchi, M. (2023). Exploring the potential of using an AI language model for automated essay scoring. *Research Methods in Applied Linguistics, 2*(2), 100050. doi:10.1016/j.rmal.2023.100050

Modgil, S., Singh, R., & Hannibal, C. (2021). Artificial Intelligence for Supply Chain Resilience: Learning From Covid-19. *International Journal of Logistics Management*. doi:10.1108/IJLM-02-2021-0094

Mohamed Hashim, M. A., Tlemsani, I., & Matthews, R. (2022). Higher education strategy in digital transformation. *Education and Information Technologies, 27*(3), 3171–3195. doi:10.1007/s10639-021-10739-1 PMID:34539217

Mohmmed, A. O., Khidhir, B. A., Nazeer, A., & Vijayan, V. J. (2020). Emergency remote teaching during Coronavirus pandemic: The current trend and future directive at Middle East College Oman. *Innovative Infrastructure Solutions, 5*(3), 1–11. doi:10.1007/s41062-020-00326-7

Monteith, S., Glenn, T., Geddes, J. R., Whybrow, P. C., Achtyes, E., & Bauer, M. (2023). Artificial intelligence and increasing misinformation. *The British Journal of Psychiatry*, 1–3. PMID:37881016

Moore, S. L. (2007, August 17). David H. Rose, Anne Meyer, Teaching Every Student in the Digital Age: Universal Design for Learning. *Educational Technology Research and Development, 55*(5), 521–525. doi:10.1007/s11423-007-9056-3

Moor, J. (2006). The Dartmouth College artificial intelligence conference: The next fifty years. *AI Magazine, 27*(4), 87–87.

Mora, H., Signes-Pont, M. T., Fuster-Guilló, A., & Pertegal-Felices, M. L. (2020). A collaborative working model for enhancing the learning process of science & engineering students. *Computers in Human Behavior, 103*, 140–150. doi:10.1016/j.chb.2019.09.008

Morandini, S., Fraboni, F., Angelis, M. D., Puzzo, G., Giusino, D., & Pietrantoni, L. (2023). The impact of artificial intelligence on workers' skills: upskilling and reskilling in organisations. Informing Science: The International Journal of an Emerging Transdiscipline, 26, 039-068. doi:10.28945/5078

Morandini, S., Fraboni, F., Puzzo, G., Giusino, D., Volpi, L., Brendel, H., & Pietrantoni, L. (2023). Examining the Nexus between Explainability of AI Systems and User's Trust: A Preliminary Scoping Review. *Proceedings*. Ceur. http://ceur-ws.org.

Mousavi, A., Schmidt, M., Squires, V., & Wilson, K. (2021). Assessing the effectiveness of student advice recommender agent (SARA): The case of automated personalized feedback. *International Journal of Artificial Intelligence in Education*, *31*(3), 603–621. doi:10.1007/s40593-020-00210-6

MTCIT. (2021). *National Digital Economy Program*. MTCIT. https://www.mtcit.gov.om/ITAPortal/Data/English/DocLibrary/202112284942713/National%20Digital%20Economy%20Program.pdf

Müller, V. C. (2020). *Ethics of Artificial Intelligence and Robotics*.

Munz, P., Hennick, M., & Stewart, J. (2023). Maximizing AI Reliability Through Anticipatory Thinking and Model Risk Audits. *AI Magazine*, *44*(2), 173–184. doi:10.1002/aaai.12099

Murdoch, B. (2021). Privacy and artificial intelligence: Challenges for protecting health information in a new era. *BMC Medical Ethics*, *22*(1), 1–5. doi:10.1186/s12910-021-00687-3 PMID:34525993

Murphy, K., Di Ruggiero, E., Upshur, R., Willison, D. J., Malhotra, N., Cai, J., Malhotra, N., Lui, V., & Gibson, J. L. (2021). Artificial Intelligence for Good Health: A Scoping Review of the Ethics Literature. *BMC Medical Ethics*, *22*(1), 14. Advance online publication. doi:10.1186/s12910-021-00577-8 PMID:33588803

Nabila, E. L.-M. O. F. F. O. C. K. (2023). Artificial intelligence as a supportive tool for digital marketing. *AL TURATH Journal*, *13*(13), 74–92.

Nair, K.R., & Kumar, S. (2021). Impact of Industry 4.0 on Digital Marketing for Higher Education. *NVEO-NATURAL VOLATILES & ESSENTIAL OILS Journal*, 5178-5208.

Nalepa, G., & Stefanowski, J. (2020). Artificial intelligence research community and associations in Poland. *Foundations of Computing and Decision Sciences*, *45*(3), 159–177. doi:10.2478/fcds-2020-0009

Namoun, A., & Alshanqiti, A. (2020). Predicting student performance using data mining and learning analytics techniques: A systematic literature review. *Applied Sciences (Basel, Switzerland)*, *11*(1), 237. doi:10.3390/app11010237

Naqvi, A. (2020). What Is Artificial Intelligence? In *Artificial Intelligence for Audit, Forensic Accounting, and Valuation* (pp. 37–49).

Naseer, F., Khalid, M. U., Ayub, N., Rasool, A., Abbas, T., & Afzal, M. W. (2024). Automated Assessment and Feedback in Higher Education Using Generative AI. In Transforming Education With Generative AI: Prompt Engineering and Synthetic Content Creation (pp. 433-461). IGI Global.

Naseer, F., Khalid, M. U., Ayub, N., Rasool, A., Abbas, T., & Afzal, M. W. (2024). Automated Assessment and Feedback in Higher Education Using Generative AI. In Transforming Education With Generative AI: Prompt Engineering and Synthetic Content Creation (pp. 433-461). IGI Global. doi:10.4018/979-8-3693-1351-0.ch021

Natale, S., & Ballatore, A. (2020). Imagining the thinking machine: Technological myths and the rise of artificial intelligence. *Convergence (London)*, *26*(1), 3–18. doi:10.1177/1354856517715164

Nazaretsky, T., Cukurova, M., Ariely, M., & Alexandron, G. (2021, September). Confirmation bias and trust: human factors that influence teachers' attitudes towards AI-based educational technology. In CEUR Workshop Proceedings (Vol. 3042).

Nazaretsky, T., Ariely, M., Cukurova, M., & Alexandron, G. (2022). Teachers' trust in AI-powered educational technology and a professional development program to improve it. *British Journal of Educational Technology*, *53*(4), 914–931.

Nazaretsky, T., Bar, C., Walter, M., & Alexandron, G. (2022). Empowering teachers with AI: Co-designing a learning analytics tool for personalized instruction in the science classroom. *LAK22: 12th International Learning Analytics and Knowledge Conference*

Nazari, N., Shabbir, M. S., & Sctiawan, R. (2021). Application of Artificial Intelligence powered digital writing assistant in higher education: Randomized controlled trial. *Heliyon*, *7*(5), e07014. doi:10.1016/j.heliyon.2021.e07014 PMID:34027198

Ndukwe, I. G., Amadi, C. E., Nkomo, L. M., & Daniel, B. K. (2020). *Automatic grading system using sentence-BERT network*. Artificial Intelligence in Education: 21st International Conference, AIED 2020, Ifrane, Morocco.

Nedelsky, L. (1954). Absolute grading standards for objective tests. *Educational and Psychological Measurement*, *14*(1), 3 19. doi:10.1177/001316445401400101

Nelson, M. M., & Schunn, C. D. (2009). The nature of feedback: How different types of peer feedback affect writing performance. *Instructional Science*, *37*(4), 375–401. doi:10.1007/s11251-008-9053-x

Ng, W. C., Lim, W. Y. B., Ng, J. S., Xiong, Z., Niyato, D., & Miao, C. (2022). Unified resource allocation framework for the edge intelligence-enabled metaverse. *ICC 2022-IEEE International conference on Communications.*

Ng, D. T. K., Lee, M., Tan, R. J. Y., Hu, X., Downie, J. S., & Chu, S. K. W. (2023). A review of AI teaching and learning from 2000 to 2020. *Education and Information Technologies*, *28*(7), 8445–8501. doi:10.1007/s10639-022-11491-w

Nguyen, A., Järvelä, S., Rosé, C., Järvenoja, H., & Malmberg, J. (2022, October 11). Examining socially shared regulation and shared physiological arousal events with multimodal learning analytics. *British Journal of Educational Technology*, *54*(1), 293–312. doi:10.1111/bjet.13280

Nguyen, A., Ngo, H. N., Hong, Y., Dang, B., & Nguyen, B. P. T. (2023). Ethical principles for artificial Intelligence in education. *Education and Information Technologies*, *28*(4), 4221–4241. doi:10.1007/s10639-022-11316-w PMID:36254344

Nguyen, A., Ngo, H. N., Hong, Y., Dang, B., & Nguyen, B.-P. T. (2023). Ethical principles for artificial intelligence in education. *Education and Information Technologies*, *28*(4), 4221–4241.

Nigam, A., Pasricha, R., Singh, T., & Churi, P. (2021). A systematic review on ai-based proctoring systems: Past, present and future. *Education and Information Technologies*, *26*(5), 6421–6445. doi:10.1007/s10639-021-10597-x PMID:34177348

Nilsen, P., Svedberg, P., Nygren, J., Frideros, M., Johansson, J., & Schueller, S. (2022). Accelerating the impact of artificial intelligence in mental healthcare through implementation science. *Implementation Research and Practice*, *3*, 263348952211120. doi:10.1177/26334895221112033 PMID:37091110

Ning, Y.-Z. (2023). Factors Affecting the Cost Savings Rate of University Procurement. *Archives of Business Research*, *11*(5), 21–27. doi:10.14738/abr.115.14540

Norova, M. (2020). Advantages And Disadvantages of Traditional and Alternative Ways of Assessment. *ЦЕНТР НАУЧНЫХ ПУБЛИКАЦИЙ (buxdu. uz)*, *2*(2).

Ntoutsi, E., Fafalios, P., Gadiraju, U., Iosifidis, V., Nejdl, W., Vidal, M. E., Ruggieri, S., Turini, F., Papadopoulos, S., Krasanakis, E., Kompatsiaris, I., Kinder-Kurlanda, K., Wagner, C., Karimi, F., Fernandez, M., Alani, H., Berendt, B., Kruegel, T., Heinze, C., & Staab, S. (2020). Bias in data-driven artificial intelligence systems—An introductory survey. *Wiley Interdisciplinary Reviews. Data Mining and Knowledge Discovery*, *10*(3), e1356. doi:10.1002/widm.1356

Nusi, A., & Zaim, M. (2023). Philosophy of Education In Digital Transformation: Ethical Considerations For Students' Data Security In Online Learning Platforms. *Jurnal Ilmiah Pendidikan Scholastic*, *7*(3), 42–50. doi:10.36057/jips.v7i3.629

O'Dea, X. C., & O'Dea, M. (2023). Is Artificial Intelligence Really the Next Big Thing in Learning and Teaching in Higher Education? A Conceptual Paper. *Journal of University Teaching & Learning Practice*, *20*(5). doi:10.53761/1.20.5.05

O'Donovan, B., Price, M., & Rust, C. (2001). The student experience of criterion-referenced assessment (through the introduction of a common criteria assessment grid). *Innovations in Education and Teaching International*, *38*(1), 74–85. doi:10.1080/147032901300002873

O'Neil, C. (2017). *Weapons of math destruction: How big data increases inequality and risks democracy*. Tim Duggan Books.

Obeid, S., & Demirkan, H. (2020). The influence of virtual reality on design process creativity in basic design studios. *Interactive Learning Environments*, *31*(4), 1841–1859. doi:10.1080/10494820.2020.1858116

OECD. (2019). Artificial intelligence in science. *Challenges*.

Oermann, E., & Kondziolka, D. (2023). On chatbots and generative artificial intelligence. *Neurosurgery*, *92*(4), 665–666. doi:10.1227/neu.0000000000002415 PMID:36779766

Oka, A., Ishimura, N., & Ishihara, S. (2021). A new dawn for the use of artificial intelligence in gastroenterology, hepatology and pancreatology. *Diagnostics (Basel)*, *11*(9), 1719. doi:10.3390/diagnostics11091719 PMID:34574060

Oliver, J. C., & McNeil, T. (2023). Undergraduate data science degrees emphasize computer science and statistics but fall short in ethics training and domain-specific context. *PeerJ. Computer Science*, *7*, e441. doi:10.7717/peerj-cs.441 PMID:33834108

Oman Observer. (2021). Oman to unveil strategy for AI, advanced technologies. *Oman Observer*. https://www.omanobserver.om/article/1108794/business/economy/oman-to-unveil-strategy-for-ai-advanced-technologies

Oman Observer. (2023). HM speech: A national programme for the adoption of AI. *Oman Observer*. https://www.omanobserver.om/article/1145635/oman/his-majesty/hm-speech-a-national-programme-for-the-adoption-of-ai

Ore, O., & Sposato, M. (2021). Opportunities and Risks of Artificial Intelligence in Recruitment and Selection. *The International Journal of Organizational Analysis*. doi:10.1108/IJOA-07-2020-2291

Orr, D., & Luebcke, M. Schmidt, J., Philipp, Ebner, M., Wannemacher, K., Ebner, M., & Dohmen, D. (2020). *Higher Education Landscape 2030 A Trend Analysis Based on the AHEAD International Horizon Scanning*. Springer. https://www.springer.com/series/8914

Orrù, G., Piarulli, A., Conversano, C., & Gemignani, A. (2023). Human-like problem-solving abilities in large language models using ChatGPT. *Frontiers in Artificial Intelligence*, *6*, 1199350. doi:10.3389/frai.2023.1199350 PMID:37293238

Ouyang, F., Wu, M., Zheng, L., Zhang, L., & Jiao, P. (2023a). Integration of artificial intelligence performance prediction and learning analytics to improve student learning in online engineering course. *International Journal of Educational Technology in Higher Education*, *20*(1), 1–23. doi:10.1186/s41239-022-00372-4 PMID:36683653

Ouyang, F., Zhang, L., Wu, M., & Jiao, P. (2024, June). Empowering collaborative knowledge construction through the implementation of a collaborative argument map tool. *The Internet and Higher Education*, *62*, 100946. doi:10.1016/j.iheduc.2024.100946

Ouyang, F., Zheng, L., & Jiao, P. (2022). Artificial intelligence in online higher education: A systematic review of empirical research from 2011 to 2020. *Education and Information Technologies*, *27*(6), 7893–7925. doi:10.1007/s10639-022-10925-9

Overgoor, G., Chica, M., Rand, W., & Weishampel, A. (2019). Letting the Computers Take Over: Using AI to Solve Marketing Problems. *California Management Review*, *61*(4), 156–185. doi:10.1177/0008125619859318

Oversold and Underused. (2004, May 1). Computers in the Classroom. *International Journal of Educational Management*, *18*(3), 205–206. doi:10.1108/09513540410527202

Owan, V. J., Abang, K. B., Idika, D. O., Etta, E. O., & Bassey, B. A. (2023). Exploring the potential of artificial intelligence tools in educational measurement and assessment. *Eurasia Journal of Mathematics, Science and Technology Education*, *19*(8), em2307. doi:10.29333/ejmste/13428

Oxford Business Group. (2023a). *Attractive Environment: Private Sector Investment and an Updated Regulatory Landscape are Supporting Increased E-Commerce Activity in Abu Dhabi*. Oxford Business Group. https://oxfordbusinessgroup.com/reports/uae-abu-dhabi/2023-report/industry-retail/attractive-environment-private-sector-investment-and-an-updated-regulatory-landscape-are-supporting-increased-e-commerce-activity-analysis/

Oxford Business Group. (2023b). *Crypto Rush: Decentralised Financing Could Play an Important Role in GCC Countries' Efforts to Diversify Their Economies*. Oxford. https://oxfordbusinessgroup.com/reports/uae-abu-dhabi/2023-report/banking/crypto-rush-decentralised-financing-could-play-an-important-role-in-gcc-countries-efforts-to-diversify-their-economies-analysis/

Oxford Business Group. (2023c). *Gulf Countries Look to Space to Harness Scientific and Commercial Opportunities*. Oxford. https://oxfordbusinessgroup.com/articles-interviews/gulf-countries-look-to-space-to-harness-scientific-and-commercial-opportunities/

Oxford Business Group. (2023d). *The Competitive Edge: Harnessing Artificial Intelligence Technology to Bolster Economic Growth and Strengthen Sustainability in Oman*. Oxford. https://oxfordbusinessgroup.com/reports/oman/2023-report/economy/the-competitive-edge-harnessing-artificial-intelligence-technology-to-bolster-economic-growth-and-strengthen-sustainability-analysis/

Oxford Business Group. (2023e). *Upward Trajectory: The Digital Economy is Helping Streamline Government Services and Support Startups and Innovation in Oman*. Oxford. https://oxfordbusinessgroup.com/reports/oman/2023-report/ict/upward-trajectory-the-digital-economy-is-helping-streamline-government-services-and-support-start-ups-and-innovation-analysis/

Oxford Business Group. (2023f). *What CEOs in the Gulf See on the Horizon for 2023 and Beyond*. Oxford. https://oxfordbusinessgroup.com/reports/oman/2023-report/country-profile/what-ceos-in-the-gulf-see-on-the-horizon-for-2023-and-beyond-overview/

Özcan, C., & Kaptan, F. (2020). Investigation of the Studies on Socioscientific Issues between 2008-2017. *Journal of Muallim Rıfat Faculty of Education*, *2*(1), 16–36.

Pagallo, U., Sciolla, J. C., & Durante, M. (2022). *The Environmental Challenges of AI in EU Law: Lessons Learned From the Artificial Intelligence Act (AIA) With Its Drawbacks*. Transforming Government People Process and Policy. doi:10.1108/TG-07-2021-0121

Paiva, J. C., Leal, J. P., & Figueira, Á. (2022). Automated assessment in computer science education: A state-of-the-art review. [TOCE]. *ACM Transactions on Computing Education*, *22*(3), 1–40. doi:10.1145/3513140

Palomares, I. (2021). *A panoramic view and swot analysis of artificial intelligence for achieving the sustainable development goals by 2030: progress and prospects.*

Papanastasiou, E. C., & Solomonidou, G. (2023). Evaluating Emergency Remote Assessment Adaptations in Higher Education due to COVID-19: Faculty Insights and Challenges. *Education Sciences*, *13*(2), 184. doi:10.3390/educsci13020184

Pappula, S. R., & Allam, S. R. (2023, December 9). LLMs for Conversational AI: Enhancing Chatbots and Virtual Assistants. *International Journal of Research Publication and Reviews*, *4*(12), 1601–1611. doi:10.55248/gengpi.4.1223.123425

Pardamean, B., Suparyanto, T., Cenggoro, T. W., Sudigyo, D., & Anugrahana, A. (2022). AI-based learning style prediction in online learning for primary education. *IEEE Access : Practical Innovations, Open Solutions*, *10*, 35725–35735. doi:10.1109/ACCESS.2022.3160177

Pardo, A., & Siemens, G. (2014). Ethical and privacy principles for learning analytics. *British Journal of Educational Technology*, *45*(3), 438–450. doi:10.1111/bjet.12152

Pardo-Garcia, C., & Barac, M. (2020). Promoting employability in higher education: A case study on boosting entrepreneurship skills. *sustainability, 12*(10), 4004.

Patra, B., Roberts, K., & Wu, H. (2020). A content-based dataset recommendation system for researchers—a case study on gene expression omnibus (geo) repository. Database, 2020. https://doi.org/ doi:10.1093/database/baaa064

Pattnaik, P. (2020). AI-Based Techniques for Real-Time Face Recognition-based Attendance System- A comparative Study. *2020 4th International Conference on Electronics, Communication and Aerospace Technology (ICECA),* (pp. 1034–1039). IEEE.

Patty, J. (2024). The Use Of Ai In Language Learning: What You Need To Know. *Jurnal Review Pendidikan dan Pengajaran (JRPP), 7*(1), 642-654.

Pedro, F., Subosa, M., Rivas, A., & Valverde, P. (2019). *Artificial intelligence in education: Challenges and opportunities for sustainable development.*

Pedro, F., Subosa, M., Rivas, A., & Valverde, P. (2019). *Artificial intelligence in education: Challenges and opportunities for sustainable development*. United Nations Education, Scientific and Cultural Organization. https://unesdoc.unesco.org/ark:/48223/pf0000366994

Pedro, F., Subosa, M., Rivas, A., & Valverde, P. (2019). *Artificial Intelligence in education: Challenges and opportunities for sustainable development.* United Nations Educational, Scientific and Cultural Organization (UNESCO). https://unesdoc.unesco.org/ark:/48223/pf0000366994?posInSet=22&queryId=9d8ca6cf-6a26-4f09-9b10-5e339c0e75da

Pedró, F. (2020). Applications of Artificial Intelligence to higher education: Possibilities, evidence, and challenges. *IUL Research*, *1*(1), 61–76. doi:10.57568/iulres.v1i1.43

Pellegrino, J. W. (2013). Proficiency in science: Assessment challenges and opportunities. *Science*, *340*(6130), 320–323. doi:10.1126/science.1232065 PMID:23599485

Peng, H., Ma, S., & Spector, J. M. (2019, September 18). Personalized adaptive learning: An emerging pedagogical approach enabled by a smart learning environment. *Smart Learning Environments*, *6*(1), 9. doi:10.1186/s40561-019-0089-y

Peng, L., Wei, W., Gong, Y., & Jia, R. (2022). University Library Space Renovation Based on the User Learning Experience in Two Wuhan Universities. *International Journal of Environmental Research and Public Health*, *19*(16), 10395. doi:10.3390/ijerph191610395 PMID:36012030

Pereira, V., & Gomes Costa, H. (2016). Linear integer model for the course timetabling problem of a faculty in rio de janeiro. *Advances in Operations Research*, *2016*, 1–9. doi:10.1155/2016/7597062

Peretz-Andersson, E., Lavesson, N., Bifet, A., & Mikalef, P. (2021, June). AI Transformation in the Public Sector: Ongoing Research. In *2021 Swedish Artificial Intelligence Society Workshop (SAIS)* (pp. 1-4). IEEE. 10.1109/SAIS53221.2021.9483960

Perifanis, N. A., & Kitsios, F. (2023). Investigating the influence of artificial intelligence on business value in the digital era of strategy: A literature review. *Information (Basel)*, *14*(2), 85. doi:10.3390/info14020085

Perret, J. K., & Heitkamp, M. (2021). On the Potentials of Artificial Intelligence in Marketing – The Case of Robotic Process Automation. *International Journal of Applied Research in Management and Economics*. doi:10.33422/ijarme.v4i4.768

Pessoa, G. J., Dias, T. M. R., Silva, T. H. P., & Laender, A. H. F. (2022). A geographic analysis of the interdisciplinary collaborations in the Brazilian scientific community. *Journal of the Brazilian Computer Society*, *28*(1), 1–12. doi:10.5753/jbcs.2022.2887

Petersson, L., Larsson, I., Nygren, J., Nilsen, P., Neher, M., Reed, J., Tyskbo, D., & Svedberg, P. (2022). Challenges to implementing artificial intelligence in healthcare: A qualitative interview study with healthcare leaders in Sweden. *BMC Health Services Research*, *22*(1), 850. Advance online publication. doi:10.1186/s12913-022-08215-8 PMID:35778736

Peyravi, B., Nekrošienė, J., & Lobanova, L. (2020). Revolutionised technologies for marketing: Theoretical review with focus on artificial intelligence. *Business: Theory and Practice*, *21*(2), 827–834. doi:10.3846/btp.2020.12313

Phanichsiti, S., Thamnita, O., & Thipphayasaeng, P. (2023). Internet of Things and Big Data for a Sustainable Smart University. *Journal of Higher Education Theory and Practice*, *23*(2).

Picciano, A. G. (2017, September 1). Theories and Frameworks for Online Education: Seeking an Integrated Model. *Online Learning : the Official Journal of the Online Learning Consortium*, *21*(3). doi:10.24059/olj.v21i3.1225

Pierdicca, R., & Paolanti, M. (2022). Geoai: A review of artificial intelligence approaches for interpreting complex geomatics data. *Geoscientific Instrumentation, Methods and Data Systems, 11*(1), 195–218. doi:10.5194/gi-11-195-2022

Pikhart, M., & Klímová, B. (2020). eLearning 4.0 as a sustainability strategy for generation Z language learners: Applied linguistics of second language acquisition in younger adults. *Societies (Basel, Switzerland), 10*(2), 38. doi:10.3390/soc10020038

Pillai, R. (2019). Technology and Talent Analytics for Talent Management – A Game Changer for Organizational Performance. *The International Journal of Organizational Analysis*. doi:10.1108/IJOA-01-2019-1634

Pisica, A. I., Edu, T., Zaharia, R. M., & Zaharia, R. (2023). Implementing Artificial Intelligence in Higher Education: Pros and Cons from the Perspectives of Academics. *Societies (Basel, Switzerland), 13*(5), 118. doi:10.3390/soc13050118

Pitarch, C., Ribas, V., & Vellido, A. (2023). AI-Based Glioma Grading for a Trustworthy Diagnosis: An Analytical Pipeline for Improved Reliability. *Cancers (Basel), 15*(13), 3369.

Plathottam, S. J., Rzonca, A., Lakhnori, R., & Iloeje, C. O. (2023). A review of artificial intelligence applications in manufacturing operations. *Journal of Advanced Manufacturing and Processing, 5*(3), e10159. doi:10.1002/amp2.10159

Pokrivcakova, S. (2019). Preparing teachers for the application of AI-powered technologies in foreign language education. *Journal of Language and Cultural Education, 7*(3), 135–153. doi:10.2478/jolace-2019-0025

Polya, G. (1957). How to solve it: A new aspect of mathematical method. N.J.: Princeton.

Popenici, S. (2023). The critique of AI as a foundation for judicious use in higher education. *Journal of Applied Learning & Teaching, 6*(2). https://journals.sfu.ca/jalt/index.php/jalt/article/view/883/605

Poth, A., Beck, Q., & Riel, A. (2019). Artificial Intelligence helps making Quality Assurance processes leaner. In *Systems, Software and Services Process Improvement: 26th European Conference, EuroSPI 2019, Edinburgh, UK, September 18–20, 2019* [Springer International Publishing.]. *Proceedings, 26*, 722–730.

Pratama, M. P., Sampelolo, R., & Lura, H. (2023). Revolutionizing education: harnessing the power of artificial Intelligence for personalized learning. *Klasikal: Journal of Education. Language Teaching and Science, 5*(2), 350–357.

Pratama, M. P., Sampelolo, R., & Lura, H. (2023, August 10). REVOLUTIONIZING EDUCATION: HARNESSING THE POWER OF ARTIFICIAL INTELLIGENCE FOR PERSONALIZED LEARNING. *KLASIKAL : JOURNAL OF EDUCATION, LANGUAGE TEACHING AND SCIENCE, 5*(2), 350–357. doi:10.52208/klasikal.v5i2.877

Prokop, E., Han, X. Y., Papyan, V., Donoho, D., & Johnson, C. Jr. (2021). AI and the Digitized Photoarchive: Promoting Access and Discoverability. *Art Documentation: Journal of the Art Libraries Society of North America*, *40*(1), 1–20. doi:10.1086/714604

Punlumjeak, W., Rachburee, N., & Arunrerk, J. (2017). Big data analytics: Student performance prediction using feature selection and machine learning on microsoft azure platform. [JTEC]. *Journal of Telecommunication, Electronic and Computer Engineering*, *9*(1-4), 113–117.

Pursnani, V., Sermet, Y., Kurt, M., & Demir, I. (2023). Performance of ChatGPT on the US fundamentals of engineering exam: Comprehensive assessment of proficiency and potential implications for professional environmental engineering practice. *Computers and Education: Artificial Intelligence*, *5*, 100183.

PWC. (2016). *AI in Education: Transforming Learning and Administrative Systems*. PWC. https://www.pwc.com/ai_in_education

Pym, A., & Ayvazyan, N. (2017). Linguistics, translation and interpreting in foreign-language teaching contexts. In *The Routledge Handbook of Translation Studies and Linguistics* (pp. 393–407). Routledge. doi:10.4324/9781315692845-26

Qadir, J. (2023). Engineering education in the era of ChatGPT: Promise and pitfalls of generative AI for education. *2023 IEEE Global Engineering Education Conference (EDUCON)*. IEEE.

Qadir, J. (2023).Engineering Education in the Era of ChatGPT: Promise and Pitfalls of Generative AI for Education. *IEEE Global Engineering Education Conference (EDUCON)*. IEEE. 10.1109/EDUCON54358.2023.10125121

Qin, Z., Ahmed, S., Sarker, M., Paul, K., Adel, A., Naheyan, T., Barrett, R., Banu, S., & Creswell, J. (2021). Tuberculosis detection from chest x-rays for triaging in a high tuberculosis-burden setting: An evaluation of five artificial intelligence algorithms. *The Lancet. Digital Health*, *3*(9), e543–e554. doi:10.1016/S2589-7500(21)00116-3 PMID:34446265

Qureshi, F. H., & Khawaja, S. (2021). THE GROWTH OF PRIVATE HIGHER EDUCATION: AN OVERVIEW IN THE CONTEXT OF LIBERALISATION, PRIVATISATION AND MARKETISATION. *European Journal of Education Studies*, *8*(9). doi:10.46827/ejes.v8i9.3896

Quy, V. K., Thanh, B. T., Chehri, A., Linh, D. M., & Tuan, D. A. (2023). AI and digital transformation in higher education: Vision and approach of a specific university in Vietnam. *Sustainability (Basel)*, *15*(14), 11093. doi:10.3390/su151411093

Raheem, B. R., Anjum, F., & Ghafar, Z. N. (2023). Exploring the Profound Impact of Artificial Intelligence Applications (Quillbot, Grammarly and ChatGPT) on English Academic Writing: A Systematic Review. [IJIR]. *International Journal of Integrative Research*, *1*(10), 599–622.

Rahman, M. M., & Watanobe, Y. (2023). ChatGPT for education and research: Opportunities, threats, and strategies. Applied Sciences (Basel, Switzerland), 13(9), 5783

Rahman, M. M., & Watanobe, Y. (2023). ChatGPT for education and research: Opportunities, threats, and strategies. *Applied Sciences (Basel, Switzerland)*, *13*(9), 5783. doi:10.3390/app13095783

Rakhimbekova, B., Seisebayeva, R., & Abdigaliyeva, G. (2022). *Higher Education in Kazakhstan: Global Trends and State Policy*. Farabi Journal of Social Sciences., doi:10.26577/FJSS.2022.v8.i2.01

Ramazan, & Gizem. (n.d.). Investigation of student views on data privacy and ethical use of data in smart learning environments. *10th International İstanbul Scientific Research Congress, July 23-25, 2022.*

Ramesh, D., & Sanampudi, S. K. (2022). An automated essay scoring systems: A systematic literature review. *Artificial Intelligence Review*, *55*(3), 2495–2527. doi:10.1007/s10462-021-10068-2 PMID:34584325

Ramprasad, R., Pacholsky, A., & Wolverton, C. (2016). Automated exploration of the materials phase diagram using Density Functional Theory calculations. *Proceedings of the National Academy of Sciences of the United States of America*, *113*(47), 1.

Rana, J., Gaur, L., Singh, G., Awan, U., & Rasheed, M. (2021). Reinforcing customer journey through artificial intelligence: A review and research agenda. *International Journal of Emerging Markets*, *17*(7), 1738–1758. doi:10.1108/IJOEM-08-2021-1214

Rapanta, C., Botturi, L., Goodyear, P., Guàrdia, L., & Koole, M. (2020). Online university teaching during and after the Covid-19 crisis: Refocusing teacher presence and learning activity. *Postdigital science and education, 2*, 923-945.

Rawat, A. (n.d). Ethical Considerations in AI for Education: Addressing Privacy and Bias Concerns. *Education Unleashed: The AI Era*, 173.

Reeves, T. C., Herrington, J., & Oliver, R. (2004, December). A development research agenda for online collaborative learning. *Educational Technology Research and Development*, *52*(4), 53–65. doi:10.1007/BF02504718

Regan, P. M., & Jesse, J. (2019). Ethical challenges of edtech, big data and personalized learning: Twenty-first century student sorting and tracking. *Ethics and Information Technology*, *21*, 167–179.

Reidenberg, J. R., & Schaub, F. (2018). Achieving big data privacy in education. *Theory and Research in Education*, *16*(3), 263–279.

Reim, W., Åström, J., & Eriksson, O. (2020). Implementation of Artificial Intelligence (AI): A Roadmap for Business Model Innovation. In AI (Switzerland) (Vol. 1, Issue 2). Multidisciplinary Digital Publishing Institute (MDPI). doi:10.3390/ai1020011

Remian, D. (2019). Augmenting education: ethical considerations for incorporating artificial intelligence in education.

Remian, D. (2019). Augmenting Education: Ethical Considerations for Incorporating Artificial Intelligence in Education. Instructional Design Capstones Collection, 52. Rights Critique of Stakeholder Guidelines. *Global Policy*, *12*(S6), 32–44.

Remian, D. (2019). *Augmenting education: Ethical considerations for incorporating artificial intelligence in education. ScholarWorks at UMass Boston*. University of Massachusetts Boston.

Renda, A. (2020). Europe: Toward a Policy Framework for Trustworthy AI. In M. D. Dubber, F. Pasquale, & S. Das (Eds.), *The Oxford Handbook of Ethics of AI* (pp. 650–666). Academic.

Research Planning and Review Committee. (2022). Top trends in academic libraries A review of the trends and issues. *College & Research Libraries News*, *83*(2).

Rezwana, J., & Maher, M. Lou. (2022). *Identifying Ethical Issues in AI Partners in Human-Ai Co-Creation*. https://doi.org//arxiv.2204.07644 doi:10.48550

Richey Jr, R. G., Chowdhury, S., Davis-Sramek, B., Giannakis, M., & Dwivedi, Y. K. (2023). *Artificial intelligence in logistics and supply chain management: A primer and roadmap for research*. Wiley Online Library.

Rivera, S. C., Liu, X., Chan, A. W., Denniston, A. K., Calvert, M., Ashrafian, H., ... Yau, C. (2020). Guidelines for clinical trial protocols for artificial intelligence interventions: The spirit-ai extension. *The Lancet. Digital Health*, *2*(10), e549–e560. doi:10.1016/S2589-7500(20)30219-3 PMID:33328049

Roccapriore, K. M., Boebinger, M. G., Dyck, O., Ghosh, A., Unocic, R. R., Kalinin, S. V., & Ziatdinov, M. (2022). Probing electron beam-induced transformations on a single-defect level via automated scanning transmission electron microscopy. *ACS Nano*, *16*(10), 17116–17127. doi:10.1021/acsnano.2c07451 PMID:36206357

Rodrigues, R. (2020). Legal and human rights issues of AI: Gaps, challenges and vulnerabilities. *Journal of Responsible Technology*, *4*, 100005. doi:10.1016/j.jrt.2020.100005

Römmele, C., Mendel, R., Barrett, C., Kiesl, H., Rauber, D., Rückert, T., Kraus, L., Heinkele, J., Dhillon, C., Grosser, B., Prinz, F., Wanzl, J., Fleischmann, C., Nagl, S., Schnoy, E., Schlottmann, J., Dellon, E. S., Messmann, H., Palm, C., & Ebigbo, A. (2022). An artificial intelligence algorithm is highly accurate for detecting endoscopic features of eosinophilic esophagitis. *Scientific Reports*, *12*(1), 11115. Advance online publication. doi:10.1038/s41598-022-14605-z PMID:35778456

Rong, G., Mendez, A., Assi, E. B., Zhao, B., & Sawan, M. (2020). Artificial intelligence in healthcare: Review and prediction case studies. *Engineering (Beijing)*, *6*(3), 291–301. doi:10.1016/j.eng.2019.08.015

Roozbahani, Z., Rezaeenour, J., Katanforoush, A., & Bidgoly, A. J. (2021). Personalisation of the collaborator recommendation system in multi-layer scientific social networks: A case study of researchgate. *Expert Systems: International Journal of Knowledge Engineering and Neural Networks*, *39*(5), e12932. Advance online publication. doi:10.1111/exsy.12932

Rosen, C. (2023). Applying Cognitive Theory to the Teaching of Programming: Metaphors, Robots and Problem-Based Learning. In Higher Education Computer Science: A Manual of Practical Approaches (pp. 51-61). Springer.

Roshanaei, M., Olivares, H., & Lopez, R. R. (2023). Harnessing AI to Foster Equity in Education: Opportunities, Challenges, and Emerging Strategies. *Journal of Intelligent Learning Systems and Applications*, *15*(04), 123–143. doi:10.4236/jilsa.2023.154009

Ross, J. (2019). The Reliability, Validity, and Utility of Self-Assessment. *Practical Assessment, Research & Evaluation*, *11*(1). Advance online publication. doi:10.7275/9wph-vv65

Rožman, M., Oreški, D., & Tominc, P. (2022). Integrating Artificial Intelligence Into a Talent Management Model to Increase the Work Engagement and Performance of Enterprises. *Frontiers in Psychology*, *13*, 1014434. Advance online publication. doi:10.3389/fpsyg.2022.1014434 PMID:36506984

Rudolf, G., & Grünbichler, R. (2023). Implementation Barriers of Artificial Intelligence in Companies. *International Odyssey: Conference on Economics and Business*. IEEE. https://doi.org/10.22598/odyssey/2023.5

Ruiz-Rojas, L. I., Acosta-Vargas, P., De-Moreta-Llovet, J., & Gonzalez-Rodriguez, M. (2023). Empowering education with generative artificial intelligence tools: Approach with an instructional design matrix. *Sustainability*, *15*(15), 11524.

Rundgren, S. N. C., & Rundgren, C. J. (2010). SEE-SEP: From a separate to a holistic view of socioscientific issues. *Asia-Pacific Forum on Science Learning and Teaching*, *11*(1), 1.

Rutner, S. M., & Scott, R. A. (2022). Use of Artificial Intelligence to Grade Student Discussion Boards: An Exploratory Study. *Information Systems Education Journal*, *20*(4), 4–18.

Sabic, A., & Azemovic, J. (2010). Model of efficient Assessment System with accent on privacy, security and integration with E-University components. *Paper presented at the 2010 2nd International Conference on Education Technology and Computer*. IEEE. 10.1109/ICETC.2010.5529579

Sadler, T. D., Barab, S., & Scott, B. (2007). What do students gain by engaging in socioscientific inquiry? *Research in Science Education*, *37*(4), 371–391. doi:10.1007/s11165-006-9030-9

Sadler, T. D., & Zeidler, D. L. (2005). The significance of content knowledge for informal reasoning regarding socioscientific issues: Applying genetics knowledge to genetic engineering issues. *Science Education*, *89*(1), 71–93. doi:10.1002/sce.20023

Sağlam, M. K., & Çoban, G. (2018). Fen bilimleri öğretmenleri ve öğretmen adaylarına yönelik akıl yürütme becerileri testi'nin geliştirilmesi. *Elementary Education*, *17*(3), 1496–1510. doi:10.17051/ilkonline.2018.466374

Sai, B., Thanigaivelu, S., Shivaani, N., Shyamala Babu, C. S., & Ramaa, A. (2022). Integration of Chatbots in the Procurement Stage of a Supply Chain. *6th IEEE International Conference on Computational System and Information Technology for Sustainable Solutions, CSITSS 2022*. IEEE. 10.1109/CSITSS57437.2022.10026367

Salvaris, M., Dean, D., & Tok, W. H. (2018). *Deep learning with azure. Building and Deploying Artificial Intelligence Solutions on Microsoft AI Platform*. Apress.

Samardali, M. F. S., & Ismael, A. M. H. (2017). Translation as a tool for teaching English as a second language. *Journal of Literature. Language and Linguistics (Taipei)*, *40*, 64–69.

Sandu, N., & Gide, E. (2019, September). Adoption of AI-Chatbots to enhance student learning experience in higher education in India. In *2019 18th International Conference on Information Technology Based Higher Education and Training (ITHET)* (pp. 1-5). IEEE.

Sandy, D. A., Ritchie, H., Adrianto, Z., & Gunardi, A. (2022). Robotic process automation in action: a use case in accounting task. Journal of Digital Innovation Studies, pp. 52–65. doi:10.24198/digits.v1i1.38534

Sapci, A. H., & Sapci, H. A. (2020). Artificial intelligence education and tools for medical and health informatics students: Systematic review. *JMIR Medical Education*, *6*(1), e19285.

Saputra, I., Astuti, M., Sayuti, M., & Kusumastuti, D. (2023, August 30). Integration of Artificial Intelligence in Education: Opportunities, Challenges, Threats and Obstacles. A Literature Review. *Indonesian Journal of Computer Science*, *12*(4). Advance online publication. doi:10.33022/ijcs.v12i4.3266

Saraswat, D., Bhattacharya, P., Verma, A., Prasad, V. K., Tanwar, S., Sharma, G., Bokoro, P. N., & Sharma, R. (2022). *Explainable AI for Healthcare 5.0: Opportunities and Challenges*. IEEE. doi:10.1109/ACCESS.2022.3197671

Sarwar, M. A., Saima, M., & Gul, A. (2024). The Role of Artificial Intelligence in Shaping the Future of Education at Higher Secondary Level. *Journal of Education and Social Studies*, *5*(1), 34–45. doi:10.52223/jess.2024.5104

Sateli, B., Löffler, F., König-Ries, B., & Witte, R. (2017). Scholarlens: Extracting competencies from research publications to automatically generate semantic user profiles. *PeerJ. Computer Science*, *3*, e121. doi:10.7717/peerj-cs.121

Sathivel, T., Raju, V., & John, P. (2005). Data Security in AI Applications in Higher Education. *Journal of Educational Data Security*, *3*(1), 12–19.

Sayers, D., Sousa-Silva, R., Höhn, S., Ahmedi, L., Allkivi-Metsoja, K., Anastasiou, D., & Catala, A. (2021). The Dawn of the Human-Machine Era: A forecast of new and emerging language technologies.

Schiff, D. (2021). Out of the laboratory and into the classroom: The future of artificial intelligence in education. *AI & Society*, *36*(1), 331–348. doi:10.1007/s00146-020-01033-8 PMID:32836908

Schiff, D. (2022). Education for AI, not AI for Education: The Role of Education and Ethics in National AI Policy Strategies. *International Journal of Artificial Intelligence in Education*, *32*(3), 527–563. doi:10.1007/s40593-021-00270-2

Schildkamp, K. (2019). Data-based decision-making for school improvement: Research insights and gaps. *Educational Research*, *61*(3), 257–273. doi:10.1080/00131881.2019.1625716

Schmohl, T., Schelling, K., Go, S., Thaler, K. J., & Watanabe, A. (2022). Development, Implementation and Acceptance of an AI-based Tutoring System: A Research-Led Methodology. CSEDU (2).

Schneider, A., Kühl, M., & Kühl, S. J. (2019). Utilizing research findings in medical education: The testing effect within a flipped/inverted biochemistry classroom. *Medical Teacher*, *41*(11), 1245–1251. doi:10.1080/0142159X.2019.1628195 PMID:31282246

Schön, E.-M., Neumann, M., Hofmann-Stölting, C., Baeza-Yates, R., & Rauschenberger, M. (2023). How are AI assistants changing higher education?.

Schuett, J. (2019). A legal definition of AI. arXiv preprint arXiv:1909.01095.

Sedenberg, E. (2016). *Recovering the history of informed consent for data science and internet industry research ethics*.

Seldon, A., Abidoye, O., & Metcalf, T. (2020). *The Fourth Education Revolution Reconsidered: Will Artificial Intelligence Enrich Or Diminish Humanity?* Legend Press Ltd.

Selenko, E., Bankins, S., Shoss, M. K., Warburton, J., & Restubog, S. L. D. (2022). Artificial Intelligence and the Future of Work: A Functional-Identity Perspective. *Current Directions in Psychological Science*, *31*(3), 272–279. doi:10.1177/09637214221091823

Sennott, S. C., Akagi, L., Lee, M., & Rhodes, A. (2019). AAC and artificial intelligence (AI). *Topics in Language Disorders*, *39*(4), 389–403. doi:10.1097/TLD.0000000000000197 PMID:34012187

Serutla, L., Mwanza, A., & Celik, T. (2024). *Online Assessments in a Changing Education Landscape Reimagining Education-The Role of E-Learning, Creativity, and Technology in the Post-Pandemic Era*. IntechOpen.

Sethi, K., Chauhan, S. S., & Jaiswal, V. (2021). *Artificial Intelligence in Higher Education*. Springer. doi:10.4018/978-1-7998-4763-2.ch001

Sethi, K., Sharma, A., Chauhan, S., & Jaiswal, V. (2020). Impact of social and cultural challenges in education using AI. In *Revolutionizing Education in the Age of AI and Machine Learning* (pp. 130–151). IGI Global. doi:10.4018/978-1-5225-7793-5.ch007

Shadbad, F., Bahr, G., Luse, A., & Hammer, B. (2023). Inclusion of gamification elements in the context of virtual lab environments to increase educational value. *AIS Transactions on Human-Computer Interaction*, *15*(2), 224–246. doi:10.17705/1thci.00089

Shadravan, A., & Parsaei, H. (2023). *The paradigm shift from industry 4.0 implementation to industry 5.0 readiness*. AHFE International., doi:10.54941/ahfe1004296

Shahnaz, K., & Mukesh, D. (2022). The role of artificial intelligence in combat against COVID-19. *IJEAST*, *7*(4), 252–256. doi:10.33564/IJEAST.2022.v07i04.040

Shanmugam, G., Rajendran, D., Thanarajan, T., Murugaraj, S.S., & Rajendran, S. (2023). Artificial Intelligence as a Catalyst in Digital Marketing: Enhancing Profitability and Market Potential. *Ingénierie des Systèmes d'Information, 28*(6).

Sharifuddin, N. S., & Hashim, H. (2019-2022). Benefits and Challenges in Implementing Artificial Intelligence in Education (AIED) in ESL Classroom. *Systematic Reviews.*

Sharma, A. K., Pareta, A., Meena, J., & Sharma, R. (2022). A long term impact of artificial intelligence and robotics on higher education. *Proceedings - IEEE International Conference on Advances in Computing, Communication and Applied Informatics, ACCAI 2022*. IEEE. 10.1109/ACCAI53970.2022.9752633

Sharma, S., Malik, A., Sharma, C., Batra, I., Kaswan, M. S., & Garza-Reyes, J. A. (2023). Adoption of industry 4.0 in different sectors: a structural review using natural language processing. *International Journal on Interactive Design and Manufacturing (IJIDeM)*, 1-23.

Sharma, A., Thakur, K., Kapoor, D. S., & Singh, K. J. (2023). *Designing Inclusive Learning Environments: Universal Design for Learning in Practice The Impact and Importance of Instructional Design in the Educational Landscape*. IGI Global. doi:10.4018/978-1-6684-8208-7.ch002

Sharma, G. (2021). A literature review on application of Artificial Intelligence in Human Resource Management and its practices in current organizational scenario. *Proceedings of the 5th International Conference on I-SMAC (IoT in Social, Mobile, Analytics and Cloud), I-SMAC 2021*, (pp. 594–600). IEEE. 10.1109/I-SMAC52330.2021.9640954

Sheehan, T. (2023). Generative AI in education: Past, present, and future. *EDUCAUSE Review*. https://er.educause.edu/articles/sponsored/2023/9/generative-ai-in-education-past-present-and-future

Sheehy, K., & Holliman, A. (2017, December 13). *Education and New Technologies*. Routledge. http://books.google.ie/books?id=HilEDwAAQBAJ&printsec=frontcover&dq=Artificial+Intelligence+in+Education:+Promises+and+Implications+for+Teaching+and+Learning&hl=&cd=3&source=gbs_api

Shemshack, A., & Spector, J. M. (2020). A systematic literature review of personalized learning terms. *Smart Learning Environments*, *7*(1), 1–20. doi:10.1186/s40561-020-00140-9

Shi, D., Wang, T., Xing, H., & Xu, H. (2020). A learning path recommendation model based on a multidimensional knowledge graph framework for e-learning. *Knowledge-Based Systems*, *195*, 105618.

Shofiah, N., Putera, Z. F., & Solichah, N. (2023). Challenges and opportunities in the use of artificial Intelligence in education for academic writing: A scoping review. In Conference Psychology and Flourishing Humanity (PFH 2023) (pp. 174-193). Atlantis Press. doi:10.2991/978-2-38476-188-3_20

Siddiqui, S. T., Sohail, M. M. A., Aftab, A., Sarfaraz, M., Alam, M. I., & Salim, A. (2023). Enhancing Efficiency and Empowering Institutions: Leveraging Wireless Sensor Devices, IoT Edge Computing, and Fog Computing in Educational Systems. *Paper presented at the 2023 7th International Conference on Computation System and Information Technology for Sustainable Solutions (CSITSS).* IEEE. 10.1109/CSITSS60515.2023.10334212

Sigfrids, A., Leikas, J., Salo-Pöntinen, H., & Koskimies, E. (2023). Human-centricity in AI governance: A systemic approach. *Frontiers in Artificial Intelligence*, *6*, 976887. doi:10.3389/frai.2023.976887 PMID:36872934

Siler, E. (2019). Collection Development and Management for 21st Century Library Collections: An Introduction. *Technical Services Quarterly*, *36*(4), 426–427. doi:10.1080/07317131.2019.1664121

Sillat, L. H., Tammets, K., & Laanpere, M. (2021). Digital competence assessment methods in higher education: A systematic literature review. *Education Sciences*, *11*(8), 402. doi:10.3390/educsci11080402

Silseth, K., Steier, R., & Arnseth, H. C. (2024, February 15). Exploring students' immersive VR experiences as resources for collaborative meaning making and learning. *International Journal of Computer-Supported Collaborative Learning*, *19*(1), 11–36. doi:10.1007/s11412-023-09413-0

Silva, M., Munk, D. D., & Bursuck, W. D. (2005). Grading adaptations for students with disabilities. *Intervention in School and Clinic*, *41*(2), 87–98. doi:10.1177/10534512050410020901

Simões, R. V., Parreiras, M. V. C., Da Silva, A. C. C., Barbosa, C. E., de Lima, Y. O., & de Souza, J. M. (2022, October). Artificial intelligence and digital transformation: analyzing future trends. In *2022 IEEE International Conference on Systems, Man, and Cybernetics (SMC)* (pp. 1462-1467). IEEE. 10.1109/SMC53654.2022.9945429

Singh, S. V., & Hiran, K. K. (2022). The Impact of AI on Teaching and Learning in Higher Education Technology. *Journal of Higher Education Theory and Practice*, *12*(13).

Sinhaliz, S., et,al. (2023). How ChatGPT Could Revolutionize Academia The AI Chatbot Could Enhance Learning, But Also Creates Some Challenges. *IEEE Spectrum.*

Slimi, Z., & Carballido, B. V. (2023). Navigating the Ethical Challenges of Artificial Intelligence in Higher Education: An Analysis of Seven Global AI Ethics Policies. *TEM Journal, 12*(2).

Slimi, Z., et, al. (2023). Navigating the Ethical Challenges of Artificial Intelligence in Higher Education: An Analysis of Seven Global AI Ethics Policies. *TEM Journal, 12*(2).

SlimiZ. (2021). *The Impact of AI Implementation in Higher Education on Educational Process Future: A Systematic Review*. https://doi.org/ doi:10.21203/rs.3.rs-1081043/v1

Snyder, H. (2019). Literature review as a research methodology: An overview and guidelines. *Journal of Business Research*, *104*, 333–339. https://doi.org/https://doi.org/10.1016/j.jbusres.2019.07.039. doi:10.1016/j.jbusres.2019.07.039

Son, J.-B., Ruzic, N. K., & Philpott, A. (2023). Artificial intelligence technologies and applications for language learning and teaching. *Journal of China Computer-Assisted Language Learning*, *0*(0). doi:10.1515/jccall-2023-0015

Soori, M., Arezoo, B., & Dastres, R. (2023). Artificial Intelligence, Machine Learning and deep learning in advanced robotics, a review. *Cognitive Robotics*, *3*, 54–70. doi:10.1016/j.cogr.2023.04.001

Sousa, M., Dal Mas, F., Pesqueira, A., Lemos, C., Verde, J. M., & Cobianchi, L. (2021). The potential of AI in health higher education to increase the students' learning outcomes. *The potential of AI in health higher education to increase the students' learning outcomes,* (2), 488-497.

Southworth, J., Migliaccio, K., Glover, J., Reed, D., McCarty, C., Brendemuhl, J., & Thomas, A. (2023). Developing a model for AI Across the curriculum: Transforming the higher education landscape via innovation in AI literacy. *Computers and Education: Artificial Intelligence*, *4*, 100127. doi:10.1016/j.caeai.2023.100127

Srinivasan, R., & Chander, A. (2021). Biases in AI systems. *Communications of the ACM*, *64*(8), 44–49. doi:10.1145/3464903

Srivastava, R. (2020). Unlocking technology for language learning: A viability at the time of transition from traditional to online teaching and learning. Arab World English Journal (AWEJ) Proceedings of 2nd MEC TESOL Conference

Srivastava, B., Rossi, F., Usmani, S., & Bernagozzi, M. (2020). Personalized chatbot trustworthiness ratings. *IEEE Transactions on Technology and Society*, *1*(4), 184–192.

Stüber, J. (2018). *Barriers of digital technologies in higher education: a teachers' perspective from a Swedish university.*

Subaveerapandiyan, A. (2023). *Application of Artificial Intelligence (AI) In Libraries and Its Impact on Library Operations Review*. https://digitalcommons.unl.edu/libphilprac

Suhail, A. H., Guangul, F. M., & Kuckian, S. (2023). Contemporary and Technology Based Assessment and Feedback for Student Enhanced Learning: A Case Study of Mechanical Engineering Department at Middle East College. *Paper presented at the SHS Web of Conferences*. IEEE. 10.1051/shsconf/202315607005

Suh, W., & Ahn, S. (2022). Development and Validation of a Scale Measuring Student Attitudes Toward Artificial Intelligence. *SAGE Open*, *12*(2). doi:10.1177/21582440221100463

Su, J., Ng, D. T. K., & Chu, S. K. W. (2023). Artificial Intelligence (AI) Literacy in Early Childhood Education: The Challenges and Opportunities. *Computers and Education: Artificial Intelligence*, *4*, 100124. doi:10.1016/j.caeai.2023.100124

Sullivan, M., Kelly, A., & McLaughlan, P. (2023). ChatGPT in higher education: Considerations for academic integrity and student learning.

Sullivan, M., Kelly, A., and McLaughlan, P. (2023). *ChatGPT in higher education: Considerations for academic integrity and student learning.*

Sullivan, M., et, al. (2023). ChatGPT in higher education: Considerations for academic integrity and student learning. *Journal of Applied Learning & Teaching*, *6*(1), 1–10.

Sultan Qaboos University. (2023). *SQU Inks Agreement to Launch First Omani AI Model to Space*. Anwaar. https://anwaar.squ.edu.om/Post/Post-Detail/ArticleID/3971/SQU-Inks-Agreement-to-Launch-First-Omani-AI-Model-to-Space

Šumak, B., Brdnik, S., & Pušnik, M. (2021). Sensors and artificial intelligence methods and algorithms for human–computer intelligent interaction: A systematic mapping study. *Sensors (Basel)*, *22*(1), 20. doi:10.3390/s22010020 PMID:35009562

Sun, Y., Liu, J., Wang, J., Cao, Y., & Kato, N. (2020). When machine learning meets privacy in 6G: A survey. *IEEE Communications Surveys and Tutorials*, *22*(4), 2694–2724. doi:10.1109/COMST.2020.3011561

Suresh, H., & Guttag, J. (2021, October). A framework for understanding sources of harm throughout the machine learning life cycle. In *Proceedings of the 1st ACM Conference on Equity and Access in Algorithms, Mechanisms, and Optimization* (pp. 1-9). 10.1145/3465416.3483305

Svitlana, T., Vasylyk, A., & Olga, B. (2022). Artificial Intelligence in HR: Practices and Prospects of the Spread in Ukraine. *The Eurasia Proceedings of Science Technology Engineering and Mathematics*. doi:10.55549/epstem.1176076

Swiecki, Z., Khosravi, H., Chen, G., Martinez-Maldonado, R., Lodge, J. M., Milligan, S., Selwyn, N., & Gašević, D. (2022). Assessment in the age of artificial Intelligence. *Computers and Education: Artificial Intelligence*, *3*, 100075. doi:10.1016/j.caeai.2022.100075

Sychev, O., Anikin, A., & Prokudin, A. (2020). Automatic grading and hinting in open-ended text questions. *Cognitive Systems Research*, *59*, 264–272. doi:10.1016/j.cogsys.2019.09.025

Tabatabai, S. (2020). Simulations and virtual learning supporting clinical education during the COVID 19 pandemic. *Advances in Medical Education and Practice*, *11*, 513–516. doi:10.2147/AMEP.S257750 PMID:32821192

Tableau Software. (2023). *Tableau: Data visualisation software*. https://www.tableau.com/

Taddeo, M., & Floridi, L. (2018). How AI can be a force for good. *Science*, *361*(6404), 751–752. doi:10.1126/science.aat5991 PMID:30139858

Taeihagh, A. (2021). Governance of artificial intelligence. *Policy and Society*, *40*(2), 137–157. doi:10.1080/14494035.2021.1928377

Tahiru, F. (2021). AI in education: A systematic literature review. [JCIT]. *Journal of Cases on Information Technology*, *23*(1), 1–20. doi:10.4018/JCIT.2021010101

Tai, M. C.-T. (2020). The impact of artificial intelligence on human society and bioethics. *Tzu-Chi Medical Journal*, *32*(4), 339–343. doi:10.4103/tcmj.tcmj_71_20 PMID:33163378

Tajane, K., Dave, S., Jahagirdar, P., Ghadge, A., & Musale, A. (2018). AI based chat-bot using azure cognitive services. *Paper presented at the 2018 Fourth International Conference on Computing Communication Control and Automation (ICCUBEA).* IEEE. 10.1109/ICCUBEA.2018.8697737

Takimoto, M., & Hashimoto, H. (2010). An" eye-opening" learning experience: Language learning through interpreting and translation. *Electronic Journal of Foreign Language Teaching*, *7*(1), 86–95.

Tanik Önal, N., & Önal, N.ÖNAL. (2023). Online learning and teaching experiences of preservice science teachers during Covid-19 pandemic. *Journal of Educational Technology and Online Learning*, *6*(2), 295–314. doi:10.31681/jetol.1078486

Tao, X., Shannon-Honson, A., Delaney, P., Li, L., Dann, C., Li, Y., & Xie, H. (2022). Data analytics on online student engagement data for academic performance modeling. *IEEE Access : Practical Innovations, Open Solutions*, *10*, 103176–103186. doi:10.1109/ACCESS.2022.3208953

Tapalova, O., & Zhiyenbayeva, N. (2022). Artificial Intelligence in Education: AIEd for Personalised Learning Pathways. *Electronic Journal of e-Learning*, *20*(5), 639–653. doi:10.34190/ejel.20.5.2597

Taylor, D. L., Yeung, M., & Bashet, A. (2021). Personalized and adaptive learning. *Innovative learning environments in STEM higher education: Opportunities, Challenges, and Looking Forward*, 17-34.

Teachflow. (2023, September 18). *The evolution of AI in education: Past, present, and future.* Teachflow.AI. https://teachflow.ai/the-evolution-of-ai-in-education-past-present-and-future/

Tekin, N., Oktay, K., & Özgül, K. (2023). Sosyobilimsel Konulara İlişkin Bir Projede Yetişen Fen Bilimleri Öğretmenlerinin Görüşlerinin İncelenmesi. *Science Insights Education Frontiers*, *14*(1), 2013–2037. doi:10.15354/sief.23.or089

Teng, Y., Zhang, J., & Sun, T. (2023). Data-driven decision-making model based on artificial intelligence in higher education system of colleges and universities. *Expert Systems: International Journal of Knowledge Engineering and Neural Networks*, *40*(4), e12820. doi:10.1111/exsy.12820

The Impact of Content Curation for Personal / Informal Learning. (2016, January 5). The Impact of Content Curation for Personal / Informal Learning. *International Journal of Science and Research (Raipur, India)*, *5*(1), 1673–1676. doi:10.21275/v5i1.NOV153170

Thilagavathy, N., & Kumar, E. P. (2021). *Artificial intelligence on digital Marketing-An overview.* NVEO-NATURAL VOLATILES & ESSENTIAL OILS Journal NVEO.

Thomas, R., Bhosale, U., Shukla, K., & Kapadia, A. (2023). Impact and perceived value of the revolutionary advent of artificial intelligence in research and publishing among researchers: A survey-based descriptive study. *Science Editing*, *10*(1), 27–34. doi:10.6087/kcse.294

Thurzo, A., Strunga, M., Urban, R., Surovková, J., & Afrashtehfar, K. I. (2023). Impact of artificial intelligence on dental education: A review and guide for curriculum update. *Education Sciences*, *13*(2), 150. doi:10.3390/educsci13020150

Tian, X., Pavur, R., Han, H., & Zhang, L. (2022). A Machine Learning-Based Human Resources Recruitment System for Business Process Management: Using LSA, BERT and SVM. *Business Process Management Journal*. doi:10.1108/BPMJ-08-2022-0389

Tian, Y., & Zhang, Y. (2022). Evaluation of Accounting Data of Water Company Based on Combination Model. *Scientific Programming*, *2022*, 1–9. doi:10.1155/2022/3373420

Timmons, A. C., Duong, J. B., Simo Fiallo, N., Lee, T., Vo, H. P. Q., Ahle, M. W., Comer, J. S., Brewer, L. C., Frazier, S. L., & Chaspari, T. (2023). A call to action on assessing and mitigating bias in artificial intelligence applications for mental health. *Perspectives on Psychological Science*, *18*(5), 1062–1096.

Tiwari, R. (2023). Explainable AI (xai) and its applications in building trust and understanding in AI decision-making. *International Journal of Scientific Research in Engineering and Management*, *07*(01). Advance online publication. doi:10.55041/IJSREM17592

Tjahyadi, H., Budijono, Y. G., Lukas, S., & Krisnadi, D. (2017, October). Android Based Automated Scoring of Multiple-Choice Test. *International Journal of Machine Learning and Computing*, *7*(5), 110–113. doi:10.18178/ijmlc.2017.7.5.630

Topping, K. (1998). Peer assessment between students in colleges and universities. *Review of Educational Research*, *68*(3), 249–276. doi:10.3102/00346543068003249

Toutain, O., Jabbouri, R., & Truong, Y. (2023). Artificial intelligence and the transformation of management education. *Management International*, *27*(2), 119–132. doi:10.59876/a-kthz-pbf0

Tredinnick, L., & Laybats, C. (2023). The dangers of generative artificial intelligence. *Business Information Review*, *40*(2), 46–48. doi:10.1177/02663821231183756

Tretow-Fish, T. A. B., & Khalid, M. S. (2023). Methods for Evaluating Learning Analytics and Learning Analytics Dashboards in Adaptive Learning Platforms: A Systematic Review. *Electronic Journal of e-Learning*, *21*(5), 430–449. doi:10.34190/ejel.21.5.3088

Tsai, S. (2024, February 1). Gradescope Review: Is It Worth It? *SCI Journal*. https://www.scijournal.org/articles/gradescope-review

Tsai, Y.-S., Perrotta, C., & Gašević, D. (2020). Empowering learners with personalised learning approaches? Agency, equity and transparency in the context of learning analytics. *Assessment & Evaluation in Higher Education*, *45*(4), 554–567. doi:10.1080/02602938.2019.1676396

Turnbull, J. M. (1989). What is… normative versus criterion-referenced assessment. *Medical Teacher*, *11*(2), 145–150. doi:10.3109/01421598909146317 PMID:2586296

Tzachor, A., Whittlestone, J., Sundaram, L., & hÉigeartaigh, S. (2020). Artificial intelligence in a crisis needs ethics with urgency. In *Nature Machine Intelligence, 2*(7). Nature Research. doi:10.1038/s42256-020-0195-0

Tzimas, D., & Demetriadis, S. (2021). Ethical issues in learning analytics: A review of the field. *Educational Technology Research and Development*, *69*(2), 1101–1133. doi:10.1007/s11423-021-09977-4

UNESCO (2023). *Ethics of Artificial Intelligence*. UNESCO.

UNESCO. (2021). *Recommendation on the ethics of artificial intelligence*. UNESCO.

UNESCO. (2022). HIGHER EDUCATION GLOBAL. *Data Report*.

Ungerer, L., & Slade, S. (2022). Ethical considerations of artificial intelligence in learning analytics in distance education contexts. In Learning Analytics in Open and Distributed Learning: Potential and Challenges (pp. 105-120). Springer Nature Singapore. doi:10.1007/978-981-19-0786-9_8

United Nations Educational, Scientific and Cultural Organization, & Organization, C. (2021). *Recommendation on the Ethics of Artificial Intelligence*. United Nations Educational. https://unesdoc.unesco. org/ark:/48223/pf0000379920.page=14

Uskov, V. L., Bakken, J. P., Gayke, K., Fatima, J., Galloway, B., Ganapathi, K. S., & Jose, D. (2020). Smart learning analytics: student academic performance data representation, processing and prediction. *Paper presented at the Smart Education and e-Learning 2020*. Springer. 10.1007/978-981-15-5584-8_1

Valladares, L. (2021). Scientific Literacy and Social Transformation. *Science & Education*, *30*(3), 557–587. doi:10.1007/s11191-021-00205-2 PMID:33867683

Valle-Cruz, D., García-Contreras, R., & Gil-Garcia, J. R. (2023). Exploring the negative impacts of artificial intelligence in government: The dark side of intelligent algorithms and cognitive machines. *International Review of Administrative Sciences*, 00208523231187051. doi:10.1177/00208523231187051

Van Belkon, A. (2020). Speeding up to keep up: Exploring the use of AI in the research process. *AI & Society*, 1–17.

Van der Heyden, B., Cohilis, M., Souris, K., de Freitas Nascimento, L., & Sterpin, E. (2021). Artificial intelligence supported single detector multi-energy proton radiography system. *Physics in Medicine and Biology*, *66*(10), 105001. doi:10.1088/1361-6560/abe918 PMID:33621962

Van der Kleij, F. M., & Lipnevich, A. A. (2021). Student perceptions of assessment feedback: A critical scoping review and call for research. *Educational Assessment, Evaluation and Accountability*, *33*(2), 345–373. doi:10.1007/s11092-020-09331-x

Vasconcelos, M. A. R., & dos Santos, R. P. (2023). Enhancing STEM learning with ChatGPT and Bing Chat as objects to think with: A case study. *Eurasia Journal of Mathematics, Science and Technology Education*, *19*(7), em2296. doi:10.29333/ejmste/13313

Vashishth, T. K., Sharma, V., Sharma, K. K., Kumar, B., Panwar, R., & Chaudhary, S. (2024). AI-Driven Learning Analytics for Personalized Feedback and Assessment in Higher Education. In *Using Traditional Design Methods to Enhance AI-Driven Decision Making* (pp. 206–230). IGI Global. doi:10.4018/979-8-3693-0639-0.ch009

Veeramuthu, P., & Periasamy, R. (2014). Application of higher education system for predicting student using data mining techniques. *International Journal of Innovative Research in Advanced Engineering, 1*(5), 31–36.

Venusamy, K., Krishnan Rajagopal, N., & Yousoof, M. (2020). A study of human resources development through chatbots using artificial intelligence. *Proceedings of the 3rd International Conference on Intelligent Sustainable Systems, ICISS 2020*, (pp. 94–99). IEEE. 10.1109/ICISS49785.2020.9315881

Verma, A., Sharma, Y., & Shekhar, S. (2021). *Artificial intelligence (AI) is used in qualitative research for theory development*. PhilArchive.

Villegas-Ch, W., & García-Ortiz, J. (2023). Enhancing Learning Personalization in Educational Environments through Ontology-Based Knowledge Representation. *Computers, 12*(10), 199. doi:10.3390/computers12100199

Vonderwell, S. K., & Boboc, M. (2013). Promoting formative assessment in online teaching and learning. *TechTrends, 57*(4), 22–27. doi:10.1007/s11528-013-0673-x

Vorobeva, D., El Fassi, Y., Pinto, D. C., Hildebrand, D., Herter, M. M., & Mattila, A. S. (2022). Thinking Skills Don't Protect Service Workers From Replacement by Artificial Intelligence. *Journal of Service Research, 25*(4), 601–613. doi:10.1177/10946705221104312

Walczak, S., & Cellary, W. (2023). Challenges for higher education in the era of widespread access to Generative AI. *Journal of Educational Technology & Society, 26*(1), 25–40.

Walczak, S., & Cellary, W. (2023). Co-creating digital art with generative AI in K-9 education: Socio-material insights. *The Journal of Educational Research, 116*(2), 124–138. doi:10.1080/00220671.2023.1234567

Waldenmaier, H. E., Gorre, E., Poltash, M. L., Gunawardena, H. P., Zhai, X. A., Li, J., Zhai, B., Beil, E. J., Terzo, J. C., Lawler, R., English, A. M., Bern, M., Mahan, A. D., Carlson, E., & Nanda, H. (2023). "lab of the future"—today: Fully automated system for high-throughput mass spectrometry analysis of biotherapeutics. *Journal of the American Society for Mass Spectrometry, 34*(6), 1073–1085. doi:10.1021/jasms.3c00036 PMID:37186948

Walker, M. E., Olivera-Aguilar, M., Lehman, B., Laitusis, C., Guzman-Orth, D., & Gholson, M. (2023). Culturally Responsive Assessment: Provisional Principles. *ETS Research Report Series, 2023*(1), 1–24. doi:10.1002/ets2.12374

Walter, S., & Lankes, R. D. (2015). The innovation agenda. In College and Research Libraries, 76(7). Association of College and Research Libraries. doi:10.5860/crl.76.7.854

Wang, Q. (2023). The Impact of COVID-19 on the Development of Online Education in Higher Education. *Journal of Education Humanities and Social Sciences*. doi:10.54097/ehss.v8i.4612

Wang, K., Lu, L., Fang, J., Xing, Y., Tong, Z., & Wang, L. (2023). The Downside of Artificial Intelligence (AI) in Green Choices: How AI Recommender Systems Decrease Green Consumption. *MDE. Managerial and Decision Economics*, *44*(6), 3346–3353. doi:10.1002/mde.3882

Wang, S., Christensen, C., Cui, W., Tong, R., Yarnall, L., Shear, L., & Feng, M. (2023). When adaptive learning is effective learning: Comparison of an adaptive learning system to teacher-led instruction. *Interactive Learning Environments*, *31*(2), 793–803. doi:10.1080/10494820.2020.1808794

Wang, T., & Cheng, E. C. K. (2021). An investigation of barriers to Hong Kong K-12 schools incorporating Artificial Intelligence in education. *Computers and Education: Artificial Intelligence*, *2*, 100031. doi:10.1016/j.caeai.2021.100031

Wang, T., Lund, B. D., Marengo, A., Pagano, A., Mannuru, N. R., Teel, Z. A., & Pange, J. (2023). Exploring the Potential Impact of Artificial Intelligence (AI) on International Students in Higher Education: Generative AI, Chatbots, Analytics, and International Student Success. *Applied Sciences (Basel, Switzerland)*, *13*(11), 6716. doi:10.3390/app13116716

Wang, T., Vargas-Diaz, D., Brown, C., & Chen, Y. (2023). *Exploring the Role of AI Assistants in Computer Science Education: Methods*. Implications, and Instructor Perspectives.

Wang, Y., Liu, C., & Tu, Y. F. (2021). Factors affecting the adoption of AI-based applications in higher education. *Journal of Educational Technology & Society*, *24*(3), 116–129.

Wang, Z. (2022). Computer-assisted EFL writing and evaluations based on artificial intelligence: A case from a college reading and writing course. *Library Hi Tech*, *40*(1), 80–97. doi:10.1108/LHT-05-2020-0113

Wan, P., Wang, X., Lin, Y., & Pang, G. (2021). A knowledge diffusion model in autonomous learning under multiple networks for personalized educational resource allocation. *IEEE Transactions on Learning Technologies*, *14*(4), 430–444. doi:10.1109/TLT.2021.3103006

Warschauer, M. (2023). *The affordances and contradictions of AI-generated text for second language writers*. SSRN.

WarschauerM.TsengW.YimS.WebsterT.JacobS.DuQ.TateT. (2023). The affordances and contradictions of AI- generated text for second language writers. doi:10.2139/ssrn.4404380

Weber, M., Engert, M., Schaffer, N., Weking, J., & Krcmar, H. (2022). Organisational capabilities for AI implementation—Coping with inscrutability and data dependency in AI. *Information Systems Frontiers*, *25*(4), 1549–1569. doi:10.1007/s10796-022-10297-y

Weegar, R., & Idestam-Almquist, P. (2023). Reducing Workload in Short Answer Grading Using Machine Learning. *International Journal of Artificial Intelligence in Education*. doi:10.1007/s40593-022-00322-1

Weng, X., & Chiu, T. K. (2023). Instructional design and learning outcomes of intelligent computer assisted language learning: Systematic review in the field. *Computers and Education: Artificial Intelligence*, 100117.

Whalley, B., France, D., Park, J., Mauchline, A., & Welsh, K. (2021). Towards flexible personalized learning and the future educational system in the fourth industrial revolution in the wake of Covid-19. *Higher Education Pedagogies*, *6*(1), 79–99. doi:10.1080/23752696.2021.1883458

Wheatley, A., & Hervieux, S. (2020). Artificial intelligence in academic libraries: An environmental scan. *Information Services & Use*, *39*(4), 347–356. doi:10.3233/ISU-190065

Widdowson, H. G. (2014). The role of translation in language learning and teaching. In *Translation: A multidisciplinary approach* (pp. 222–240). Palgrave Macmillan UK. doi:10.1057/9781137025487_12

Wiley, J., Hastings, P., Blaum, D., Jaeger, A. J., Hughes, S., Wallace, P., Griffin, T. D., & Britt, M. A. (2017). Different approaches to assessing the quality of explanations following a multiple-document inquiry activity in science. *International Journal of Artificial Intelligence in Education*, *27*(4), 758–790. doi:10.1007/s40593-017-0138-z

Wiliam, D. (2011). What is assessment for learning? *Studies in Educational Evaluation*, *37*(1), 3–14. doi:10.1016/j.stueduc.2011.03.001

Williamson, B. (2020). Making Markets Through Digital Platforms: Pearson, Edu-Business, and the (E)valuation of Higher Education. *Critical Studies in Education*. doi:10.1080/17508487.2020.1737556

Williamson, B. (2024). Eğitimde Yapay Zekanın Sosyal Hayatı. *International Journal of Artificial Intelligence in Education*, *34*, 97–104. doi:10.1007/s40593-023-00342-5

Williamson, B., Bayne, S., & Shay, S. (2020). *The datafication of teaching in Higher Education: critical issues and perspectives* (Vol. 25). Taylor & Francis.

Winfield, A. F. T., & Jirotka, M. (2018). Ethical Governance Is Essential to Building Trust in Robotics and Artificial Intelligence Systems. *Philosophical Transactions. Series A, Mathematical, Physical, and Engineering Sciences*, *376*(2133), 20180085. doi:10.1098/rsta.2018.0085 PMID:30323000

Winstone, N. E., & Boud, D. (2022). The need to disentangle assessment and feedback in higher education. *Studies in Higher Education*, *47*(3), 656–667. doi:10.1080/03075079.2020.1779687

Wirtz, B., Weyerer, J., & Geyer, C. (2018). Artificial intelligence and the public sector—Applications and challenges. *International Journal of Public Administration*, *42*(7), 596–615. doi:10.1080/01900692.2018.1498103

Wood, P. (2023). Oxford and Cambridge ban AI language tool GPT-3 over fears of plagiarism. *inews.co.uk*.

Wood, D. F. (2013). Formative assessment. In T. Swanwick (Ed.), *Understanding Medical Education: Evidence, Theory and Practice* (pp. 317–328). The Association for the Study of Medical Education. doi:10.1002/9781118472361.ch23

Wu, X., Duan, R., & Ni, J. (2023). Unveiling security, privacy, and ethical concerns of ChatGPT. *Journal of Information and Intelligence*.

Wu, C., & Monfort, A. (2022). Role of Artificial Intelligence in Marketing Strategies and Performance. *Psychology and Marketing*. doi:10.1002/mar.21737

Wu, Y., Hu, Q., Liang, H., Wang, A., Xu, H., Wang, L., & He, X. (2023). Electrostatic potential as a solvent descriptor enables rational electrolyte design for lithium batteries. *Advanced Energy Materials, 13*(22), 2300259. Advance online publication. doi:10.1002/aenm.202300259

Xia, X., & Li, X. (2022). Artificial Intelligence for Higher Education Development and Teaching Skills. *Wireless Communications and Mobile Computing, 2022*, 1–10. doi:10.1155/2022/7614337

Xiufeng, L.,(2009). Beyond Science Literacy: Science and the Public. *International Journal of Environmental and Science Education, 4*(3), 301-311.

Xu, W., & Ouyang, F. (2022). The application of AI technologies in STEM education: A systematic review from 2011 to 2021. *International Journal of STEM Education, 9*(1), 59. doi:10.1186/s40594-022-00377-5

Xu, Y., Liu, X., Cao, X., Huang, C., Liu, E., Qian, S., Liu, X., Wu, Y., Dong, F., Qiu, C.-W., Qiu, J., Hua, K., Su, W., Wu, J., Xu, H., Han, Y., Fu, C., Yin, Z., Liu, M., & Zhang, J. (2021). Artificial intelligence: A powerful paradigm for scientific research. *Innovation (Cambridge (Mass.)), 2*(4), 100179. doi:10.1016/j.xinn.2021.100179 PMID:34877560

Yadlapally, D. K., Vasireddy, B., Marimganti, M., Chowdary, T., Karthikeyan, C., & Vignesh, T. (2023). *A Review on the Potential of AI Voice Assistants for Personalized and Adaptive Learning in Education.*

Yang, Q., Steinfeld, A., Rosé, C., & Zimmerman, J. (2020). *Re-examining whether, why, and how human-ai interaction is uniquely difficult to design*. doi:10.1145/3313831.3376301

Yang, S., & Evans, C. (2019, November). Opportunities and challenges in using AI chatbots in higher education. In *Proceedings of the 2019 3rd International Conference on Education and E-Learning* (pp. 79-83). 10.1145/3371647.3371659

Yang, X., Hao-wen, L. I., Ni, L., & Li, T. (2021). Application of Artificial Intelligence in Precision Marketing. *Journal of Organizational and End User Computing, 33*(4), 209–219. doi:10.4018/JOEUC.20210701.oa10

Yangyang, W. (2023). Teaching Ability, Performance and Professional Development Among Artificial Intelligence Chinese Professors. *Asia Pacific Journal of Management and Sustainable Development, 11*(1).

Yan, L., Sha, L., Zhao, L., Li, Y., Martinez-Maldonado, R., Chen, G., Li, X., Jin, Y., & Gašević, D. (2024). Practical and ethical challenges of large language models in education: A systematic scoping review. *British Journal of Educational Technology*, *55*(1), 90–112. doi:10.1111/bjet.13370

Yanli, X., & Danni, L. (2021). Prospect of Vocational Education under the Background of Digital Age: Analysis of European Union's "Digital Education Action Plan (2021-2027)". *Paper presented at the 2021 International Conference on Internet, Education and Information Technology (IEIT)*. IEEE. 10.1109/IEIT53597.2021.00042

Yao, G. (2022). Application of higher education management in colleges and universities by deep learning. *Computational Intelligence and Neuroscience*, *2022*, 2022. doi:10.1155/2022/7295198 PMID:35990163

Yathiraju, N. (2022). Investigating the use of an Artificial Intelligence Model in an ERP Cloud-Based System. International Journal of Electrical. *Electronics and Computers*, *7*(2), 1–26.

Yau, C., & Chan, K. (2023). University of Hong Kong temporarily bans students from using ChatGPT, other AI-based tools for coursework. South China Morning Post, 17.

Yousefi, M., & Abdullah, A. G. K. (2019). The Impact of Organizational Stressors on Job Performance Among Academic Staff. *International Journal of Instruction*, *12*(3), 561–576. doi:10.29333/iji.2019.12334a

Yu, R., Li, Q., Fischer, C., Doroudi, S., & Xu, D. (2020). Towards Accurate and Fair Prediction of College Success: Evaluating Different Sources of Student Data. *International educational data mining society*.

Yu, K., Guo, Z., Shen, Y., Wang, W., Lin, J. C.-W., & Sato, T. (2021). Secure artificial intelligence of things for implicit group recommendations. *IEEE Internet of Things Journal*, *9*(4), 2698–2707.

Yurkofsky, M. M., Peterson, A. J., Mehta, J. D., Horwitz-Willis, R., & Frumin, K. M. (2020). Research on continuous improvement: Exploring the complexities of managing educational change. *Review of Research in Education*, *44*(1), 403–433. doi:10.3102/0091732X20907363

Zadorozhnyi, Z. M., Muravskyi, V., Pochynok, N., Muravskyi, V., Shevchuk, A., & Majda, M. (2023). Application of Chatbots with Artificial Intelligence in Accounting. *2023 13th International Conference on Advanced Computer Information Technologies, ACIT 2023 - Proceedings*, (pp. 196–200). IEEE. 10.1109/ACIT58437.2023.10275395

Zawacki-Richter, O., Marín, V. I., Bond, M., & Gouverneur, F. (2019). Systematic review of research on artificial intelligence applications in higher education–where are the educators? *International Journal of Educational Technology in Higher Education*, *16*(1), 1–27. doi:10.1186/s41239-019-0171-0

Zeidler, D. L., Herman, B. C., & Sadler, T. D. (2019). New directions in socioscientific issues research. *Disciplinary and Interdisciplinary Science Education Research*, *1*(11), 1–9. doi:10.1186/s43031-019-0008-7

Zemanova, L. (2015). AI and Its Impact on Educational Administration. *Journal of Education Policy*, *30*(4), 531–546.

Zembylas, M. (2023). A decolonial approach to AI in higher education teaching and learning: Strategies for undoing the ethics of digital neocolonialism. *Learning, Media and Technology*, *48*(1), 25–37. doi:10.1080/17439884.2021.2010094

Zhai, X., & Wiebe, E. (2023). Technology-based innovative assessment. *Classroom-based STEM assessment*, 99-125.

ZhaiX. (2022). ChatGPT user experience: Implications for education. Available at SSRN 4312418.

Zhai, X., Chu, X., Chai, C. S., Jong, M. S. Y., Istenic, A., Spector, M., Liu, J.-B., Yuan, J., & Li, Y. (2021). A Review of Artificial Intelligence (AI) in Education from 2010 to 2020. *Complexity*, *2021*, 1–18. doi:10.1155/2021/8812542

Zhai, X., He, P., & Krajcik, J. (2022). Applying machine learning to automatically assess scientific models. *Journal of Research in Science Teaching*, *59*(10), 1765–1794. doi:10.1002/tea.21773

Zhai, X., Yin, Y., Pellegrino, J. W., Haudek, K. C., & Shi, L. (2020). Applying machine learning in science assessment: A systematic review. *Studies in Science Education*, *56*(1), 111–151. doi:10.1080/03057267.2020.1735757

Zhang, K., & Aslan, A. B. (2021). AI technologies for education: Recent research & future directions. *Computers and Education: Artificial Intelligence*, *2*, 100025. doi:10.1016/j.caeai.2021.100025

Zhang, W., Cai, M., Lee, H. J., Evans, R., Zhu, C., & Ming, C. (2023). AI in Medical Education: Global situation, effects and challenges. *Education and Information Technologies*, •••, 1–23.

Zhang, W., Wu, Y., & Calautit, J. K. (2022). A review on occupancy prediction through machine learning for enhancing energy efficiency, air quality and thermal comfort in the built environment. *Renewable & Sustainable Energy Reviews*, *167*, 112704. doi:10.1016/j.rser.2022.112704

Zhang, Z., & Xu, L. (2022). Student engagement with automated feedback on academic writing: A study on Uyghur ethnic minority students in China. *Journal of Multilingual and Multicultural Development*, 1–14. doi:10.1080/01434632.2022.2102175

Zhang, Z., Zhou, X., Zhang, X., Wang, L., & Wang, P. (2018). A Model Based on Convolutional Neural Network for Online Transaction Fraud Detection. *Security and Communication Networks*, *2018*, 1–9. doi:10.1155/2018/5680264

Zhao, K., Cheng, M., & Guo, Y. (2020). Artificial intelligence in social and human sciences: An overview. *International Journal of Human-Computer Interaction*, *36*(8), 609–623.

Zheng, Y., Niu, S., Shang, Y., Shao, Z., & Jian, L. (2019). Integrating plug-in electric vehicles into power grids: A comprehensive review on power interaction mode, scheduling methodology and mathematical foundation. *Renewable & Sustainable Energy Reviews*, *112*, 424–439. doi:10.1016/j.rser.2019.05.059

Zheng, Y., & Wen, X. (2021). The application of artificial intelligence technology in cloud computing environment resources. *Journal of Web Engineering*. doi:10.13052/jwe1540-9589.2067

Zhou, J., Chen, F., Berry, A., Reed, M., Zhang, S., & Savage, S. (2020). *A survey on ethical principles of AI and implementations*. IEEE. doi:10.1109/SSCI47803.2020.9308437

Zhu, D. (2020). *Research on the Transformation From Financial Accounting to Management Accounting in the Age of Artificial Intelligence*. Probe - Accounting Auditing and Taxation., doi:10.18686/aat.v2i2.1335

Zhu, K., Li, L. D., & Li, M. (2021). School Timetabling Optimisation Using Artificial Bee Colony Algorithm Based on a Virtual Searching Space Method. *Mathematics*, *10*(1), 73. doi:10.3390/math10010073

Žigienė, G., Rybakovas, E., & Vaitkienė, R. (2020). Challenges in applying artificial intelligence for supply chain risk management. *International Journal of Economics and Business Administration*, *VIII*(4), 299–318. doi:10.35808/ijeba/589

Zitnik, M., Azuaje-Flores, L., Mac Jones, D., & Lengauer, T. (2012). Biomarker discovery platform: An R/Java framework for analysis of high-throughput proteomic data. *Journal of Proteome Research*, *11*(3), 1421–1432.

Zou, D., Huang, Y., & Xie, H. (2021). Digital game-based vocabulary learning: Where are we and where are we going? *Computer Assisted Language Learning*, *34*(5-6), 751–777. doi:10.1080/09588221.2019.1640745

About the Contributors

Nasser Al Harrasi is an accomplished senior lecturer of Business Studies at the University of Technology and Applied Science-Muscat. With over a decade of diverse experience, he has held various roles in teaching, consultancy, and corporate management in Oman. Dr. Al Harrasi received his PhD in Human Resources Management from Binary University, College of Management & Entrepreneurship, Malaysia in 2020 and is also a Fellow of the UK Higher Education Academy. As a dedicated researcher, Dr. Al Harrasi is passionate about investigating topics related to HRM practices, organization behavior, and higher education. He has a successful track record of securing external funding and grant research opportunities and leads and supervises several research teams. His research has been published in reputable journals such as the Journal of Social Science and Business Management. Dr. Al Harrasi is a dynamic professional who is committed to excellence in teaching, research, and community service. He is well-respected by his colleagues and students for his inspiring leadership, mentoring, and contributions to the field of business studies.

Mohamed Salah El Din, a driven lecturer and researcher, pioneers AI applications in management and higher education. His master's in international Transport & Logistics from Arab Academy for Science, Technology and Maritime Transport (AAST), and extensive industry experience in shipping and logistics, bridge academic rigor with practical expertise. Certified by the Association for Supply Chain Management (ASCM) and having taken several courses on AI and digital transformation, Mohamed adds industry validation and cutting-edge knowledge to his research. Mohamed's accomplishments include publishing peer-reviewed articles, securing multiple research grants, and winning several research competitions. He has published on AI adoption in management, including a groundbreaking book on using ChatGPT in academia, and currently co-edits a book on the broader scope of AI use in higher education.

***

Sajeel Ahmed joined the Business School in January 2015 as a full-time Lecturer in September 2019 and Senior Lecturer in Business Systems and Management in July 2021. He has taught various business-related subjects at the university. Mainly my expertise is in teaching and researching in subjects related to digital technologies, information management, information systems, computer-mediated communication, digital marketing, and digital business management.

Ali Younis Al Bolushi is Lecturer in the Faculty of Business Management. Ali holds a bachelor's degree in Banking and Finance from the University of Bahrain and an MBA from the New York Institute of Technology. In addition to his previous work as a lecturer in Gulf College, Ali brings industrial experience through his work as an assistant researcher in UNDP - Bahrain, and as an executive manager in Enjaz Business & Projects Co, Oman. Ali has a Train-the-Trainer, AMIDEAST training certificate, and has received coaching and certification for mentoring from Radiant Sail Management Consulting. This expertise has allowed him to conduct training in various public and private sectors such as the Ministry of Defence and Bank Muscat. His research interests are in the fields of Entrepreneurship, Management, Marketing, and Strategy.

Salim Al Daraai stands out as an inspiring figure in the academic and research communities, particularly in the fields of Business and Accounting. Currently a lecturer at Muscat College in the Sultanate of Oman, Salim has dedicated himself to fostering the next generation of leaders and innovators. Salim has pursued excellence in education and research throughout his career. His academic journey led him to earn a Master's degree in Management from the University of Liverpool in 2017, where his dissertation focused on delegation's influence on the success of SMEs in Oman. He is currently a PhD candidate at the University of Plymouth, United Kingdom. Salim's professional journey is marked by significant contributions to the oil and gas industry, where he worked in various capacities, including as a Petroleum Engineer Assistant Workshop Manager, & Engineers Leader at Ray International Oil & Gas. His transition from the industry to academia in 2021 as a lecturer at Muscat College showcases his passion for teaching and mentoring students. Salim's research interests lie in human resources and innovation. He actively involves students and the community in his research, aiming to make a tangible impact through his work. His publications and conference presentations reflect a deep commitment to advancing knowledge in his field, with topics ranging from the automation revolution in recruitment to the synergies between innovation and internationalization in family firms. Beyond his academic and research pursuits, Salim is actively involved in service roles within Muscat College, contributing to exam and training committees and taking leadership roles in student learning platforms.

His dedication to student engagement and practical learning experiences form the core of his teaching philosophy.

Khoula Al Harthy is an esteemed researcher with a focus on information security and a keen interest in Blockchain technology. Her career is dedicated to the empowerment of local expertise in cutting-edge technologies. As a recognized speaker, she contributes her insights at both national and international events. In a significant leadership role, Khoula serves as the President of the Oman Blockchain Club for 2 years . This organization is pivotal in disseminating knowledge and education about blockchain applications across Oman, fostering a deeper understanding of this revolutionary technology. In the academic realm, Khoula holds a PhD in Risk Management. She is the Head of computer science and Creative Technologies department in GCET. Notably, she is the initiator of the Blockchain Research Thematic Group, driving forward the academic exploration and application of blockchain technology. Her work in this area highlights her commitment to integrating advanced tech into academia and beyond, shaping the future of information cybersecurity security and AI in the region.

Sulaiman Al Hasani received a B.Eng. (Hons) in Electrical and Computer Systems Engineering and a PhD. In Electrical and Electronics Engineering from Monash University, Melbourne, Australia, where he focused primarily on signal processing and deep learning and their application to enhance and accelerate Magnetic Resonance Imaging (MRI), and received a post-graduate certificate in academic practice from the University of the West of England, Bristol, UK. During his academic journey, Dr. Sulaiman Al Hasani actively engaged in collaborative projects with esteemed institutions such as Monash Biomedical Imaging, Monash Centre for Synchrotron Science in Australia, and the University of Glasgow in Scotland and received research training from Siemens Healthcare, North Carolina, USA. His professional journey began at Monash University's Department of Electrical and Computer Systems Engineering as a demonstrator and then a lecturer. He later joined the Global College of Engineering and Technology (GCET) in Muscat, Oman, as a lecturer and then as the head of the Electronics and Telecommunication Engineering department. Currently, Dr. Sulaiman Al Hasani holds the position of Deputy Dean (Academic Affairs and Resources) at the (GCET). With a passion for signal processing, compressive sensing, deep learning, and robotics. And an increasing interest and dedication to leadership in higher education to address aspects of quality education, accessibility, and inclusivity within higher education.

Mallak Al Maqurshi is a final-year student specializing in human resources at Muscat College. She is actively engaged in research, particularly focusing on issues related to workforce diversity and its impact on organizational performance within the higher education sector. Her proactive approach to research highlights her dedication to contributing valuable insights to human resource management.

Zahir Al Shaikh brings over a decade of industrial experience to his current role in academia, having held various leadership positions. With a Master's Degree in Project Management, Zahir shifted his career path from the industry to education, driven by his passion for teaching and development. He is currently a lecturer at the University of Technology and Applied Science in Muscat, specializing in Project Management.

Mohammed Al Zakwani is a seasoned professional with over 20 years of experience in the oil and gas industry, where he held various leadership roles in both local and international companies. With an MBA and a deep passion for knowledge sharing, Mohammed transitioned from industry to academia. He currently serves as a Senior Lecturer at Muscat College, specializing in Project Management. His extensive industry background enriches his teaching, providing students with valuable real-world insights into project management within the dynamic context of the energy sector.

Md. Al-Amin, a dedicated researcher from the University of Dhaka, delves into the realms of distance learning, AI, and STEM, advocating for inclusive learning methodologies. Through his scholarly articles, Al-Amin showcases his deep commitment to advancing educational practices, inspiring future scholars and educators alike. With hands-on experience in empirical research and data analysis, he contributes valuable insights to the evolving landscape of educational technology integration. Al-Amin's belief in the transformative power of education drives his passion for advocating for inclusive and equitable learning opportunities for all.

Ammar Abdulrahman Al Balushi is the Head of the Faculty of Business Management at Majan University College, Oman. He plays a key role in strategic, financial, and HR decisions, leading the largest faculty and initiating key programmes like BSc Business Analytics with AI and Fintech. His experience spans marketing, tourism development, quality assurance, teaching, and senior management roles in academia and industry. Dr. AlBalushi emphasizes continuous learning and innovation in leadership, aiming to foster a culture of intellectual curiosity and academic excellence.

Yongmei Bentley is a Principal Lecturer in Logistics at the University of Bedfordshire Business School, capstone leader of MSc programmes and link coordinator of

BA and MBA programmes delivered overseas. Yongmei is also a visiting professor of Yichun University in China, and a chartered member of the Chartered Institute of Logistics and Transport, UK.

Dina Ghandour is an esteemed Assistant Professor of Accounting and Finance at the Faculty of Business Management in Majan University College (MUC),affiliated with the university of Bedfordshire, UK, holds a Doctorate degree in Accounting and a Master's degree in Finance. She is a distinguished academic and respected researcher. Previously taught at the University of Medical Sciences & Technology (UMST) in Sudan, at the Postgraduate, MBA, and undergraduate programs. Internationally, she made her mark in the Global MBA in Impact Entrepreneurship Program in Milan, Italy. Also, was an assessor in Edexcel BTEC Level 5 HND in Business in the UK, and a Financial Training Officer at Symap Consultancy. Besides that, Dr. Ghandour excelled in administrative leadership, worked as an Academic Counselor, Coordinator of Postgraduate studies (including DBA and MBA programs), and Director of External Relations at UMST. Currently, she serves as the chair of the Faculty of Business Management research committee at MUC, and also an editorial board member at the International Journal of Social & Educational Sciences in Turkey, member at the African Network of Social Entrepreneurship Scholars (ANSES) in South Africa, and previously at UNICEF. Furthermore, she has Participated in different International/National trainings, workshops, and conferences. She has Published a number of articles in Top-Ranking journals and Conference proceedings. Two of the publications are listed on Social Science Research Network-Elsevier Top Ten download list. Dr. Ghandour Awarded the best paper at an International Conference in Kuala Lumpur, Malaysia, and Nominated as a Professional Public Speaker at Zurich/Switzerland while presenting a scientific paper at International Conference. She presented a paper and served as a discussant at the American Chapter Conference of the Academy of Sustainable Finance, Accounting, Accountability and Governance (ASFAAG), held at Florida International University, Miami, USA. Dr. Ghandour has been recognized in the AD Scientific Index 2023 as a top researcher. Her research interest revolves around FinTech, banking, finance, financial accounting, and auditing.

Fiseha Mekonnen Guangul, an Assistant Professor of Mechanical Engineering at Middle East College in Oman, obtained his Ph.D. in Mechanical Engineering from Universiti Teknologi PETRONAS. His academic journey includes earning BSc and MSc degrees in Mechanical Engineering from Addis Ababa University, Ethiopia. Furthermore, he holds a Higher Diploma in Professional Teacher Education from Adama Science and Technology University. Recognized as a Chartered Engineer (CEng, MIMechE) by IMechE, he is an active member of ASME, IAENGR, and the

Oman Society of Engineers. Dr. Fiseha has over 25 years of expertise encompassing industry, research, teaching, and academic governance. His professional background includes managerial roles in both manufacturing and service sectors. Post-doctorally, he led the Hybrid Energy Systems Research Laboratory at Universiti Teknologi PETRONAS. His diverse research interests cover renewable energy, thermofluids, gasification, project management, total quality management, and teaching quality. With a prolific record, Dr. Fiseha has authored over 34 papers published in journals and conferences. Additionally, he has contributed four book chapters to Springer.

Rabbi Khan is a Lecturer in the Department of Educational Technology at Bangabandhu Sheikh Mujibur Rahman Digital University, Gazipur, Bangladesh. He earned his Bachelor of Education (Hons.) and Master of Education degree from Institute of Education and Research (IER), University of Dhaka. Md. Rabbi Khan's research interests include Educational technology, Pedagogy, Instructional Design, Global citizenship etc.

Abdul Nazeer specialized in areas of Composite Materials, Design simulation and Engineering, Management. He received B.E. (Mechanical), Visvesvaraya technological university. M.Tech (Machine Design), Visvesvaraya technological university INDIA. Ph.D. (Composite Materials), Visvesvarya Technological University, INDIA. He has 13 Years of Teaching, Research and Administration experience with 11 publication in national and international journals and 06 conferences.

Fatematuz Zahra Saqui is a lecturer at the Institute of Business Administration (IBA), University of Dhaka, Bangladesh. Before joining academia, she worked extensively as a researcher in various multinational research companies. Her industry experience includes multiple managerial roles where she managed and led a team of researchers. Her research expertise lies in market research involving market segmentation, brand health, product development, customer satisfaction, etc., across industries such as FMCG, telecom, and mobile financial services. She has led multiple cross-country studies for global businesses. Her research interests lie in poverty, inequality, and education, along with exploring decolonized methodologies.

Abira Zaki is an accomplished professional with an MBA in Human Resource Management from Iqra University. She excels in the fields of Data Analysis and SEO, showcasing her versatile skill set. With a keen eye for detail and a passion for optimizing outcomes, Abira is dedicated to leveraging her expertise to drive success in the realms of human resources and digital marketing.

Index

D

E

F

G

H

I

L

M

O

P

R

S

U

V

Premier Reference Source
The Use of Artificial Intelligence in Digital Marketing
Competitive Strategies and Tactics
IGI Global

Premier Reference Source
Innovations in Materials Chemistry, Physics, and Engineering Research
Eugene de Silva and Pramudi Abeydeera
IGI Global

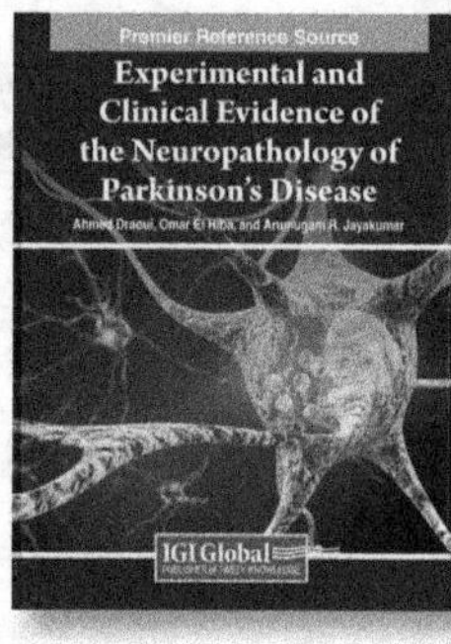

Premier Reference Source
Experimental and Clinical Evidence of the Neuropathology of Parkinson's Disease
Ahmed Draoui, Omar El Hiba, and Arumugam R. Jayakumar
IGI Global

Premier Reference Source
Balance and Boundaries in Creating Meaningful Relationships in Online Higher Education
Sarah H. Jarvie and Cara Metz
IGI Global

www.ingramcontent.com/pod-product-compliance
Lightning Source LLC
LaVergne TN
LVHW080341011026
849161LV00009B/2143